# PARNELL
## AND HIS PARTY

CHARLES STEWART PARNELL

# PARNELL
## AND HIS PARTY
## 1880—90

BY

CONOR CRUISE O'BRIEN

OXFORD
AT THE CLARENDON PRESS
1957

*Oxford University Press, Amen House, London E.C.4*

GLASGOW NEW YORK TORONTO MELBOURNE WELLINGTON
BOMBAY CALCUTTA MADRAS KARACHI
CAPE TOWN IBADAN NAIROBI ACCRA SINGAPORE

---

PRINTED IN GREAT BRITAIN

IN MEMORY OF
DAVID SHEEHY
AND OF
HENRY HARRISON

# PREFACE

WHEN I began work on this book, more than fourteen years ago, some members of Parnell's party
still survived; many people were living—and some
still are—who had followed the debates in Committee Room
15 with the passionate partisanship of the time. To this day
in Ireland, certain families are apt to regard each other with
an animosity derived from the events of 1890 and fading
only slowly from generation to generation. Few bloodless
struggles in modern times can have produced such intense
and lasting loyalties and resentments as did the crisis over
the leadership of the Irish party and people after the verdict
in the divorce case, *O'Shea* v. *O'Shea and Parnell*. If, as some
distinguished historians tell us, the proper theme of history
is 'the dead past'—a past which can evoke no emotions in
our contemporaries—then Parnell's time is not yet ripe for
the historian. Not only do its angry echoes still reach us
through several living traditions, but it has not yet reached
that blessed state of total irrelevance to our own problems
which would qualify it for the attention of the ideal historian. The writer on this period may be tempted, for example, to ask himself such a practical question as whether
the Gladstone–Parnell attempt at a home rule settlement
could have led to a united Ireland within the Commonwealth. The mere fact that such a temptation can arise,
even if it is immediately suppressed, would be sufficient, in
some eyes, to expel our subject from the proper field of the
historian. A less austere school might hold, however, that a
period which is close enough for us to share many of its
interests and assumptions, and far enough away for us to be
able to extricate ourselves at least from its cruder forms of
partisanship, may usefully be studied, and that whether we
call the result history or not is of no great importance. To
have talked with so intelligent and charming and cheerfully
partisan a survivor as was Henry Harrison, is upsetting to
the impartiality, but also to the ignorance; one tended to
become involved, but one got to know more. Yet it is true

that the nearness of the time and its passions makes all the more necessary, in listening to such reminiscences, not indeed detachment but a fascinated scepticism.

The present work is based as little as possible on such reminiscences—although probably coloured by them here and there, not always in the same sense—and as much as possible on contemporary evidence, and on the measurement of whatever was susceptible of being even roughly measured. Such measurements—as of the composition of the party and some of its factions—can seldom yield results which are either precise or surprising, but they serve as a check against certain biased statements by contemporaries and as a spiritual exercise in objectivity.

From the beginning of this work, as a thesis for the degree of Doctor of Philosophy in the University of Dublin, I had the great benefit of the guidance of Professor T. W. Moody, S.F.T.C.D., whose lucid judgement and experience in the assessment of historical evidence saved me from errors of emphasis and direction, as well as of plain fact. It gives me great pleasure to acknowledge here my debt to his wise and tactful counsel. I have pleasure also in thanking Professor R. Dudley Edwards, of University College, Dublin, for many stimulating criticisms, as a result of one of which I re-examined, not without benefit, some important source-material.

I should like to thank also the directors and staff of the various repositories in which I worked—including the Manuscripts Room of the British Museum, the State Paper Office in Dublin Castle, the Dublin Public Record Office, the Royal Irish Academy and the Library of Trinity College, Dublin—for their unfailing helpfulness. A special tribute is due to the Director of the National Library of Ireland, Dr. R. J. Hayes and to his staff, notably Mr. James Carty, Mr. Patrick Henchy, and Mr. Tom O'Neill, who gave me very valuable help over a number of years.

I am grateful to Dr. Myles Dillon, for letting me examine the large and valuable collection of papers left by his father, the late John Dillon and to Dr. C. S. Andrews, Mr. G. E. Hetherington, Mr. John Muldoon, and the Librarian of the National Liberal Club for making possible access to other material; and to Mr. A. R. Foster, Mr. John J. Horgan, Mr. Lawrence Kettle, Mrs. Mary S. Kettle, Mr. Patrick Lynch, Dr. R. B. McDowell, Dr. Eoin MacWhite, and Mr. J. K. Walton for their help and criticisms. I record with sadness my debt to some who are now dead—to Henry Harrison and J. P. Hayden for their reminiscences and to P. S. O'Hegarty for letting me use freely his splendid collection of nineteenth-century Irish books and pamphlets.

Finally, I should like to thank my wife, not only for her great patience with this slowly developing project but for her help with the gathering of the facts and her good advice.

C. C. O'B.

*Paris, August 1956*

# CONTENTS

# ABBREVIATIONS

| | |
|---|---|
| B.M. | British Museum. |
| *D.N.B.* | *Dictionary of National Biography* |
| *F.J.* | *Freeman's Journal.* |
| *I.H.S.* | *Irish Historical Studies.* |
| I.R.B. | Irish Republican Brotherhood. |
| *I.T.* | *Irish Times.* |
| N.L.I. | National Library of Ireland. |
| P.R.O. | Public Record Office, Dublin. |
| S.P.O. | State Paper Office, Dublin Castle. |
| *U.I.* | *United Ireland.* |

# INTRODUCTION

## *Background:* The New Departure and the Irish party in 1880

THE fear of famine, or rather of having to choose between starvation and eviction, was the great underlying political reality of the late seventies and early eighties of the nineteenth century in Ireland. The famine of 1845–7, as a result of which a million people died and many thousands were evicted, was present either in the memory or in the imagination of every Irishman. From 1878 on, partial failures of the potato crop—still the staple diet of thousands of Irish tenant-farmers—and falling prices for other crops threatened a recurrence of the pattern of the forties and fifties: mass-starvation, mass-evictions, mass-emigration. At the time of the Great Famine this pattern had not been resisted: many had paid their landlord his rent until they could pay no longer, then resigned themselves to die. But now, although the social and economic framework remained very much the same, several important new political factors gave a quite different twist to events. The same sort of economic crisis as had, in the late forties, destroyed the old Gaelic-speaking Ireland was now to shake the foundations of the seventeenth-century land-settlement itself, the basis of English rule in the greater part of the country.

Of the new factors an essential one—although the least important from the point of view of its direct action on the people—was the Irish Republican Brotherhood, the secret oath-bound revolutionary society, founded in the fifties and generally known as 'the fenians'. Following a pattern familiar in Europe, this movement was better organized, less scrupulous about its methods, and more determined, than the earlier separatist movements, inspired by the romantic enthusiasm of 'Young Ireland', which had issued in the quixotic and hopeless rising of 1848. The actual

B

achievements of the fenian movement, in organizing armed
revolution, were not much greater than those of their
predecessors; 1867 was a failure as 1848 had been. But as
a political school the Irish Republican Brotherhood was effective; very effective for those who were able to meditate
its lessons later in the harsh penal servitude of that day without having their spirit broken thereby. Michael Davitt, the
founder of the Land League, was one of these.

The second factor, and the most obvious to hostile observers, was the rising influence of the Irish in America. The
famine emigrants, and especially their children, had attained
in America a relative prosperity which enabled them to send
money home; they retained at the same time, and even increased, a bitter resentment against landlordism and Britain;
their money and their propaganda were ready to help those
in Ireland who seemed to be doing the most effective work
to end the British rule and landlord ascendancy in Ireland.
The fenians got help from America; then the Land League
did so; then the parliamentarians; later Sinn Féin and its
offshoots: all in proportion as they seemed to be making
progress in 'getting England out'. It became increasingly
difficult for the British authorities to cope with this situation. 'In former Irish rebellions', wrote one of the more
coercion-minded of Gladstone's lieutenants, 'the Irish were
*in Ireland*. Now there is an Irish nation in the United States,
equally hostile, with plenty of money, absolutely beyond
our reach and yet within ten days of our shores.'[1] The
character of this American aid was sometimes misunder-
stood; it was not true, as unionist propagandists sometimes
claimed, that nationalist leaders in Ireland were merely pup-
pets worked on financial strings by 'paymasters' in Chicago,
New York, or Philadelphia. Under the leadership of Parnell
the national movement in Ireland was—after 1882—to ignore for long its 'paymasters', and then to recover their
co-operation on its own terms. But 'America' did remain a
great resource, in money and encouragement, whenever an
Irish movement was on a leftward line; a fact that gave Irish
politics a greater depth, and Irish leaders a much wider
range of choice than they would otherwise have had. The

[1] See Chap. VI, p. 161.

fenians were the first Irish movement to rely to any great extent on American support and it was the fenian-trained politicians, like Michael Davitt and—in America—John Devoy, who first brought the Irish in America to support an 'open' movement at home and so made them a force in constitutional politics.

The third new factor, on which the first two converged, was the Land League. The Land League was a combination of which the immediate aim was to keep rents down by bringing public opinion to bear on particularly hard cases of eviction for arrears of rent, and by making life difficult for those—known as 'grabbers'—who became tenants of 'evicted land'. The source of the movement's strength was the almost universal popular support for this programme; the league 'boycott'—although it was yet to win that name —was already a most formidable force. The league had come into being in 1879. It was the creation of Michael Davitt, the fenian who had recently emerged from Dartmoor, and of other advanced nationalists who—unlike the majority on the fenian supreme council—favoured 'a policy of parallel action between the revolutionary and constitutional movements'.[1] Fenians and ex-fenians made up 'the hard core of the league.'[2] The police, indeed, saw the league primarily as a device for recruiting members for the I.R.B. According to Superintendent Mallon of the Dublin Metropolitan Police, the league was meant to be 'the medium of organizing the peasantry for fenian purposes. This is borne out by the notorious fact that when fenianism was rife it was chiefly confined to the artisan and shop-boy classes in the towns while the rural population were decidedly hostile and revived ribbonism.'[3] 'Ribbonism' was the name given to the sporadic, ineffective, and usually violent agrarian combinations which had preceded the Land League; those who disliked the ex-fenian promoters of the new league often referred to them as 'ribbon-fenians'. Through its fenian connexions in the American Clan-na-

---

[1] T. W. Moody, 'Michael Davitt, a Survey and Appreciation' (*Studies*, June–Sept. 1946). A member of the supreme council, O'Connor Power, was expelled for his support of this policy.
[2] Ibid.         [3] S.P.O., Mallon Report (see Bibliography).

Gael, and because of its obvious effectiveness, the league could draw heavily on American aid, which enabled it to sustain its chosen evicted tenants, those who were willing to resist—'the wounded soldiers of the land-war'. This financial aid, disbursed by shrewd, courageous, and honest organizers, working on a national scale, gave the new movement a very different character from the poor, local, badly led, and desperate agrarian resistances of earlier days.

So far, the new movement, as we have described it, might be seen as an off-shoot of fenianism. It is doubtful, however, whether the fenians and ex-fenians—Davitt, Devoy, Egan, O'Connor Power, John Barry, and the others—with all their talent and devotion could have successfully formed a great national movement. No one of them would easily have accepted the leadership of any of the others; they were divided by personal jealousies, and especially by the gulf which separated the members of parliament from the others. Certain ex-fenians—Barry, O'Connor Power, Biggar—had 'broken their fenian oath' by entering parliament and swearing allegiance to the English Queen. These were particularly obnoxious to subscribing fenians, and often secretly despised even by those ex-fenians who had not broken their oath. The 'fenian parliamentarians', for their part, would certainly have found it hard to accept an extra-parliamentary leadership, which would have been censorious of parliamentarians generally, and particularly severe on ex-fenians. It was natural, therefore, that 'the fenians' themselves should prefer a non-fenian leader. They found that leader in a young Irish landlord, Charles Stewart Parnell.

Parnell had been elected to parliament as member for Meath in 1875, as a member of Isaac Butt's very moderate and constitutional home rule party, which contained many landlords,[1] was conservative on social questions, and more sensitive to 'the tone of the House' at Westminster than to the feelings of its constituents in Ireland. It was on this last point that Parnell first distinguished himself. He was from the beginning, and remained, indifferent to what was thought of him in Westminster, provided that he could secure and retain the confidence of the Irish. He became a

[1] See Chap. I, p. 18, Table 3.

member, and soon the most conspicuous member, of the so-called 'active' or 'obstructive' section of Butt's party,[1] and by 1877 had won the confidence of fenian and ex-fenian elements to such an extent that, with their aid, he ousted Isaac Butt from the chairmanship of the Irish organization in England, then called the Home Rule Confederation of Great Britain. In June 1879, after Butt's death, Parnell first publicly associated himself with Davitt's Land League of Mayo, the first 'non-fenian' member of parliament to do so.[2] This Westport meeting showed, for the first time, something of Parnell's mettle as a leader. The meeting had been condemned in strong terms—probably because the 'rack-renting' landlord in this case was a Catholic priest—by the Archbishop of Tuam, John McHale, 'one of the most nationalist and one of the most respected of the Irish hierarchy'.[3] Davitt expected, after the archbishop's letter, that Parnell 'would follow the example of other invited guests by pleading some excuse to remain away'.[4] But Parnell held firm: 'I have promised to be there and you can count upon my keeping that promise.'[5] It was at this meeting that Parnell reduced the policy of the Land League to a clear and simple formula. 'You must show the landlords that you intend to hold a firm grip on your homesteads and lands. You must not allow yourselves to be dispossessed as you were dispossessed in 1847.'

In October 1879 the Irish National Land League was formed in Dublin, with Parnell as its first president. The then chairman of the home rule party in parliament, William Shaw—Butt's successor—held aloof from the league, as did most of the members of the party. With Parnell's assumption of the leadership of the land movement there was completed what was known, in fenian language, as 'the New Departure'—the association in one great national movement of an agrarian agitation, the progressive (or opportunist) elements in fenianism both in England and in Ireland, a strong Irish-American section led by Devoy, and the most

[1] See Chap. I, pp. 21–23.
[2] The only other M.P. in the Land League at this time was the ex-fenian O'Connor Power.
[3] O'Hegarty, *Ireland under the Union*, p. 485.
[4] *Fall of Feudalism*, p. 153.                    [5] Ibid., p. 154.

determined and aggressive section of the Irish representation in parliament, led by Parnell.[1] The New Departure has
been accurately assessed, both as to its force and as to its
tendency, by J. L. Garvin: 'Nothing less than the strongest
native revolt for over two hundred years, it sought to dis-
rupt the bases of the Cromwellian settlement and of British
rule.'[2]

Parnell was now leader of the Irish in Britain and leader
also, at least in title, of the agrarian agitation in Ireland. He
was not yet leader of the Irish representation in parliament,
or even of any sizeable section of it, and the great political
question, in the spring of 1880 in Ireland, was whether the
general election in April would give him enough followers
to make him leader of the party also. If it should do so he
could claim, with more reason than any man since O'Connell, the title of leader of the Irish people.

Superficially there was a paradox in the rise of a Protestant
landlord to the leadership of a Catholic people in its fight
against landlordism. Yet in reality Parnell's social superiority
was one of his claims to leadership. The House of Commons
in the eighties was still an aristocratic assembly and it was a
great advantage for the Irish to have a leader who would
neither 'misunderstand its tone' nor let himself be overawed
by it. Inside the national movement the fact that Parnell was
socially 'different' was also an advantage in his progress
towards the leadership, in that this difference placed him
above the resentments which men feel at the advancement
of their own equals. The political advantage of his status
was consciously appreciated by his contemporaries.[3] 'They
wanted a county gintleman', sneered a disgruntled ex-
member of the party.[4] They did, and for good reason.

Protestant landlords who supported home rule, as a
rather vague aspiration, were fairly numerous. Landlords—

---

[1] For the origins and development of this movement see T. W. Moody,
'The New Departure in Irish Politics, 1878–9' (*Essays in British and Irish
History in honour of J. E. Todd*, 1949).

[2] *Life of Chamberlain*, i. 318–19.

[3] Cf. *Irish World* (New York), 1 July 1882 (interview with Michael Davitt);
also interview with T. M. Healy in *Pall Mall Gazette*: 'Story of the Parnell
Crisis' (1891), p. 90.

[4] F. H. O'Donnell, *History of the Irish Parliamentary Party*, i. 256.

Catholic or Protestant—who supported the Land League were, in the nature of things, very rare indeed. It was the good fortune of the Irish movement that one of the very few individuals who possessed this combination of qualifications for leadership happened also to be endowed in a most exceptional degree with the less tangible qualities of leadership: prudence and daring, firmness and flexibility, farsightedness and tactical sense. That he should have been also—as he was—gifted with imposing stature and great physical beauty makes it easier to understand the almost superstitious veneration with which many of his followers —especially his remoter followers—regarded him. Few leaders in modern times have looked so very like a leader.

There are then reasons enough—and even a superfluity of reasons—why Parnell, having taken up the Irish cause, should have become its leader. His own motives and intentions in taking up that cause are less plain. Some writers have seen him simply as an Irish patriot of no complicated kind, working for his country's freedom and the fulfilment of Tone's ambition: 'to break the connection with England'. Others have expressed much the same idea with different emotions, regarding him as infected by a hysterical American mother with a pathological hatred of England and a craving for destruction. Others again—and these included some who knew him well—saw him as a daring but profoundly conservative politician, aiming at the economic and political regeneration of a very sick country. Cecil Rhodes thought that he and his party could become, after home rule, an important force for the development of the British Empire.

The present study is not directly concerned either with Parnell's ultimate motives or with his long-term intentions, but with his political behaviour, and that of the party which he led, during the decade in which he was leader. I believe that the study of this behaviour does point to certain conclusions as regards Parnell's intentions, but it is better not to anticipate the evidence by discussing the conclusions at this point. Parnell's actions were, in any case, determined, not only by his long-term intentions—whatever they may have been—but by the changing political context in which

he worked. Part of that context has been considered: the
deep agrarian and political unrest, the fenians, the Land
League, the Irish Americans. These were the great forces
making for change, and Parnell showed that he understood
their strength—and weakness—better than any man. But
there were also relatively conservative forces in Irish
nationalism, and these forces were represented politically
by that very ambiguous body, the Irish parliamentary
party.

The whole of this book deals with the Irish party, and it
is therefore not necessary to make more than a few general
comments on it in this Introduction. It was, when Parnell
first rose to prominence in it in the years 1875–80, a very
loose association of Irish members, who were supposed in
principle to help Isaac Butt in the work of convincing the
imperial parliament that it should confer a measure of self-
government on Ireland.[1] These members included many
landlords and other gentlemen who in fact, though not in
theory, were little more than a Catholic and faintly particu-
larist fringe to the English liberal party. Such members
were known in Ireland as 'whigs' and were detested by
those ex-fenians, land leaguers, and other active nationalists
who were already coming to be known as Parnellites. On
the other hand, the 'whigs' enjoyed the esteem and protection of many though not all of the senior Catholic clergy, a
fact which was of great importance since the Irish party did
not have—until Parnell had been leader for some years—
any election machine, and the clergy in many areas took the
place of such a machine even as late as the general election
of 1880. The whigs tended to show more practical activity
in parliament on Catholic than on Irish national issues and
it was believed of many of them—unfairly in some cases—
that they had only two political principles: to stay in with
the clergy in order to keep their seats and to stay in with the
liberals in order to get jobs.

After the general election of 1880, landlords and whigs
did not long remain a preponderant factor in the party—
although they left their mark on it—but the influence of the
clergy on elections survived them, and another conservative

[1] See Chap. I, pp. 21 sqq.

influence was also permanent.[1] This was the influence of
parliament itself. The gap between Irish public opinion and
the public opinion of the rest of the United Kingdom was
enormous, and the Irish party had, usually, to make some
attempt to span it. An Irish home rule member in Westminster came from among constituents who not only disliked British rule in the abstract but cherished a peculiar
personal detestation for Queen Victoria, 'the Famine Queen';
from this atmosphere he stepped into a House where the
constitution and the person of the monarch were above all
controversy, on an almost religious plane. To flout the
traditions of the House of Commons took great moral courage; to make allies there, and hold them, while also holding
one's own constituents, took ingenuity of a particularly
tenacious kind.

The Parnellite movement differed from earlier and later
Irish movements of importance, by reason of the primacy
in it of the parliamentary principle. It convinced the Irish
people that, through their representation at Westminster,
they could secure the agrarian and political reforms which
they desired. 'The party' under Parnell's leadership achieved
an importance which no political party in Ireland had ever
had before, and it came to exercise a decisive influence, for
a time, on the politics of the United Kingdom. It could
never have won such a position without the prestige and
leadership of Parnell, but it was not 'created' by him. It had
its own traditions from the days of Butt—although they
rapidly suffered change; its own necessities, of recruitment,
election, and maintenance; its own tendencies which were,
for the earlier period we have to consider, to the right of its
leader, and for the later period, in agrarian matters, somewhat to the left. In relation to public opinion in Ireland the
party probably always tended to hold a right-of-centre
position.

Parnell directed a movement of revolutionary inspiration,
from within a relatively conservative and constitutional

---

[1] Other 'conservative factors' at work in the elections of 1880—the restricted state of the franchise, the cost of election, the expense for members
of travelling to London and maintaining themselves there, &c.—are discussed
in Chap. II, pp. 39–42.

party. This is the peculiarity that made 'Parnellism' such an equivocal term and so elusive and effective a force. The relative importance of the terms 'revolutionary movement', 'party', and 'Parnell' we shall see shifting, and shifting decisively, during the period we are to cover, but neither Parnell nor the party lost in importance, until the catastrophe. Their importance was indeed interdependent. 'We created Parnell', one of the ablest members of the party was to write, 'and Parnell created us. We seized very early in the movement the idea of this man with his superb silences, his historic name, his determination, his self-control, his aloofness—we seized that as the canvas of a great national hero.'[1]

Healy's idea of the party as a kind of collective Pygmalion is certainly excessive, but his remarks are worth quoting, if only to counterbalance the more traditional myth of the leader as an isolated and self-sufficient phenomenon. The many 'lives' of Parnell[2] have, by the natural inclination of biography, tended to set him apart. The object of the present study is to restore him to his immediate political context and to describe that context; to examine how the Irish party at Westminster in the eighties was made up; how it developed and what it did; how it was led and how, finally, it and its leader destroyed each other.

[1] Interview with T. M. Healy in *Pall Mall Gazette*: 'Story of the Parnell Crisis', p. 90.
[2] See Bibliography.

# I

# THE MEMBERSHIP OF THE PARTY, 1880

Those who hold and those who are without property have ever formed distinct interests in society. . . . . A landed interest, a manufacturing interest, a mercantile interest, a moneyed interest, with many lesser interests, grow up of necessity in civilized nations and divide them into different classes, actuated by different sentiments and views. The regulation of these various and interfering interests forms the principal task of modern legislation, and involves the spirit of party and faction in the necessary and ordinary operations of the government.
                                        JAMES MADISON (*The Federalist*, No. X)

It is unfortunately exceedingly rare to find a tenant farmer with sufficient means to enable him to go over to parliament. That is because that parliament is in London instead of in Dublin. The class from which we can select our candidates under the circumstances of parliamentary representation in London is an exceedingly limited one.
                                        C. S. PARNELL (Reported in *F.J.*, 30 Mar. 1880)

THE general election of April 1880, of which the main result as far as the United Kingdom was concerned was to replace Disraeli by Gladstone, was, in Ireland, mainly interesting as a stage in the rise of Parnell. The home rule party in parliament had come into existence at the previous general election, in 1874, and was now led by the moderate William Shaw. The main subjects of political speculation were whether the home rule party could hold together at all, and whether the 'active' section in it, supported by the Land League, could become sufficiently strong to make Parnell leader of the party. These, however, were by no means clear-cut issues in the campaign, and it was not even always quite clear which candidates were home rulers at all. Indeed in this very loose and confused campaign a home ruler might have been defined as any person who chose to call himself such, irrespective of whether or not he also belonged to some other political party.

More precise definitions were available but were little used, except by politicians wishing to be pedantic at an opponent's expense. A home ruler, the purists said, was one who subscribed to the resolutions passed at the Home Rule Conference of 1873, and therefore one who advocated the establishment of a native legislature, with an executive responsible to it, to deal with the domestic affairs of Ireland, leaving the imperial parliament to deal with all other questions.

As there was at that time no strong party machine to enforce copyright of the home rule label, and as the electorate had at best only a hazy recollection of the conference of 1873, it was natural that the distortions and evasions of electioneering, and the simplifications of the press, turned home rule into something as vague as possible. The Irish press in general tended to put the letters 'H.R.' after the names of anyone whose election address, previous record, or speeches seemed to show sympathy with popular aspirations. As support of one or other of the great English parties where purely English questions were concerned was not then regarded as incompatible with home rule,[1] the descriptions 'liberal home ruler' or, much more rarely, 'conservative home ruler'[2] were in use, helping further to blur the already difficult distinction between a true, though whiggish, home ruler and an ordinary liberal who hoped to catch votes by waving some sort of green flag.

This being so it is not surprising that the number of home rulers returned at the election of 1880 has been variously estimated. Most authors, probably following the *Annual Register*, give the number of home rulers elected as 60, but the contemporary press, when the results were announced, gave it as 63. Two members—H. V. Stuart and R. P. Blennerhasset—whom the press treated as home rulers showed by their actions immediately after election that they were ordinary liberals, who had allowed a beneficial ambiguity to prevail during the campaign. The remaining 61

---

[1] By a resolution of 4 Mar. 1874 home rulers had pledged themselves that 'we should individually and collectively hold ourselves aloof from and independent of all party combinations . . .' (see Chap. IV, p. 140). Most home rulers at this time, however, interpreted this pledge with the minimum of strictness. The pledge of 1874 is not to be confused with the much more severe and effective one introduced in 1884 (Chap. IV, pp. 142–3).

[2] One gentleman, J. O. Lever of Galway, described himself as 'A liberal-conservative and in favour of home rule' (*Dod's Parliamentary Companion*, 1880). The Parnellite organ *The Nation* described him more concisely as 'an arrant humbug' (13 Apr. 1880).

were all, in some sense, home rulers and constituted the Irish parliamentary party, at this time a very loose association.

One or two members had indicated precisely what they meant by home rule and what their supporters were voting for. Thus, the address of H. J. Gill[1] for Westmeath, pledged support to home rule 'as defined by the national conference of 1873'. Most candidates preferred a vagueness. Few were so happy as Justin McCarthy, admittedly a professional man of letters, in reducing imprecision to a lapidary formula. 'I am', he said to his constituents, 'thoroughly in agreement with you on all questions.'[2]

The party elected on so unregulated a ticket was naturally lacking in any kind of uniformity. None the less it was apparent that, taken as a whole, it was greatly different from the party elected at the previous election in 1874. Before examining the different factions within the party in 1880 it may be well to contrast its membership generally with that of the 1874 party, and some comparisons with the non-home rule Irish members of 1880 may also be useful. As the crucial issue in 1880 was the land,[3] the first question to be asked about the elected members is, naturally: How many of them owned Irish land, and how much land did they own?

The question, fortunately, can be answered with a considerable degree of accuracy. The so-called Irish domesday book,[4] a return of all the owners of land in Ireland, was made in 1876, and so, in the stable conditions of land tenure

---

[1] *Freeman's Journal*, 15 Mar. 1880. Gill was the owner of the well-known publishing house of Gill & Son, and a graduate of Dublin University. His election address pledged support to 'an active parliamentary policy.'

[2] *F.J.*, 13 Mar. McCarthy was even then quite an eminent Victorian, but as a novelist and popular historian, not as a politician. His *History of Our Own Times* had already appeared (1877) and novels like *Dear Lady Disdain* (1875) had found a big public among the English middle classes. In one of his numerous volumes of reminiscences he gives the clue to his politics: 'I had been invited to stand [for Longford, April 1879] by some of the leaders of the local nationalist party on the ground that I was not likely to go into extremes on the one side or the other. They felt that I would neither refuse to leave Butt an opportunity to mend his ways nor deny any recognition of the rising claims of Parnell' (*Story of an Irishman*, London, 1904).

[3] See Introduction.

[4] *Land owners in Ireland. Return of owners of land of one acre and upwards in the several counties of cities and counties of towns of Ireland . . . Presented to both houses of parliament by command of her majesty. Printed by Alex Thom for H.M. stationery office. Dublin 1876.*

in that epoch, probably presents, generally speaking, a correct picture both for 1874 and for 1880.

In outline, that picture is as follows: Amongst them all, the 61 home rulers of 1880 owned 62,608 acres of Irish land, at a total annual valuation of £23,050. If this had been divided equally among all the members, which it was not, it would have given each over 1,000 acres, a very sizeable estate, by modern Irish standards, if not by the measurement of those times. In fact only 25 members owned any land at all—giving a real average of over 2,500 acres per landowning member. Of the 25, 14, who had also been elected at the general election of 1874, owned far more than half of the total land. They had 54,337 acres, at a total valuation of £17,330, leaving the remaining 11 landowners with a total of 8,271 acres—which included Parnell's own estate of 4,678 acres. The most significant fact which emerges, however, is that, of the 23 home rule members who were elected to parliament for the first time at the general election of 1880, only 3 owned any land in Ireland, and these 3 had only 1,000 acres amongst them. No men who could properly be described as landlords were newly elected in 1880 for home rule constituencies, and 'the landlords' had largely, although not entirely, lost their grip on the home rule party.[1]

That grip had once been considerable. The 56 home rulers returned in 1874—the first 'home rule' election—had included 34 landowners who amongst them had owned over 150,000 acres—an average of over 4,700 acres each—valued at over £63,000. As we know, only 14 of these landowners, owning 54,337 acres, survived the general election of 1880, so that in the interval, almost 100,000 acres of Irish land, valued at £40,000, disappeared from the political scene. Indeed this rather underestimates the decline in the landed interest since it takes no account of the disappearance of

---

[1] Only 19 presented themselves as candidates in 1880. Three large landowners of the 1874 parliament, the O'Conor Don of Sligo, George Browne of Mayo, and K. T. Digby of Queen's County, as well as two smaller ones, Purcell O'Hanlon and Nicholas Murphy, were defeated by Parnellites. Another large landowner and early home ruler defeated was Colonel King-Harman, who had entered parliament after 1874. It is safe to assume that others of the 1874 landowners, or their successors in title, refrained from seeking election because they realized the political power of the Land League.

men with important landlord connexions like Lord Francis Conyngham, whip of the home rule party and younger son of a very great landlord, the Marquess of Conyngham.[1]

The above figures, obviously, do not show, except very roughly, the relative strength of the landed interest in the party of 1874, as compared with that of 1880. The outlook of the party on the land question would tend to be determined, not by the gross total of land owned by its members, nor even by the total number of members owning some land, but by the number of members owning a considerable quantity of land. A gentleman who owns 9 acres in Co. Dublin, from which he is drawing ground rents, may take the most radical views on the necessity for the immediate establishment of a peasant proprietary. Conversely, a very great landlord did not necessarily wield a proportionate influence.

For these reasons, the following table, showing the numbers of landlords of various sizes, is probably a better guide to the declining power of the landlord in national politics. In order to put the matter into perspective I have included also the figures for the Irish non-home rule (liberal and conservative) M.P.s of 1880:

TABLE I[2]

| Section | Owners of 500– 2,000 acres | Owners of 2,000– 5,000 acres | Owners of 5,000– 10,000 acres | Owners of 10,000– 15,000 acres | Owners of over 15,000 acres | Total owners of over 500 acres |
|---|---|---|---|---|---|---|
| Home rule members, 1880 (61 members) | 5 | 4 | 4 | 1 | 0 | 14 |
| Home rule members, 1874 (56 members) | 5 | 11 | 5 | 3 | 2 | 26 |
| Liberals and conservatives, 1880 (40 members) | 4 | 0 | 6 | 3 | 3 | 16 |

[1] The Marquess of Conyngham owned over 150,000 acres of Irish land —nearly three times as much as was owned by the whole home rule party of 1880.

[2] The analyses of nominal lists on which this and the other tables in this book are based have been deposited in Trinity College, Dublin.

The above figures, as far as they suggest a comparison between home rulers and other Irish members, are misleading in that they do not show the true extent of the gap. One might assume from them, wrongly, that there was very little difference in point of landlordism between the liberals and conservatives of 1880—who were very much the same as the conservatives and liberals of 1874—and the home rulers of 1874. The true situation as regards this point is better shown below:

TABLE 2

| Section | Total acreage of land owned | Total annual valuation | Average annual valuation per acre |
|---|---|---|---|
| Home rulers, 1880 . | 62,608 | £23,050 | 7/- per acre approx. |
| Home rulers, 1874 . | 144,364 | £63,597 | 8/- per acre approx. |
| Liberals and conservatives, 1880 . | 177,570 | £165,532 | 18/- per acre approx. |

This shows quite clearly that the home rule landlords as a class were much less wealthy than the landlords of the other parties, even though their estates at one time were not much smaller. The wealth of the non-nationalists was based, of course, on the relative prosperity and stability of eastern Ulster, where five-sixths of all their land was situated. On the other hand, about half of the land owned by home rule members was the poor land of the western seaboard —the so-called Congested Districts. It is probable also that the 'connexions' of those members who belonged to the nobility or gentry, but were not landlords themselves, were with western land to a greater extent among home rulers than among Irish members.

That crucially important section of the 1880 party that was elected for the first time in 1880 is not treated separately in the above tables for the reason that it included no one who owned more than a thousand acres, and only one man who owned more than five hundred. That man was Captain William Henry O'Shea.

Still looking at the matter from the point of view of the main issue, at this date the land-struggle, it may be useful to attempt an analysis from the social and economic point of view of the three sections dealt with above. This would be an impossible thing to do, if a very fine degree of accuracy were required, for we obviously cannot know, except very roughly, how rich or poor every member was in 1880 or 1874. Fortunately, great accuracy is not really required here, and it will be sufficient if we can obtain an imprecise but coherent impression of the variations in social standing of the different sections. It may be assumed that a man's political outlook is conditioned much more by his general position in society, his 'caste', profession, or employment, than by the state of his purse at a given moment. On this assumption one may divide employments into six classes (see Table 3, p. 18), three of which may be labelled 'upper' and three 'lower'. It is true, of course, that some bankers go bankrupt, that the private means of some gentlemen are straitened, that not all barristers have briefs, and not all doctors patients; true also that some journalists are wealthy men, and many serve the interests of wealth, that not quite all farmers, even in Ireland then, were poor, and that some vague and shadowy callings are lucrative. None the less, one may hold that the main dividing line of economic interest, especially in questions of land tenure, ran between the two groups indicated. The three classes above the line have this in common—they are 'capitalists', in the sense that they have inherited or acquired capital—classes I and II—or have had an education so costly that it amounts to a capital asset— class III; the lower group, on the other hand, is nearer to the proletariat in that it has no known capital, or very little.[1] Small shopkeepers are obviously borderline cases, generally speaking, but for our present purposes they definitely belong below the line, their prosperity was closely linked with the fortunes of the people on the land, they had themselves often risen from the peasantry, and they were still, by the standards of that time, undoubtedly 'lower class'.

[1] Halford Mackinder made a similar division of English society in 1919: 'In England the upper professional classes go to the same schools and universities as the landed classes and the merchants and captains of industry also send their sons to these schools. Therefore the line of social cleavage, as shown by speech and bearing, is between the upper and the lower middle-classes' (*Democratic Ideals and Reality*, Penguin edition, p. 141).

To give a present-day point of comparison I include in the table (column 6) the membership of the Tenth Dáil.[1] The comparison shows the position of the 1880 party as a stage in the democratization of the parliamentary representation of the Irish people.

TABLE 3

| (1)<br><br><br><br>Group | (2)<br><br><br><br>Class | (3)<br>Home<br>rulers<br>of 1874<br>(56) | (4)<br>Home<br>rulers<br>of 1880<br>(61) | (5)<br>Non-home<br>rulers<br>1880<br>(40) | (6)<br><br><br>Tenth Dáil<br>(138 T.D.s) |
|---|---|---|---|---|---|
| 'A'<br><br>Upper<br>group | 1. Landowners (of over 1,000 acres) | 17 | 8 | 13 | 0 |
| | 2. Merchants, industrialists, bankers, rentiers, &c. | 16 | 19 | 14 | 9 |
| | 3. Higher professions | 21 | 21 | 13 | 35 |
| | Total group 'A' | 54 | 48 | 40 | 44 |
| 'B'<br><br>Lower<br>group | 1. Lower professions | 0 | 8 | 0 | 22 |
| | 2. Farmers, shopkeepers, wage-earners, &c. | 2 | 2 | 0 | 57 |
| | 3. Undefined occupations | 0 | 3 | 0 | 15 |
| | Total group 'B' | 2 | 13 | 0 | 94 |

The liberal and conservative members of 1880 were 100 per cent. upper group, on this definition; the home rulers of 1874 96 per cent. upper group, the home rulers of 1880 79 per cent. upper group, and the Tenth Dáil 68 per cent. lower group.

[1] Particulars taken from *Flynn's Parliamentary Companion*, 1939. The classification of T.D.s made in column 6 of the table has no pretensions to strict accuracy (on such points, for instance, as whether a given T.D. is a 'large merchant' or a 'small shopkeeper') but it is sufficiently correct to serve as a rough standard of comparison. The Tenth Dáil included forty farmers; many of these, no doubt, are technically 'landowners' in the sense that they hold their land in fee simple, subject to the payment of a land annuity, but real 'landowners' in the 1880 sense have ceased to exist in Ireland since the Land Act of 1923.

Of the thirteen lower group members of the 1880 party, ten had been elected for the first time at the general election of that year.

From the purely statistical point of view, therefore, all that happened to the balance of classes at the 1880 election was the 'replacement' of about ten landlords by the same number of individuals from the 'lower group', which may be roughly identified with the lower middle class. Yet this change seemed cataclysmic to some contemporaries. 'Gone', lamented Frank Hugh O'Donnell,[1] 'were all the colleagues who symbolized the union of Ireland under Isaac Butt; gone Lord Francis Conyngham . . . gone O'Conor Don . . . gone Hon. Charles ffrench and Hon. Wilfred O'Callaghan . . . Penny-a-liners from New York and Lambeth, from Mallow and Drumcondra; out-of-works from half a dozen modest professions had come in their place to earn the wages of Mr. Patrick Egan[2] and Mr. Patrick Ford.'[3]

From the tone of these words one would think that something on the scale of the Russian revolution had occurred. In fact, however, we have seen that, on one definition at least, the 1880 party was still predominantly upper class. How far they were from what we now regard as a popular assembly is shown by the very rough analysis I have given of the Tenth Dáil, and even that assembly would have been surprised to hear itself compared, in O'Donnell's catching phrase, with 'the sparkish ranks of the gay and desperate disclassees round Lucius Sergius Catilina'.[4]

The upper-class nature of the 1880 party as a whole is

---

[1] *History of the Irish Parliamentary Party*, i. 467. O'Donnell had been the most intelligent exponent of obstruction from 1877, when he entered parliament, up to 1880, and was elected on the 'active' or 'Parnellite' ticket at the general election of the latter year. He soon broke with the Parnellites, however, partly through dislike of the Land League (his avowed motive) and partly through jealousy of Parnell, whom he later described as his 'runaway errand-boy'. He himself was a journalist in London and so ranks with the 'lower group' in our classification, among the 'penny-a-liners' whom he so despised. For a description of his work see Bibliography.

[2] Treasurer of the Land League. It was widely believed that the Land League was paying a stipend to poor and 'extreme' M.P.s. On this point see Chap. IV.

[3] Owner and editor of the New York *Irish World*, through which large quantities of American money had come to the Land League.

[4] O'Donnell, *Irish Parliamentary Party*, i. 468.

confirmed by an analysis of its members from the point of view of education. Of the 61, 45 are known to have had at least a secondary education—this includes 6 of the 'lower-group' members—and some of those who, like Justin McCarthy[1] and A. M. Sullivan,[2] had received little formal education, clearly rank as belonging to the educated classes. The finer shades of social status, however, which would be accurately shown in England by 'school', are best adumbrated for nineteenth-century Ireland by 'university'. Table 4 shows, and sets in perspective, the number of university men in the 1880 parliament, and the types of university from which they came:

TABLE 4[3]

| University | 1874 *home rulers* (56) | 1880 *home rulers* (61) | 1880 *non-home rulers* (40) |
|---|---|---|---|
| Oxford or Cambridge . . | 3 | 2 | 11 |
| Dublin . . . . | 15 | 13[4] | 7 |
| English provincial . . | 5 | 4 | 1 |
| Queen's University or Catholic University . . . . | 1 | 5 | 0 |
| Total university men . . | 24 | 24 | 19 |

[1] p. 13, n. 2.
[2] A. M. Sullivan, b. 1830, a brother of T. D. Sullivan and a foundation member of the celebrated 'Bantry band', was one of the best-known members of the Irish party at this date. He had been a Young Irelander, and had later edited *The Nation*, had been sentenced (Feb. 1868) to six months for seditious libel on the government (an article on the Manchester Martyrs). As well as having a 'national record' he was a man of considerable ability. He received the honour of a special call to the English Bar in 1877, and was the author of a popular history, *The Story of Ireland* (1870), as well as other works. One of his books, *New Ireland*, evidently helped to mould the Churchillian conception of Ireland (Winston Churchill, *Lord Randolph Churchill*, i. 81).
[3] The materials for this table are drawn from *Dod, Boase, D.N.B.*, Burtchaell and Sadleir (*Alumni Dublinenses. A register of the students, graduates &c. of Trinity College in the university of Dublin*), and Foster's *Alumni Oxonienses* (1715–1886).
[4] Of the 13 Trinity men, 11 were Catholics, and 11 of middle-class origin. Two, William Archer Redmond and The O'Gorman Mahon, are sons of persons described as *generosus*, the rest of various *pragmatici* and *mercatores* (Burtchaell and Sadleir, op. cit.). It will be noted that nearly 25 per cent. of the whole Irish representation in 1880 were Trinity men, a phenomenon which has not since been repeated.

Though these figures are too small to bear any great weight of presumption, they tend to confirm our previous impression that the social gap between the home rulers of 1874 and those of 1880 was much less than that between all the home rulers and the Irish conservatives and liberals. From the point of view of education, as distinct from social status, there was probably little to choose between the groups. F. H. O'Donnell admits that even the twenty-three new-comers of 1880 had 'brains'—there were nine university men among them as well as some unacademic talent—but concludes that brains without property are a danger to the state.

We have examined the social position of the party as a whole. But this party was on the point of disintegration, was, indeed, in process of disintegration during the general election. One of the factions into which it divided was to become a dominating force in the politics of the United Kingdom for a decade; the others were to be absorbed, or disappear from politics rapidly. What was the political nature of these factions? What was their social make-up?

The first question has been answered very often, usually with acrimony. It may be well to set out the main facts here, briefly and with an attempt at objectivity.

The home rule party of Isaac Butt, which entered parliament in 1874, was, it is clear, a fairly prosperous body of Irish gentlemen. The aim of these gentlemen was to persuade an assembly of English gentlemen that the cares of Irish government could safely be devolved upon them. Their code was a liberal one; they believed both in the persuasive powers of human reason and in the virtues of enlightened oligarchy. It is often stated that their policy of convincing the House by reasoned argument was a failure, but it is only fair to add that it was not given a long or unimpeded test. As early as 1875 Joseph Biggar[1] had decided

---

[1] Joseph Gillis Biggar (b. 1828) was a wealthy Belfast provision merchant, son of a chairman of the Ulster Bank. He was a Presbyterian by origin, and was educated at Belfast Royal Academy, but had become, in 1877, a Catholic. He had been a member of the supreme council of the I.R.B., and was active in incitement at Land League meetings, but the centre of his interests was certainly parliament. 'Probably', claims his biographer in the *D.N.B.*, 'no member with less qualifications for public speaking ever occupied so much of the time of the House of Commons.'

to act on his, probably well-founded, conviction that conciliation was not getting anywhere. He tried a policy of
irritation; he bored the House with blue-books, insulted
Gladstone, insulted the Prince of Wales,[1] exasperated the
English gentry by his self-confident ungentlemanliness and
harsh, untiring garrulity. His only aims seem to have been
to keep the Irish question to the front, to make the English
wish the Irish had a parliament of their own, and to annoy.
In the first and third aims he was certainly successful and his
success aroused emulation. Obstruction was continued and
extended, and by the late seventies a little group of activists
had become the bane of parliament and the best-known men
in Ireland.

Frank Hugh O'Donnell, who entered parliament in 1877,
later claimed to have been the directing brain of the group.[2]
Certainly he was its most imaginative, as well as its most
articulate, member. He believed in constant well-informed
interference both in English affairs—to voice the feelings
and rouse the sympathy of the English masses—and in
imperial affairs—to act as a mouthpiece for the whole un-
enfranchised empire.[3] To this positive development of the
obstruction policy England owes, it is claimed, so important
a reform as the abolition of flogging in the army, and India,
according to O'Donnell, owes the formation of her Congress
party.[4]

---

[1] Not all these feats were performed as early as 1875, but the policy of
which they were the instruments began to come into operation in that year.
It was in the spring of 1875 that Biggar became notorious by 'espying
strangers' in the gallery of the House—one of the strangers being the Prince
of Wales.                                    [2] Op. cit., *passim*.

[3] O'Donnell tells us, for instance, that in 1874 he had been approached by
Indian political leaders to offer the Irish parliamentary party the 'political
and pecuniary support of a great Indian movement, on condition that Ireland
should elect some representatives of India to speak for India in the House and
that India in her turn was to endorse the Irish demand for self-government'
(op. cit., ii. 428). Butt, according to O'Donnell, had 'warmly approved the
idea' but was afraid of irritating English conservative opinion. Parnell 'could
not understand how such a proposal could excite interest in Ireland'. The
project was revived in 1883, when Davitt suggested an interventionist programme including the allocating of an Irish seat to Dadabhai Naoroje, the
Indian nationalist. Parnell after due consideration 'liked the plan very much'
but feared 'it would not be clearly understood in Ireland and might lead to
trouble within the party' (*Fall of Feudalism in Ireland*, p. 447).

[4] It is hardly within the scope of the present study to assess the truth of

The third of the principal obstructionists was politician enough to keep his eye on the Irish—whether in Ireland, England, or America—rather than on the English, the Indians, or the South Africans. Parnell did not care, at this stage, what happened to a measure, provided that the watching 'extremists' and their numerous associates were impressed. He was playing, very successfully, to the gallery.

The majority of his colleagues did not care for either the success or the gallery. Obstruction came to seem to them a form of rabble-rousing; some, we may reasonably assume, became jealous of the fame of the obstructionists, many fearful of its consequences. As early as July 1877, the founder of home rule, Isaac Butt, rebuked Frank Hugh O'Donnell in the House for his obstruction of the South Africa Bill. From that time on, the crack in the party, which was to develop into a split after the general election, was plain. On one side was the great bulk of the representation, priding itself on its loyalty to Butt, order, and the original principles of home rule; on the other was a little group, numbering not more than seven or eight,[1] which prided itself on its activity and its contempt for English institutions. The group could not, at this stage, be called Parnellite; Biggar and O'Donnell were too individualistic to be reliable followers of any man, and at least one other member[2] was a personal enemy of Parnell's. The tremendously rapid growth of Parnell's prestige was soon, however, to impose that label both upon the obstructionists and upon their policy.

The general election of 1880, therefore, was fought out, not merely between home rulers and anti-home rulers, but

this claim. In the reports of the first and second Indian National Congresses I can find only one reference to the home rule movement and that not an important one—the statement that 'in Ireland, where the religious antagonism of Protestants and Roman Catholics far exceeds that anywhere existing in India between Mahomedans and Hindus, a Protestant like Mr. Parnell represents a Catholic constituency' (Dadabhai Naoroje, Introductory article to the Report of the Second Indian National Congress, 1886).

[1] R. Barry O'Brien tells us that in 1877 'Parnell's force all told numbered five men—Biggar, O'Donnell, Kirk, O'Connor Power and himself': op. cit., p. 109. To these must be added Lysaght Finigan (elected 1879) and Philip Callan, and possibly also Captain Nolan.

[2] Callan, whom Parnell tried to drive out of politics in 1880 and did drive out in 1885. O'Connor Power was also on bad terms with Parnell.

within the home rule party, by 'whigs' and 'Parnellites'.[1]
As Parnell represented the link between the land agitation
and parliamentary obstruction,[2] those who were known to
be active in either of these movements tended to be called
Parnellites. The 'whigs', for their part, regarded both movements merely as different aspects of demagogy; they showed
their contempt for the emotional side of politics by grouping
themselves round the dim figure of the Congregationalist
banker, William Shaw.[3] Although feeling was strong between the two factions, open hostility during the campaign
was not widespread. Only six home rulers (in *seven* constituencies) were actively opposed by the Parnellites, who
denied 'the skilfully spread assertions of a wholesale intention to attack the seats of the present representative body'.[4]
Their declared policy, determined by the length of their
purse and by their fear of the common enemy, was to let
alone 'any M.P. who has been fairly or tolerably observant
of his pledges and attentive to his duties'.

It followed naturally that only in seven constituencies—
Sligo, Wexford, Dundalk, Louth, Mayo, Cork City and
County—did antagonisms become open.[5] In these areas the
Parnellites, according to the whigs, were communists, Gari-
baldians, atheists, and criminal conspirators:[6] and the whigs,
according to the Parnellites, were traitors to their country,
either asleep at their post or bought by English gold. In the
other constituencies the unity of the home rule movement
was stressed. Some whigs, in their anxiety not to have a
Parnellite sprung on them at the last moment, went so far

---

[1] These terms are used purely for convenience; they are the names by
which each faction was known to the other. As to the character of the 'whigs'
see Introduction, p. 8.                    [2] See Introduction.

[3] b. 1823, son of Rev. Samuel Shaw. He was minister of the Independent
church at Cork for four years (1846–50), later went in for business and became chairman of the Munster Bank. He was elected sessional chairman of
the Irish party after Butt's death in 1879. To do him justice he was perfectly
aware of his lack of glamour. 'I have not', he declared at the 'leadership'
meeting in 1880, 'the slightest intention of competing in popularity with
Mr. Parnell. Mr. Parnell is a good-looking young man' (*F.J.*, 19 May 1880).
He was not more successful at banking than at politics; the Munster Bank
collapsed in 1885, and remains the last Irish bank to have done so.

[4] *The Nation*, 13 Mar. 1880.

[5] The liveliest fights were those in Wexford and Cork County.

[6] See, for instance, *F.J.*, 12 Apr. 1880.

as to profess an admiration for the capacities and usefulness of Parnell, or announced their intention to pursue 'a truly active policy in parliament'.[1]

Even after the election no one could be quite sure immediately whether the Parnellites had 'won' or not. They had obviously made great gains; Parnell himself had been elected for three constituencies, and a number of young men of whom little was known except that they were recommended by him, had been returned.[3] But no one could be quite sure how these young men once elected would vote, or how actively whiggish the 'whigs', still numerically strong, would prove.[4]

These questions were partly solved when on 17 May 1880 a meeting was held in the city hall, Dublin, to elect a sessional chairman. The meeting was attended by 43 members: Parnell was elected by 23 votes as against 18 for Shaw.

Our analysis of the composition of the Parnellite, as opposed to the whig, group in the party must be based on this division, incomplete though it is. It would be dilution to include among the Parnellites those who later associated themselves with the victorious group.[5] It is legitimate,

[1] D. F. Gabbett, for example, a whiggish lawyer who later voted for Shaw against Parnell, declared in a campaign speech that 'it was only through fear of Parnell that the government did anything at all' (*F. J.*, 13 Mar. 1880). Even Shaw had gone so far as to say that he never saw a bailiff's cart without wanting to pull the linch-pin out of it. One aged whig, The O'Donoghue, issued an election address in which he announced, not only his support for Parnell, but also, very candidly, his motive: 'It will not surprise you to hear that at the end of so many years in parliament I should be sorry to lose my seat' (*I.T.*, 15 Mar. 1880).

[2] Cork County, Meath, and Mayo.

[3] For instance, T. P. O'Connor, Thomas Sexton, Garrett Byrne, and Arthur O'Connor.

[4] The newly elected members seem even to have been in doubt as to whether there would be a contest for the leadership. T. P. O'Connor later recalled that 'Up to a few days before the meeting there was practically no intention of proposing Mr. Parnell as leader' and that some gentlemen— John Barry, Richard Lalor, J. J. O'Kelly, Dr. Commins, Biggar, T. P. himself, and J. C. McCoan—staying in the Imperial Hotel a few days before the meeting on 15 May, had 'discussed the question of leadership and decided to nominate Parnell' (*Parnell Movement*, p. 370). Parnell's own idea—to which, however, he cannot have held very strongly—was apparently to have Justin McCarthy elected to prevent a split (Sherlock, *Parnell*, p. 83).

[5] Or those, who like F. H. O'Donnell were Parnellites before the election but not after it.

however, to place among the Parnellites John Dillon, who had been with Parnell on his American tour and was still in America at the date of the meeting, and to place with the whigs three members who a few days after the fatal division publicly associated themselves with the supporters of Shaw by sitting along with them on the government side of the house.[1]

This gives us 24 definite Parnellites, 21 definite whigs, and 14 home rulers of indefinite affiliation. Most of the last group—and indeed two of the second—were gradually drawn to the side which had enthusiastic popular support, good leadership, a coherent (though flexible) policy, and the probability of victory in the next general election. The intransigent whigs no longer took an active part in home rule politics after Parnell became chairman; most of them formally seceded early in 1881,[2] and none of them survived the landslide election of 1885. After May 1880 the Parnellite group tends to become for most practical purposes, the home rule party.[3]

The first and most striking feature about the group is that it consisted almost entirely of new members of parliament. Nineteen of our 24 Parnellites were members who had been elected for the first time at the general election; 2 others were sitting only since 1879. The whigs, on the other hand, were comparative veterans; only 2 of them were 'new members', and 14 had been sitting since, at least, 1874.

A second feature is implicit, in some degree, in the first. The Parnellites were, on the whole, slightly younger than the whigs. This difference was, however, by no means so dramatic as is sometimes assumed. References to Parnell's 'brilliant young men' and the general tone of Parnellite

---

[1] The Parnellite policy was, of course, one of permanent opposition. The whigs believed in general support for a liberal ministry.

[2] Twelve members—Shaw, Blennerhassett, Brooke, Collins, Colthurst, Errington, Mitchell Henry, Meldon, O'Beirne, P. O'Brien, O'Conor, and Smyth—seceded in Jan. 1881 (*F.J.*, 18 Jan. 1881).

[3] Davitt later estimated that this election gave Parnell 'a following of 36 nationalist members' (*Fall of Feudalism in Ireland*, p. 238). Parnell himself, when questioned ten years later, put the figure at 'about 40' (*Report of the Special Commission*, vii. 27, 58, 488). These estimates exaggerate considerably; both Parnell and Davitt were probably unconsciously including the results of subsequent by-elections and 'conversions'.

Memoirs[1] tend to give the general impression that the clash was one between fiery youth and palsied age. In fact, the average age of fiery youth was 45·6 and that of the palsied party was 46·8. Nine of the whigs were over fifty: nine of the Parnellites also were over fifty. The over-sixty and under-thirty age groups had each one whig and one Parnellite.[2] It is obvious that the comparative ages of the groups do not supply any clue to their political adherences.

Nor does a comparison of religions give a much better clue. Both sections consisted, as might be expected, largely of Catholics; and both had Protestants for their leaders. There were two Protestants among the followers of Parnell and five among the followers of Shaw. Admittedly a mere division into Protestant and Catholic is not sufficient, and it must be conceded that there was an Erastian tinge in some of the Catholic Parnellites that was not to be seen in any of the Catholic whigs. In the seven disputed constituencies the clergy, or at any rate the politically vocal part of the clergy, had generally taken the side[3] of the whiggish candidates. Parnell's own candidature for the city of Cork was condemned at a meeting of the bishop and clergy of Cork,[4] and Parnell himself was stigmatized as a 'self-elected dictator'. In the Cork county election Canon J. V. Cullinane disclosed that 'one of Mr. Parnell's followers boasted that he ate meat on Good Friday and that he was the follower of Garibaldi the assassin'.[5] In the Wexford contest, where the issue was whether the whiggish Chevalier O'Clery, a 'soldier of the Pope', was to be allowed to keep his seat, the people's mind became so inflamed by differing emotions and irreconcilable loyalties that an exceptionally violent free fight occurred, at

---

[1] The various reminiscences, for instance, of T. P. O'Connor, or William O'Brien (see Bibliography).

[2] The oldest man in the party. The O'Gorman Mahon (b. 1803), was a Parnellite.

[3] Many of the clergy at this time considered it their duty to intervene actively in election campaigns. The venerable Archbishop McHale, for instance, issued the following formidable warning in the form of an advertisement: 'The present representatives of this county [Galway] have given so much satisfaction to their constituents that I should consider any attempt at a contested election . . . both unwise and ungrateful to its excellent members. Faithfully yours, John, Archbishop of Tuam' (*F.J.*, 13 Mar. 1880).

[4] Ibid., 2 Apr. 1880.

[5] Ibid., 13 Apr. 1880.

Enniscorthy, in which Parnell was assaulted.[1] In these circumstances, and although, in constituencies where there was no clash between the two home rule groups, the clergy supported Parnellites and whigs alike, it was not surprising that the Parnellites sometimes raised the cry 'No priests in politics', which was so often to recur in a harsher struggle ten years later. Lysaght Finigan, one of the younger and 'wilder' Parnellites, declared at Macroom[2] that, although himself a Catholic, he was 'determined, so long as there was no religious question intervening, to dispute the right of the priests to interfere against the interests of the people'. Three or four of the Parnellites seem to have been suspected with some reason of anti-clericalism, and of being influenced by the more dangerous currents of French or British radicalism.[3] This suspicion tended to be confirmed by the fact that, as will be seen below, many of the Parnellites lived in the great cities of England, in what was believed to be an atmosphere of irreverence and irreligion. None the less, the great majority of them seem to have been of unchallenged orthodoxy, although their political convictions, or the party line, sometimes compelled them to differ in non-essential matters from the leaders of their church. Clerical hostility to Parnellism at this time sprang not so much from any doubts as to the religious bona fides of the candidates, as from the church's general suspicion of all movements of a revolutionary or semi-revolutionary character—a suspicion which was particularly marked in the years closely following the European disturbances of 1870–1. 'Parnellite dictation' was resented and denounced because it reflected the growing strength of the New Departure—with the Land League and 'the fenians' behind it. The shade of apparent 'religious'

[1] The Chevalier's chairman, Father Murphy, made a stirring appeal to local, national, and religious traditions—'Here in the shadow of Vinegar Hill is it to be told that the priests and the bishop and the people of Wexford cannot select their own candidate?' (F.J., 29 Mar. 1880).

[2] Ibid., 13 Apr. 1880.

[3] J. J. O'Kelly, for instance, who had fought in France, was proud of his acquaintance with such dangerous characters as Rochefort and Clemenceau. T. P. O'Connor was a self-avowed 'advanced radical' (Dod) and, according to Tim Healy, was 'opposed to the priests' (Letter to Maurice Healy, 22 Oct. 1879, quoted in Letters and Leaders of my Day, i. 76). Lysaght Finigan, whose views are quoted above, had also been in France.

difference that existed between whigs and Parnellites was, therefore, not a cause but a result of politico-economic differences.

Closely allied with this quasi-religious difference, but more fundamental than it, was a difference in the degree of association with 'extreme nationalist' movements, i.e. movements which had contemplated or attempted separation from England by force of arms. Only one of the whigs, P. J. Smyth,[1] had been associated with any such movement. Smyth had taken part in the Young Ireland movement of 1848—which by 1880 had become almost respectable—and was among those who organized the escape of John Mitchell in 1854. This political extremism was balanced, however, by social conservatism, and it was his aversion from the doctrines of the Land League[2] which drove him to join with a group of men who seem to have been unanimous in their loyalty to the crown. Mitchell Henry, of Manchester and Kylemore, undoubtedly expressed the feelings of his fellow whigs when he declared that 'If rebellion broke out in Ireland (which is stuff), home rulers . . . would support the authority of the Queen in the most loyal manner.'[3]

This statement certainly did not hold good, at this time, for all the Parnellite members. Two of these, Joseph Biggar and John Barry, had been members of the supreme council of the Irish Republican Brotherhood,[4] and four others were described by the Dublin Metropolitan Police, in their

[1] b. 1823, M.P. since 1871. The extremism was, even as late as the sixties, genuine enough to attract police attention—there are brief factual references to him in S.P.O., Irish Crimes Records, 1862–5 (see Bibliography).

[2] He had admitted even before the election that he 'did not approve of all the League's doctrines' (F.J., 18 Mar. 1880).

[3] Undated letter to The O'Gorman Mahon, quoted in Denis Gwynn, Life of The O'Gorman Mahon, p. 227. Mitchell Henry (b. 1826) was a Manchester magnate who had failed three times (1865, 1867, and 1868) to be elected for an English constituency as a liberal. Then, his biographer in the D.N.B. tells us, 'his interest in angling brought him to the west of Ireland', where he bought Kylemore castle and 9,000 acres of land. He was elected for Co. Galway as a home ruler in 1871.

[4] Special Commission Act 1888, Report &c. 1890, viii. 365. Biggar admitted he had joined the fenians in 1875 or 1876 and had been expelled from the supreme council in 1877. He also stated that Barry had been a member of the supreme council.

confidential communications, as 'fenians'. John Dillon, according to the D.M.P., was 'a cool fenian ... trusted by the American branch';[1] J. J. O'Kelly was 'decidedly a fenian';[2] T. D. Sullivan had been 'an active agent in 1864–5'[3] and was 'suspected of propagating fenianism during election';[3] W. H. O'Sullivan[3] had been arrested under the Suspension of Habeas Corpus Act in 1867 because his house was at one time said to be 'the rendezvous of Captain Dunne and other active fenians'[3] and because 'he acts in concert with other well-known conspirators and the D.I. looks on him as most dangerous'.[3] John Barry himself was 'by common repute an advanced fenian, openly associated with low members of the society'.[4] Even allowing for the fact that the D.M.P. definition of fenianism was probably not pedantic, we may take it that they had developed a good nose for disloyalty, and that the five gentlemen they named—four of whom, it is worth noting, belong to the 'lower group' in our system, and four of whom were new members, were or had been extreme nationalists of one sort or another. With Biggar, we have six 'extremists', or one-quarter of the total Parnellites, a fairly high proportion. Parnell himself, of course, did his best to conciliate fenians, without committing himself to much and was apparently successful in this.[5] The

[1] S.P.O., Mallon Report: 'Student for the medical profession, not very industrious. ... Trustworthy persons who know him say he fully agrees with J. Devoy's principles and is really a cool fenian, trusted by the American branch.' For an assessment of Dillon as a constitutional politician, see Chap. VIII, pp. 250 sqq.

[2] S.P.O., Mallon Report: O'Kelly uses very 'fenian' language in his correspondence with John Devoy (see, for example, letter of 21 Sept. 1882 in Ryan and O'Brien, *Devoy's Postbag*, ii. 140). The tendency of his advice is, however, towards moderation.

[3] S.P.O., Irish Crimes Records, 1862–5.

[4] S.P.O., Mallon Report.

[5] R. Barry O'Brien, *Parnell*, p. 110, reports that a certain fenian (anonymous) was deputed, c. 1877, 'to ask Parnell to join us. He said "No" without a moment's hesitation.' F. H. O'Donnell reports a conference in the spring of 1878 between two fenian leaders, John O'Leary (Ireland) and Dr. Carroll of Philadelphia, and the two leaders of the 'active party' in parliament—Parnell and O'Donnell himself, and states that Parnell's comment after the meeting was 'The fenians want to catch us but they aren't going to' (*Irish Parliamentary Party*, i. 271). At a somewhat later stage a Clan na Gael emissary, W. M. Lomasney, reporting to John Devoy on a meeting with Parnell in Paris said: 'I feel that he is eminently deserving of our support and that he means to go as far as we do in pushing the business. . . . John O'Leary is

supreme council of the I.R.B. had, it seems, condemned parliamentarianism afresh in 1877, and had expelled Biggar for not supporting the resolution. The parliamentarians, however, were not so much interested in the supreme council as in the votes and active support of rank-and-file fenians and 'fellow travellers'. By putting forward men with a 'national record', by the example of their own activity, by the use, occasionally, of theatrical gestures of intransigence, and above all through the land movement, the Parnellites succeeded in getting that support, which had been almost completely lacking during the 'whiggish' stage of the home rule movement.[1]

On the land question itself, the cleavage was sharp and clear. The Parnellites favoured the Land League programme —the key to which at the moment was the stopping of evictions—the whigs, although most of them paid verbal tribute to the remote 'principle of a peasant proprietary', feared and disliked the league. Indeed it was primarily by reason of their fear that most of them were whigs at all. Yet it is an over-simplification to say, as F. H. O'Donnell did, that 'one-third of the parliamentary representation' i.e.

pleased with him but doesn't like his associates' (letter of 18 Feb. 1881, in O'Brien and Ryan, *Devoy's Postbag*, ii. 40). Mr. Ryan holds that at this time 'it is arguable that Parnell may, for a short and certainly last time, have contemplated a guerrilla phase of the struggle or even insurrection'. The argument would be founded mainly on an alleged, and at any rate inconclusive, interview in Paris with the spy Le Caron in Apr. 1881 (ibid., ii. 80–87). Dr. Moody's statement in his essay on *The New Departure in Irish Politics* which Mr. Ryan quotes (p. 87) that Parnell 'used the fenians in the interests of parliamentary action and did not permit himself to be used in the interests of revolutionary action' is fully borne out by a study of Parnell's actions, as distinct from his reported conversations, at this crucial period.

[1] The following commentary from a police informer may supply a clue to what a few of the more teleologically minded among the fenians were aiming at in associating themselves with parliamentarianism at a still earlier date: 'They (the exiles in America) indorse the agreement entered into by Smyth and others to support the home rule movement in every way both at elections and in getting up demonstrations so as to convulse the country as far as possible in order that the home rule idea may be carried out without fighting and then they argue that they can easily procure arms and make a bid for total separation' (1871) (S.P.O., Fenian Papers, 7531). The parliamentarian idea in flirting with fenianism was more tersely expressed by Biggar: 'What I thought I could do was to direct the parliamentary election by the assistance of the (fenian) organization' (*Special Comm. Proc.*, viii. 365). Some deduction must be made from both these statements, for persuasive bias.

roughly speaking all the Parnellites—were leaguers. The only members who had played, at this time, at all prominent parts in league affairs were O'Connor Power, who was by no means a Parnellite, Parnell himself, Biggar, Dillon, Sexton, and Lysaght Finigan. The others seem to have been only leaguers by contingency,[1] inasmuch as they were 'Parnell's men' and Parnell was president of the league. The distinction was to prove of some importance.

We have done something by now to establish the general political and social orientation of the Parnellites. They were, as compared with the whigs, fresh to politics; they had a streak of 'fenianism', a streak of more exotic radicalism; and they were committed to a very advanced land programme, which they had not themselves evolved. These are all fairly well-recognized facts. But we have yet to answer the questions; where did they live, and what did they do for a living?

During the election campaign the cry 'Parnellite carpetbagger'[2] was frequently raised by the whigs, and with some justice as the result was to show. Only two of the whigs lived permanently in England—some others had residences in both countries—but no less than ten of the Parnellites lived there, mostly in London and Liverpool. Ten of the whigs lived in the constituencies which they represented; only four of the newly elected Parnellites did so. It was easy, in these conditions, for opponents of Parnell to view with alarm the overthrow of an old paternal system, under which a county had been represented by a local man of standing, who knew and loved his people, in favour of a soulless machinery which gave the county a man completely ignorant of local conditions, and not even living in the same country. The complaint was understandable but futile; the people were ceasing to vote for local representatives and beginning to vote, through party nominees, for a national leader and a national programme. As the party, at that time, had hardly any money, the leader had to look for nominees who could afford to leave their businesses and go to West-

---

[1] Within a few months of the election many of them, of course, were in the thick of the league agitation.

[2] 'Carpet-baggers' was the phrase of the *Freeman's Journal*; the *Irish Times*, retorting for the landlords, preferred 'absentee representatives'.

minster, or, alternatively, men whose businesses lay close enough to Westminster to enable them to combine a parliamentary career with the earning of a living. As the programme of the Land League was not attractive to many members of the former class, he was forced to fall back in many cases on his 'carpet-baggers'—the Irish in England.

The question: what did they do for a living? may first be answered in tabular form, on the same lines as the comparison between the parties of 1880 and 1874 (Table 3 above).

TABLE 5

| Group | Class | Whigs ('21) | Parnellites ('24) |
|---|---|---|---|
| 'A'<br>Upper<br>group | 1. Landowners (over 1,000 acres) | 5 | 0 |
| | 2. Industrialists, large merchants, rentiers    .    .    .    . | 8 | 6 |
| | 3. 'Higher' professions    .    . | 8 | 7 |
| | Total group 'A'    .    .    . | 21 | 13 |
| 'B'<br>Lower<br>group | 1. 'Lower' professions    .    . | 0 | 7 |
| | 2. Farmers, small shopkeepers, wage-earners    .    .    . | 0 | 2 |
| | 3. Undefined occupations or 'no occupation'    .    .    . | 0 | 2 |
| | Total group 'B'    .    .    . | 0 | 11 |

On this analysis the 'whigs' are all 'upper class' and the Parnellites are about half-and-half. Even if we admit that the division is not likely to be perfectly correct, it still appears that the cleavage along class-lines is more definite than any other difference we have yet remarked, except for the differences in views on the land question and newness to Westminster. And yet, looking back from our own point in time we are struck rather by the number of wealthy and successful men among the Parnellites, than by their general comparative poverty. There were among them two rich merchants, a prosperous Dublin publisher, a very popular London novelist, and two members of the English Bar. Although none of them could claim to rank primarily as 'landlords', four of them owned more than 200 acres of Irish land. And their leader was an Irish landlord.

Yet to unfriendly contemporary eyes, the total impression they conveyed was one of squalor. The fastidious Sir Henry Lucy, for example, was shocked out of the amused disdain with which he had hitherto affected to regard most of the Irish representation, into positive alarm. Parliament, he exclaimed in his diary, had been invaded by the manners of the Irish peasant. Several of the new Parnellites—and even more of those elected after 1880—were not content with simply 'not being gentlemen', they were dynamically, noisily, plebeian, and demonstrated to those who had always suspected a connexion between obstruction and 'the mob', how right they had been. Those who criticized, often in bitter language, the manners of the new representatives were, however, also paying an unwilling tribute to their determination and activity.

The change in the character of the representation can probably be attributed in the main to two causes, the Ballot Act of 1872 and the agricultural depression of 1879. The Ballot Act, which introduced the system of secret voting, had been in force at the previous general election, but suspicious country folk seem to have been slow to believe that their landlords would really have no opportunity of inspecting their ballot-papers. The crop failure and low prices of 1878 onwards, however, certainly exacerbated their anti-landlord feelings and perhaps tended to make them less in dread of eviction; also the spirit of resistance fostered by the Land League, and the operation of the boycott, were beginning to rob the landlord of the power of arbitrary eviction; again, even some of the more faint-hearted were no doubt moved to an electoral revolt by the assurance, given by men whom they trusted and respected, that the ballot really *was* secret.[1] The most obvious effect of this was that, as we have seen above, no landlord gained a seat and many landlords lost their seats, being replaced by individuals from various strata of the middle classes who had declared their opposition to landlordism.

This description is colourless and so, to some extent, misleading. Many of the Parnellites were men whose careers or

[1] Assurances by the Parnellites that the 'secret ballot' really meant what it said were a marked feature of the campaign (*F.J.*, Apr.–May 1880).

personalities were picturesque and bellicose; swashbucklers or fighters, with something theatrical and even stage-Irish about them, suitable for the excited mass-meetings and the generally turbulent semi-revolutionary atmosphere of the time. Such a man was the anti-clerical Lysaght Finigan who peppered his election speeches with reference to his battles in distant lands when he had served in the French Foreign Legion and campaigned against the Germans with the army of the Loire. Such also was J. J. O'Kelly, who had been a war-correspondent in Cuba, had also fought the Germans in 1870, and was a well-advertised duellist. The classic example of the type was, of course, the O'Gorman Mahon who had nominated O'Connell in the Clare election and afterwards quarrelled with him, had married an heiress and squandered her money, had fought innumerable duels and been a soldier of fortune in Russia, Turkey, Austria, Uruguay, Chile, Brazil, and the United States, had been a general in one country and an admiral in another, and had in short done almost everything but practise his own profession of the law.[1] The appeal of such men was not so much their mere 'opposition to landlordism' as their capacity for surrounding the unromantic agrarian and electoral struggles with a haze of battle; the orators, Dillon and Sexton, made the same appeal with their storming denunciations and martial metaphors;[2] Parnell himself, in more subtle ways, managed to communicate the feeling that war was being waged against England.[3] In this way repressed instincts of violence, which might have burst out into open rebellion were enlisted in 1880, into the service of a Parnellism, the content of which, whether 'constitutional' or 'revolutionary', was still equivocal.

[1] Denis Gwynn, *The O'Gorman Mahon*.

[2] As Tim Healy, years afterwards, observed to Labouchere: 'the English with their bayonets to rely on need not grudge us Billingsgate'. It is fair to observe that the language of Dillon and Sexton, violent as it was, was always chivalrous in tone. The 'Billingsgate' was the contribution of Healy and William O'Brien, after 1880.

[3] The equivocal association with fenianism was of course calculated to give the same impression, with an added touch of conspiratorial excitement.

# II

## THE PARTY AND THE LAND WAR (1880–2)

*To those who apprehend that Mr. Parnell may be carried away from the regions of practical commonsense into visionary and utterly unworkable theories, we would say—wait! Nothing so moderates a sensible man as success. . . .*

F.J., 14 Apr. 1880

### 1. *From the Election to the Land Bill*

BEFORE attempting to analyse the part played by the Irish parliamentary party in the crucial years 1880–2 it may be well to set out in a general way the main forces operating in the political context of which Parnell and his party were part. For the sake of vividness, I am presenting these forces in diagrammatic form. This diagram is, of course, very incomplete, and it cannot, for instance, indicate the relative importance of the factors shown, or the constant shifting of the whole complex under the impact of economic change, political decisions, and the turning of the seasons. It will be of some use, however, if it serves as a reminder that Parnell was by no means as free at this date as the later composite popular image of him represents.

He had risen to his position of leadership by becoming the very symbol of defiance and agitation, but the fact of being leader forced him to become something else again. As chairman of the party, and a man who had been returned for three constituencies, he now carried all the responsibility of being leader of the national movement. He had become the nodal point connecting a number of different groups and movements, with different objects and ideals, but having a minimum of agreement in so far as they all desired some measure of Irish emancipation from English control. He could not step far outside the minimum of agreement, by word or deed, unless he could be sure that the huge amorphous group at the bottom of the structure, the Irish farmers and their associates, would follow him against whatever pressure group, or combination of groups, he had offended.

He could not, during this early phase of his leadership, step outside it at all, unless he exercised tactical care, moving now a little to the left, now a little to the right, watching the while to see how the country was taking it. There was nothing peculiarly Irish about his dilemma; on the contrary it is the basic problem of all politicians in democratic countries. It is only because of the dramatic fiction that has grown up

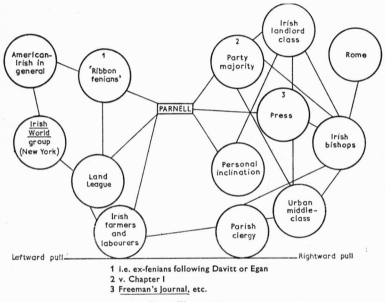

1 i.e. ex-fenians following Davitt or Egan
2 v. Chapter I
3 Freeman's Journal, etc.

Parnellism, 1880–2.

round Parnell, and pervades even the best biographies of him, that one finds it necessary to emphasize his cramped political position at this time. Certain personal characteristics of Parnell—'aloofness', 'inscrutability', &c.—were well suited to his political situation. A political leader must, after all, be a little aloof, unless he either possesses the stamina of a Dan O'Connell to be hail-fellow-well-met with all the world, or is willing to lose his leadership by being confounded in one section of his following. Parnell was inscrutable, but then inscrutability is an occupational disease of successful politicians. It really refers to phenomena, of which the causes are fairly clear. A leader is subject to fits

of silence, and that on the most important topics; when he
does speak his utterances are very likely to be partly self-
contradictory, strangely varying in emphasis, or subject to
revision in a short time. To the reader studying the period
afterwards, it becomes plain that he was silent at such a
time because he was waiting to see which way public opinion
was moving, and that his speech at $X$ differed from his
speech at $Y$, because his speech at $Y$ had offended the $Z$
interest, which he now wished to reassure. In the heat of
the struggle, however, and in the mind of the people, these
things are not so plain, and the leader is apt to become a
sphinx-like figure, and to accept the awe with which his
followers regard him as a welcome by-product of a difficult
situation. This acceptance of course may in turn result in a
certain self-dramatization as a man of mystery, but that is
a secondary phase. A difficulty with Parnell, as with other
leaders, is that his inscrutability and aloofness have accompanied him out of politics into history divorced from their
true context, as signs of an almost supernatural domination
over his environment, rather than as intelligently applied
techniques of power. The tragedy of his fall has made this
sort of deification—which blurs the real greatness of the
man—all the easier and more persuasive. The tendency of
his biographers to set him against a generalized 'background
of his time'—i.e. a panorama of fenianism and the land
movement—and to forget about his immediate political
surroundings has accelerated the process.

April 1880 was a period of crisis and the 'surroundings'
at that date accordingly constituted an exceptionally difficult
environment for the political leader. One complex set of
forces had supplied much of the drive to bring Parnell to
the top: these were the leftward groups and institutions
and individuals of the 'New Departure': the Land League
with its vote-catching power, the American Irish with their
money the enthusiasm of certain fenians under the influence
of Davitt and Egan, the propagandist power for votes and
money of Patrick Ford's *Irish World* in New York. A second
set of forces, on the right, was coming into play, now that
the New Departure under the symbol of Parnell, had scored
a success. The *Freeman's Journal*, the nationalist daily paper,

middle class in tone, and responsive to expressions of clerical opinion, very soon after the election gave Parnell a guarded salutation, and uttered a very sensible editorial forecast, quoted at the head of this chapter. Schematically, it might be said that the object of the 'left' was to carry out its various aims (of separation, land revolution, &c.) through the development of the land crisis, the organization of the Land League, and the general commanding force of its supposed 'figurehead', Parnell; it was the aim of the 'right' to oust what anarchic forces there might be on the left, by getting control over the league organization as far as possible, inducing the British government to mitigate the land crisis by means of ameliorative legislation, and appropriating, if possible, Parnell, using the Land League's symbol to charm away the Land League's power.[1] It was Parnell's own immediate aim—whatever his long-term object was—to keep the whole movement as powerful and united as possible and under his own leadership.

In this situation, one element of vital importance was the semi-rejuvenated parliamentary party, of which Parnell was now chairman. In the most literal sense the party constituted his immediate political context and to a great extent it must have been through its members that the other factors at work operated on him. He must have had to gauge public opinion largely by the reactions of the party, and, whether he did or not, he had, for the sake of prestige and of effective parliamentary action, to be able to command at all times the support of a considerable group of members. This being so, it was among the deciding factors at this crucial period that the party as a whole stood considerably to the right of the country in general.

There was a number of excellent reasons why this should be so.

Prominent among these was the restricted state of the franchise. The parliamentary constituencies of Ireland consisted of 32 counties and 31 boroughs, some of which returned two members. As regards both counties and

---

[1] It is not intended to imply that anyone necessarily thought exactly along these lines. The reference is to the tendency of the actions of the parties involved.

boroughs the franchise was confined to a far wealthier class, relatively, than that which possessed it in Britain.[1] In the counties the most important difference was that, in Ireland, the 40-shilling freehold vote, still valid in Britain, no longer existed. In the boroughs a valuation of more than £4 was required of an Irish voter, but any valuation served in England. Nationalists often drew attention to the anomalies resulting from these and other differentiations,[2] and pointed out, for instance, that Leeds had nearly four times as many parliamentary electors as Dublin, a city of approximately the same size, or that the east riding of Sussex and the east riding of Yorkshire, with a population just equal to that of Dublin and Limerick counties, had twice as many parliamentary electors. All the differential restrictions—the 'security' motive for which is obvious enough—were abolished by 1885, but not before they had been able to exercise a very powerful influence on the course of Parnellism. They had a double effect. One, that which was no doubt intended, was to keep out nationalists and home rulers of all tints. The other, and more insidious, was to bring in 'safe' men with a 'home rule' label—many of them local gentlemen of means who added 'H.R.' to 'liberal' in order to swing round the marginal votes against their conservative opponent. Thus Youghal's 289 votes put in the whiggish (but adaptable) landlord, Sir Joseph Neale McKenna; Tralee's 355 returned The O'Donoghue, whose political gyrations we have already observed; Galway, with its 875 voters, had a safe seat for a

---

[1] *Franchise and Registration Law* by Henry Hunt (1885, Dublin) is the most detailed work dealing with the franchise at this period. Although its main purpose is to state the law as it existed in 1885 it also gives an adequate account of what the law regarding the franchise was before the passing of the Representation of the People Act, 1884, &c.

[2] An examination of parliamentary papers reveals the degree of rottenness of the Irish boroughs to have been not less than the nationalists claimed. The average number of electors per borough in England and Wales was 8,000; the corresponding figure for Ireland was about 1,850. British boroughs had one member for every 40,000 of population; the 31 Irish boroughs had a member for every 25,000. It would appear that about one-fifth of the total English and Welsh borough-population were electors whereas in Ireland the proportion was lower than one-tenth. As is well known, Ireland became over-represented in the imperial legislature but at this date any over-representation was monopolized by these supposedly safe boroughs (see Parliamentary Papers, 1880 (382), lvii–1; 1884–5 (259), lxii–271).

shipowner, J. O. Lever, whose obeisances to home rule were perfunctory to the point of cynicism. Of the twenty-one 'borough' members returned on 'home rule' principles only five voted for Parnell at the crucial leadership election.[1] In the counties the dice were less heavily loaded, but even there the gap between 'public opinion' and 'voters' opinion' existed. The whigs could not have held their ground in a large electorate, as the results of the first elections held on a reformed franchise—in the much less revolutionary atmosphere of 1885—were to prove. But even before the reform of the franchise, Parnell seems to have captured the restricted electorate, at least to the extent of ousting whigs, as the by-election results 1880–4 show.

Another factor, of minor, but distinct, importance was the actual cost of getting returned. At this time there was no party machine in working order to pay candidates' expenses, and although a certain amount of Land League money appears to have found its way into the war-chests of candidates favoured by the league—and in at least one case the expenses of a candidate were met by popular subscription—the great majority of would-be parliamentarians must have had to pay their own expenses. These expenses were fairly heavy. A parliamentary return[2] gives the figures for twenty-three of the home rulers: they average out at £414 per man, and we shall probably not go far wrong in assuming that the expenses of the other home rulers were near that average. Such an expenditure—especially when it led to a totally unremunerative and time-wasting occupation—would be a heavy deterrent to any member of the Irish

---

[1] After the election, when a bill for the assimilation of the Irish borough franchise to the English was going forward, an intelligent nationalist observer gave an indication of what a handicap the differentiation had been to the home rule party. The bill, said Tim Healy, would 'secure nearly a dozen more seats for the H.R. Party in places like Athlone, Bandon, Derry, Drogheda, Dublin, Dundalk, Galway, Portarlington, Mallow, Newry, Dungannon, while in five or six others it will enfranchise a class of men who will hardly consider their views adequately represented by the type of Collins or Moore' (London letter in *Nation*, 29 May 1880). For the period from the general election to Oct. 1880, this 'London letter' provides a friendly but illuminating running commentary on the actions of the party. Healy was elected to parliament in Nov. 1880.

[2] *Return of charges made to candidates at the late elections &c.*, Parliamentary Papers, 1880 (382), lvii–1.

middle class, and an impassable barrier to anyone of lower status. This must have had a double effect, similar to that of the restricted franchise described above, and although the data available are inadequate to base any conclusions as regards the expenditure of whig and Parnellite home rulers, it is fairly clear that 'unionist' candidates—to employ a term that did not come into fashion until some years later—were sometimes able to compensate for lack of popular enthusiasm by generous expenditure. The non-home rulers for whom we have figures averaged an expenditure of £1,699 per head, as against the home rule average of £414. The non-home ruler had to pay nearly twice as much per vote—although we may assume it did not often represent a direct purchase—as did the home ruler.[1] Such a situation placed a political premium on wealth, and made it almost impossible for Land League views to be directly represented, except by candidates whose expenses the league was willing to pay. This step it was generally, perhaps unwisely, unwilling to take.

When to the restricted franchise and the cost of election we add the expense of travelling to London, and maintaining oneself there while engaging in unpaid work, we have a fairly formidable list of reasons why members should have tended to be drawn—as we have seen that they were in fact drawn—from the wealthier classes of the community. But in addition to simple economic motives, there were more subtle conservative pressures at work. For one thing the absence of a party machine left a gap which was often filled, rather incongruously, by a different organization—the church. The home rule nomination was often in practice decided by meetings of 'the bishop and clergy' of the diocese in which the constituency was situated, In Co. Meath, for example, the diocese of Dr. Nulty, the earliest friend of the New Departure among the hierarchy, the 'clerical system' was seen at its most democratic. Before a by-election in February 1882 the bishop summoned his clergy to 'take counsel at once with your parishioners and inform yourself on the opinions they may have formed and the preferences

[1] The non-home ruler averaged about 1·7 votes per £1 expended: the home ruler got 3·1 votes for his £1.

they may entertain for individual candidates, in order that the choice the clergy will make at the coming meeting of bishop and clergy may be as nearly as possible . . . what the electors desire.'[1] Earlier a parish priest of this diocese had stressed in connexion with a similar meeting that the bishop made no attempt to impose his own views on it, and also pointed out that the decision of such a meeting should not be regarded as authoritative: 'The clergy did not assume at all the right to nominate a candidate, but to recommend to the constituency a certain individual.'[2] As we have seen, however, clerical guidance could take a different tone in other areas (cf. Archbishop McHale's intervention in the Galway election—p. 27, n. 3). As regards the general tendency of clerical action in politics over the whole home rule period, F. H. O'Donnell has some interesting remarks: 'Though the Irish Catholic clergy were ready to make use of the popular agitation in the first place for the purpose of procuring reforms which they believed to be necessary and in the second for shaking or destroying the ascendancy of the Protestant gentry, they were never in any doubt of the danger to society . . . and to the Christian religion . . . which underlay the explosion.'[3] 'Meetings of the bishop and clergy' were likely to pick the least revolutionary among those who were 'available'—i.e. those persons who had the time and money to stand, and who were willing to subscribe to the ideals of home rule and 'a peasant proprietary'. Again, the principal 'home rule' paper, the *Freeman's Journal*, was at this time distinctly right-of-centre—it was covertly anti-Parnell during the campaign of 1880—and members were more likely to get 'a good press' for moderation than for extremism. The most subtly powerful influence of all was that exercised by Westminster itself. The 'tone of the House' had a fascination that was all the more fatal to extremism in that it was precisely the ablest members who were most liable to be affected by it. A representative from Louth, another from King's County, might be indifferent to the Commons' opinion of them; but then their insensitiveness was only a concomitant of drunkenness in one case and

---

[1] *The Nation*, 18 Feb. 1882.  [2] Ibid., 22 Apr. 1881.
[3] *Irish Parliamentary Party*, ii. 363.

buffoonery in the other. The pick of the parliamentarians, however—Frank Hugh O'Donnell, O'Connor Power, Sexton, Tim Healy—tended to be won over by the gentlemanly atmosphere of debate, and by the good opinions won by an effective speech. In such an atmosphere members' ideas of what constituted 'extremism' tended to shift.

We have observed in Chapter I that for various reasons popular opinion had been able to effect a perceptible amount of 'downclassing' in the representation, and to extract Land League professions at least from a number of candidates who proved successful. But such a radicalizing and democratizing change could not, in the conditions of 1880, take place without the aid of exiles. As we have also seen, almost half of the Parnellites—that is to say the supposedly extreme wing of the party—lived in England. They were therefore particularly close to the moderating influence of Westminster, out of touch with the feeling of their constituents, and exposed to all sorts of pressures which tended to make them regard an 'extreme' period with anxiety, and a moderate one with relief.[1]

The first period of the new parliament, a period which lasted up to the beginning of August, was, with good reason, a moderate one. The home rule party, it must be remembered, had from its parliamentary inception, in 1874, existed under a tory government from which nothing could be hoped and which could therefore be flouted with impunity. None the less, the majority of its members had confined themselves to opposition of the most parliamentary and 'loyal' variety. Now, although the obstructionist section had been greatly reinforced, there was, as yet, no occasion for obstruction. A liberal government was in power, not responsible for the mistakes of its predecessor, and headed by Gladstone, venerated as the author of two great measures of Irish reform. The people of Ireland naturally looked with hope to this government for some measure that would

---

[1] An example of a very real form of pressure, not unlike boycotting, which could be applied to Irish members having a living to make in England is given by Justin McCarthy: 'During these troublous times of obstruction (1879–82) I found that the intense feeling raised among the general English public against the Irish obstructionists had a distinct effect on the sale of my books' (*Story of Ireland*, p. 251).

alleviate their terrible condition, and it would have been folly from every point of view for the Irish party to have begun by obstructing the working of the government. To impute the party's restraint at this period solely to the pressures listed above would therefore be wrong. But the character of the party was such that periods of peace like this were bound to encourage constitutionalism and weaken the convictions of the extreme men. In such a period the tone of the House became more binding, the party orators had a welcome chance of pleasing, and therefore of being won over, and the young extremist began to despise his former associates.[1]

This process of assimilation, or, as Sinn Féin was later to say, corruption, was a slow and interrupted one and certainly was not a matter of grave concern to many people in May 1880. The burning political question then was : would the new government put a stop to the evictions, which were rapidly increasing in number, just as they had increased after the great famine and for the same reasons. The action of the Irish members was considered in relation to this immediate problem, and not to the remote consideration of home rule. Although the followers of Shaw differed sharply from the Parnellites on the evictions question and on the land question generally, the trend of the parliamentary policy of the two factions during this session was very similar. 'Our attitude towards the liberal party', wrote Mitchell Henry, 'should be that of watchful expectation', and this slogan of the whiggish section, expressed in effect the feelings of the Parnellites also, although their motives and their execution of the policy were different.

At the very beginning of the session the two varieties of expectation were well displayed. When the Queen's address was read, O'Connor Power, on behalf of the Parnellites,

[1] A fine example of the latter phenomenon is furnished by Tim Healy. 'The sum received by the Land League for political purposes', he wrote to his brother, 'is about £40,000, but, as I tell Parnell, it is the greatest farce for him to have exhausted himself raising this in order that it may be pieced away by a little knot of nobodies in Dublin—Heaven knows how' (letter dated 18 July 1880, quoted in *Letters and Leaders of my Day*, i. 95). And at this date Healy was attending parliament merely in the capacity of a reporter and political secretary. For an assessment of him, as the prominent politician he later became, see Chap. VIII, pp. 254 sqq.

moved a moderately worded amendment, the purpose of which was to draw attention to the seriousness of the land crisis in Ireland, and to force the government into making some statement of policy in the matter.[1] Other Parnellites supported him in very temperate language, of which the keynote was given by Justin McCarthy: 'Two or three lines couched in sympathetic terms in the Queen's speech . . . would have prevented the great disappointment of the Irish people who usually looked to a liberal government for relief for their grievances.'[2] One would have imagined that no representative of a half-starving country could have spoken with greater moderation. But, the chief secretary Forster having spoken in a negative but vaguely conciliatory fashion, Shaw rose to support him: 'The rt. hon. gentleman had given a sufficient reason why legislation should not be strongly urged at present. It was a very large question. It required to be looked at all round . . . better that the rt. hon gentleman should wait for a year and try to make a bill of his own.'[2] It was clear from this that the whiggish home rulers would not only not put pressure, even of the most constitutional kind, on the government to remedy the land crisis, but would supply them with excuses, of the 'home-rulers-themselves-admit' variety, for inaction. Their group very definitely represented landlord interests[3] which no doubt calculated that an 'interim measure' involving, as it inevitably would, compensation for eviction, would mean a heavy drain on their resources, whereas a full-fledged Land Bill would enable them to draw off securely from the ex-chequer whatever might be lost in claims against their tenantry. The importance of this attitude was not merely that it played into the hands of the government but that it influenced the content of Parnellism itself. For the home rule party had not yet definitely split, and Parnell was still theoretically at the head of a party of over 60. Shaw himself had not yet unequivocally dissociated himself from Parnell's leadership,[4] and as long as he and his supporters remained

[1] F.J., 15 May 1880.          [2] Hansard, v. 252, col. 150.
[3] See Chap. I.
[4] After his deposition from the sessional chairmanship Shaw had stated that he 'would not quarrel with Mr. Parnell's election, provided it is under-stood that this is not a sanction of the principles that Mr. Parnell has been

in some sort of association with the Parnellites, the party still carried a great deal of rightist ballast. It is significant that Parnell did not take any steps, as he could easily have done, to expel the Shawites from the party—for example, for disobeying the majority decision to continue sitting on the opposition side of the House. Whether the failure to carry out such a 'purge' was due to forces at home, like the church and the *Freeman's Journal*, or to a politic judgement that the longer the theoretical unity of the party was preserved the more time there would be for right-of-centre waverers to climb on the Parnellite 'bandwagon',[1] it is certain that the ambiguous position was of advantage to Parnell against the leftward pressure of the Land League elements. His spokesman, Tim Healy, could tell the country, through the columns of *The Nation*, that, if the post-election Parnell was not so aggressive as of old, the fault was not his own. 'Since his election to the leadership Mr. Parnell seems to keep mindful of the fact that he has been placed at the head of . . . a composite party. He is obliged to remember that the whole of his flock is not so advanced as he.'[2]

The token amendment to the address having been 'by leave withdrawn', the next action of the Parnellites was to introduce a bill having for its object the compensation of tenants ejected for non-payment of rent. Once more the intention was to force the government to show its hand, and once more the mover was O'Connor Power. This strange character contained within himself many of the varying currents of the national movement. Once an active fenian, and the first M.P. to be associated with the Land League, he was by now an ardent parliamentarian, and had a personal grudge against Parnell. It was no doubt not merely

advocating in America and through this country for the last six or eight months. If that is the meaning of Mr. Parnell's election, I must declare . . . that I cannot follow in the wake of these principles and cannot be a member of the party' (*F.J.*, 19 May 1880).

[1] In the first session of the new parliament there was, as well as the Shaw and Parnell factions, a fairly large 'centre party' consisting largely of individualists with comparatively long experience of parliament, eccentrics incapable of forming part of any coherent grouping, and opportunists beginning to edge out of their allegiance to Shaw.

[2] London letter, 5 June 1880. The theme was more than once repeated in this column (e.g. 26 June 1880).

for his undoubted debating skill and knowledge of the land question, but also because of his neutral position, isolated from both factions of the party, that he was selected as chief spokesman on these occasions. O'Connor Power's bill had its second reading on 4 June, and the Parnellite manœuvre soon had the success intended. On 15 June the chief secretary indicated the government's intention of introducing a measure for the purpose of mitigating evictions, and on 18 June the government's Compensation for Disturbance Bill was introduced.

The introduction of this measure, the essence of which was that certain distressed evicted tenants might receive compensation out of the Irish church surplus, was a great victory for the cause of moderation among the Irish and a great reinforcement of it. The government had been brought to notice the land crisis—for the matter had been ignored in the Queen's speech—and this had been effected by thoroughly constitutional means, no use having been made of obstructive tactics. This seemed to show that, with a Gladstonian government in power, all that was required from home rulers was a Buttite policy of reasonable debate —a conclusion very palatable to many members of the party. As a matter of immediate practical politics within the home rule party, it meant that whigs and Parnellites would now in effect be collaborating on the most important Irish measure of the session.

The second reading of the bill was carried on 5 July by 295 to 217, the majority including 51 home rulers, representing a most unusually large and united attendance of the party. On the committee motion, as was natural, the union between the two home rule factions tended to dissolve.[1] The Parnellites believed that certain clauses (the so-called 'permission to sell' clause and the omission from the operation of the bill of all tenancies over £30) would not have the intended effect but would lead to clearances and consolidation. Failing to secure the deletion of the obnoxious

[1] Parnell, however, remained anxious to keep the whigs at least partially within the fold. On 14 July 1880 he 'welcomed (Shaw's) appearance in this debate, as he saw in that the prospect of receiving from him valuable assistance in the discussion which might take place upon the bill on a future occasion' (*Hansard*, 254. 428).

clauses, they decided to abstain from voting on the motion that the House of Commons go into committee, a decision not obeyed by the whig minority. This decision to abstain, which of course angered the liberal party, was to be described by the *Annual Register* as 'Mr. Parnell's declaration of war on the bill', but in fact it was not more than a token resistance. Parnell was well aware that the abstention of his followers did not endanger the passage of the bill, and in fact the Parnellites voted in strength for the third reading on 26 July.

On 3 August the House of Lords by an enormous majority threw out the Compensation for Disturbance Bill, and this period of moderation came to an end. Of this rejection, Joseph Chamberlain's biographer wrote: 'No more foolish vote is recorded in the annals of the Upper House, nor upon them rests a deeper stain.'[1] At the time the Queen was pleased. 'Dear Lord Beaconsfield', she wrote on 5 August, 'I cannot be entirely silent now the *event* has taken place. I hope you are *not* the worse. Do you *ever* remember so many voting against the government to whose party they belong? *I* do *not*.'[2]

Looked back at from a later point in time, that short period seems in some ways more illustrative of the party's real position than were the more exciting years immediately ahead. The story of the Compensation Bill was in some ways an epitome of the coming home rule struggle: the same patient and constitutional pressure by the Irish members, the same deceptive triumph, the same ultimate destruction. And even among the Parnellites the great liberal party already exercised powerful fascinations, though not yet the full hypnotism of 1890–1918. They were not of course quite the same fascinations that told on the followers of Shaw: members of the Parnellite faction tended to become attached, not so much to the liberal party as an institution, as to the person of Gladstone himself[3] or, in several cases at this time,

---

[1] J. L. Garvin, *Life of Joseph Chamberlain*, i. 322.
[2] *Letters of Queen Victoria*, G. E. Buckle, 2nd series, iii. 127.
[3] The following passages from *Hansard* show the trepidation with which two 'moderate' Parnellites followed Parnell's lead on abstention from voting on the Compensation Bill:
'Mr. DALY said he was one of those Irish members who under ordinary

to the radical wing of the liberal party under Chamberlain and Dilke. The famous Bradlaugh case first revealed the extent of these sympathies. In the first division (24 May 1880) as to whether the 'notorious atheist' should be allowed to take his seat, 13 home rulers, including 7 Parnellites, voted in his favour, and it later became clear that 5 other Parnellites supported him.[1] Such opinions, so remote from the views of the constituencies represented by these men, may not have been entirely due to the influence of English radicals, but they certainly revealed a mental atmosphere among certain Parnellites favourable at this time to a rapprochement with a section of Gladstone's party.

The action of the Lords had immediate repercussions in Ireland. The *Annual Register* tells of 'most disquieting reports . . . riots at evictions, assaults on grabbers . . . during the first weeks of August'. Queenstown saw a fenian arms raid on 11 August and elsewhere there were less spectacular disturbances.

The reaction of the parliamentary party was more cautious. One could hardly get a better illustration either of Parnell's fine political touch or of the nature of his leadership than what he did, and did not do, in this crisis. He did not denounce the House of Lords or call for its abolition; he did not hasten back to Ireland to address mass meetings; he did not incontinently set in to obstruct the civil service estimates. He simply, within two days of the rejection of the bill, asked the chief secretary for Ireland the following parliamentary question:

circumstances would have at once complied with the wish of the respected Premier. . . .'

'Mr. DAWSON said he should have been willing to surrender his judgement upon the question to the direction of the Prime Minister, but for . . .' (*Hansard*, 254. 72–73). Other home rulers spoke in similar vein.

[1] The twelve Parnellites of Bradlaugh sympathies were: Byrne, Finigan, Leahy, T. P. O'Connor, O'Gorman Mahon, O'Connor Power, Isaac Nelson, Biggar, Barry, McCarthy, O'Kelly, and Parnell. The first seven voted 'aye' on the first Bradlaugh division in the House, and the remaining five voted at a party meeting in favour of supporting him (*F.J.*, 5 July 1880). T. P. O'Connor had been a radical before he was a home ruler at all: F. H. O'Donnell blames him as the chief 'radicalizer' of the Parnellite party; O'Donnell, however, exaggerates the extent, and misconceives the nature, of Parnellite 'radicalism' which was much more opportunist than ideological—as the tory alliance was to prove (see Chap. III below).

'Whether in view of the rejection by the House of Lords of the Compensation for Disturbance Bill he proposes to employ the constabulary and military forces of the Queen for the purpose of assisting at the eviction of tenants who can be proved to be unable to pay their rents?'[1]

This neat manœuvre put the onus and odium of the coming evictions squarely on to the chief secretary's shoulders, while it also gave a hint of coming obstruction on the R.I.C. estimate, and above all—this was most characteristic of Parnell—gained valuable time during which the country's reaction could be properly appraised. The chief secretary, for his part, gave the only possible reply: 'We shall protect the officers of the courts of law in the execution of the law.'[2] On the following day, 6 August, a meeting of the Irish party —at which only seventeen members, almost all Parnellites, attended—resolved to 'oppose' the constabulary estimates and 'to place themselves at the disposal of the country' at the end of the session.[3] Obstruction and agitation were definitely in the air but the party was not yet irretrievably committed to these policies. No member had yet made anything approaching a violent or seditious speech, and the first such speeches which occurred were certainly not made as a part of Parnellite policy. On 10 August John Dillon—fresh from America, new to the House, and still indifferent to its tone— used a type of language which had not been heard from Irish members since the advent of the liberal government to power. He hinted, not very delicately, at the uses of obstruction; shocked the House to its core by declaring that he did not share the chief secretary's confidence 'either in the forbearance of Irish landlords or the cowardice of Irish tenants'; and warned of 'bloodshed and massacre' to come.[4] He followed this up by returning to Ireland and delivering at a Land League meeting on Sunday, 16 August, one of the most inflammatory speeches of the whole land campaign.[5] He advised that in every parish 'two active young men' on behalf of the Land League should visit each farmer who still remained outside that organization and persuade him to join

[1] *Hansard*, 255. 314 (5 Aug. 1880).
[2] Ibid. 315.
[3] *F.J.*, 7 Aug. 1880.
[4] *Hansard*, 255. 786.
[5] *F.J.*, 17 Aug. 1880.

it, and he foreshadowed a general strike against rent. This one-man 'New Departure', taken at a time when the rest of the Irish party were engaged in humdrum parliamentary activities of a highly constitutional character, pending the introduction of the constabulary estimate, probably caused almost as much consternation among the Parnellites as it did in government circles. Certainly, when the matter was raised in the House on the following day, only one Parnellite, T. P. O'Connor, rose to defend the absent Dillon, and he did so in the most apologetic fashion, not without reference to 'violent language' and 'exaggerated hopes'.[1] Clearly the Parnellites were anxious to hear the last of the 'two active young men', and the natural short-term result of Dillon's impetuousness would have been to induce even greater caution among them. But the chief secretary himself turned it instead into an occasion of further agitation. Forster would have been neglecting his duty had he failed to denounce Dillon's speech; it was his misfortune, however, that, with the first of those flashes of unearthly folly that were to wreck his career, he picked the one term in the whole vocabulary of denunciation that could infuriate the Irish people, stimulate the progress of the Land League, and goad the members of the Irish party to support their reckless colleague. 'Its wickedness', he blurted out, in his attack on the speech, 'can only be equalled by its cowardice.'[2] The incredible tactlessness of taunting the representative of a subject people, in an excited time, with cowardice, was quickly rewarded. The *Freeman's Journal*, not previously much taken with Dillon or his policy, now sprang hotly to his defence, and on 23 August, when the matter next came up in parliament, Dillon found not one defender but fourteen, few of whom disowned anything said by him.[2]

As it happened the long-awaited constabulary estimate was introduced on the following day, and the Dillon–Forster episode with the consequent rise in the party temperature, made it certain that the 'opposition' to the estimate would be of an obstructive nature. Nineteen home rule members joined in the discussion on the estimate, some of them, in particular A. M. Sullivan, returning again and again with

[1] *Hansard*, 255. 136.                    [2] Ibid., 1373.

admirable pertinacity, so that the House was forced into an all-night sitting. It was the first genuine piece of obstruction in the new parliament, and the first intimation of how power-ful the weapon was in the hands of an expanded active party.[1] And yet it was still no more than a token display and the Parnellite policy was still one of wait-and-see. In the very midst of obstructing the estimate, on 24 August, Parnell had indicated that he was not engaged in any very serious attempt to defy the House. 'It is idle to charge us with ob-struction', he explained quaintly, 'when we have waited until the last days of the session to commence a course of obstruction.' Later, when the estimate was being allowed to pass, he was more explicit: 'He wished to say that sub-sequently to a speech which [Forster] delivered on Tuesday, the Irish members abandoned their intention to use the forms of the House to oppose the vote. . . . They considered that two nights' discussion would be sufficient for the pur-pose of putting the ground of their opposition to these esti-mates before the English public.'[2] As Forster's speech of Tuesday, 23 August, had contained nothing more promising than a hint of both a Land Bill and a Coercion Bill for the coming session, it was evident that the Irish party were still giving appreciable signs of willingness to be concili-ated. The brief remainder of the session passed without further signs of obstruction, or verbal violence of any kind, from the Irish party, and parliament was prorogued on 7 September.

In accordance with their promise to 'place themselves at the disposal of their country' the leading Parnellites returned without delay to Ireland. Parnell himself arrived in Dublin on 9 September, but adjourned immediately to the Wicklow hills for the shooting[3] without giving any lead on the land question. It was not until 19 September, ten days after his return and nearly seven weeks after the rejection of the Compensation Bill, that he at last spoke without ambiguity

[1] T. M. Healy said in his London letter that 'about five members of the party—Biggar, Barry, Dillon, Finigan and A. O'Connor—used active pres-sure on their leader to influence determined hostilities on this estimate' (*Nation*, 4 Sept. 1880).      [2] *Hansard*, 256. 658.
[3] Letter from Parnell to Mrs. O'Shea, quoted in Katherine O'Shea, *Charles Stewart Parnell*, i. 141.

and proclaimed at Ennis the Land League policy. The policy of the 'moral Coventry' for land-grabbers, the policy which was shortly afterwards to take, triumphantly, the name of 'boycotting', was not new—indeed 'peaceful picketing' had been the essence of the league's doctrine, if not always its practice, from the first—but Parnell's cold and systematic description of it at that Ennis meeting gave it a new and tremendous impetus. It rapidly became apparent, as the tempo of agitation quickened, and all the most important sections of Irish nationalist opinion—the Land League, the priests, and the *Freeman's Journal*—followed Parnell unswervingly, that he had taken the right line, whatever English or conservative opinion might say of him. He had apparently taken care not to advance without securing his right flank. There were no fewer than eight priests on his platform at Ennis[1] and the other league meetings of that and following Sundays were also well patronized by the clergy. Lysaght Finigan (the leading anti-clerical of the general election campaign), following Parnell at Ennis, referred significantly to 'the priests and the people united once more'. The *Freeman's Journal*, usually certain either to hedge or adopt a conservative line in presence of any new development, had, as if inspired, its first really eulogistic leader on Parnell the day after the Ennis meeting. A month afterwards it adverted editorially to the fact that 'Slowly, but surely and steadily, the priests of Ireland are taking up their position in masses on the right centre of the army of agitation.'[2]

The Ennis meeting was synchronized with other great Land League meetings at Loughrea, Cork, Galway, and Cahir. These Sunday meetings, usually attended by one or more Parnellite M.P.s—most frequently Dillon, Sexton, Biggar, O'Kelly, T. D. Sullivan, Lysaght Finigan, T. P. O'Connor, or A. O'Connor—and with many clergy on the platform, became the main feature of the autumn agitation. Parnell spoke, always on the same lines, at New Ross on the following Sunday, and at a great processional 'tar-barrel' demonstration at Cork on the Sunday after (3 October) which probably marked the climax both of the land agitation and of his own popularity as a semi-revolutionary leader.

[1] *F.J.*, 20 Sept. 1880.                    [2] Ibid., 22 Oct. 1880.

Further meetings on 11 and 17 October continued the agitation without opening any really new lines. On 24 October at Galway Parnell delivered a speech in which he seemed to appeal to the political rather than the social extremists and stated candidly that he 'would not have taken off his coat' over the land war if he had not thought it would lead to the independence of Ireland.[1] On 31 October at Tipperary, and again at Athlone on 9 November with O'Sullivan, he spoke on more orthodox Land League lines. By this time the success of the agitation was beyond all doubt. Its most splendid advertisement was the excursion to Mayo (11–26 November) of fifty Orange labourers under military guard to gather belatedly the crops of Captain Boycott, but far more significant than this Humpty-Dumpty-like escapade was the sharp falling-off in evictions.[2] The landlords, through the general fear whether of outrage or of boycotting, had temporarily lost their power.

For the purposes of distraction, and as a demonstration of the necessity for a measure of coercion, the government decided to prosecute the leaders of the Land League on charges of conspiracy to prevent the payment of rent. On 2 November five M.P.s—Parnell, Biggar, Dillon, T. D. Sullivan, and Sexton, along with Egan, Brennan, and other prominent leaguers, were so prosecuted. These 'demonstration trials'—brought on for the edification of English public opinion, in order to prove to critics on the right that the government was 'doing something' and to critics on the left that the ordinary law was really inadequate for Irish purposes—had the usual effect of political prosecutions in Ireland.[3] Enthusiasm for the 'traversers' rose; a defence

[1] Ibid., 25 Oct. 1880.
[2] 'Under the pressure of the land agitation the figure for the numbers evicted decreased from 3,447 in the third quarter of 1880 to only 954 during the last three months of the year' (Palmer, *The Irish Land League Crisis*, p. 271).
[3] A memorandum of Forster's to Gladstone (dated 8 Oct. 1880) makes it clear that he plainly foresaw all the adverse effects of the prosecutions, in arousing enthusiasm for Parnell, healing 'the quarrel between the land leaguers and the nationalists', driving more moderate home rulers over to Parnell, and, finally, Parnell's acquittal. None the less he advised proceedings 'to make it clear that we are not in league with them' (T. Wemyss Reid, *Life of W. E. Forster*, ii. 255–8). This is a classic example of the self-defeating nature of the attempt to combine colonialism and democracy.

fund was organized by the *Freeman's Journal* and showed eventually a handsome surplus which was used for continuing agitation;[1] the ranks of the national movement closed, and some whiggish or otherwise anti-Land League members of parliament—Molloy, Smithwick, McKenna—indicated in various ways their solidarity. On 28 December, when the proceedings opened, the traversers were accompanied to their trial by an imposing escort of twenty-four M.P.s and a great miscellaneous following. The twenty-days trial, with the prosecution stressing the power of the league and the defence showing the reasons for that power, made excellent propaganda, and the almost inevitable disagreement of the jury which took place on 23 January appeared a definite victory for the national cause.

Advantage was taken of the favourable situation in order to consolidate and discipline the Irish party. A meeting of the party held in the city hall on 27 December at which 38 members were present, resolved unanimously, *inter alia*,[2] 'that all home rule members should henceforward sit in opposition.'[3] This presented whiggish members with a clear 'come in or get out' alternative. Shaw and 11 of his followers chose the latter course and formally seceded from the home rule party, in January 1881.[4] It is perhaps significant that of the 12 seceders, 9 were owners of Irish land. Some whigs

---

[1] It was revealed in 1882 that £21,000 had been received for the defence fund (£6,500 through the Land League, and £14,500 through the *Freeman's Journal*) and that only £15,000 was spent on the state trials. The balance formed part of the famous Paris funds (*F.J.*, 18 Oct. 1882; Davitt, op. cit., p. 373; see also Chap. IV, § 3). Several bishops, Cashel, Limerick, Cloyne and Ross, Clonfert, and Tuam, and the lower clergy in great numbers subscribed through the *Freeman's Journal*. If, however, the recollection of Peter O'Brien, later Lord O'Brien, better known as 'Peter the Packer', is to be trusted on such a point, relations between Parnell and the hierarchy were not, even in this crisis, really cordial. O'Brien, who was counsel for T. D. Sullivan, recalled in after years that he had suggested to Parnell that bishops should be called to give evidence 'But Parnell who even in those days had little affection towards the Catholic church said: "Don't produce the bishops; they would hedge" ' (*Reminiscences of the Rt. Hon. Lord O'Brien*, &c., ed. Hon. Georgina O'Brien, p. 29).

[2] For the other decisions of this meeting see Chap. IV, § 6.

[3] *F.J.*, 28 Dec. 1880.

[4] Ibid., 17 Jan. 1881. The seceders were Shaw, Blennerhassett, Brooks, Collins, Colthurst, Errington, Mitchell Henry, Meldon, O'Beirne, O'Brien, O'Conor, and Smyth.

ignored the decision altogether, some sat now on one side and now on the other, a few crossed the House and sat among the 'active section'[1] thus increasing the right-wing element in Parnell's following. 'You would be astonished', wrote Davitt to Devoy about this time, 'to find the class of men who are now joining us inside a movement with which I am connected. There is a danger, however, of this class and the priests coalescing and gaining control of the whole thing and turning it against us.'[2]

Parliament opened on 7 January 1881. Ireland, ignored in May 1880, was the main topic of the Queen's speech, which having referred to the 'extended system of terror' in that country, developed Forster's hint of the previous session by promising an 'Additional Powers' Bill and a Land Bill. But the months of agitation which intervened between Forster's remarks and the Queen's promise had so changed the temper of the country and the party that the programme which had once been a reason for abandoning obstruction was now a reason for beginning it. Parnell, still on his trial, began his obstructive campaign by what appeared to be a piece of pure 'constitutional opposition'. His amendment to the address[3] was to the effect that coercion was not required; he argued that the Land Bill should come first, also that the Land League provided a peaceful outlet for feelings which would otherwise break out in crime. Several Irish whigs and a few English radicals supported him and he was able to muster 57 votes (against 435) in favour of his amendment. His party then passed over into open obstruction, proposing amendment after amendment and renewing, in Gladstone's words, 'night after night . . . spontaneous debate aimed at no practical conclusion'.[4] The debate on the address did not end until 20 January, having taken eleven nights. On 24 January Forster brought in his coercion measure, the Protection of Person and Property (Ireland) Bill, and obstruction increased in intensity. The intensity of the obstruction

[1] 'The only members I noticed who sat on the government side last year and who have gone over to the opposition in consonance with the resolution of the party were Messrs. O'Shea, Smithwick, M'Kenna, Macfarlane . . . Mr. Brooks and Major Nolan seemed undecided' (*F.J.*, 8 Jan. 1881).

[2] Letter of 16 Dec. 1880 (*Devoy's Postbag*, ii. 23).

[3] *Hansard*, 257. 192.

[4] Ibid., 869.

was a measure of the fears entertained about the effects of the bill. 'I am necessitated', Davitt had written to Devoy in the letter already quoted, 'to take a conservative stand in order to stave off coercion, for if the Habeas Corpus is suspended the whole movement would be crushed in a month.'[1] It was, in the view of such an old hand as F. H. O'Donnell, a crude variety of obstruction; the intention of speakers was hardly camouflaged at all; the technique was uninspired, consisting simply of endlessly renewed motions for adjournment and 'that the speaker do now leave the chair'; only two of the industrious obstructives, A. M. Sullivan and his young kinsman T. M. Healy showed any debating skill or ingenuity in the handling of red herrings. Sullivan was a really fine debater, with great inventiveness and spontaneity as well as tenacity. The original contribution of Healy, whose first experience of parliament this was—he had just been returned at a by-election, for Longford—was a series of short, dogged, savagely insulting speeches, which could be relied on to stimulate some government supporter to reply indignantly and thus waste his own time. Because of the sheer weight of the numbers engaged in it, this obstruction, lacking in finesse though it generally was, was the most effective which the House had ever encountered. An active section of six or seven members had been vexatious in the parliament of 1874–80, but now there were about thirty members with the will to obstruct and the work of the House became, under its existing rules, impossible. The sitting of January 25 took twenty-two hours: and on 31 January a sitting began which lasted forty-one hours: 'the longest', according to the *Annual Register*, 'on record in the history of the House of Commons and probably of any other legislative body'. It became plain that a band of obstructives numerous enough to work in shifts could 'use the forms of the House', as the Parnellite euphemism went, to block the bill for the whole session, even if the House sat continuously. The inevitable remedy was applied more quickly than anyone expected. On 2 February the speaker's intervention brought the forty-one hour sitting to an end: 'A crisis has arisen which demands the prompt intervention

[1] O'Brien and Ryan, *Devoy's Postbag*, ii. 233.

of the chair. . . . The usual rules have proved powerless to ensure orderly and effective debate. . . . I decline to call upon any more members to speak and will at once proceed to put the question from the chair.'[1] The House divided and the first reading of the bill was passed. This was the death-blow to the obstruction policy but its agonies were somewhat protracted. On the following day (3 February), the home secretary having announced the arrest of Michael Davitt, the 'active party' made their last dramatic stand. Dillon, as usual the spearhead of 'extremism', was suspended for disregarding the authority of the chair. Parnell, not to be outdone, interrupted the prime minister with the proposal that he 'be no longer heard' and scenes of 'indescribable confusion'[2] followed, culminating in the suspension and ejection from the House of thirty-six Irish members.[3]

This was a turning-point in the history of the party and the country. If previous hints of secession from parliament had meant anything, now surely was the time to secede. The country had never been so united behind Parnell, nor had so much attention ever been focused upon the party. The land crisis and agitation, the state trials, the threat of coercion, the fight put up by the obstructives, and finally Davitt's arrest had worked Irish opinion up to a point at which the semi-revolutionary gesture of secession would have been more acceptable than ever before. And, most important of all, the 'active policy' as hitherto known was dead, the speaker's action having smashed what was, in the absence of a command of the party balance of power in the House, its only effective weapon. One of the key ideas of

---

[1] *Hansard*, 257. 2038. On the following day the prime minister moved, 'That if upon notice given a motion be made by a minister of the crown that the state of public business is urgent and if upon the call of the speaker 40 members shall support it by rising in their places, the speaker shall forthwith put the question, no debate, amendment or adjournment being allowed' (ibid., 258. 103). This resolution, somewhat amended, formed the core of new rules framed by the speaker and presented to the House on 9 Feb. (ibid., 435).

[2] Ibid., 257. 2038.

[3] Dillon, Parnell, Finigan, Barry, Biggar, Byrne, Corbet, Daly, Dawson, Gill, Gray, Healy, Lalor, Leamy, Leahy, M'Carthy, McCoan, Marum, Metge, Nelson, A. O'Connor, T. P. O'Connor, O'Donoghue, O'Gorman Mahon, O'Sullivan, O'Connor Power, Redmond, Sexton, Smithwick, A. M. Sullivan, T. D. Sullivan, Molloy (withdrew), O'Kelly, O'Donnell, R. Power, O'Shaughnessy (ibid., 258. 80–81).

the New Departure, according to Davitt, had been the eventual secession of the home rulers from parliament,[1] and Parnell though not committing himself to such a policy, had, if we are to believe Davitt, held out the hope that the Irish members might 'get themselves expelled'.[2] Now they had been ejected and it was open to them to treat that ejection as an expulsion. Further, had not Parnell promised[3] that the first arrest under the Coercion Act would be the signal for a general strike against rent, and was not Davitt's arrest just as surely coercive as if the Person and Property Bill were already law?

The Land League policy, as presented by Davitt and Andrew Kettle to Parnell and a group of his colleagues just before Davitt's arrest, was that 'on the day when coercion should become law the whole Irish party should rise and leave the House, cross to Ireland and carry out the no-rent campaign'.[4] Parnell gave Davitt the impression that himself 'was favourable to such a fighting policy at the time but he could not command the allegiance of more than half his nominal following to so extreme a course'.[5] The combination of secession with a general strike against rent, both taking place a little before the passage of a Coercion Bill or an Arms Bill, and long before the passage of any measure of redress, would have presented the already embarrassed liberal government with a situation of appalling difficulty and have called forth an unparalleled degree of support from America. Whether this fulfilment of the New Departure would have resulted in the victory of home rule it is

[1] Davitt, *Fall of Feudalism*, p. 112.
[2] Ibid. I see no reason to doubt Davitt's account on these two points.
[3] On 16 Jan. 1881 (*Annual Register*).
[4] This meeting took place in the Westminster Palace Hotel, London, just before Davitt's arrest, which occurred on 3 Feb.; Davitt (*Fall of Feudalism*, pp. 302–3) gives the date of the meeting itself as 3 Feb., and the date of his arrest as 4 Feb., but this is clearly a slip of memory. Mr. Lawrence J. Kettle, son of the late Andrew Kettle, corroborates Davitt's account of the meeting, and informs me that the Land League proposal, that the party should return to Ireland was adopted by the league on Andrew Kettle's initiative, Davitt's original idea having been 'that some of them should go to America and elsewhere—a policy of dispersion' (letter of 22 Feb. 1955, in response to a query from the present writer). The 'American' plan was revived very shortly afterwards, by Dillon (below, p. 61).
[5] Davitt, *Fall of Feudalism*, p. 310.

impossible to say. It is probable, however, that if Parnell
had been the crypto-revolutionary which some of his contemporaries and some more modern writers have taken him
to be, he would have seceded, with what following he could
muster, from parliament in February 1881. As it was, he
barely considered the possibility of doing so. On the morrow of the ejection of the Irish members, a representative of
the *Freeman's Journal* asked him the momentous question:

'Will your party go back to parliament after last night's proceedings?' And he replied:

'If we consulted our own feelings we should retire, but we
must do our duty.'[1]

It is probable that Parnell himself was not the man to
take a really revolutionary step, unless the pressure of events
absolutely obliged him to do so; it is certain that his party
as a whole was even less inclined for anything that might
lead to revolution. Had a considerable number of the party
been ripe for secession, Parnell might have been forced to
give them a lead, but in fact I estimate that, although 36
members had been expelled, not more than 20 would have
obeyed a party decision to secede and certainly not more
than 5 would have advocated such a policy.[2] Pressure from
outside, from the Land League, was firmly resisted. On
14 February at a meeting of the Land League executive in
Paris, Dillon, according to the *Freeman's Journal*, 'conveyed
to Mr. Parnell the desire of the Land League that he should
go to America'.[3] Such a course would have speeded up the
agitation by putting Parnell in a position where he would
have to make separatist speeches, by removing his controlling hand from the movement, and by lining still more
deeply the coffers of the Land League. Parnell declined the
gambit, stating that 'his first duty was to return to parliament, while Egan should remain in Paris to maintain relations with America'.[3] Both Davitt and Egan, the two great

---

[1] *F.J.*, 5 Feb. 1881.

[2] Dillon, according to Davitt, was in favour of the general strike against
rent, if coercion was passed (*Fall of Feudalism*, p. 301). Barry and Biggar
might also have supported extreme measures. The course of the Land Bill
was to show that the bulk of the party, and even of the 36 ejected members,
stood somewhat to the right of Parnell.

[3] *F.J.*, 15 Feb. 1881.

non-parliamentary land leaguers, were now out of the way. Parnell then wrote, from Paris, an open letter to the Land League, which was a further illustration of his mastery of political tactics. It contained three points:

1. It was his duty to stay at his post, not to go to America.
2. He could not agree with the Land League proposition 'that for the present very little is to be expected from parliamentary action'.
3. On the suspension of the members there had been two alternatives: (*a*) to 'retire' in a body and possibly 'appeal to force' or (*b*) to 'go on widening the area of the agitation . . . to include the English masses . . . and effect . . . a junction between the English masses and Irish nationalism'. The latter alternative was to be adopted.

The idea of 'widening the area of the agitation' to include the English masses was not altogether new, but hitherto Parnell himself does not seem to have shown much interest in it. Outside the party, Michael Davitt, and, within the party, T. P. O'Connor, had been its principal advocates. As early as February 1880 Davitt had proclaimed that the cause of Ireland was also that of humanity and labour throughout the world.[1] In September 1880, a month after the defeat of the Compensation for Disturbance Bill by the House of Lords, T. P. O'Connor, John Barry, and J. J. O'Kelly conducted a Trafalgar Square demonstration against the Lords.[2] Some English 'advanced radicals', led by H. M. Hyndman, rallied to the support of the Irish agitation, and established an Anti-Coercion Association, with a weekly paper, the *Radical*, which attacked the liberals for their treatment of Ireland.[3] T. P. O'Connor, Hyndman, and others spoke at a meeting of this association in February 1881.[3] A few months later, in June 1881, the Anti-Coercion Association developed into the Democratic Federation, continuing for some time to hold as 'the principal cause of its existence . . . the action

---

[1] T. W. Moody, 'Michael Davitt and the British Labour Movement, 1882–1906', *Transactions of the Royal Historical Society*, 5th ser., vol. iii, 1953.
[2] *F.J.*, 17 Feb. 1881.
[3] Pelling, *Origins of the Labour Party*, p. 15.

of the Government in relation to Ireland'.[1] As the immediate precursor of the Social Democratic Federation and, as it were, a grandparent of the British labour party, the Democratic Federation, with its close Irish connexions, is of considerable historical interest. But, in the circumstances of the 1880's, an alliance with such a body was of little or no immediate value. Even some years later, in 1884, the Social Democratic Federation had no more than 500 members;[2] in 1880–1 the 'advanced radicals' were probably even fewer in number. Representative trade unionists of the day, like Broadhurst, opposed the Irish claims and in general the British workers 'shared the hostility of the British governing class towards the Land League'.[3] It may also be doubted whether the two movements, both then unpopular in Britain, stood to gain much by pooling their forces, and creating an increased stock of unpopularity for each of them. Parnell himself, some years later—in 1884—cast scorn on the whole idea, to which Davitt still held faithful. 'We are told', said Parnell at this later time, 'of some great wave of English democracy, which is coming over here to assist the Irish democracy. The poor Irish democracy will have, I fear, to rely upon themselves in the future as they have had to do up to the present.'[4] It is not very likely that Parnell was of a fundamentally different opinion in 1881, but there were sound tactical reasons for adopting a different tone in public. Parnell had just rejected the really revolutionary choice—that of secession of his party from parliament—and it was highly desirable for him to be able to present the Irish public with an alternative that would look 'strong' instead of 'weak', without being revolutionary in any real sense. This alternative lay to hand in Davitt's scheme for bringing into the agitation (in theory) 'the English masses' and (in fact) a handful of English middle-class advanced radicals. It was fortunate that this programme was particularly attractive to that radical wing of Parnell's own party which had been pressing him to go to America, where he

[1] Ibid., p. 17.
[2] Ibid., p. 47.
[3] Moody, 'Michael Davitt and the British Labour Movement'.
[4] R. Barry O'Brien, *Parnell*, p. 316; see also Moody, 'Michael Davitt and the British Labour Movement'.

would have been under constant moral pressure to speed up
the agitation. His action at this time, as at so many others,
was that of a master of constitutional politics, adept at the
cape-work of the pseudo-revolutionary gesture. During this
same stay in Paris he ostentatiously visited Victor Hugo and
the 'notorious Communard' Rochefort. The 'castle' Archbishop of Dublin, McCabe, denounced these visits in the
strongest language: 'A calamity more terrible and humiliat-
ing than any that has yet befallen Ireland seems to threaten
our people to-day. Allies for our country in her struggle for
justice are sought from the ranks of impious infidels, who
have plunged their own unhappy country into misery and
who are sworn to destroy the foundations of all religions.'[1]
But the archbishop's thunder and its echoes only increased
Parnell's prestige among those revolutionaries whose movement he had, at this time of crisis, diverted away from their
objective, and whose independent influence he was soon to
sap and destroy.

It was during this visit to Paris that he gave the impression to the Clan na Gael emissary Lomasney that he
meant 'to go as far' as the fenians.[2] Within ten days of his
interview with Lomasney, and on the day on which the
Coercion Bill passed the Commons, Parnell sent the following telegram to Devoy: 'You are reported to have sent
threatening telegram to home secretary. If true your action
most censurable. If untrue should cable contradiction.'[3] The
Paris visit increased Parnell's reputation, abroad as well as
at home, for being a dangerous, if impractical, revolutionary.
'Parnell's Paris expedition', wrote Cardinal Manning at the
time (18 February 1881) to Archbishop Vaughan, 'is a showing of cards which has damaged him and his works.'[4] But
close political observers were not long in discerning the
spurious nature of the association. Archbishop Croke informed Cardinal Manning a few months later—in August

---

[1] Lenten instructions of 23 Feb. 1881 quoted in *Nation*, 26 Feb. 1881.
A. H. Bellingham and George Errington, whiggish home rulers, and the
respected A. M. Sullivan also protested against these visits. Parnell himself
after the archbishop's attack disclaimed any political intention in seeing
Rochefort (*F.J.*, 25 Feb. 1881).                                    [2] p. 30, n. 5.
   [3] Telegram of 28 Feb. 1881 quoted in O'Brien and Ryan, *Devoy's Postbag*,
ii. 45.                                    [4] Shane Leslie, *Manning*, p. 383.

1881—that there was 'nothing to be dreaded from the so-called "French alliance" for the very valid reason that it is an alliance *in nubibus*'.[1]

Meanwhile, under the new rules of procedure, the Coercion Bill moved more rapidly towards enactment. It took eight nights in committee, three on consideration, four on third reading, and was passed by the Commons on 28 February. Immediately its complement, the Peace Preservation (Ireland) Bill, better known as the Arms Bill, was introduced and went through without a hitch, being passed by the Commons on 11 March. The rest of March was occupied almost exclusively with English business, and any remarks made by the Irish members were constitutional in the highest degree.[2]

## 2. *The Land Bill*

On 7 April 1881 Gladstone introduced his Land Bill. This bill, which was, as Parnell had prophesied, the measure of the tenants' activities during the winter, went farther to meet the tenants' demands than had been generally expected, and tended therefore to divide the Parnellite movement, just as repression and refusal had tended to unite it. The great concessions which the bill contained, especially the provisions for judicially fixed rents, were the substance of the national demands of a few years ago, but it was not clear how the country would take them now. The Coercion Act, which had become law on 2 March, was spreading its beneficent shade over the landlords, and evictions were rising sharply;[3] correspondingly, spasmodic outbreaks, as opposed to the disciplined demonstrations organized by the league, were becoming more frequent;[3] on the left, some land leaguers, mindful of the occurrences of February, were muttering against Parnell's moderation.[4] It would, therefore, hardly be safe for him to support any government measure. And yet it was certain that, this being undoubtedly

[1] Ibid., p. 385.
[2] With the exception of Dillon who made a very fiery anti-coercion speech on 3 Mar. (*Hansard*, 259. 156) which was deprecated by Parnell on the following day (ibid., 336).
[3] Palmer, *Irish Land League Crisis*, p. 271.
[4] O'Donnell, op. cit., ii. 24.

'a good bill', the 'moderate nationalists', for whom the still powerful *Freeman's Journal* spoke, would urge support for it. This was a situation which Davitt had predicted as early as 16 December 1880 in that important letter to Devoy from which we have already quoted: 'The government land bill', he had said, 'will not be enough but it will satisfy a great number inside the league and be accepted by the bishops and priests almost to a man. I anticipate a serious split in the league when the government measure comes out'.[1]

In these circumstances Parnell did exactly what he had done in August 1880; he played for time. 'It would not be fair', he declared after the prime minister had spoken, 'either to the government or the bill to express any opinion on it until they saw the measure in print.'[2] Once again, however, his hand was to be forced. On parliament's rising for the Easter recess, the thunder-stealing Dillon went back to Ireland and at Dublin made a direct attack on the bill.[3] He followed this up by other inflammatory speeches in various parts of the country, while Parnell was still hesitating to commit himself. A Land League convention meeting in Dublin under Parnell's chairmanship passed on 22 April a resolution, of a rather academically extreme variety, to the effect that nothing but the abolition of landlordism would satisfy the Irish people.[4] The convention left the parliamentary party free, however, to support the government bill or not, as they pleased. Parliament reassembled on 26 April but Dillon continued the agitation in Ireland, and on 2 May, after a violent speech at Grangemockler, was arrested under the Coercion Act.[5] It was now up to Parnell to do something, or forfeit the confidence of his, still important, left wing. There were two courses open: to launch the general strike against rent which he had promised in the event of the first such arrest,[6] or to refrain from voting on the second

[1] O'Brien and Ryan, *Devoy's Postbag*, ii. 23.

[2] *Hansard*, 250. 933 (7 Apr. 1881).

[3] He said in the Rotunda, Dublin, on 12 Apr. that 'no consideration would induce me to vote for this bill, knowing as I do that I would be only helping to rivet the collar of the master around the tenants' (*F.J.*, 13 Apr. 1881). In Donegal on 18 Apr. he told the farmers that if they accepted the bill 'they were going blindfolded into a worse state of slavery than they ever were in before' (ibid., 19 Apr. 1881).     [4] Ibid., 23 Apr. 1881.

[5] Ibid., 3 May 1881.     [6] Above, p. 60.

reading on the Land Bill. He chose the more constitutional alternative. On 5 May, at a meeting of the party, he moved to resent Dillon's arrest by not voting on the second reading, and this motion was carried by 18 votes to 11 after Parnell had threatened to resign if it was defeated.[1] It is clear that if such a considerable minority of the 'active party'—for of course no full-fledged whigs were present—opposed this harmless gesture of intransigence (which could not endanger the bill), even more would have opposed the revolutionary policy of secession. In Ireland the 'right centre of the army of agitation' showed signs of mutiny. The *Freeman's Journal*[2] immediately condemned the party decision, *The Nation*[3] regretted it, and, most important of all, the famous Land League archbishop, Croke of Cashel,[4] pronounced definitely against it. The 'serious split' which Davitt had foreseen was beginning to appear. Parnell, to check it, had to explain the unimportance of his gesture. The abstention policy, he stated, in an open letter to the archbishop, was merely intended to 'mark a sense of the imperfections of the bill' by 'making a demonstration . . . which . . . will not affect the division.'[5] When the division actually came, on 19 May, no fewer than fourteen members —excluding those who had seceded with Shaw—disobeyed the party decision and voted in favour of the bill.[6] The

[1] R. Barry O'Brien, *Parnell*, p. 228; *F.J.*, 6 May 1881. The division was as follows: *For abstention*: Parnell, O'Kelly, Lalor, Commins, Leahy, Byrne, Corbet, Redmond, Leamy, Finigan, Biggar, Healy, Dawson, Sexton, T. P. and A. O'Connor, Barry, O'Donnell. *Against*: T. D. Sullivan, Marum, Daly, Macfarlane, O'Shaughnessy, O'Sullivan, McCarthy, M'Coan, Blake, Smithwick, O'Connor Power. This division does not reveal the full strength of dislike felt within the party for the abstention policy. T. P. O'Connor who voted for it reveals that 'the proposal came as a shock to most of the members. . . . I consulted Sexton and his answer was that Parnell had acted badly but we were bound to support him' (*Memoirs of an Old Parliamentarian*, i. 177); R. Barry O'Brien (*Parnell*, pp. 227–8) dates this meeting before 25 Apr. but this is not correct.

[2] *F.J.*, 6 May 1881.    [3] *Nation*, 14 May 1881.
[4] *F.J.*, 7 May 1881.    [5] Ibid., 11 May 1881.
[6] The 12 seceders all voted for the bill also, making the total home rule vote for it 26. The subscribing members who voted for it were: Bellingham, Blake, Daly, Fay, Gabbett, M'Coan, Martin, Moore, The O'Donoghue, O'Shaughnessy, O'Shea, O'Connor Power, Synan, and Whitworth (*Hansard*, 262. 928). It is noteworthy that all these, except O'Shea, disappeared from home rule politics after 1885.

thunder on the right continued; Archbishop Croke took advantage of the situation to stress the supreme importance of the clergy in the campaign. 'Mr. Parnell,' he revealed at Holycross, 'in Dublin, more than two years ago . . . literally went upon his knees to me . . . to use all my influence to have the priests join the movement.'[1]  And he reminded his hearers, not quite accurately, that Davitt and Parnell were then 'a convict and an unknown man'.[1] He urged upon the party restraint and 'a policy of judicious flexibility'.[2] With Davitt and Dillon in jail and Egan in Paris, there was no one near to counteract this sort of pressure. Parnell refrained for the moment from any further gestures to placate the left. Throughout the long committee stages of the bill, 26 May–27 July, his party, led in this respect by Healy, settled down in earnest, and in good faith, to the business of amending the act, and defending the government text against amendments from the right, proceedings in which they were assisted by almost all the Irish whigs.[3] It even seems that, already at this stage, Parnell, through O'Shea, had proposed to Gladstone, in exchange for concessions on certain aspects of the bill—arrears, improvements, and purchase—the ending of the agrarian agitation. It was, however, to take a year more of agitation before the substance of this proposal was accepted in the famous Kilmainham treaty.[4] Meanwhile on the parliamentary stage any display of intransigence was carefully avoided; when Gladstone, on one occasion signified that a particular amendment was time-wasting, Parnell

[1] *F.J.*, 2 June 1881.
[2] Ibid., 10 June 1881. Archbishop Croke's reputation with the people was now at its height, due to his defence in the previous March of the newly founded Ladies' Land League against the imputations of the famous 'castle archbishop', McCabe. Cardinal Manning at this time saw in Archbishop Croke the hope of moderating a movement which he disliked. 'My desire', he wrote on 13 July 1881, 'is to see you and the Irish episcopate leading and uniting the people as in old times and all the more because we are now not dealing with Ireland in Ireland but with America in Ireland, as I fear' (Manning to Croke: in Shane Leslie, *Manning*, p. 385).
[3] A liberal member remarked that 'nothing was more wonderful than the unanimity shown by the Irish members' (*Hansard*, 263. 312—7 July 1881).
[4] In *Joseph Chamberlain: a Political Memoir*, edited by C. H. D. Howard, a letter of O'Shea's to Gladstone, dated 13 Apr. 1882—during the Kilmainham treaty negotiations—refers to these earlier proposals (June 1881) of which every detail, according to O'Shea, had obtained Parnell's assent.

got its mover, Biggar, to withdraw it, and carefully disclaimed any intention to obstruct.[1] When the time came for
the bill's third reading (29 July) Parnell left it to the individual discretion of members to decide whether or not they
would abstain. Twenty-seven home rule members (excluding seceders) voted in favour of the bill this time.[2] A few
days later, on 1 August, Parnell, having protested against
'the farce of a division' on a government motion managed
to get himself suspended for the remainder of the session.[3]

Parnell had, however, been disturbed by the 'bolting' of
so many of his party on the abstention issue, and, in particular, by the defection of the nationalist press. He decided to
launch a weekly paper, Parnellite-Land League in complexion, under the editorship of a brilliant young ex-fenian[4]
journalist and agitator, William O'Brien. *United Ireland*,
which began publication on 13 August, and speedily
reached a wide public, served Parnell in two ways. It denounced, with picturesque invective, the members who had
'ratted on the land bill'[5] and, more important, its stirring
language and boundless enthusiasm served without doubt
to combat the general tendency towards apathy in the ranks
of the Land League, and especially the declining popularity
of Parnell on the left. 'Violence', O'Brien once said, 'is the
only way of securing a hearing for moderation.'[6] Those
words might well have been inscribed on the masthead of
*United Ireland*.

The Land Act, amended but not crippled by the Lords,
received the royal assent on 22 August. The tendency towards disintegration which the Gladstonian combination
of redress on top of coercion had induced in the national
movement was now intensified, and Parnell's dilemma was
correspondingly acute.[7] The agrarian war was raging

---

[1] *Hansard*, 262. 362.　　　　　　　　　　　　[2] Ibid., 264. 192.

[3] This incident is recounted in detail by R. Barry O'Brien (*Parnell*, p. 230).

[4] 'Willie O'Brien used to be one of our young men [fenians]. He left the
I.R.B. about six years ago and I did not much blame him' (T. H. Ronayne to
John Devoy, 24 Sept. 1881: O'Brien and Ryan, *Devoy's Postbag*, ii. 104).

[5] Members denounced in early issues of *United Ireland* included, as well as
the seceders, Fay, Gabbett, O'Shaughnessy, Corbet, W. H. O'Sullivan, Blake,
Nelson, McCoan, and O'Shea.

[6] McDonagh, *Life of William O'Brien*.

[7] Cf. R. Barry O'Brien, *Parnell*, p. 233.

unabated, and American opinion was as militant as ever, yet
the clergy welcomed the Act—the hierarchy issued a manifesto describing it as 'a great benefit . . . for which the
gratitude of the country is due to Mr. Gladstone'[1]—and it
was probable that, whatever they might feel at the moment,
the farmers would accept it in the end. The 'Kilmainham
party' of suspects, headed by Dillon, Father Sheehy, and
Matthew Harris, did not conceal their contempt for Parnell's
moderation—Dillon had bluntly refused Parnell's invitation
to become a director of *United Ireland*.[2] Patrick Egan was
urging 'vigorous measures' against the 'whig reactionary
movement'.[3] On the other side, most of the parliamentary
party were suspicious of Parnell's extremism.

These conflicting elements met at a great Land League
conference which opened at the Rotunda, Dublin, on
11 September. Telegrams poured in from America to the
conference, all to the effect that the bill should be ignored
and the harvest held.[4] The delegates themselves appeared
to be about equally divided as to acceptance or rejection
when Parnell produced his famous formula: *test the Act* (i.e.
the league in each area, to hold back the tenants from a rush
into the land courts and submit only selected cases). This
compromise was accepted unanimously, as it deserved to be,
for it was undoubtedly the wisest course. Patrick Ford and
his friends were too remote from Ireland to know that it
was now too late to achieve anything by 'unfurling the banner of No Rent'. All that was left now was to put the land
courts in the position of bidding for the tenants' support,
an operation that was very well carried out under the Parnell
formula.

The 'testing' policy had the grave political drawback,

---

[1] *F.J.*, 27 Sept. 1881.

[2] William O'Brien, *Recollections*, p. 297.

[3] 'Now that the Land Act has passed the house of commons and is likely
soon to become law it behoves the forces of the land movement throughout
the country to be ready to take vigorous measures to meet the whig reactionary movement which will assuredly be attempted' (Egan to Timothy
Harrington, 31 July 1881: N.L.I., Harrington MSS.: folder, Egan correspondence).

[4] Patrick Ford, the influential and militant editor of the New York *Irish
World*, wired: 'Unfurl the banner of No Rent. . . . Hold the harvest. . . . If
this is not done America will be disheartened' (*F.J.*, 16 Sept. 1881).

however, that it left the 'American allies' dissatisfied. It was necessary, in order to dispel the atmosphere of undue moderation, to cover the reality of qualified acceptance with a cloak of verbal defiance. Parnell in his wire to the president of the Land League of America at the end of the conference stressed that the tenants were advised to 'rely on the old methods to reach justice' and alleged that the new formula had been devised 'in order that tenants . . . may realize . . . the hollowness of the Act'.[1] Whether because of the 'tone of the House' or, much more probably, the conservative influences within his own party, Parnell's utterances generally tended to become fairly moderate when parliament was sitting; during the recess, however, addressing audiences in Ireland, his language was much stronger. This time the intransigence of speech was particularly marked. At Dublin on 25 September, at Maryborough on 26 September, and at Cork on 2 October,[2] he stressed 'the hollowness of the Act' and linked the land question closely with 'legislative independence'. The release of Dillon and Father Sheehy speeded up the agitation, and finally, on 7 October, Gladstone got Parnell out of most of his difficulties by denouncing and threatening him and the Land League together in his famous speech at Leeds.[3] The attack of the English prime minister had a tonic effect on the reputation of the Irish statesman. Parnell, according to Barry O'Brien, had been deliberately 'drawing the fire of the English enemy upon himself'[4] and now the main barrage had come. He replied at length from Wexford, light-heartedly, briskly, and insultingly, in words that were aimed across the Atlantic as well as across the Irish Sea—'the perfidious English enemy', the 'masquerading knight-errant'—and concluded with appeals to the fighting tradition of '98 and '67 and a tribute to the shooting abilities of the Boers.[5] He must have known very well, when he used this language, that Gladstone with his boasted 'resources of civilization', would be forced to arrest him, and it is difficult to resist F. H. O'Donnell's contention[6]

---

[1] Ibid., 18 Sept. 1881.    [2] Ibid., 27 Sept. 1881; 3 Oct. 1881.
[3] *The Times*, 8 Oct. 1881.
[4] *Parnell*, p. 233.    [5] *F.J.*, 10 Oct. 1881.
[6] Op. cit., ii. 32 sqq. On the other hand, references in letters to Mrs. O'Shea (*Parnell*, i. 217, 235) seem to indicate that he considered going to America

that he was deliberately trying to get himself arrested, in order to re-unite the national movement behind him. He was arrested on 13 October.

Looking back on the eventful period of February–October 1881, one sees that the leaders of the New Departure, that amalgam of revolution and constitutionalism, had been forced on 2–3 February, by the speaker's coup and the inevitability of coercion, to choose between the two elements of their programme, and that Parnell, speaking for the great majority of his parliamentary party, had decided in favour of the non-revolutionary element. The political history of the subsequent months consisted, as far as the Parnellites were concerned, in earnest efforts along constitutional lines (e.g. the amendment and defence of the Land Bill in committee) camouflaged by quasi-revolutionary demonstrations; the appeal to the English working-class, the ostentatious but harmless abstention on the second reading of the Land Bill, Parnell's demonstrative protest against 'the farce of a division' with his consequent suspension, and, finally, the manœuvre of exposing 'the hollowness of the [Land] Act'. All these were no more than masking operations, more or less successful and sometimes contested, covering the slow and cautious retreat, following the by no means inconsiderable achievement of the Land Act, into a purely parliamentary policy. The final and most fortunate of these operations was that by which Parnell induced the government to transmute him, by imprisonment, into a symbol of the Irish nation.

### 3. *Kilmainham*

Parnell's arrest aroused, as was expected, intense feeling in Ireland, and his lieutenants—Sexton, O'Kelly, and O'Brien—as well as John Dillon, found themselves, after organizing indignation meetings, in Kilmainham also.

after the Wexford meeting (as the Land League had requested him to do in Feb.).

[1] A great meeting, at which Dawson, Gray, Dillon, Biggar, T. D. Sullivan, O'Kelly, Sexton, and Metge spoke was held in the Rotunda on 14 Oct. (*F.J.*, 15 Oct. 1881). The intensity of the general feeling is revealed in the almost seditious tone of the usually cautious *Freeman*.

It was then[1] that the 'general strike against rent', long
discussed in Land League circles, was called by means of a
'No Rent Manifesto', signed by the 'suspects' in Kilmainham. None of the various explanations which have been put
forward for this act is completely satisfactory. According to
Mrs. O'Shea,[2] Parnell was 'really opposed to it', but bowed
to the decision of the 'majority of the leaders in Kilmainham'. The 'leaders in Kilmainham' who signed the manifesto, besides Parnell, were Kettle, Brennan, Dillon, and
Sexton. Sexton was a Parnellite parliamentarian rather than
a leaguer, and Dillon was not in favour of the issue of the
manifesto. It is improbable—to say the least of it—that
Kettle and Brennan, even with the assistance of William
O'Brien,[3] could have coerced Parnell into signing something which he did not want to sign. F. H. O'Donnell's
allegation that Parnell did it with the deliberate design of
getting the league suppressed is hyper-Machiavellian and on
the whole unlikely.[4] It is even more unlikely that he had any
hopes of its being a success. It would have been more than
clear to such a politician as Parnell that the manifesto would
not stand a chance against the combined pressure of the
Coercion Act, the Land Act, and the condemnation of the
church—certain in view of the hierarchy's commendation
of the Land Act.[5] Yet William O'Brien, who, as the draughts-
man of the manifesto, ought to know, tells us that Parnell
in Kilmainham was the 'most resolute' in favour of 'extreme
measures'.[6] This at a time when, as we know from his
letters to Mrs. O'Shea, he believed the movement to be in a
state of collapse.[7]

The most likely explanation seems to be that, having
realized that the arrests rendered it impossible for the
moment to carry through his compromise formula of

---

[1] On 18 Oct.                                    [2] *Parnell*, i. 209.
[3] Ibid.; R. Barry O'Brien, *Parnell*, pp. 246–7; William O'Brien, *Recollections*, pp. 353–5.
[4] Op. cit., ii. 39.                              [5] Above, p. 70.
[6] *Recollections*, p. 353; R. Barry O'Brien, however (*Parnell*, p. 246), asserts
that Parnell was really opposed to the manifesto but relented to appease Ford
and Egan.
[7] 'Politically it is a fortunate thing for me that I have been arrested, as the
movement is breaking fast and all will be quiet in a few months when I shall
be released' (letter of 13 Oct. 1881, quoted in Mrs. O'Shea, *Parnell*, i. 207).

'testing the act', and it being now out of the question to accept the act openly, he had as a *pis aller* to allow the supporters of Patrick Ford their head—which he could do with every confidence that their policy would fail and that thereby his hand would be strengthened in any future course of moderation.[1]

The manifesto was in due course condemned by Archbishop Croke[2] and the *Freeman's Journal*,[2] and gently deprecated by *The Nation*;[3] the Land League was suppressed immediately (20 October); the tenants in most areas either paid their rents or went to the land courts to have a fair rent fixed. 'No Rent' was a failure, as Parnell no doubt expected. Under the vague auspices of the Ladies' Land League and 'Captain Moonlight', sporadic local terror and outrage increased, while the direction and purpose of the old league and of the New Departure years were gone. These lengthy and futile lacerations also prepared the way for a moderate policy to come.

As for the parliamentary party, it had no corporate existence during this period.[4] Its leader and two of its sub-leaders were in jail; some of its more active members—Healy, T. P. O'Connor, sometimes A. O'Connor and Biggar—were engaged in 'widening the area of the agitation' in England, outside the range of the Coercion Act; most members quietly awaited the reopening of parliament, which did not occur until February. Any new lines of policy would have to be worked out in Kilmainham.

[1] In an interview with a *Freeman's Journal* reporter after the issue of the manifesto Parnell stated that it was issued because the arrest of so many 'subordinate leaders' had made 'the complicated task' of testing the act impossible (*F.J.*, 24 Oct. 1881). Immediately after his own arrest and before the other arrests Parnell had recommended the league 'to make no change in the policy declared at the convention' (ibid., 14 Oct. 1881). William O'Brien (op. cit., 353) says that Parnell had sent to the Rotunda 'indignation meeting' on 14 Oct. a letter (which was not read) warning that if the league were suppressed the consequence would be a general refusal of rents. The arrest of the 'subordinate leaders' was of course similar in effect.

[2] *F.J.*, 20 Oct. 1881.

[3] *Nation*, 5 Nov. 1881. The whole press, except *United Ireland*, deplored it in varying keys.

[4] Of the five parliamentarians consulted about the manifesto, three (Biggar, O'Kelly, and T. D. Sullivan) were definitely hostile, one (Dillon) was hesitantly opposed, and one (Sexton) apparently in favour. Cf. W. O'Brien, *Recollections*, p. 353.

The idea of some sort of a 'treaty' was mooted as early as December 1881, for we find Parnell, on 16 December, writing to Mrs. O'Shea: 'I could not very well make any arrangement or enter into any undertaking with government unless I retired altogether from politics.'[1] About the same time we learn—but on doubtful authority—that the Kilmainham group rebuked a nationalist member for endeavouring to have the Land Bill amended to cover tenants who were in arrears. 'I was plainly told', alleges F. H. O'Donnell, 'that the arrears were a complication which was most welcome as it increased the difficulty of keeping Ireland orderly under Mr. Forster.'[2] January 1882 saw no apparent alteration in this intransigent attitude, but after the opening of parliament, on 7 February, by which date, at the latest, Parnell had expected to be released, his letters to Mrs. O'Shea—who was using all her influence on the side of conciliation[3]—show some signs of a desire to come to terms. 'I think', he wrote on 10 February, 'that we shall probably be released by the middle of March, as it will be known by then which way the tenants intend to go, and we shall be able to decide whether it is worth our while remaining here any longer.'[4] On 14 February he betrayed his private attitude towards the Land League and its successor: 'When I was arrested', he wrote petulantly, 'I did not think the movement would have lasted a month, but this wretched government have such a fashion of doing things by halves that it has managed to keep things going in several of the counties up till now.'[5]

Meanwhile the party in the new parliament had, inevitably, re-elected him sessional chairman.[6] Only nineteen

---

[1] O'Shea, *Parnell*, i. 226.

[2] O'Donnell, op. cit., ii. 128.

[3] W. S. Blunt, who was fairly well informed on both the English and Irish sides, strongly emphasizes Mrs. O'Shea's personal influence in this matter. 'The first trace of the new [O'Shea] influence which is recognizable in his conduct as party leader is, I think, that of the Kilmainham treaty. This was a new departure which, without consultation with his most trusted followers, he decided on through the instrumentality of the O'Sheas with Gladstone' (*Land War in Ireland*, p. 457).

[4] O'Shea, *Parnell*, i. 235.

[5] Ibid., p. 236.

[6] *F.J.*, 7 Feb. 1882.

members[1] attended the meeting and it was clear that the party, diminished from its swollen size of February 1881, now consisted of no more than the 'active section'. The breach with the whigs and semi-whigs was aggravated by the action of the activists in passing a vote of censure on the 'nominal home rulers'.[2] By these developments and above all by the absence of Parnell, the parliamentary effectiveness of the home rule party at the beginning of the new session was greatly lessened.

On 10 April 1882 Parnell took advantage of his release on parole, in connexion with the death of his nephew, to begin the negotiations leading to the so-called 'Kilmainham treaty'. The course of these negotiations has been analysed elsewhere in great detail[3] and it is unnecessary to do more than indicate their salient features here. On the evening of 10 April, Parnell discussed the political situation with the vice-chairman, Justin McCarthy, who probably was as near the dead centre of the party as anyone could be.[4] From him he apparently received an encouraging report as to the probable reaction of the party to the conclusion of a nego- tiated peace, for he promptly entered into negotiations, at first through O'Shea with Gladstone and Chamberlain, and later through McCarthy with Chamberlain. It is doubtful how far Parnell kept his colleagues in Kilmainham in- formed of his negotiations. Davitt claims that all of them— except perhaps O'Kelly—were kept in the dark.[5] On the other hand, O'Shea, after the release of Parnell, Dillon, and O'Kelly, informed Gladstone that 'Parnell *had* communi-

[1] Biggar, Lalor, Gill, R. Power, Callan, Gray, Byrne, Finigan, Leahy Corbet, Metge, Barry, McCoan, Leamy, Redmond, O'Donnell, A. O'Connor, T. D. Sullivan, O'Gorman Mahon.

[2] This action was deplored by the *Freeman's Journal* which suggested that 'the guiding hand of Mr. Parnell has been frequently missed' (*F.J.*, 14 Mar. 1882).

[3] See R. Barry O'Brien, *Parnell*, pp. 258–69; Henry Harrison, *Parnell Vindicated*, app. C, and also *Joseph Chamberlain: a Political Memoir* (ed. C. H. D. Howard), chap. ii. The full text of the memoir, with the letters quoted from O'Shea and Justin McCarthy, was not available to Harrison. Harrison erred, I think, in his suggestion that O'Shea was no more a member of Parnell's party than were Blennerhassett, Errington, or Shaw. All these had already seceded from the party, which O'Shea had not done. O'Shea was fairly regular in his attendance at party meetings. He had voted for Parnell on 17 May 1880 for the chairmanship of the party.

[4] See Chap. I, p. 13, n. 2.          [5] Davitt, *Fall of Feudalism*, p. 353.

cated with his fellow prisoners before writing to O'Shea',[1] and implied that there had been differences on the subject: 'He intimated he has now got his hand upon Dillon who is difficult to manage and intensely ambitious.' It seems reasonable to suppose that he confided, to some extent at least, in the two prisoners who were members of his party, but not at all in the purely Land League group, including Davitt. Eventually, in return for an understanding that the arrears question would be dealt with and leaseholders admitted to the benefits of the Land Act, and a contingent understanding that coercion would be abandoned, he agreed that the act, thus amended, would be 'a practical settlement of the land question' and would enable the home rule party 'to co-operate cordially for the future with the liberal party in forwarding liberal principles and measures of general reform'.[2] Parnell, Dillon, and O'Kelly were released on 2 May.

In the wording of his undertaking, perhaps indeed in the giving of a written undertaking at all, Parnell may have gone farther than many of his parliamentary colleagues of the active section would have been prepared to go.[3] But the substance of the Kilmainham treaty, the abandonment as far as possible of the land war, and revolutionary agitation, in favour of the constitutional struggle for home rule, was emphatically agreeable to the parliamentary party. Indeed it

[1] B.M., Gladstone Papers, 33766, f. 71. Memorandum dated 5 May 1882 of conversation with O'Shea. O'Shea also stated that Parnell was 'now in earnest about putting down lawlessness, as he feels himself in danger of being supplanted by more violent men'. This was the day before the Phoenix Park murders.

[2] Letter to O'Shea of 28 Apr. (text in Joseph Chamberlain, *A Political Memoir*, pp. 49–50). A previous letter (24 Apr.) to McCarthy was to a similar effect, but did not contain the celebrated 'hors d'œuvre' about the liberal party (B.M., Gladstone Papers, 44125, f. 134); the text is so quoted in O'Brien, *Parnell*, pp. 262–3.

[3] Healy, *Letters and Leaders*, i. 155, recollects that on the news of the treaty 'Gloom at Parnell's surrender filled our hearts' and that 'We felt that the chief had lowered the flag' (i. 162). 'We' apparently consisted of Healy, Sexton, and the O'Connors, none of whom seems to have made any protest or acted in defence of the land movement. Chamberlain, while the Kilmainham negotiations were going on, acknowledged the desire of Healy and Sexton— as shown in their parliamentary conduct—'to come back to a more moderate policy' (memorandum of 21 Apr. 1882 in *A Political Memoir*, p. 51). Healy publicly defended the Kilmainham policy (below, p. 84).

was with the full support of the party that the substantial decision in this regard had been made over a year before. Once the moment when a revolutionary policy stood a reasonable chance had been refused, and once a good Land Act had been secured, it would have been merely mischievous for politicians to go on stirring up the land agitation. The Kilmainham treaty was essentially a business-like recognition of this situation. The policy which had long been decided upon had now to be enforced if the movement was not to disintegrate.

The dangers of that policy Parnell himself had prophetically described. He had warned the people not to put too much trust in parliamentary agitation;[1] he had warned them that even the best Irish party could not long remain completely independent;[1] he had pointed—as he was to do again in 1890—to the fate of 'Grattan's parliament' after 'Grattan's volunteers' had been disbanded.[2] Yet it was by his own decision and that of his party that in 1881 the New Departure had in effect dropped its weapons, and a purely parliamentary policy had been decided on. It was he now who gave the undertaking that the Irish party would 'co-operate with the liberal party'.[3]

However distasteful Parnell's constitutional policy was to the inventors of the New Departure, however much it clashed with certain past (and future) pronouncements of his own, however many dangers for the future it contained, he would be a bold man who would say that the alternative policy—a crescendo of agitation culminating in open rebellion—would have had any better results in the eighties. That a revolution would have been crushed seems over-

[1] R. B. O'Brien, *Parnell*, p. 199.
[2] In his speech at Wexford (9 Oct. 1881).
[3] The extent to which he actually did collaborate with the liberal party after Kilmainham is shown in numerous communications with Gladstone over the period 1882–5 quoted in Mrs. O'Shea, *Parnell*. See also Thorold, *Labouchere*. The process of collaboration, or bargaining, was of course severely hindered on the liberal side by the Phoenix Park murders and, on the Parnellite side, by the consequent new Coercion Act, and was interrupted towards the end of 1885 by the brief tiff of the so-called 'Carnarvon treaty' with the tories (Chap. III). It was in the nature of the purely parliamentary policy, however, that it involved prolonged dealings with the liberals and a consequent tendency towards the absorption of the Irish party.

whelmingly probable; that it could not have achieved anything better than partial independence for a partitioned Ireland seems certain. An ably led constitutional movement,
with the drive behind it of *repressed* agrarian and political
revolution, offered better hopes. It had obtained a great
measure of land reform, the beginning of the end of landlordism. It was to 'capture' for home rule one of the two
great English parties with the greatest statesman of the day.
Having done so, it seemed likely—up to the end of 1890—
to win self-government, though not absolute independence,
for all Ireland, in unprecedented harmony with England.

# III

## CONSTITUTIONAL POLITICS (1882–85)

THE years immediately following the Kilmainham treaty were politically uneventful compared with those that had preceded it. The Irish party, which was now a Parnellite group numbering effectively about thirty members,[1] had become thoroughly constitutional in aims, although orators and journalists to disguise that fact were not lacking. As a small constitutional party it could do little except prepare its machinery against election day, a task to which, as we shall see (in Chapter IV), it applied itself most skilfully. In parliament, under the new rules, obstruction had ceased to be practicable on a serious scale, and critical opposition was only moderately effective from a party which, gaining in discipline, had diminished both in numbers and in debating brilliance. Parnell himself, at this period, rarely came to the House; Dillon left Ireland for America; T. P. O'Connor's journalistic work did not often allow him to attend; F. H. O'Donnell ostentatiously resigned,[2] and O'Connor Power attached himself to the liberal party.[3] Healy and Sexton became the caretakers of the parliamentary party, which, under them, quietly applied itself to obtaining small Irish reforms.

In Ireland itself, the people seem to have turned for leadership and incitement not to the parliamentary party, but to William O'Brien's newspaper *United Ireland*, now freed from censorship. O'Brien had a marvellous combination of pure fanaticism and journalistic flair; the language

---

[1] In the summer after Kilmainham it was rather less than this. *United Ireland* (17 June 1882) credits only 14 members with 'resolutely opposing' the Crimes Bill. Only 22 members had opposed the introduction of the bill (11 May), and when it was finally decided to obstruct it, only 25 members were suspended (30–31 June). The last figure probably represents the approximate total of loyal party members at this time. It sank to about 20 in the early part of 1883 and rose again to over 30 in 1884 and 1885.

[2] See *Nation*, 30 June 1883.

[3] In the general election of 1885 he ran as a liberal for an English constituency and was defeated.

he used was more effectively violent than that of Patrick Ford's *Irish World* (New York), his sources of information were better, and he was far closer to the popular mind. The aura of the election meetings of 1881 was kept vivid by him, almost alone, in the grey years, 1882 to 1885. And yet, however violent his language, however audacious his attacks upon the castle administration, the parliamentary party could always count on him in an emergency. *United Ireland*, unlike the moderate *Nation*, was totally uncritical of Parnell,[1] and the ingenious irrelevancies of its vocabulary[2] undoubtedly did much to keep national opinion in Ireland solid behind him, and much also to prevent mass defections among Irish-American nationalists. Dillon, who withdrew temporarily from the scene of Irish politics after the Kilmainham treaty and went to America, also did his part in preventing such defections. To American audiences he explained the new policy (with which he personally did not sympathize) in the following words:

Mr. Parnell wishes—considers it best—that the movement in Ireland should be conducted on moderate lines till the present coercion act is exhausted. It may be that this is the wisest policy. He believes that after the next election his power in parliament to resist coercion will be increased ten-fold. There can be no doubt that this will be so. He prefers that for the next year the Irish race should devote itself to organization and preparation and that the final step in advance should not be made till after the next election. Well, let it be so. But be assured that when the time comes and he gives the word the Irish people will rise up and sweep the wretched mockery of the land court into oblivion and with the final effort recover the land that belonged to their fathers for so many centuries.[3]

[1] Compare, for example, the following quotations: 'If it be hero-worship to follow [Parnell] as trustfully as a Pillar of Fire, the Irish people are not likely to shrink from the imputation' (*U.I.*, 23 Dec. 1882); 'Mr. Parnell, they [the Irish people] are convinced, is a wise and sagacious champion; they would regard his loss as most serious, but he is not indispensable' (*Nation*, 30 Sept. 1882).

[2] *United Ireland* made free use of battle-metaphor in its parliamentary correspondence. On the participation of 36 members in a vote of censure it wrote: 'it was a moment of exultation comparable to a Benburb or a Fontenoy' (17 May 1884). And a debate on constabulary redistribution made 'one of those rare nights of hot eager man-to-man conflicts with the foe which have something of the excitement of a battle-charge' (21 Mar. 1885).

[3] R.I.A. Dillon MSS.: lecture notebook, undated entry, probably early 1883.

J. J. O'Kelly also did his bit, managing, in his correspondence with John Devoy, to keep up the 'fenian' tone while
defending the new policy.[1]

External accidents also helped to disguise and distort the
basic trend. Of these the first and most important was the
strange and tragic anachronism of the Phoenix Park murders. All accounts agree[2] that when Parnell, only a few days
after the pact and his release, learned that the new chief
secretary for Ireland, Lord Frederick Cavendish, and the
under-secretary, T. H. Burke, had been cut to death in the
park with surgical knives, his reactions included, along with
natural human horror, a deep political dismay. He felt that
the blows had been aimed at him; that their effect would be
to wreck his policy and discredit his leadership. So far indeed was he carried away by this conviction that he offered
Gladstone his resignation; an offer which that matchless
politician wisely declined. But the actual effect of the murders was the contrary of what Parnell had feared. By drawing
down on him and his party the abuse of English politicians,
the murders caused the national ranks to close behind
him, as had happened before under Gladstone's attacks in
the autumn of 1881; at the same time attention was drawn
away from the fact of the Kilmainham treaty, and the revolutionary wing of the national movement was discredited by
the ill-judged act of terrorism. The futility of political
assassination was seldom better illustrated than by this
event, in which the assassins actually rescued their bitter
opponents, the constitutional politicians, from a position of
some danger and difficulty.[3]

[1] O'Brien and Ryan, *Devoy's Postbag*, ii. 140–3 : letter of 21 Sept. 1882.
[2] e.g. R. Barry O'Brien, *Parnell*, p. 274; Davitt, *Fall of Feudalism*, pp.
357–8; Katherine O'Shea, *Parnell*, i. 262–4; F. H. O'Donnell, op. cit. ii., 121–2.
[3] An eminent historian has made a strange judgement about the effect of
the Phoenix Park murders on Parnell's prestige: 'Parnell's authority in
Ireland and influence in England never quite survived the blow' (George
Macaulay Trevelyan, *Sir George Otto Trevelyan*, p. 108). Whatever (the truth)
about Parnell's influence in England—always subject to parliamentary contingencies—his authority in Ireland survived very healthily over the next
eight years. The error derives from the habit of mind, prevalent among
English writers for this period, of assuming that Irish public opinion was
really, at bottom, very like English public opinion. It would be truer to say
that the two were radically opposed. What injured an Irish politician's
reputation in England was likely to help it in Ireland and vice versa. But it

The liberal government which had intended to drop coercion was driven by popular feeling in Britain to reintroduce it in the form of a Crimes Bill, and the Irish party was thus given the opportunity for a display of spirited but constitutional opposition. The second reading was carried without difficulty (18 May), but a score or so of Irish members, led on this occasion by Biggar and Sexton, succeeded in prolonging the committee stages for over a month (1 June to 4 July). This process, the climax of which was an all-night session (30–31 June) and the suspension of twenty-five members on the ground of obstruction, was not, however, obstruction in the old sense. In the words of a writer in *The Nation*: ' "Obstruction" there has been none—that is, the clumsy device of moving adjournments has given place to a process of opposition and scrutiny equally prolonged but not open to parliamentary censure.'[1] The writer proved unduly sanguine about the censure but his general description was correct; obstructive tactics had lost the flamboyancy which had characterized them a year before, when they had been an accompaniment to a quasi-revolutionary policy in Ireland. This, at any rate, was to be the last flare-up and when it had failed, the party resolved to take no further part in the proceedings and to 'cast upon the government the sole responsibility'.[2] The Crimes Act became law on 12 July.

The Arrears Bill—i.e. the inclusion of tenants in arrears in the benefits of the Land Act of 1881—which had been the Gladstonian *quid pro quo* for Parnell's abandonment of the New Departure, passed the Commons on 21 July. The incident in the Phoenix Park had disturbed the outward semblance of the Kilmainham settlement, but the settlement itself endured. Parnell was now in constant negotiation with the liberal leaders; with Gladstone and the liberal whip, Lord Richard Grosvenor, through Mrs. O'Shea[3] and with

is true that *English* feeling about the murders probably played a part in the defeat at the polls of the Gladstonian liberals in 1886.

[1] 17 June 1882.
[2] *Hansard*, 271. 1400. Two or three Parnellites, including Biggar, did, however, take part in subsequent debates on the bill.
[3] Katherine O'Shea, *Parnell*, ii. 7 sqq. The Gladstone Papers in the British Museum include several short letters from Mrs. O'Shea to Grosvenor, and from

Chamberlain through Labouchere;[1] at the same time he was throttling the land agitation at home and liquidating the Ladies' Land League. He could and did imply in all his communications with the liberals that he was their main bulwark against revolution in Ireland, and his requests for concessions were founded upon this principle. The parliamentary party, although most of them were probably unaware of the extent of Parnell's co-operation with the government, acquiesced almost unanimously in the general line. Healy, at this time next to Parnell the most important man in the party, did know what was going on and although in later life he professed to regard Parnell's 'surrender' at this time with disgust,[2] he was in fact a supporter and propagandist of 'Kilmainham'. In a significant article published in an English magazine, at a time when Parnell had already implemented his Kilmainham promises, Healy having explained that 'the agrarian question and the national question are two different things', argued that, under home rule, England would find it easy to suppress rebellion in Ireland, and that home rule was the best way of circumventing desires for separatism.[3] This, from the principal spokesman of the Parnellite party, was much nearer to the old argument of Butt and Mitchell Henry than to the proud claims of Parnell's followers in the pre-Kilmainham period. At the same time *United Ireland*, representing the 'extremist' wing of Parnellism, hailed the same policy in the language suited to its readers: 'Our people have a tendency to underrate the importance of attacking English rule in detail . . .'[4] These declarations coincided with measures of reorganization and discipline inside the national movement, culminat-

Grosvenor to Mrs. O'Shea (44315, f. 94, f. 119, f. 149, &c.). These corroborate Mrs. O'Shea's account in her book.

[1] Algar Thorold, *Life of Labouchere*, pp. 160–70. Letters dated 16 and 22 May and 9 June from Labouchere to Chamberlain shed some light on the close collaboration of both Parnell and Healy with the liberals at this time.

[2] *Letters and Leaders*, i. 162.

[3] 'The Irish Parliamentary Party', in *Fortnightly Rev.*, xxxii. 625–33, 1 Nov. 1882.

[4] 28 Oct. 1882. *The Nation* also condemned this tendency of public opinion: 'Some people seem to think that the Irish party are not doing their duty unless they are perpetually engaged in hostilities with the government or with the House' (4 Nov. 1882).

ing in the establishment of the National League, under parliamentarian control, in place of the old independent Land League.[1]

In fact, the land agitation being safely shelved, coercion a fact, and the election still far distant, the parliamentary party entered on a prolonged spell of relative inactivity. The *clôture* in its decisive form was introduced in October, and the debates on this resolution gave the party its last chance of genuine obstruction; it was content, however, to signify perfunctorily its dislike of the measure, and to recede for a time into the background.

For two years, from the summer of 1880 to the summer of 1882, Ireland had held a foremost position in the politics of the United Kingdom. By the end of 1882 she had ceased to be a major concern; the Irish party's effectives dwindled to about twenty,[2] and its policy became purely a waiting one. In America, eager for 'results', the credit of Parnellism fell to its lowest point;[3] in Ireland, however, the strange streak of luck which for so long favoured Parnell, and of which he never failed to make effective use, preserved his reputation with two providential attacks. A melodramatic denunciation by Forster linking Parnell with the Phoenix Park murderers gave the Irish leader once more the stature of a symbol of rebellion; a stature which he increased by the cold disdain with which he declined to refute the suggestions of the embittered ex-chief secretary.[4] The effect of this could hardly have worn off, when what was seemingly a far more formidable attack was delivered, this time from Rome. The so-called Roman letter from the Propaganda commanding the Irish bishops and priests to refrain from associating themselves with the National League was clearly seen in Ireland as a blow directed, through English influence in Rome, at the Parnellite movement.[5] Once more Parnellism and Irish

[1] See Chap. IV.
[2] The party organs for this period are full of complaints about absenteeism and defections. See *U.I.*, 10 Mar., 7 Apr., 30 June, 1 Sept.; *Nation*, 10 Mar., 21 Apr., 11 Aug. 1883.      [3] See Chap. IV.
[4] F. H. O'Donnell, op. cit., ii. 147–8, claims, rather improbably, the credit of having devised this piece of tactics.
[5] *The Nation*, a journal which devoted much space to matters of religious interest, and was deeply respectful to the church, declared editorially: 'We shall stand for the national rights and liberties of Ireland against Rome and

independence were identified, to the benefit of Parnellism. The 'tribute', the national collection which had just been organized for Parnell, was sharply stimulated;[1] the Irish clergy and the Irish press remained loyal to the league; and the 'Roman letter' was from the point of view of its instigators a fiasco, as indeed all England's previous attempts to govern Ireland through Rome had been. The Irish party, however, was enabled to retain the people's loyalty without any special effort of its own at a time when the initiative had passed from its hands, and its activities in parliament were confined to such non-emotive matters as fisheries and tramways.

The beginning of the session of 1884 (6 February) saw stirrings of greater activity. The government introduced a Franchise Bill which was controversial as regards its application to Ireland. It proposed to extend the household franchise, which already existed in the British boroughs, to British counties, and also to both Irish boroughs and counties which had hitherto had a property franchise. The main effect of the measure in Ireland would be to enfranchise the agricultural labourers; the electorate would expand from about 200,000 to over 600,000. Most tories—excluding, except initially, Lord Randolph Churchill and his friends, who were already beginning to see tactical merit in an Irish alliance—opposed the bill, unless it could be accompanied by a reduction in the Irish representation at Westminster; a suggestion which the government rejected.

It has been argued that it is to this impending franchise legislation that we should ascribe Parnell's 'moderation' in the post-Kilmainham years: 'His first objective', wrote Henry Harrison, 'was to hold the liberals to electoral reform without discrimination against Ireland. It was to this end that his influence in slowing down the agitation during this period was exercised.'[2] It is certainly a factor to be noted,

England' (19 May 1883). The 'Roman letter' was believed to have been obtained by the exertions of Sir George Errington, a former whiggish home ruler, who went on an unofficial mission to the Vatican on behalf of the British government.

[1] In the week after the publication of the 'Roman letter' £2,000 was collected—double the previous rate of collection (figures weekly in *Nation*, Mar.–May 1883).

[2] Harrison, *Parnell, Joseph Chamberlain and Mr. Garvin*, pp. 85–86.

but the policy of moderation dates openly from May 1882, and has its roots as far back as the fateful period of February 1881—periods at which the question of electoral reform was not dominant in anybody's mind. The importance of the reform itself for Ireland could be exaggerated, as even the restricted franchise was already returning Parnellites steadily at by-elections. The situation, as Joseph Chamberlain—no mean electoral calculator—saw it at this time, has been expounded by J. L. Garvin: 'On all mechanical calculations his [Parnell's] phalanx in the next House would be something over 80 with the franchise reform but of something under 80 without it, unless the total Irish representation were indeed reduced to a strictly proportionate figure [to population] and this no responsible British politician proposed.'[1] An estimate of Parnell's was very similar—about 75 without the bill, about 85 with it (*U.I.* 29 March 1884).

The Irish party supported the bill, not by speeches—indeed they expressed indifference to it—but by their votes. Their parliamentary strength was rather greater now, partly as a result of by-elections, partly of better attendance as the general election and Parnell's supremacy over the new electorate—which had at first been questioned[2]—came into better view. The party press was becoming increasingly merciless with absentee members, semi-whigs, and 'irregulars' of all types. The leader of the 'nominal home rulers', Shaw, acknowledged the defeat of his faction, by predicting a large Parnellite party as the result of the next election. In a word the excitement of approaching victory was in the air.

And as victory approached and discipline grew tighter—it was at this time that the party pledge was drawn up[3]—so also the political position of the party was clarified. It was early in 1882 that the party line had decisively swung to the right; in the latter part of 1882, and in 1883, the left wing of the national movement had been deprived of influence; its

[1] *Chamberlain*, i. 463. See also below, Chap. V, p. 151, n. 3.
[2] Notably by the fenian, James Stephens, in an article 'Ireland and the Franchise Bill' (*Contemporary Review*, May 1884).
[3] See Chap. IV. The Dungarvan convention, at which the pledge was first imposed, took place in Aug. 1884. Earlier in the year Parnell, in an interview, had forecast the introduction of the pledge in substantially the form later adopted (*U.I.*, 29 Mar. 1884).

members had become discouraged or had taken to aimless and sporadic violence. It was not until 1884, however, that the degree of the change was made apparent. In April of this year Parnell first made a definite open breach with Davitt, by a speech attacking his theories on land-nationaliza-tion and his association with English radicals.[1] This, of course, had far more significance than its direct application; it implied that the parliamentary party was now so confident of its control over the forces formerly led by the Land League, that it did not feel obliged to use its old diplomacy towards the Land League's founder. At the same time it was a solid piece of reassurance for any propertied nationalists who still feared revolutionary elements in Parnellism.[2] The immediate pretext for the rebuff to Davitt was well chosen so as to alienate as few as possible of his supporters; of all Davitt's ideas, that of land-nationalization in the Ireland of the eighties must surely have been the least popular as well as the least practicable.

The party's detachment from its 'disreputable' past favoured also, for the time being, a new attitude to the Eng-lish radicals with whom in former days some Parnellites had given signs of aligning themselves. Now the most extreme of the nationalist organs proclaimed that 'a sense of meanness is the nearest approach to shame of which the liberty-loving English radical is capable';[3] nationalist organs and speakers[4] went out of their way to sneer at the radicals, and in parlia-

[1] This speech, delivered at Drogheda on 15 Apr., dismissed the nationaliza-tion idea as 'a will o' the wisp . . . which may lead to serious disunion' (F.J., 16 Apr. 1884). The timing of this speech would fit in with Harrison's theory associating 'moderation' with the Franchise Bill: the division on whether to admit Ireland to the benefits of the bill (for admission, 332, against, 137) took place in the following month, on 21 May. It is by no means clear, however, why anxiety to 'hold the liberals to electoral reform' should necessitate attacks on the radicals who, after all, advocated such reform, and the inclu-sion of Ireland in it.

[2] A series of dynamite explosions in England, beginning in the spring of 1883 and lasting, with intermissions, to the beginning of 1885, was generally ascribed to the fenians and applauded by the fenian press in America. The campaign culminated, on 24 Jan. 1885, in simultaneous explosions in the Tower of London, Westminster Hall, and the House of Commons. This background has to be borne in mind in considering the parliamentary party's moderate policy at the same period.                    [3] U.I., 19 July 1884.

[4] See, for example, a speech by Matthew Harris, quoted in ibid., 23 Aug. 1884.

ment, the party had turned solidly against them on an important issue where previously it had been divided. On the question of the admission of the atheist Bradlaugh, 43 home rulers—a record muster—came to vote against him in February 1884[1] and not one home ruler voted for him; in May 1880 almost half the Parnellite party, including Parnell himself, had favoured his admission.[2]

This coldness towards the radicals had, no doubt, part of its origin in disappointment at, for example, radical failure to provide serious opposition to coercion bills,[3] but this alone would hardly quite account for the bitterness of nationalist anti-radicalism. A contributory cause, at least, was that the flirtations with English radicals in the pre-Kilmainham period had aroused alarm among the Irish clergy and that now, with the new alliance between priests and party to be embodied in the structure of the National League,[4] it was essential not to offend the church. The clergy stood firm against the Roman letter, but the very fact of that rebuke from the Holy See made it all the more desirable to give reassurances that there was no tincture of dangerous continental unrest in the Irish national movement. The radicals, and especially Bradlaugh, on whom *United Ireland* now lavished such terms as 'filthy humbug', provided convenient occasions for such reassurances.

That the clergy were in fact effectively reassured was soon magnificently proved, when, in October 1884, the Irish hierarchy unanimously called upon the Irish party to urge upon the House of Commons the claims of Catholic Ireland as regards education.[5] Catholic interests in what is, from the

[1] The Irish members from the time of Parnell's release in May 1882 voted solidly against Bradlaugh. Davitt, however, continued to favour his admission to parliament.

[2] See Chap. II, p. 50.

[3] Such disappointment would of course have been intensified by the false hopes aroused by the campaigns of 1881 in England 'to rouse democratic public opinion' on Ireland's behalf (see Chap. II). From an excessive trust in radical sympathy it was easy to swing to an equal excess of disillusionment.

[4] See Chap. IV, esp. pp. 128 sqq.

[5] *United Ireland* hailed this as 'one of the most momentous events in recent Irish politics' (4 Oct. 1884). The actual words used by the hierarchy were: 'That we call upon the Irish parliamentary party to bring the above resolutions [grants for Catholic schools] under the notice of the House of Commons, and to urge generally upon the government the hitherto unsatisfied claims of

religious point of view, the most important of political questions, were thus entrusted to a group which, less than five years before, the majority of bishops had regarded as dangerously subversive. Parnellism was now accepted; from now on in Catholic Ireland no one but a crank could condemn it as revolutionary. There is evidence, however, that, in this period between the hierarchy's commission to the Irish party and the general election, some of those around Parnell were beginning to fear the preponderance of clerical influence in the party. 'The adhesion of the bishops', wrote J. J. O'Kelly to John Devoy in America, 'is a source of great immediate strength for the present—whether or not it will continue to be so in the future is not so clear. One thing is certain: the mistaken attitude [of non-co-operation] taken up by the leading men representing your friends in this country [i.e. the fenians] has thrown back an enormous power into the hands of the church party.'[1] There can be little doubt that the fear here implied was present to Parnell's own mind.[2]

The general climate of Irish politics had, then, become, for various reasons, distinctly hostile to radicalism by the time the radical leader, Joseph Chamberlain, saw his way, in December 1884, to make his first definite overtures to the nationalists.[3] Chamberlain may perhaps have come to be

Catholic Ireland in all branches of the education question . . .' (*F.J.*, 2 Oct. 1884).

[1] Letter of 17 Sept. 1885 (O'Brien and Ryan, *Devoy's Postbag*, ii. 265).

[2] R. Barry O'Brien describes O'Kelly as 'the one personal friend Parnell had in the party—the one man to whom he freely opened his mind—when indeed he opened it at all' (*Parnell*, p. 513).

[3] See J. L. Garvin, *Joseph Chamberlain*, i. 579 sqq. Henry Harrison has shown (*Parnell, Joseph Chamberlain and Mr. Garvin*) that Garvin's account is not wholly candid. Chamberlain's long retrospective and self-justificatory account of his proposals and their reception has recently been published in full; its editor records the view that Garvin's extensive use of this document was 'not always careful' (Chamberlain, *A Political Memoir*). The doubtful points relate almost entirely to Chamberlain's good faith, a question not of primary importance for the present study. Mr. C. H. D. Howard the editor of *A Political Memoir* has given an exhaustive account of the 'local government negotiations' ('Parnell, Joseph Chamberlain and the Irish Central Board Scheme, 1884–5' in *Irish Historical Studies*, vol. viii, no. 32 (Sept. 1953)). He has also published (*I.H.S.*, Mar. 1953, vol. viii, no. 31) a number of documents from the Chamberlain, Spencer, and Manning papers relating to these negotiations. The whole question of the 'central board' bulked much larger on the English side—where it presented itself as a potential substitute for

persuaded, as was his friend Labouchere, 'that the only effective way to "dish the whigs", whom he hated even more than the conservatives, was to use the Irish vote'.[1] He certainly appreciated the signs of the future, as revealed in the Irish by-elections and the implications of the Franchise Act. His proposal now, which he chose to embody in a letter to an Irish friend[2] not prominent in politics, was for Irish local government reform—local government in Ireland was still to a great extent undemocratic and controlled by the 'ascendancy'—and for a central Irish board which would control, in effect, a department of local government. Through Captain O'Shea—his usual intermediary in Irish affairs—Chamberlain was in touch, or rather at cross-purposes, with Parnell. Parnell's attitude was both sensible and clear-cut; he was prepared to accept the local government board, but not as a substitute for home rule. 'In talking to our friend [Chamberlain]', he instructed O'Shea on 5 January, 'you must give him clearly to understand that we do *not* propose this local self-government plank as a substitute for the restitution of our Irish parliament.'[3] Chamberlain afterwards claimed that O'Shea suppressed this and similar messages and gave him a partial and misleading account of Parnell's position. However that may have been, he now approached other leading Irishmen; Garvin records that Parnell thought that Chamberlain was trying to divide his following. Thus we learn from Chamberlain's retrospective account that while O'Brien and others were entirely hostile, Gray, representing the right centre, was personally well disposed to it. Healy—sounded by both Dilke and Labouchere—was equivocal.[4] More important, Cardinal

home rule—than on the Irish side, where Parnell and his followers saw it as a piece of proposed local government legislation to be treated on its merits. The two sides were put at cross-purposes by O'Shea's diplomacy and perhaps also by the over-eagerness of both Chamberlain and Manning.

[1] Thorold, *Labouchere*, p. 205. See also Elliott, *Goschen*, i. 264, who mentions a belief that some ministers (Chamberlain and Dilke) were looking to a political combination between advanced English radicals and the nationalists of Ireland.

[2] Letter of 17 Dec. 1884 to W. H. Duignan (Garvin, *Chamberlain*, loc. cit.).

[3] Garvin, *Chamberlain*, i. 588.

[4] Chamberlain, *A Political Memoir*, p. 138 (for O'Brien), p. 149 (for Gray), app. B (for Labouchere on Healy). See also, for Healy's attitude, Gwynn

Manning took a hand with the Irish bishops as they opportunely passed through London on their *ad limina* visits to Rome. If Manning's account is to be trusted, Chamberlain's suggestions were better received by the churchmen than by the lay leaders: paradoxically enough, considering the traditional ecclesiastical distrust and dislike of the radicals. But apparently the churchmen, even such nationalists as Archbishop Croke, were in a mood—perhaps influenced by the activities of the dynamiters—to consider any moderate proposals, from any quarter, which might extinguish the dangerous embers that had been smouldering since 1879. 'Monsignor Croke', wrote Manning to Leo XIII, 'asserted in the most explicit terms his own conviction that the union should be left untouched, and that the whole Irish episcopate is unanimously of that same opinion.'[1] Manning—presumably briefed by Chamberlain, or at least after discussion with him —informed the Irish bishops of Chamberlain's proposals.[2] He called—20 April—on Sir Charles Dilke, Chamberlain's closest associate at this time, to convey the results of his diplomacy. 'He spoke in the name of Croke and another Roman Catholic Irish archbishop [McEvilly of Tuam] and of five Irish Roman Catholic bishops who had been staying with him. . . . He said that Croke had become frightened of the extreme nationalists. The cardinal declared that the Roman Catholic clergy were ready to pacify Ireland if we would pass Chamberlain's local government scheme with a central board. The bishops would be prepared to denounce not only separation but an Irish parliament.'[3] Chamberlain, in his turn, called on Manning and received similar in-

and Tuckwell, *Dilke*, ii. 124. Healy gave little direct encouragement to the local government scheme, but his conversation fostered the impression that the Irish party could be divided.

[1] Letter of 12 Apr. 1885 in Leslie, *Manning*, p. 403.

[2] Garvin, *Chamberlain*, i. 596. It may well have been Manning who briefed Chamberlain on the whole local self-government idea. As early as 1883 he had written to Leo XIII: 'Amministrazione domestica, ma Parlamento no: sarebbe preludio di conflitto e di separazione!' (Purcell, *Manning*, p. 579).

[3] B.M., Dilke MSS., 43931, f. 122; reproduced in Gwynn and Tuckwell, *Dilke*, ii. 129. Manning called again on Dilke two days later to volunteer that if the bishops got the board they would 'denounce as revolutionary' the idea of an Irish parliament. On the same day Dilke wrote to Gladstone that Manning had 'got a pledge from the R.C. bishops and from Davitt to denounce separation' (B.M., Dilke MSS., 43931, f. 124).

formation which he immediately conveyed to his cabinet colleagues:

They [the Irish bishops] were all opposed to separation between the two countries. Some of the bishops were in favour of a separate parliament . . . [but after Manning had argued with them] . . . they were inclined to accept these [local self-government] proposals as satisfying all just and reasonable demands. . . . He said that there were practically two influences powerful in Ireland at this moment,—Mr. Parnell's . . . and the bishops'.[1]

Manning, then, was thinking in terms of driving a wedge, so as to weaken the Irish demand; or, perhaps more accurately, he wanted to use the bishops' influence to neutralize that of Parnell. Chamberlain's own conception was more realistic, in that he saw Parnell not as a magnetic extremist—which seems to have been Manning's idea—but as the centre of a political complex. If, he seems to have reasoned, he could come to terms with the right wing of the nationalist movement—represented by the bishops—he could move the whole complex, or system, and its chief representative with it, farther to the right and nearer to English public opinion. 'I added that in my view the difficulty would not lie in [Parnell's] personal objections to such a scheme, but in his hesitation to commit himself in face of possible opposition from members of his own party.'[2] About a week later (30 April) Manning saw Parnell and told him of the bishops' attitude; according to O'Shea (whose unreliability is notorious) and the account given by Chamberlain to the cabinet, Parnell promised to support the local government proposals, and also not to obstruct the Crimes Bill, which the liberal government proposed to revive.[3] This is

[1] Chamberlain's memorandum for the cabinet, 24 Apr. 1885, in Garvin, *Chamberlain*, i. 598, and Chamberlain, *A Political Memoir*, pp. 144–5.

[2] Garvin, *Chamberlain*, i. 599. Garvin says this shows Chamberlain's ignorance of Parnell's 'vital letters suppressed by O'Shea'. This does not necessarily follow; Chamberlain might well have believed that the attitude taken by Parnell in these letters was determined by the 'possible opposition' in the party; it was this opposition, and not Parnell himself, which Chamberlain, as distinct from Manning, wished to use the bishops to neutralize.

[3] B.M., Dilke MSS., 43931, f. 126; also in Gwynn and Tuckwell, *Dilke*, ii. 130. Morley (*Gladstone*, iii. 194) says that at the cabinet, on 9 May, 'ministers were aware from the correspondence of one of them with an eminent third person that Mr. Parnell approved the scheme and in consideration of it would even not oppose a very limited Crimes Bill'.

not very likely—at least as a complete account—since Manning, on the following day, having mentioned to Dilke his interview with Parnell, spoke of 'a more completely satisfactory interview with Sexton',[1] and Sexton himself, later recalling this conversation in a friendly talk with Dilke, said that 'he had agreed to the Chamberlain plan in conversation with Manning, but it was as a local government plan, not to prevent, so far as he was concerned, the subsequent adoption of a parliament'.[2] As this accords with Parnell's position, recorded in his written instructions to O'Shea, and as Sexton was one of those members whose loyalty and integrity were never in any doubt, we are justified in accepting this recollection as accurate, and in treating with reserve the Dilke–O'Shea–Chamberlain account of the Manning–Parnell conversation. The interview with Sexton was probably 'more completely satisfactory' in tone, but the substance of both interviews was probably the same.

To summarize these rather complicated (because indirect) negotiations, the position was now that the radical leader had tried out, with his local government proposals, both the political and the ecclesiastical leaders of the Irish people. The political leaders were ready to accept them, but not as a substitute for an Irish parliament; the ecclesiastical leaders were ready to use their influence to get them accepted as a final settlement, and to moderate the demand for home rule.[3] There is something faintly comic, and at the same time instructive, in this situation, when the general background is taken into account. The lay political leaders had, over the past year, denounced atheistic radicalism, and the English radicals specifically, at every opportunity; and their

---

[1] B.M., Dilke MSS., 43931, f. 126.

[2] Dilke's diary, 22 Mar. 1886, in Gwynn and Tuckwell, *Dilke*, ii. 211.

[3] We have only Manning's word for this, and it is necessary to discount something for Manning's optimistic memory. It is not likely, for instance, that the Irish bishops undertook to denounce an Irish parliament as 'revolutionary'; they knew their Irish public opinion too well for that, and in any case the idea of such a denunciation would probably have been repugnant to many of them personally. But they must have shown themselves ready to accept local self-government instead of home rule—unless we are to reject Manning's testimony wholly, and assume that he was deliberately and gratuitously lying in his communications not only with Dilke and Chamberlain, but with Leo XIII.

primary object in this was probably to reassure the Irish hierarchy and enlist its support, as they successfully did. Yet now these same English radicals—and Chamberlain's reputation as a dangerous man was still growing at this date— were trying, with much initial success, to outflank the Irish lay leaders, *on the right*, by means of an agreement with the Irish hierarchy itself. The readiness of the bishops to do business, politically speaking, with Chamberlain at this time was probably directly related to the abhorrence with which they regarded his ideas. 'Local self-government' would take Irish education safely—and quickly—out of the reach of such irreligious innovators as Joseph Chamberlain; home rule, on the other hand, might take years, and violent political convulsions, to accomplish, and might in the end bring Irish Chamberlains to power. The 'anti-radicalism' of the Parnellites, however, was neither ideological nor deep-rooted, and in this it resembled their 'radicalism' of an earlier period. They had used 'radicalism'—foreign radicalism—as a means of diverting an impending agrarian and national revolution; they were prepared to use 'anti-radicalism' as a cement in the conserving dykes which now held the same revolutionary forces safely behind the constitutional home rule movement. Many of them, even those who personally disliked radicalism, were probably pleased enough at the apparent rise of English radicalism, as helping the Irish bishops to see the merits of a measure of autonomy for Ireland. But Parnell and his followers, committed to home rule and—for the most part at least—passionately desiring it, were relatively indifferent to the inroads that the English radical philosophy might, in the meantime, make in Ireland. It was of the ingenuity of Chamberlain's proposals—later imitated by others—that they struck at this point of difference between the spiritual and temporal leaders of the Irish people.

Ingenious though the proposals were, it is hard to believe that they ever had much chance of success. The great majority of the Irish people wanted the greatest degree of separation from England that they could get; this demand had gradually crystallized, over the last ten years or so, into the form of 'home rule', not clearly defined, but understood as meaning nothing less than an Irish parliament, whatever the powers of that parliament might be, preferably sitting in 'the old House in College Green'. This parliament was now firmly established as the minimum demand and essential test of nationalism. It had been regarded, since 1882 at any rate, as commanding at least the tacit approval of the Irish bishops, and if these bishops had now been so imprudent as to denounce it, in favour of local self-government, their advice would certainly have been rejected and their influence would have suffered. English politicians realized that the authority of the church in Ireland was very great, but what they did not always realize was that the church's direct political influence was very much less than her spiritual and moral authority; indeed, if this had not been the case, the Land League, the New Departure, and the Parnellite movement would never have been successful. Even if—what is even more unlikely—Chamberlain's scheme had met with the best reception possible, and Parnell with Gray and the other 'moderates' had joined the bishops in abandoning home rule, the net result could only have been the destruction of Parnell's own influence, the wrecking of the movement which bore his name, and the growth of more extreme movements. This was hardly what Chamberlain, at this time, desired. When these fundamental facts are taken into account, the clever initiatives of Chamberlain, and the assiduous diplomacy of Cardinal Manning and Captain O'Shea, seem ill-informed and misdirected. A more sagacious mind than Chamberlain's or Manning's was not elated at these dealings. 'I do not reckon with any confidence', wrote Gladstone to Hartington, 'upon Manning or Parnell. I have never looked much in Irish matters at negotiation and the consultation of leaders. I look at the question in itself.'[1]

At the beginning of May 1885, however, Chamberlain was well enough satisfied with the progress he had made to try to get cabinet approval for his scheme. He wanted a local government offer to be combined with a limited Coercion Bill—which O'Shea and probably Manning had convinced him Parnell would not in these circumstances oppose. The cabinet rejected the scheme on 9 May, but went ahead with

[1] Letter of 30 May 1885 in Morley, *Gladstone*, iii. 197.

the Crimes Bill.[1] Gladstone announced on 15 May his intention of continuing 'certain clauses of a valuable and equitable description' in the existing Coercion Act, and held out no hope of ameliorative legislation. As Morley says, 'no parliamentary situation could be more tempting to an astute opposition';[2] for the radicals, and some moderates, could not be relied on to support the government which had rejected Chamberlain's pleas, and Chamberlain himself tendered his resignation despite an effort by Harcourt to patch up the cabinet conflict on the basis of a programme which must have appealed to many English hearts: 'no home rule, no coercion, no remedial legislation, no Ireland at all.'[3] Once that failed, the liberals ceased for the time to be capable of concerted action, and it became clear that a determined thrust by tories and Parnellites together might bring them down.

The opposition, or at least a section of it, had been astute enough to be tempted already. Lord Randolph Churchill, as early as May 1884, had defended, wittily and with effect, the inclusion of Ireland in the benefits of the Franchise Bill. Lord Randolph's humorous and reckless personality, and his 'Fourth Party's' adoption of 'Irish' obstruction tactics had predisposed Irish opinion in his favour. From the time of the Franchise Bill the tone of the nationalist press was more cordial to him than to almost any other leading English politician.[4] He now angled for Irish support to overthrow the government. In a speech at the St. Stephen's club, on 20 May, he 'intimated that a conservative government would not think it necessary to renew the [Coercion] Act'.[5] He privately, and probably in more definite words, gave the same assurances to Parnell.[6] On 8 June, 39 Parnellites combined with the tories to defeat the government (264–252) on a budget point, more than 70 liberals, mostly followers of

[1] Morley, *Gladstone*, iii. 194; Gardiner, *Harcourt*, i. 524. The journal of the young Harcourt mentions that Chamberlain explained his scheme 'from Mrs. O'Shea's manuscript'.

[2] Morley, *Gladstone*, iii. 188.

[3] B.M., Dilke MSS., 43931, f. 146.

[4] With the exception of Gladstone who, even at this date, commanded the admiration of the *Freeman's Journal* and the respect of *The Nation*.

[5] Winston Churchill, *Lord Randolph Churchill*, i. 391.

[6] Ibid., p. 395; Gwynn and Tuckwell, *Dilke*, ii. p. 133.

Chamberlain, abstaining. On 13 June the government resigned and on 15 June Lord Salisbury took office.

Winston Churchill in his *Life* of his father stresses that
there could have been no treaty or arrangement between
Lord Randolph and the Parnellites. It is indeed clear that it
needed no such incentive to induce the Parnellites to vote
against the government; early in the session and before Lord
Randolph's speeches they had joined in a vote of censure on
the government, from which, the Franchise Bill once passed,
they had, for the moment, no more to gain. Further, it was
sound tactics, on the brink of the election, to indicate to the
liberal party that it would require something concrete to
win over the Parnellites and the block of votes in England
which they were believed to control through the National
League of Great Britain; also, no doubt, there was a certain
emotional satisfaction to be derived from overthrowing the
jailers of Kilmainham.[1] The hypothesis of a compact is
therefore not required, although the unusually large muster
of Parnellites on the decisive vote certainly suggests advance
planning.

In the short run, the 'tory alliance' paid the expected divi-
dends; the Crimes Act was not renewed and the new lord
lieutenant, Lord Carnarvon, indicated that his policy, unlike
that of his predecessor, Lord Spencer, would be conciliatory. The new government assumed no responsibility for
the acts of the Spencer régime, and, under pressure, promised careful inquiry into charges of maladministration in
a particular agrarian murder case.[2] Lord Carnarvon was
toying with ideas not very dissimilar to those of Chamberlain; and the same tactical approaches also suggested themselves. Even before he had become lord lieutenant he had
come to feel that English government in Ireland had broken
down. He had learned with interest of Sir Charles Gavan
Duffy's scheme for a central parliament with four provincial
assemblies and of Sir Charles's guarantee that, if the tories
took up this scheme, 'he would canvass the Roman Catholic

---

[1] On the news of the fall of the government *The Nation* exclaimed: 'At last
they [the Irish party] had got their vengeance upon the jailers of the suspects'
(13 June 1885).

[2] The proceedings against the 'Maamtrasna murderers'.

bishops and all the moderate party and he felt certain that though Parnell and many of his demagogic supporters would object they could not withstand it'.[1] The indefatigable Manning, now dropping the radicals, approached Carnarvon with a scheme which combined features of the Chamberlain and Gavan Duffy proposals, to make something less advanced than either. The Irish bishops, Manning told Carnarvon, 'were all agreed in favour of union with England, and of local self-government in the different provinces, but not of a central parliament. This they feared, as they held it would weaken the influence of the church by the introduction of an anti-Christian spirit in the representative body and of Protestants in the House of Lords.'[2]

Meanwhile the radical leaders, now out of office, but more interested than ever in an Irish settlement, found doors closing against them. Chamberlain and Dilke proposed to visit Ireland, 'to visit the Catholic archbishops and bishops', Dilke told Manning, 'and find out what they want'.[3] But Manning was afraid of 'your Midlothian in Ireland' and 'to their indignant amazement'—according to Chamberlain's biographer—refused their request for introductions. 'The prince of the church preferred to deal rather with members of government than with men in opposition.'[4] They were even more unlucky in the reception by lay opinion of the suggestion of their visit. The response of the nationalist press was as contemptuous as if a satisfactory bargain with the tories had already been sealed. *The Nation* gave a grudging consent to the visit, added some strictures on radicals in general, and concluded with a foolish piece of frankness: 'We shall be glad to get a good measure of home rule from the greatest rascal among them.'[5] The *Freeman's Journal* took a similar line, but *United Ireland*, more influential than either, launched a definite campaign against the visit. Not long before—and after the Duignan letter—it had characterized Chamberlain as 'a sort of shop-keeping Danton',[6] now it

---

[1] Hardinge, *Carnarvon*, iii. 149. This conversation took place in Oct. 1884.
[2] Ibid., p. 161.  This conversation took place shortly after the Salisbury government took office.
[3] Gwynn and Tuckwell, *Dilke*, ii. 149.
[4] Garvin, *Chamberlain*, ii. 14.
[5] 27 June 1885.                                    [6] 24 Jan. 1885.

dwelt on the 'cynical hypocrisy', of his present plan, abused
him and his colleague and the radical party together, and
concluded: 'We plainly tell Messrs. Chamberlain and Dilke
that if they are wise, they will keep out of our country. . . .'[1]
This advice carried some weight coming from *United Ireland*
which had declared a very effective boycott against a royal
visitor earlier in the year. Chamberlain had held out, his
biographer tells us, 'a generous and manly hand. The hand
he thought would be clasped was bitten to the bone.'[2]
Despite this injury, he held on for a while, to see what
would be the results of a direct approach, by-passing the
unfaithful Manning, to the new nationalist Archbishop of
Dublin, Walsh. These were hopeful at first; Dilke received
two non-committal but friendly letters at the beginning of
July.[3] But near the end of July his Irish hopes received the
*coup de grâce*. Archbishop Walsh wrote to say that he, like
Manning, could give no introductions, as such an action
'would be interpreted as hostile to the excellent tenor and
promise of Lord Carnarvon's conservative regime.'[4] Im-

[1] 27 June 1885. Davitt, more friendly to the radicals than were any of the
parliamentary leaders, immediately wrote to Chamberlain to say that it was
*The Nation* which really represented the Irish view: 'The attitude of *United
Ireland* on the contrary *does not* reflect the opinion of Irish nationalists in this
matter and I am glad to learn since my arrival in London that *most* of Mr.
Parnell's party in the house strongly condemn the article in the last issue of
*United Ireland*' (Garvin, *Chamberlain*, ii. 18). It seems that Healy wrote this
fateful article; so, at any rate, O'Shea told Chamberlain (letter of 13 July 1885
in Chamberlain, *A Political Memoir*, p. 154). Healy already discerned and
detested 'the O'Shea influence'—through which Chamberlain had worked—
and would probably not have been averse from embarrassing Parnell through
an attack which alienated Chamberlain and ruined the personal hopes of
Captain O'Shea (who rather wildly hoped to be made chief secretary for
Ireland in an eventual Chamberlain cabinet). That, however, is speculation;
and Healy later (22 July) told Labouchere (or so Labouchere wrote to
Chamberlain) that 'those who wished that you [Chamberlain] should be ill
received in Ireland should not have their way' (Thorold, *Labouchere*, p. 232;
Chamberlain, *A Political Memoir*, app. B). This was not necessarily either
sincere on the part of Healy or accurate on the part of Labouchere.

[2] Garvin, *Chamberlain*, ii. 12.

[3] Gwynn and Tuckwell, *Dilke*, ii. 154. Davitt at this time still hoped for
the Chamberlain–Dilke visit (Davitt MSS.: McGhee correspondence; letter
of 14 July 1885).

[4] Garvin, *Chamberlain*, ii. 27. Dilke was by this time under a cloud (because
of the impending Crawford divorce) and his biographers—certainly in-
correctly as far as Chamberlain is concerned—ascribe the cancellation of the
joint tour to this cause (Gwynn and Tuckwell, *Dilke*, ii. 181).

mediately, Chamberlain, through O'Shea,[1] informed Parnell of his decision to drop local self-government for Ireland from the famous 'unauthorized programme' with which he was preparing to shake Great Britain. From now on, Chamberlain was a bitter enemy of Irish aspirations. 'The nationalists', says his biographer, 'he nevermore trusted or liked.'[2] It was to be, for both sides, a costly hostility. 'The repulse', as William O'Brien wrote long afterwards, 'of Chamberlain's essay to enthrone himself as our national patron saint had its drawbacks'[3]—a very moderate estimate, seeing that it was Chamberlain's defection that brought about the defeat of the first Home Rule Bill. O'Brien's view in retrospect was that it was 'a choice between Gladstone and Chamberlain' and this accords with one statement of Parnell's policy at the time.[4] It is not clear that, at this point, any such choice was necessary, especially as the tory negotiations were now in full swing. A more recent interpretation is somewhat more convincing: that the tour 'savoured too much of a semi-abdication by Parnell and a radical attempt to capture the bishops and the Irish moderates for the policy outlined in the Duignan letter'.[5] This assessment of the nature of the radical attempt is undoubtedly correct but, since the tories were doing something very similar with Parnellite approval, it does not in itself seem to provide an adequate motive for the hostile manner in which the radical

[1] Garvin, *Chamberlain*, ii. 26. O'Shea had already informed Chamberlain of Parnell's view that it would not be worth while to 'encumber the Irish question at present', with a local government scheme (letter of 13 July quoted by Howard in his article on the central board scheme in *I.H.S.*, viii. 32).

[2] Garvin, *Chamberlain*, ii. 28. Garvin adds that he was not actuated by personal resentment. This suggests a degree of sanctity in Chamberlain that has not been discerned by any other writer.

[3] O'Brien, *Evening Memories*, pp. 87–88.

[4] See Gwynn and Tuckwell, *Dilke*, ii. 152 n.: 'He [Parnell] discussed the [Irish tour] project with one of his colleagues, Mr. John O'Connor, to whom he expressed the view that Mr. Chamberlain was aspiring to replace Mr. Gladstone in the leadership, and that he would do nothing which could assist him in this purpose because he thought that he "could squeeze more out of Gladstone than he could out of Chamberlain"' (MS. note by Dilke, June 1885).

[5] Henry Harrison, *Parnell, Joseph Chamberlain and Mr. Garvin*, p. 105. He might have added certain 'extremists'—Davitt was very well disposed to the proposed Chamberlain–Dilke visit.

overtures were received. This is a question to which we shall have to return, after considering the history of the negotiations with the tories.

Lord Carnarvon lost little time after his appointment in pursuing the strategy which Sir Charles Gavan Duffy, months before, had outlined. The sympathetic hearing which he seems to have given to Archbishop Walsh, on behalf of the hierarchy, on the education question,[1] was no doubt the basis of that prelate's impression about 'the excellent tenor and promise' of his régime. It was plain to Lord Carnarvon that, as Sir Charles Gavan Duffy had said, the clergy would support a settlement on moderate lines. At the same time he was making contact, as Sir Charles had also advised, with the moderate Parnellites. Justin McCarthy, whom he saw on 6 July, was, if the phrase may be used, moderate in the extreme: 'Mr. McCarthy repudiated any desire of separation, any disloyalty to the crown, any culpable connexion with the National League and insisted on the patriotism [apparently British patriotism] of many, if not most, of the Irish members.'[2] These views were pleasing to Lord Carnarvon; they would have been less so to the electors of Longford, who had five years before accepted McCarthy's simple assurance that he was 'thoroughly in agreement with them in all questions'. However, McCarthy left Carnarvon in no doubt that the master of the situation was Parnell: 'he really stood in front of the Irish people and . . . wielded them'. Parnell was not intransigent; he was 'ready to come to a compromise, to give and take'. This view, after consideration, and even before meeting Parnell himself, Carnarvon accepted. 'I do not believe', he wrote to Salisbury on 26 July, 'that [Parnell] is disposed to be immoderate. On the contrary, as the final struggle draws near, he seems to me, as far as I can learn, to grow more moderate in his objects than could perhaps be expected. Further, I think that he can carry with him perhaps all, and certainly the most influential, of his party.'[3] A few days later he saw Parnell. The circumstances of that famous interview, in a house in Grosvenor square, with the carpets up and the

---

[1] See P. J. Walsh, *Archbishop Walsh*, p. 199.
[2] Hardinge, *Carnarvon*, iii. 163–4.          [3] Ibid., p. 175.

blinds down, have often been described. The conversation was less conspiratorial than the setting. Carnarvon had, in advance, informed Parnell—as he wrote to Salisbury on 1 August—'that the only point from which I could speak or consider any question—to which also I understood he was an assenting party—was the union of the two countries. . . . In this Mr. Parnell also concurred, adding some words as to his desire that a better government should provoke the loyalty of the people.'[1] Parnell was, indeed, 'singularly moderate' throughout; spoke of his influence in quieting violence, and keeping the National League in bounds; 'indicated plainly his fear of the extreme party', and named Davitt. He would prefer a 'central chamber' with smaller powers to a 'board' with larger; he agreed as to the need for 'real protection for property and especially landed property'; he also spoke of his 'desire to improve the industrial resources of Ireland as his great object'. Carnarvon was impressed both by Parnell's strong position and by the possibility of coming to a reasonable arrangement with him. Parnell, he informed the cabinet early in October, 'was holding in check for the time both Davitt and the American extremists'. As for a local parliament, 'it might be possible in agreeing to such a demand to satisfy the nationalists' aspirations and to give the shadow without giving the substance, or at least the substance of that which would be perilous'.[2]

There can be little doubt that from the point of view of tory principles—of the preservation of the empire—Lord Carnarvon's conception was statesmanlike and strategically sound. Unfortunately, Lord Carnarvon's colleagues were interested not in strategy but in tactics: the use that could be made of the Irish for the discomfiture of the liberals. Lord Salisbury had, very early in Lord Carnarvon's régime, been able to reassure Queen Victoria that there was no danger of what the Queen dreaded, a repetition of the 'so-called treaty of Kilmainham': 'He entirely agrees with your majesty in thinking that the nationalists cannot be trusted and that any bargain with them would be full of danger.'[3]

[1] Ibid., p. 178–9.　　　　　　　[2] Ibid., p. 194: 6 Oct. 1885.
[3] Letters of Queen Victoria, 2nd ser., iii. 689 (20 July 1885).

For Lord Salisbury's biographer, Lord Carnarvon's ideas on home rule are simply 'the imaginative preoccupations to which [Carnarvon] was subject' and the prime minister's doubts about him were stilled by the fact that his appointment was 'only a caretaker one'.[1] The imaginative preoccupations of Lord Randolph Churchill were more characteristic of the tory leadership: 'Let us only'—if returned to office again with Irish aid—'be enabled to occupy a year with the education question. By that time I am certain Parnell's party will have become seriously disintegrated. Personal jealousies, government influences, Davitt, fenian intrigue will all be at work . . . and the bishops who in their hearts hate Parnell and don't care a scrap for home rule will complete the rout.'[2]

To Parnell, however, the tory advances seemed, with another important consideration, sufficiently promising to justify a serious commitment. Shortly after the end of the session Gladstone had issued (18 September) an election address, vaguely conciliatory on Ireland. On 10 November Parnell, speaking at Liverpool, invited Gladstone to make a specific declaration on home rule, and indicated that the Irish vote in Britain would go to the highest bidder. A week later (17 November) Gladstone replied, declining to go farther until Ireland should have made clear its wishes. The organization of the Irish in England, the Irish National League of Great Britain, had already, on 1 November, pledged itself 'to hold aloof from all British parties . . . but to await the advice of the executive of the National League of Great Britain and to stand by that advice when given'.[3] This

---

[1] Lady Gwendolen Cecil, *Salisbury*, iii. 153.

[2] Letter of 14 Oct. 1885 'to a friend of mark' in Winston Churchill, *Lord Randolph Churchill*, ii. 4. Lord Carnarvon, in the midst of his 'imaginative preoccupations' had also considered this tactic. In a memorandum of 11 Dec. he refers to the hope of tiding over difficulties by 'a large scheme of higher education . . . it was the question by which we trusted to satisfy and win over to the side of order the Roman Catholic bishops; it was one which separated them in a religious point of view from a large part of the Irish parliamentary party'. But he concluded that this approach alone could not be successful, and referred to Archbishop Walsh's 'alliance' with Parnell (Hardinge, *Carnarvon*, iii. 260).

[3] *F.J.*, 2 Nov. 1885. The members of the party present were T. P. O'Connor (president of the I.N.L., G.B.), Biggar, William O'Brien, John Redmond, and Justin McCarthy. The resolution was passed in response to an appeal

advice was given, on 21 November: 'to vote against the men who coerced Ireland'.[1] Parnell, speaking at Liverpool, endorsed the manifesto and gave an additional and probably the decisive reason: that if Gladstone got a big majority he would not introduce a Home Rule Bill.[2] It is important to note that the wording of both the manifesto and its endorsement is negative and contingent: the Irish in Britain were not told 'vote *for* the tories' but 'vote *against* the liberals', and this not on account of any tory merits or promise, but because of the record of the liberals, and their probable future performance.

It is well known that, in the event, Gladstone's majority was not to be large enough to make him independent of the Irish, but was to be too large to make the Irish vote of any real use to the tories. The results were: liberals 335; tories 249; Parnellites 86. How many tory seats had been won as a result of the Irish manifesto cannot be certainly known, but a very good political observer at the time put it at 25.[3]

Parnell's decision was resisted at the time by Michael Davitt, who campaigned in favour of radical candidates on Clydeside and in northern England. Indeed, one of Parnell's lieutenants later blamed Davitt's campaign for the 'failure'

from Biggar that when the time came they should 'give a solid vote in favour of the party that Mr. Parnell had decided'.
[1] Ibid., 23 Nov. 1885. This document which became famous as the 'vote tory manifesto' was signed by T. P. O'Connor, Justin McCarthy, Sexton, Healy, Redmond, O'Kelly, and Biggar. It was not signed by Parnell but no one doubts that it was issued on his decision. There were four individual exceptions to the manifesto—Cowen, Labouchere, Storey (radicals friendly to Ireland), and Captain O'Shea.　　　　　　　　　　　　　[2] Ibid.
[3] The estimate is Joseph Chamberlain's, according to a letter of A. J. Balfour's to Salisbury (Garvin, *Chamberlain*, ii. 189). E. R. Russell, M.P., in a letter to *The Times* (3 Dec. 1885) attributed to Parnell's influence the loss by the tories of '3 seats in Liverpool, besides Warrington, St. Helen's, Stockport and several in Manchester and some county divisions in Lancashire'. Liberal speakers, immediately after the elections, said that the Irish vote had given 50 seats to the tories, but they had an obvious interest in exaggerating its importance. Their estimate was, however, lower than that of Parnell himself who claimed in a letter to the National League that the National League of Great Britain 'controlled' 97 English and Scotch seats (N.L.I., Harrington MSS.: letter of 11 Nov. 1883). T. P. O'Connor, the president of the league in Britain, informed the House during the debate on the second reading of the Home Rule Bill that: 'The branches of the National League in England and Scotland were committee rooms for tory candidates at the last general election' (*F.J.*, 4 June 1886).

of the manifesto, in so far as it failed to bring the tory strength into sufficiently even balance with that of the liberals.[1] Davitt at the time—and even before the issue of the manifesto—attributed the party's pro-tory orientation to clerical and internal conservative influence. 'The priests and bishops', he wrote to Labouchere on 9 October, 'would rather have the tory party attempt the solution of the home rule problem owing to the fact of the conservatives being in favour of denominational education.' Certain members of the party—he named Healy—were pro-tory because they feared that the land question might be solved by 'the radical or democratic element in the Irish nationalist movement . . . on more advanced lines than those of the parliamentary party'.[2] There is little doubt that the church's influence favoured the tory alliance, and the motive of agrarian semi-conservatism may also have played its part. Certainly when Parnell learned that the tories would not, after all, take up home rule, one of his first thoughts was for the Irish land-lords. 'The conservatives', he wrote to Justin McCarthy on 17 December, 'in shrinking from dealing with the question . . . are little regardful of the interests of the Irish land-owning class, since they might have obtained guarantees . . . which the liberals will have no interest in insisting upon.'[3]

Yet to say that these considerations exerted an influence is not to say that that influence was decisive. There were good strategic grounds for the 'tory policy', even if the clergy had been opposed to it and tory principles had been anathema to all the members of the party. It was, after all, an Irish interest, of the highest and most obvious kind, that the two great English parties should be as evenly balanced as pos-sible. The Parnellites correctly foresaw that the liberals would win in the general election of 1885, and it was clearly desirable to keep their margin of victory as low as possible. This did not necessarily imply any faith in the tories, and the intention to cast the vote of the Irish in England on the

[1] William O'Brien, Evening Memories, p. 92.

[2] Thorold, Labouchere, p. 234. The belief that the 'vote tory manifesto' was issued because of clerical influence was widely held at the time. The Times referred (24 Nov. 1885) to 'the action of the Irish party or the Irish Catholic bishops' in issuing the manifesto.

[3] R. Barry O'Brien, Parnell, p. 373.

tory side apparently existed before Carnarvon's conversations with Parnell. Healy told Labouchere on 22 July that 'the party' had already taken this decision, and that it had done so, not because there was a treaty[1] or belief in the tories, but 'in order to hold the balance', adding as a subsidiary reason the fact that, since the tories controlled the House of Lords, anything that could be got from them would be of more value.[2] The 'balance' policy has been retrospectively discredited by the rather *simpliste* argument that if Gladstone's majority had been larger he might have been able to carry his Home Rule Bill.[3] He would, however, be a bold man—or a loyal liberal—who would maintain that

---

[1] It is reasonably certain that no such treaty existed. The situation has been obscured by statements made by Parnell and others *after* the tories had come out definitely against home rule, and especially after the liberals had come out for it. It was then in the Irish—and liberal—interest to exaggerate the tory flirtation with Ireland and make it appear a definite promise of marriage. The situation was embarrassing for the tories because of the rather discreditable use they had made of Lord Carnarvon's sincerely held beliefs. Parnell, in his speech on the second reading of the Home Rule Bill, claimed—in what was clearly a last-moment attempt to influence the decisive impending vote—that, before the general election when he had made a speech calling for a parliament with power to protect Irish industries, 'we had every reason to know that the conservative party if they should be successful at the polls would have offered to Ireland a statutory legislature with the power to protect her own affairs' (*loud Irish and ministerial cheers in which Mr. Gladstone warmly joined*). This intention, in the course of subsequent exchanges, he claimed to have been communicated to him by 'a minister of the crown', whom the house assumed to be Lord Randolph Churchill, but who later emerged as Lord Carnarvon. But when Carnarvon denied that he had entered into any treaty, or done anything which could bind his colleagues, this was conceded. Parnell admitted that Carnarvon had said 'we were not engaged in making any treaty or bargain whatever'; Justin McCarthy remembered 'distinctly' that 'he said he spoke only for himself' (see daily papers, 11–14 June 1886, for this exchange of letters). These admissions make it clear that Parnell's claim, in his second reading speech, was an exaggerated one.

[2] Letter of Labouchere to Chamberlain in Thorold, *Labouchere*, pp. 230–2; Chamberlain, *A Political Memoir*, app. B. Healy added that his own sympathies were with the radicals. This conflicts with Davitt's opinion quoted above. Neither statement need be taken very seriously.

[3] Davitt (*Fall of Feudalism*, p. 481) says that Parnell afterwards—no doubt in reply to some such argument—confessed he was wrong. One may suspect here a desire to terminate the discussion rather than an actual conviction of error. R. C. K. Ensor (*England, 1870–1914*, p. 95) states that Parnell's manifesto 'turned into a terrible blunder; for he had handed between 25 and 40 seats to the tories'. It is hard to see how a given action can 'turn into' a blunder. Parnell's decision was either a blunder in the first place or not a blunder at all. No one has shown it to have been a blunder.

if Gladstone's majority had been large enough to make him independent of the Irish party, he would have introduced a Home Rule Bill at all.[1] However sincere his own 'conversion' to home rule, he could hardly have carried—or attempted to carry—his followers with him, if the marginal importance of the 86 Parnellite votes had not made the question 'practical politics'. Moreover, the tory interlude itself, quite apart from the 'balance', had a powerful effect in helping on the liberal 'conversion'.[2] The negotiations with the tories and the 'vote tory manifesto' are therefore justifiable on grounds of political strategy alone, and it is not necessary to introduce the factors mentioned by Davitt in order to account for them.

If, however, the 'Davitt factors' are not required to account for the 'tory' policy, are they also irrelevant to the consideration of the rebuff that was administered to the radical leaders? This is an important question, for it was the radical, or rather Chamberlainite, defection that later tipped the scales against home rule. If that defection can be attributed to any Irish action, then that action, unlike the tory alliance itself, might be hard to explain on grounds of political strategy. It is not possible to say simply that the 'tory alliance' in itself necessitated alienation of the radicals.[3] As we have seen, the fact that the Irish had combined with the tories to put the liberal government out in no way diminished Chamberlain's eagerness to come to terms with the Irish, an eagerness which continued up to the enforced can-

[1] It is well known that the three liberal governments which introduced Home Rule Bills—in 1886, 1893, and 1912—depended on Irish support to hold office. The one liberal government that had a majority big enough to ignore the Irish—that of 1906—did so.

[2] 'When long afterwards [23 Jan. 1893] Harcourt was talking with Churchill at Lord Rothschild's house at Tring, Churchill said "Gladstone was obliged to take up home rule the moment he heard of Lord Carnarvon's interview with Parnell, which was Salisbury's doing" ' (Gardiner, *Harcourt*, i. 546). A similar view is implied in a letter from Harcourt himself to Chamberlain, on Christmas Day 1885: 'From the moment that the tories sold the pass to Parnell for office in June, it [the union] has been a lost cause' (Garvin, *Chamberlain*, ii. 147).

[3] Some high tories, even at the end of 1885, thought an understanding possible between Mr. Chamberlain and the extreme radicals, Lord Randolph Churchill and his tory democrats and Mr. Parnell and his nationalist following (Elliott, *Goschen*, i. 35–36).

cellation of his Irish tour. Nor can his subsequent hostility be related to the 'vote tory manifesto', for already towards the end of October, before the issue of that document, he was writing to Gladstone: 'I cannot see my way at all about Ireland. Parnell has shown he is not to be depended on. . . . On the whole I think the only choice is to let the Irishmen stew in their own juice.'[1] What did he mean by 'Parnell has shown he is not to be depended on'? A letter of his to Labouchere about the same time makes this clear by a reference to his 'local self-government' proposal which had, he said, practically been agreed to by Parnell and yet 'he threw it over at the last moment. It is impossible to depend on him. . . .'[2] If Chamberlain's true views are here expressed, his hostility therefore dates from the events of July, which have been described above (pp. 99–102). It is my belief that this is the case, but it may be well to consider an alternative hypothesis which has been advanced, in strong terms, by a recent Marxist historian. According to Mr. E. Strauss, in his stimulating and original work, *Irish Nationalism and British Democracy*, 'the factor which seems to have determined [Chamberlain] in his opposition to [home rule] was Parnell's rashly avowed intention to use home rule in the first place for the protection of Irish industries against British competition'.[3] What foundation is there for this interpretation?

It is certainly true that Parnell attributed great potential

---

[1] Garvin, *Chamberlain*, ii. 114, letter of 26 Oct. 1885. In a by-election contest the 'Parnellites' had already favoured a tory candidate (Sexton at Wakefield on 1 July—see *The Times*, 5 July 1885).

[2] Letter dated 23 Oct. 1885, in Thorold, *Labouchere*, p. 241.

[3] Op. cit., p. 176. Mr. Strauss attributes the 'vote tory manifesto' to a cognate factor: 'This will o' the wisp'—the possibility of the tories granting home rule with Protectionist powers—'may well have influenced Parnell's fateful decision before the general election of 1885.' A few pages later, the 'may well' is thrown to the winds and we have 'the advocacy of Protection and his consequent support of the tories' (p. 180). Mr. Strauss condemns the 'tory alliance' in unqualified terms: 'From the Irish point of view this episode was a political catastrophe which showed Parnell in the most unfavourable light. The man who had played a consummate game of cat-and-mouse with his own left wing and who had proved himself the most cautious and sceptical negotiator in his dealings with the "grand old spider" was easily bamboozled by an unscrupulous demagogue like Lord Randolph Churchill and deceived himself in a singularly sanguine manner about his true relations with the tory viceroy, Lord Carnarvon' (pp. 168–9). This language is not warranted by the facts.

importance to a tariff-imposing power, and it is natural that he should have hoped for less resistance, on this specific point, from the tories—if after the elections another tory government should depend on Irish votes—than from the liberals. His insistence, in his talks with Carnarvon, on the importance of developing Irish industries (above, p. 103) points in that direction. It is also true that, in the pre-election period, in a speech at Wicklow, he gave strong expression to his 'protectionist' views:

> I claim this for Ireland, that if the Irish parliament of the future considers that certain industries can be benefited by Protection, nursed by Protection, until they can be placed by Protection in a position to compete with similar industries in other countries . . . then Ireland's parliament ought to have the power to carry out such a policy. . . . I tell English liberals and radicals it is useless to talk of their desire to do further justice to Ireland [when they refuse] the power we think would be sufficient to build up our industries.[1]

We may agree with Mr. Strauss that this suggestion was not likely to please, and did not please, Joseph Chamberlain. Within a few days, in an important speech at Warrington, Chamberlain took up the point.

> What is Mr. Parnell's programme? He says that in his opinion the time has come to obtain altogether all demands, to obtain no further remedial measures or subsidiary reforms and to concentrate the efforts of the Irish representatives upon the securing of a separate and independent parliament which is to consist of a single chamber, whose first object is to be to put a protective duty against all English manufactures (cries of 'No, no' and cheers). . . . I say that if these and these alone are the terms upon which Mr Parnell's support is to be obtained I will not enter into them.[2]

Months later, in his crucial speech of opposition to the second reading of the Home Rule Bill, he again referred specifically to these remarks of Parnell's at Wicklow, and observed that 'unless the member for Cork has changed his

[1] The Times, 6 Sept. 1885. A little earlier, on 27 Aug., speaking at Arklow, Parnell had already referred to the desirability of 'power to protect [Ireland's] struggling industries as part of a home rule settlement'. This speech was, however, much more tentative than the Wicklow one.

[2] Ibid., 9 Sept. 1885.

opinion, it is perfectly useless for British liberals and radicals to give him this bill unless they are prepared to go further and give him power by Protection to build up special industries'.[1]

The potential demand for Protection, then, was in Joseph Chamberlain's mind when he opposed home rule. To see in it, as Mr. Strauss does, the determining factor, is quite another matter. Chamberlain, as we have seen, had quarrelled with the Irish, or rather been rebuffed by their lay and clerical leaders, as early as July, well before 'Protection' had become any sort of issue. It is to the events of July that he harks back when he insists—as in his letters, quoted above, to Labouchere and Gladstone—that the Irish are untrustworthy. His opposition to the Home Rule Bill continued even after it was quite clear that control of customs and excise would still be vested in the imperial parliament. In his lengthy negotiations with Gladstone between his resignation and the vote on the second reading of the Home Rule Bill, the crucial question was not Protection—which Gladstone had dropped with Parnell's explicit though reluctant assent—but that of the retention of the Irish members in the imperial parliament.[2] Even in his decisive speech on the second reading, the point about Protection was not the principal one; it was only one illustration of his main theme —that the Parnellites were not to be trusted in their assertion that the bill would be a final settlement—and it bulked less large than Ulster, and the potential persecuting tendencies of the Catholic church. Neither he himself, in his 'political memoir', nor his biographer, J. L. Garvin, attaches predomi-

---

[1] *F.J.*, 2 June 1886. Parnell's reply to this was to produce his 'trump' about the Carnarvon conversations (see p. 107, n. 3) and to indicate that this particular demand was aimed exclusively at the tories: 'I should never have thought, I never did think and I do not think now of claiming a right of Protection from the liberal party. I never expected it (liberal cheers). Therefore I recognize this settlement as final, a settlement without Protection' (*F.J.*, 8 June 1886). Those who hold to Mr. Strauss's theory can point to the fact, for what it is worth, that Chamberlain's two 'let the Irish stew in their own juice' letters to Gladstone and Labouchere date from after Parnell's Wicklow speech. 'Customs and excise' was also among the four questions on which Chamberlain immediately before his resignation from the cabinet, in March 1886, failed to get satisfactory assurances from Gladstone (Chamberlain, *A Political Memoir*, p. 199).

[2] Ibid., p. 208.

nant importance to the 'Protection' question, and there seems no particular reason why they should diminish its importance—or why we now should differ from them in tracing the roots of Chamberlain's hostility not to the Wicklow speech in September but to the events of July (above, p. 99) and notably to his feeling that Parnell had first accepted his 'local self-government' plan and then caused it to be denounced. The importance which Chamberlain attached to the local self-government idea may, in its turn, be traced to his conviction that England was hostile to home rule and that the liberals, if they took up that cause, would sustain a tremendous defeat in the country.[1]

'Ah, but', it may be said, 'may not the rebuff of July itself have been caused by the Protectionist tendencies of the Irish leaders?' After all, the Irish middle class, according to Mr. Strauss, were now beginning 'to clamour for a change in the economic relations between Ireland and England'.[2] What more natural than that this clamour should have affected every phase in the political negotiations both with the tories and the radicals? What peace could there be between Parnell, representing the Irish middle class, and Chamberlain, the spokesman of the British middle class?

These questions are based on false premisses, for the Irish middle classes were not clamouring for Protection, or any other economic change, and, even if they had been, Parnell did not represent them. They have been best defined by, strangely enough, Mr. Strauss himself, in another part of his study. 'The Irish *bourgeoisie* existed only as a collection of minor vested interests within the framework of British [rule]. The handful of undertakings which had survived or grown within this cage were so closely connected with the British market and dependent on British interests that their owners were to a man staunch unionists.'[3] Allowing for a very slight element of exaggeration, the definition is admirable, and strictly pertinent to this period. A class so constituted could not be expected to 'clamour', and did not

[1] Letter to Gladstone of 19 Dec. 1885 (Chamberlain, *A Political Memoir* p. 171).          [2] Op. cit., p. 173.
[3] Ibid., p. 220. Mr. Strauss is here referring to a period about twenty years *later* than the one we are dealing with, but his remarks apply *a fortiori* to the earlier period.

clamour, for Protection. When Parnell, at Wicklow, claimed control over customs for an Irish parliament, the newspapers that represented the middle classes—the *Irish Times*, *Dublin Evening Mail*, &c.—naturally did not endorse his claim, since they, like, for example, the whole Dublin chamber of commerce, were opposed to an Irish parliament. The *Freeman's Journal*, representing, as well as other sections, the weak and mostly non-industrial section of the middle class that favoured home rule, felt bound to follow Parnell's lead, as it now did on all occasions, but its editorial was hardly a clarion call to the Irish *bourgeoisie*: 'Protection may be short-sighted, fallacious, injurious, but that does not confer upon English traders the right to force their manufactures upon us if we think fit, to our own detriment, not to take them.'[1] Michael Davitt was undoubtedly right, in his assessment of current public opinion, when he wrote to Labouchere a few days later: 'Parnell's attitude on Protection is absurd. If we had a national assembly in Dublin to-morrow he could not carry a measure in favour of Protection.'[2] The 'national *bourgeoisie*', what there was of it, was dreaming, not of Protection but of capital investment, under an Irish government, in rich, untapped natural resources: 'in twenty years, Ireland would return from judicious treatment and use of her own capital the enormous sum of £765 millions'.[3]

Parnell, in desiring Protection, was not obeying any 'clamour', or responding to the pressure of any section, but simply planning logically ahead towards what had probably always been his goal: a prosperous industrialized Ireland, with a social and political structure very similar to that of contemporary Britain, and functioning as an autonomous

[1] *F.J.*, 6 Oct. 1885.
[2] Thorold, *Labouchere*, p. 234. Healy, who may certainly by this date be regarded as a *bourgeois* member took a similar attitude to that of Davitt (below, Chap. VI, p. 186, n. 2).
[3] Charles Dawson, ex.M.P., speaking to 'a splendid attendance' in the Mansion House, Dublin, on 'The influence of an Irish parliament on Irish industries' (*F.J.*, 5 Jan. 1886). The M.P.s present included three of the leading 'middle-class' members—Blake, Esmonde, and Chance. Throughout the meeting there was no reference to Protection. One of the principal *bourgeois* members-to-be of the party, William Martin Murphy, in his election address to a Dublin constituency, spoke at length about the evils of landlordism and said nothing about Protection (*F.J.*, 24 Nov. 1885).

unit, rather more independently than Canada, within the British empire. He had to drop the demand—for the time at least—when he found it strongly opposed in Britain and only apathetically supported in Ireland. As for Chamberlain, he *may* have feared that, once Ireland had home rule, she would demand, and get, Protection, and that her example would be imitated by Canada and other portions of the empire. It seems unlikely, however, that such a remote and contingent consideration should in itself have determined so momentous a step as his break with the liberal party, and there is no evidence that it did so.

Would we, then, be justified in saying that the Irish leaders' treatment of tories and radicals at this crucial period—the only period in which a momentous diplomacy was possible —was motivated solely and soundly by political strategy directed at home rule, and was not affected by strategically irrelevant social, economic, or religious factors? Such a view would, I think, be more nearly correct than the schematic Marxist one proposed by Mr. Strauss, and yet it is not altogether adequate. There were, as we have seen, the soundest of strategic reasons for the tory alliance, and even for the 'vote tory manifesto', and it was not the greed of the Irish *bourgeoisie* for tariffs that led to the alienation of the radicals. But mistakes—in the strategic sense—were made, and they were mistakes of a kind that was favoured by the internal social and political climate of Ireland. The editorial in *United Ireland*, denouncing Chamberlain's tour, and to a lesser extent the editorial in *The Nation*, grudgingly agreeing to it, were important factors in alienating Chamberlain; taken in conjunction with Archbishop Walsh's letter and with Captain O'Shea's diplomacy they were decisive, at least in the sense that they accounted adequately for Chamberlain's subsequent hostility to the Irish and to home rule; in actually breaking with the liberal party he may have had other motives outside the scope of this study. To turn a possible ally into a determined enemy can hardly be justified on grounds of political strategy. But the abuse of *United Ireland*, the sneers of *The Nation*, and the coldness of the *Freeman's Journal* expressed, in different keys, what had now become the tone of Irish public life. Although the clergy, as

we have seen, were not altogether unwilling to negotiate
with the radicals, the lay leaders, and leader-writers, seemed
to feel that they could propitiate the clergy by abusing radicals and radicalism. Another, though less tangible, force at
work was a curious type of mimetic snobbery which affected
writers on the nationalist press and several of the parliamentarians, notably Healy. This was the assumption, by middle-
class professional people who were often of peasant origin,
of the aristocratic contempt for persons 'in trade'. Many of
the nationalists were, as we have seen, themselves open to
social snubs and wounding quips from people like Sir
Henry Lucy, and some of them, by a natural human reaction,
'took it out on' that section of the English representation
which was itself vulnerable.[1] This was, mainly, a radical
section, symbolized in the person of Joseph Chamberlain.
'Brummagem' was a favourite term of contempt in the
nationalist press and the 'shop-keeping Danton' was more
despised for keeping a 'shop' than he was abhorred for being
a 'revolutionary'. Today, when snobbery is no longer an
overt political force, it is not easy to convey how completely
it saturated political commentary, on almost all sides, in the
eighties and how, in this specific instance, it informed a
certain nationalist response to Chamberlain's proposed
Irish tour.

In the atmosphere of the tory alliance, both the 'clerical'
and the 'snobbish' forms of 'anti-radicalism' flourished. The
bishops themselves soon forgot their earlier guarded negotiations with the radicals, got on famously with Lord
Carnarvon and spoke to him—so he reported to the Queen—
'very openly on the state of the country and of public feeling
and appeared to him extremely anxious to support your
majesty's government and to uphold the law'.[2] In these
conditions ideological anti-radicalism easily became vocal.

[1] The parliamentary correspondent of *United Ireland*, for example, was
capable of writing, in the manner of Sir Henry Lucy, about 'unknown pitmen
from Wales . . . [in the new parliament of 1886] trampling through the
elementary rules of order with the most beautiful rustic unconsciousness'
(16 Jan. 1886). It is perhaps revealing that in the party minute books, in
attendance lists, the names of knights and baronets are written out in full
(Sir Joseph Neale McKenna, &c.) whereas the untitled get a bare surname
(Carew, Condon, &c.).

[2] Hardinge, *Carnarvon*, iii. 182 (letter of 26 Aug. 1885).

On 18 November, three days before the 'vote tory manifesto', Dr. Nulty, Bishop of Meath, one of the oldest clerical friends of the 'New Departure', published a denunciation of the radicals as being 'fanatically anti-Christian', stating that 'the Irish parliamentary party are the bulwark of religious freedom against them'.[1] This followed on the radical demand for 'free schools'—endorsed by Chamberlain in his Warrington speech on 8 September—and on Cardinal Manning's call to Catholics, in effect, to vote against the supporters of 'free schools' (*The Tablet*, 24 October 1885). Mr. C. H. D. Howard has shown that, for Irish Catholics in England, the clergy's attitude on the 'schools' question was an influence not less important than Parnell's manifesto in producing anti-liberal votes.[2]

[1] *F.J.*, 19 Nov. 1885. Cf. Winston Churchill, *Lord Randolph Churchill*, i. 455–6: 'The menace [from the liberal left wing] to the established church and to denominational teaching . . . provided a new and perfectly unimpeachable bond of union between them and the Irish nationalists.' The 'vote tory manifesto' itself made a reference to the menace to liberty in the schools which the liberal party contained.

[2] 'A study of what actually occurred in the constituencies after the publication of the manifesto does not confirm the story of Parnell's omnipotence. It shows on the contrary that Parnell was obeyed only in so far as his orders to vote against liberals and radicals coincided with the advice that Irish Catholics were receiving from their clergy; and the clergy were primarily concerned not with the demand for home rule, but with the threat which the "unauthorized programme" of Joseph Chamberlain constituted to the church's schools' (C. H. D. Howard, 'The Parnell Manifesto of 21 November, 1885, and the Schools Question', in *E.H.R.*, Jan. 1947). In this very interesting and searching paper, Mr. Howard gives good—though not conclusive—grounds for the above statement. Two minor criticisms are possible. In explaining the violence of the manifesto by the personal opinions of T. P. O'Connor, who is supposed to have 'viewed the liberals . . . as a menace to the Christian religion' (p. 47), Mr. Howard is, in the present writer's opinion, mistaken (see Chap. I, p. 28, n. 3) and his interpretation is not borne out by the sources which he cites (p. 47, n. 3). Mr. Howard seems disposed to exaggerate both the importance and the extent of the manifesto's truculence when he says that 'the extraordinary violence of the abuse which it heaped upon the liberal party astonished people accustomed only to the gentlemanly conventions of English politics' (p. 43), and that it left behind it serious rancour among the liberals. Political invective in the eighties was vigorous even in gentlemanly England. Lord Randolph Churchill's election address of 1886 (below, p. 194, n. 3) is an example. The Irish had no particular respect for conventions of which the benefit was not extended to them. The following is a not very extreme example of the language used about Irish members in a powerful section of the English press all through the eighties: 'On the Irish benches it seemed as if a nest of cobras had been roused to sudden anger. Such writhings and squirmings, such cobra rattling and splutter and angry passions, such

As for snobbery, Lord Randolph Churchill had struck exactly the right note from the beginning, in the move that was the tory overture to the Irish. When a member of his own party, the bookseller W. H. Smith, had questioned the wisdom of admitting Irish peasants, who lived in 'mud-cabins', to the benefits of the act, Lord Randolph had made common cause with the peasant over the head of the *bourgeois*:

I suppose that in the minds of the lords of suburban villas, of the owners of vineries and pineries, the mud cabin represents the climax of physical and social degradation. . . . The difference be-tween the cabin of the Irish peasant and the cottage of the English agricultural labourer is not so great as that which exists between the abode of the right honourable member for Westminster and the humble roof which shelters from the storm the individual who now has the honour to address the committee.'[1]

Language like this went straight to the hearts of men like Healy—whose 'pro-toryism', of which Davitt speaks, was primarily a social attitude rather than a political outlook—and it is significant that even after Churchill had utterly abandoned his Irish alliances, and had become far more violently and inflammatorily anti-home rule than Chamber-lain ever was, there was never any such personal bitterness towards him in Ireland as there was towards Chamberlain.[2] It *may* be significant also that, whereas Parnell dealt with Chamberlain through an intermediary—the disastrous

flushings of faces, such spasmodic jerking forward of heads hooded with alarm and hate, such snaky sibilations sharpened into spiteful scoffs, had rarely been known in the House, even among the reptile brood introduced to parliament and there self-exhibited—by grace of American dollars—uncaged' (*Sheffield Telegraph*, 29 Feb. 1885 : quoted in Healy, *Letters and Leaders*, i. 278). The 'vote tory manifesto' was an aggressive piece of polemics, but neither hysterical nor personally wounding.

  [1] Winston Churchill, *Lord Randolph Churchill*, i. 345.

  [2] Immediately after the fall of the liberal government in June 1885 Captain O'Shea informed Chamberlain that he thought Churchill would be appointed chief secretary for Ireland and that he would make a success of it as he was 'on such good terms with the boys' i.e. the Irish party (letter of 11 June in Garvin, *Chamberlain*, ii. 15). The fact that Churchill is always mentioned affectionately in Parnellite memoirs is due rather to his charm and humour—qualities in which Chamberlain was deficient—than to 'mimetic snobbery'; but one sometimes senses that his belonging to a ducal family was not, in the opinion of these writers, a drawback.

O'Shea—he saw Churchill,[1] and later Carnarvon, himself. There is, at any rate, an undercurrent of eagerness in the Irish dealings with the tories, and there is an undercurrent of contempt in their dealings with the radicals. The undercurrents have their sources in social prejudices, to some extent in religious convictions, but most of all in the past history of the Parnellite movement itself, and in the internal semi-conservatism that followed the Kilmainham treaty.[2] It was these undercurrents, and the incalculable momentum that accompanies any grave political choice, that carried the perfectly correct policy of a tactical alliance with the tories out to the extreme of administering an insulting rebuff to a radical section, whose secession was to defeat the Home Rule Bill.

[1] Gwynn and Tuckwell, *Dilke*, ii. 153. Chamberlain may himself have preferred to deal through O'Shea whom, as Henry Harrison has demonstrated, he knew at this time to be the husband of Parnell's mistress. The fact that O'Shea was Chamberlain's henchman may have given Parnell a personal, and non-political, reason for 'anti-radicalism'.

[2] The non-revolutionary nature of Parnellism was heavily stressed at this time, especially by the nationalist clergy: 'In the beginning of Mr. Parnell's career it was whispered that he was determined to get on without the assistance of the Irish clergy and bishops, that he kept bad company in Paris and New York and that he would slowly but surely lead the Irish people into revolution and communism. Mr. Parnell has outlived these calumnies' (Very Rev. A. Phelan, P.P., chairman of Queen's County Convention of the National League—quoted in *F.J.*, 8 Oct. 1885).

# IV

## THE MACHINE (1880–5)

Historiquement les partis sont nés quand les masses populaires ont commencé à entrer réellement dans la vie politique: ils ont formé le cadre nécessaire qui leur permettait de recruter en elles-mêmes leurs propres élites.                    MAURICE DUVERGER, *Les Partis politiques*

THE history of modern political parties is rich in examples of the law that a sharp change in the party line involves a tightening in party discipline, often including a structural reorganization. The Parnellite movement did not escape the operation of this law. The Kilmainham treaty, which marked the transmutation of Parnellism from a quasi-revolutionary movement into a completely constitutional one, could not have been implemented without a drastic subordination of the branches of the movement to central control, i.e. the control of the parliamentary party itself. As the party had been reduced by secessions until it contained, for all practical purposes, no opponents of Parnell, this meant that the whole great movement of the 'New Departure', or what was left of it, was now to be turned, by the little group of Parnell's lieutenants, out of land-agitation into the more or less peaceful ways of electioneering. It was not immediately necessary to tighten the internal organization of the party itself, partly because of the secessions and partly because its make-up was such that it was inclined to welcome rather than oppose the new rightward tendency. What was needed was to discipline the 'peripheral organizations', as they would now be called, one or two of which had in the past not merely acted independently of the parliamentarians, but exercised some control over them. Before going farther with the description of how the party machine was perfected in the years following the Kilmainham treaty, it might be well, for the sake of clarity, to list these organizations and indicate briefly their relation to the parliamentary party in the immediate pre-Kilmainham era.

1. *Peripheral Organizations before the Kilmainham Treaty*

(*a*) *The Land League*

This was, of course, apart from its own independent role, by far the most important institutional ally of the Parnellite group or party in the years 1879–81. It served the party, or rather the party's 'active section' in the general election of 1880 by helping to arouse general enthusiasm for Parnell, by issuing a manifesto[1] urging land leaguers to vote against landlords' candidates, by secret financial subvention,[2] and, sometimes, by the electoral support of its local branches.[3] But this help, though valuable, was very limited in proportion to the great power and considerable resources of the league. The manifesto, beneficial as it was, took care to indicate that the Land League considered its own direct action more effective than any parliamentary programme, and took no notice of home rule; as regards finance, although the Land League was carrying forward at the end of March 1880 an unexpended balance of over £20,000, of which about £6,500 was earmarked for political purposes,[4] it

---

[1] *F.J.*, 13 Mar. 1880.

[2] The advance had to be secret because of the resolution passed on the formation of the National Land League against using any Land League money for parliamentary purposes. Davitt (*Fall of Feudalism in Ireland*, p. 173) states that this resolution was a concession to extremist prejudices in the U.S.A. Parnell admitted before the Special Commission that he 'did not approve of it at all' but claimed that, in 1880, 'Mr. Egan took a large view of it and he met me and I think the resolution was rescinded and he gave me a cheque for £2,000' (*Special Comm. Proc.* vii. 27). I have been unable to find any corroboration of the statement that the resolution was rescinded. Davitt afterwards told McGhee that no moneys were voted by the Land League for parliamentary purposes in his presence, but that he knew it had been done to the extent of £1,000—'lecture expenses' of O'Kelly, Sexton, Healy, and others (Davitt MSS.: McGhee correspondence, Jan. 1883).

[3] The branches were not supposed to take any part in electioneering, but there were ways of getting around this. The Tullow branch of the Land League, for instance, met, during the campaign, to hear the home rule candidate, E. D. Gray, deliver an address on the land question. When he had finished speaking the Rev. Chairman moved 'that the meeting of the Land League be now dissolved, the league having pledged themselves not to take part in the election, as a body. They could then resume as a meeting of electors and ratepayers'. They did this, and the meeting then unanimously adopted Gray as home rule and tenant right candidate (*F.J.*, 20 Mar. 1880).

[4] See *Special Comm. Proc.* vi. 276. The evidence given by Hardcastle, accountant, regarding the Land League bank accounts is, so far as I know,

would only produce £2,000 for the electoral expenses of the
Parnellites, and even that was classified as a loan. The
league, furthermore, at the request of some of its local
branches,[1] published a flat denial that it was 'co-operating
with the Home Rule League or any other body in promoting
the election of members of parliament'.[2] It was a grave drawback for the parliamentary party to be semi-dependent on
an organization which had been founded for quite a different
object, had so vigorous a life of its own, and was, for most
practical purposes, directed by men who were not themselves members of parliament and tended to regard parliamentarianism with suspicion. The original promoters of the
Land League—who included not a single M.P.—were
mostly fenians or ex-fenians, and the league never quite lost
the characteristic fenian distrust of constitutionalism. Its
original objects also, at its inception in Mayo, included
acting as a vigilance committee on the local M.P.,[3] and this
sort of attitude, although useful to Parnell in the 1880 election, tended still further to make the league not so much an
auxiliary of the party as its tutor. This relationship was not
without bitterness for men who, having risen from obscurity
to sudden parliamentary honour, found themselves sneered
at as 'Land League items' and suspected of having their
clothes and their railway-tickets bought for them out of
'Egan's wages'.[4] Parnell himself, although chairman of the
league, was by no means its master, as he was of his own
parliamentary followers, and was manifestly unable to over-
come completely its suspicion of the constitutional movement. What was true of the Irish Land League was true

the only authoritative information now available on Land League finances.
I applied to the banks concerned (the Hibernian Bank and the National Bank)
for permission to examine these accounts, but this was refused in both cases.
The books of the Land League are, of course, 'missing' since before 1888,
and may perhaps be presumed destroyed.

[1] Balla branch of the Land League, and Westport Tenant Union (*F.J.*,
12 Mar. 1880).

[2] Ibid., 20 Mar. 1880.           [3] Davitt, *Fall of Feudalism*, p. 163.

[4] An English observer noted in his diary that the production of the
accounts of the Land League should clear up 'many little mysteries of hotel
accommodation, first-class railway-travelling and unaccustomed suits of
clothing' (Sir Henry Lucy, *A Diary of Two Parliaments*, ii. 314). These taunts
were not altogether without foundation, but contemporaries were inclined
to exaggerate the extent of the 'dole'.

*a fortiori* of the American Land League[1] and the other organizations through which the money was coming from
abroad. They tended to be less patient of compromise, in
the degree of their remoteness from practical Irish politics,
as they were, of course, totally independent of any parliamentary control, other than the spell exerted by Parnell's
personal prestige. The necessity in which the Land League
stood of keeping up the flow of American money helped to
ensure, as long as the agitation lasted, its continued freedom
from parliamentary control.

### (b) The Irish Home Rule League

This was a much more docile and less important auxiliary.
It was founded by resolution of the Home Rule Conference
of 1873,[2] its 'only object being to obtain the self-government
claimed in these resolutions',[3] i.e. federal home rule. It was
designed to supersede the old Home Government Association, which dissolved itself shortly after the conference, and
to put the movement on a broader basis. Membership was
open to all who were willing to subscribe to the resolutions
and pay £1, and those who were not able to pay the full
subscription could for a fee of 1s. be enrolled as supporters
of the principles of the league.

The subscribing members elected annually, by ballot, 50
members of the council of the league and these in turn co-
opted a further 50.[4] The council—or rather, in practice,
those of its members who lived near the place of meeting,
Sackville Street, Dublin—met weekly, for the purpose of
accepting new members, keeping the 'national roll' of supporters up to date, and, occasionally, expressing opinions.
The part played by the league as an organization in the election campaign of January–February 1874 was negligible,
and its supporters claimed that the election had been deliberately put forward so as to take place before the league

---

[1] I do not deal with the Ladies' Land League, which played no part in the
constitutional movement and therefore cannot be regarded as a 'peripheral
organization'.
[2] Resolution 10, *F.J.*, 22 Nov. 1873.
[3] Ibid.
[4] Ibid., 20 Feb. 1874; *Nation*, 28 Feb. 1874. The council had consisted
initially of 75 members (ibid., 27 Dec. 1873).

council could have organized the country.[1] In fact, however, the council never did proceed, in the work of organization, beyond the point which it had reached in January 1874. This failure may be attributed in part to Isaac Butt's lack of political realism.

A resolution (no. 14) of the Home Rule Conference had provided that 'in addition to the normal resources of the league it is essential to raise a large special fund (vested in trustees) for the purpose of promoting the organization of the movement throughout Great Britain and Ireland'. Mitchell Henry made, at the conference, the very sensible suggestion that this fund should be used to defray the expenses of candidates, but Isaac Butt rejected this idea, saying: 'I most earnestly hope that not a penny of the fund will be expended on electioneering purposes.'[2] This decision greatly impaired the political efficacy of the league, and the league's total failure to form a network of local branches— in itself an index of the popular apathy at this time regarding pure home rule, as distinct from the New Departure programme—completely wrecked it as a 'machine' in the modern sense.[3] By 1880 the league council, the large unwieldy directorate of an almost non-existent organization, was dominated by the Parnellites and was useful to them for specific propaganda purposes. It helped to preserve their continuity with the Butt movement, which no doubt went some way to reassure middle-class electors dubious about the revolutionary element in the New Departure, and it provided a good mouthpiece through which to defend

[1] Ibid., 31 Jan. 1874.
[2] F.J., 22 Nov. 1873. This hope was not completely fulfilled. The league seems to have spent some money on the 1874 campaign and is said to have offered Parnell £300 to cover his election expenses in that year (Katherine O'Shea, *Parnell*, i. 128).
[3] During the 1880 campaign, Parnell, speaking at a Home Rule League meeting, deplored 'the want of local preparations which somehow or other always seems to be one of our failings at times of crisis' (F.J., 27 Mar.). Many months later the council of the league attempted to remedy this defect, and issued a circular urging 'the formation of local associations'. This suggestion collapsed under heavy fire from left and right; Egan replied without delay for the Land League: 'The country has outgrown the Home Rule League' (ibid., 23 Nov. 1881). Shaw, on behalf of the whigs, was no less crushing: 'The league, as at present constituted, is unfit to produce any effect on Irish opinion' (ibid., 24 Dec. 1881).

Parnell against attacks from the right.[1] It had in fact become
what would now be called a 'front'. It voluntarily merged
itself with the Irish National League shortly after that body
was constituted.[2] The 'central branch' of that body, meeting
fortnightly in Dublin, continued the propaganda work of
the old Home Rule League Council.

## (c) The Home Rule Confederation of Great Britain

This organization, a much more formidable one than the
Irish Home Rule League, was yet built up from the same
foundations—the home rule associations founded at the
instigation of Isaac Butt in the early seventies. In January
1873, i.e. considerably before the great Home Rule Conference in Dublin, John Barry, then secretary of the Manchester Home Rule Association, conceived the idea of a
federation of the existing associations in Great Britain,
numbering about twenty.[3] The number soon rose, according
to one account,[4] to about 150. The structure of the confederation was highly integrated; an annual convention of
branch delegates elected an executive council of about
twenty, plus officials (president, honorary secretary, paid
general secretary); continuity of direction was assured by
an understanding that half the executive should be drawn
from the 'capital' of the confederation (first Manchester,
then Liverpool, later London). The primary function of
the confederation was to obtain home rule pledges from
English candidates through the control of the Irish vote in
the great English cities. It differed therefore from the Irish
Home Rule League in having a well-ramified organization
and immediate practical objectives. Like the Land League,
and unlike the Irish Home Rule League, it contained a
strong fenian element,[5] and so was able to draw on deep
reserves of conspiratorial enthusiasm. Although its principal

[1] For example, the council came out immediately after the Enniscorthy
incident with a denunciation of 'the sham nationalist' O'Clery and his supporters (F.J., 31 Mar. 1880). Such a manifesto against the right-wing 'clerical'
party obviously sounded better from the league founded by Butt than it
would have from the organization of Davitt and Egan.

[2] Ibid., 25 Nov. 1882.

[3] John Denvir, History of the Irish in Great Britain, p. 265.

[4] F. H. O'Donnell, A History of the Irish Parliamentary Party, i. 162.

[5] R. Barry O'Brien, Parnell, p. 100.

functions were of necessity related more to the general home rule movement than to the parliamentary party, it rendered great service to Parnellism. By deposing Isaac Butt in favour of Parnell as its president in 1877, it gave the young leader his first great political victory, and not long afterwards, in the general election of 1880, it proved its value as a training-ground for 'available' young parliamentarians of the 'active section'.[1] From the party point of view it was probably a more admirable institution than either the Land League or the Home Rule League, combining the activity of the one with something of the docility of the other. The loyalty of the fenian element in it was not, however, unconditional, and after the 'Kilmainham treaty' the confederation did not escape reorganization.[2]

## (d) Local associations

Neither in its first general election (1874) nor in its second (1880) did the home rule party possess a national organization. The business of selecting candidates was left in some places to *ad hoc* meetings of 'the clergy and laity' summoned by the bishop or some other influential ecclesiastic; in others to similar meetings of electors convened by the lord mayor and meeting in the town hall; in a third category, the nomination was decided, provisionally or finally, by some permanent local body representing nationalist opinion. The principal bodies of this type which were active in the 1880 election were: the Queen's County Independent Club, Wexford County Independent Club, Kilkenny Tenant Farmers' Association, Carlow County Registration Association, Tipperary Independent Club, Edenderry Home Rule Club, Louth Independent Club, Ballinasloe Tenants' Defence Association, North Kerry Farmers' Club, Mallow Farmers' Club, and Clare Farmers' Club.[3] Most of these bodies were relics of the tenant right movement of the fifties, and on the

[1] Almost all the young 'English-Irish' Parnellites returned in that election were members of the confederation.

[2] It had previously been merged in the 'Land League of Great Britain' (Davitt, *Fall of Feudalism*, p. 227), but this does not seem to have amounted to more than a change of title. It was not until 1883 that its constitution was altered, in a 'parliamentary' sense (see below).

[3] *F.J.*, Mar.–Apr. 1880.

whole they seem to have represented a more prosperous class of farmers than did the Land League, with which, however, some of them co-operated electorally.[1] They were all unrelated and not amenable to control from any central headquarters;[2] some of them did the sort of local political work that would now be considered essential[3] (e.g. scrutiny of the register of electors, organization of meetings, publicity, &c.); most did nothing but signify their approval or disapproval of a candidate. Such a system or systems told, of course, in favour of local men, and it says much for the prestige of Parnell and the power of the Land League, that so many Parnellite 'carpet-baggers' were in fact returned in 1880. The chief value of the associations was that in areas where other means were lacking (e.g. where the bishop was supporting some whig landlord or the lord mayor was a tory) they could convene electoral meetings and ensure that a nationalist was in fact nominated. The Land League with its ostensible dissociation from electoral politics could not perform this service. Almost all the local associations were due to fade from the political scene after the national machine for which they were local makeshifts had made its appearance.[4]

## 2. *The Irish National League and the Election Machine*

The process of subordinating the national movement to the parliamentary party might have proved a difficult one,

[1] e.g. the Carlow Registration Association corresponded with local branches of the Land League in the matter of Gray's candidature (*F.J.*, 16 Mar. 1880).

[2] One or two such associations (e.g. the Queen's County Independent Club) had resolved at an earlier date to 'support the Home Rule League' but no organizational nexus seems to have developed. In the 1874 election a number of local 'home rule associations', presumably affiliated to the Home Rule League, had taken part (at Middlesborough, Drogheda, Cavan (3 branches), and Wexford), but by 1880 the array seemed to have dwindled to the Edenderry Home Rule Club (ibid., Jan. 1874; Mar.–Apr. 1880).

[3] Some of them had developed quite a high degree of organization. The honorary secretary of the Carlow Registration Association, for instance, induced 'the priests and lay members to form in their respective parishes local committees appointing a secretary to correspond with him' (ibid., 15 Mar. 1880).

[4] The only one which retained a vigorous life was the Dublin Registration Association, which sent 140 delegates to the National League Convention in Dublin City on 16 Nov. 1885 (ibid., 17 Nov. 1885).

but for three circumstances. The first of these was the pro-
clamation of the Land League as an illegal organization in
October 1881. The Ladies' Land League which took its
place never had the same solidity, and it was easier for Parnell to extinguish it, and prescribe the form under which the
old Land League should be resurrected, than it would have
been to force a change of constitution on the living Land
League. The second circumstance was the pacifying influence of the new land courts and the general mitigation of
the land crisis. The third was the shock of the Phoenix Park
murders, and consequent discredit of the semi-revolutionary
movement. Parnell's original idea after the 'Kilmainham
treaty' seems to have been not to revive the league at all in
any form, and in fact for several months (May–Oct. 1882)
the country remained without any such organization. In
October 1882, however, he was prevailed on to assent, on
conditions, to the setting up of a new organization, the
National League.

The new league was not, like the old one, an autonomous
agrarian organization. Its programme as approved by its
foundation conference[1] was essentially a home rule one; its
first object was 'national self-government', 'land-law reform'
coming only in the second place. Its organization was to be
dominated by the parliamentary party, which was to have
the nomination of 16 members out of a council of 48. The
remaining 32 were to be elected by county conventions composed of delegates from the local branches, meeting under
the chairmanship of a member of the party.

The council envisaged in the National League's constitution was, in fact, never elected, and the government of the
league remained in the hands of the 'organizing committee',
a supposedly temporary body, set up pending the election of
the council.[2] The committee consisted of thirty members,[3]

[1] Conference at the Antient Concert Rooms, 17 Oct. 1882 (reported in
*F.J.*, 18 Oct. 1882).
[2] N.L.I., Harrington MSS., p.c. 50. Harrington's affidavit, 30 Mar. 1892.
[3] Parnell (chairman), Biggar, M.P., and Alfred Webb (treasurers), T.
Healy, M.P., T. Brennan, and T. Harrington, M.P. (hon. secs.), Dawson,
M.P., Gray, M.P., T. D. Sullivan, M.P., J. E. Redmond, M.P., Leamy, M.P.,
Sexton, M.P., Davitt, William O'Brien, Matt Harris, Judge Little, A.
Shackleton, G. Delany, T. Mayne, J. J. Clancy, W. F. Moloney, D. Histon,
D. Sheehy, Louis Smith, J. B. Walshe, W. Abraham, John O'Connor, J.

twelve of whom were, at the date of the league's foundation, already members of parliament. Seven other members of the committee were later elected to parliament. The chairman of the committee was Parnell, Biggar was one of the treasurers, and Healy and Harrington were two of the three secretaries. It is probable that the committee showed itself so amenable to the party's influence that the election of a council was deemed unnecessary.

The committee's powers were not clearly defined by the constitution; it had 'all the powers of a Central Council until the Council is elected', but the powers of a Central Council were not defined.[1] Being itself the rule-making body, it interpreted these powers widely, including among them the power to dissolve refractory branches.[2] Despite the appearance of democracy, the National League remained throughout the period an autocratically controlled body, ruled by a committee which it had not elected, and whose powers were undefined.

What the new league really provided was the smooth-running national electioneering machinery that had hitherto been lacking to the parliamentary party. The selection of candidates, which had been largely in the hands of impromptu meetings and local clubs, was now entrusted at least nominally to conventions of the National League.

These county conventions for the selection of parliamentary candidates consisted of four delegates from each branch of the National League in the county, along with any of the Catholic clergy of the county who wished to attend and two or three representatives of the parliamentary party.[3] The

Cardiff, R. Lalor, M.P., and Metge, M.P. (list from a copy of the Address of the Irish National League to the people of Ireland—undated, probably Nov. 1882—among the Harrington Papers). Under the constitution this committee consisted of 'five members of the Mansion House Committee for the Relief of Evicted Tenants, five members of the executive of the Labour and Industrial Union, five members of the Council of the Home Rule League and fifteen other gentlemen' (from a copy of the constitution among the Harrington Papers). The 'fifteen other gentlemen' were probably nominated by Parnell.

[1] Constitution of the Irish National League: Rules.

[2] It dissolved the Waterford branch during the election period by the simple method of sending it a telegram: 'Branch dissolved by order' (*F.J.*, 21 Oct. 1885).

[3] The constitution of the league provides for country conventions for the election of the members of the league's 'Central Council', which in fact was

attendance of the Catholic clergy—which is not provided for in the league's constitution—was invited for the Wicklow Convention of 1885, the first of the general election series, and similar invitations were issued for the rest of the series. Expressing his gratification at the Wicklow invitation, Archbishop Walsh emphasized that the clergy attended, not as members of a political organization, but as the clergy of the county. What, he speculated, would be the feelings of the Archbishop of Paris if he could receive a like invitation?[1] In his confidential instructions to his clergy—of whom he assumed, correctly, that many would deem it their duty to attend—Archbishop Walsh, with characteristic prudence, laid down four principles: (1) To help the two candidates of most satisfactory antecedents among those known in advance; (2) to block surprise candidates; (3) failing that, 'to use every effort to secure an adjournment'; (4) failing that, to withdraw from the proceedings.[2] These instructions show that clerical participation in the conventions was by no means a mere formality.

Davitt, at whose friends and policies these proceedings were probably in part aimed, naturally deplored the 'clerical franchise' which he described to his friend Richard McGhee as a 'great blunder' which, in northern and western areas where the league was not strong, would mean that 'if the priests so choose they can run their own candidates'.[3] A more detached observer, T. W. Rolleston, noted that the clerical franchise 'astonished a good many Protestant and

never set up. It does not provide for the attendance of the clergy at such conventions; nor does it mention conventions for the nomination of parliamentary candidates. It seems that the preliminary arrangements for the 'parliamentary' conventions must have been settled by the organizing committee which, under the constitution, had the power to frame rules and also 'all the powers of a Central Council until the council is elected and no longer' (see above, p. 128). 'Rules for the guidance of county conventions' were read at the Wicklow convention by Timothy Harrington (*U.I.*, 10 Oct. 1885) and were accepted for the series. It was not made clear whether Harrington was speaking as secretary of the league, or on behalf of the organizing committee, or even of the party, but no one questioned his authority or credentials. Parnell was in the chair (see p. 127, n. 3).

[1] Speech at Enniskerry, 20 Sept. 1885, copy among the Dillon Papers.

[2] Copy of letter dated 25 Sept. 1885 to Canon Dillon, P.P., Wicklow (Dillon MSS., 7).

[3] Copy of letter dated 23 Sept. 1885 (Davitt MSS.: McGhee correspondence).

even Catholic nationalists' but on the whole felt that it had 'no very sinister significance'. His explanation of it is interesting and probably sound:

The Parnellites want the help of the clergy for the National League and the clergy, who never cared very ardently for nationalism, want the help of the Parnellites for their views on education, on the admission of atheists into parliament and so forth. A bargain is struck and the consequence is that at the parliamentary conventions, where it was always highly desirable and sometimes highly difficult to secure the return of the Parnellite candidates, the priests as a numerous body which in virtue of the compact aforesaid could be thoroughly depended on to vote solid and straight were thrown into the scale by a sort of *coup de main*.[1]

The conventions, which consisted on a rough average of 150 laymen and 50 priests,[2] met in some hotel of the county town and went immediately into private session, under the chairmanship of one of the members of parliament. It was at this private meeting, an 'official' account of which was afterwards furnished to the press, that the candidates were selected. This done, another delegate, usually a priest, took the chair, and a public session began, at which both the selected candidates and those who had 'withdrawn their names in the interest of unity' were eulogized. The city conventions were conducted in the same way, the only difference being that they were attended by the nationalist members of the local corporations as well as by the National League delegates and clergy. The size of these assemblies, and the fact that most of those present were unacquainted with each other, made them fairly easy to control, and if they did 'bolt' once or twice, they could be curbed by the prestige of the national leader, more potent than ever since the collapse of the radical land movement. In fact when the first real testing time, the general election of 1885, came

[1] Article, 'The Archbishop in Politics', in *Dublin University Review*, Feb 1886. This thoughtful and well-balanced article should be consulted by anyone interested in the subject.

[2] These figures are based on an analysis of the attendance at the 32 county conventions held during the general election campaign of 1885 (Oct.–Nov. 1885). The total attendance ranged from nearly 500 (Cork Convention, 12 Oct. 1885) down to a mere 7 (Antrim Convention, 18 Nov. 1885). The latter was merely a symbolic gathering which pledged itself 'to support only the candidates recommended by Mr. Parnell'.

round, the selection of candidates was already controlled by a caucus, consisting of ten or eleven M.P.s, who met for the purpose usually at Morrison's Hotel, Dublin.[1] When a candidate had been selected, an M.P. was deputed to take the chair at the appropriate county convention and went there, according to T. P. O'Connor, 'with his written instructions, the first of which was to get the man through who had been chosen by the committee in Dublin. He had also in many cases a second or third name up his sleeve. . . . In some cases where a candidate was known as somewhat undesirable, the chairman was expected to take any and every measure to prevent his being chosen.' 'Any and every measure' ranged from a straightforward intimation that the Irish parliamentary party would not be willing to work with the undesirable candidate to some very subtle devices. O'Connor[2] records with pride that before a county convention where the party knew that the name of an 'undesirable' was going to be proposed, it was arranged that his proposer should be a certain clerical delegate, who actually agreed with the party view on the person in question. When the convention was held, and the name proposed, the proposer listened gravely to the arguments against his nominee, and then rose to announce that the name was withdrawn. The approved candidate was declared unanimously elected. Again, if it was thought that a convention was in danger of bolting, it was possible for the organizing committee to arrange for the admission of suitable new branches in the menaced county, whose delegates would vote in a 'regular' fashion.[3] A third method of managing a somewhat refractory convention was described by one of the 'undesirable candidates', P. J. Louden of Mayo, who was disapproved of by the party as an intransigent land leaguer and general nuisance, and whose candidature was rejected by the Co. Mayo Convention on 3 November 1885. There were four constituencies in this county, and therefore four names to be selected by the convention. Five names, including Louden's, were proposed.

[1] T. M. Healy, *Letters and Leaders of my Day*, i. 230; T. P. O'Connor, *Memoirs of an Old Parliamentarian*, ii. 14. As regards the caucus, see § 4 (*b*), below. [2] Ibid., p. 16.
[3] See, for instance, the account of the Co. Louth Convention in the *Irish Times*, 24 Nov. 1885.

Parnell, who was in the chair, put three of them to the convention, and declared them selected on a show of hands. He kept the name of the strongest candidate, John Dillon, until the end and then announced that for the fourth seat the convention had to choose between Dillon and Louden. Naturally Dillon was selected, although Louden stated afterwards that the voting took place 'amid confusion and uproar'.[1] Railroading of this kind was facilitated by the fact that the conventions had no standing orders, other than a very general set of 'Rules for the guidance of county conventions', drawn up by Harrington.[2] This left a very wide discretion to the chairman. On one occasion when 'any and every measure' failed, and the party nominee was rejected by a Tipperary Convention, Parnell summoned another convention and got the party man nominated.[3] Such episodes were rare, however, and generally speaking the system combined the appearance of local spontaneity with the reality of centralized control.[4]

The National League effectively superseded the Home Rule League as well as 'replacing' the Land League; and in England the Irish National League of Great Britain, with headquarters in London and an executive composed of parliamentarians, took the place of the old Home Rule Confederation.[5] The effectiveness of the National League for the purposes for which it was intended proved high,[6] as the time for a general election approached. By July 1885 the police already noted 'a perceptible increase in the power of the

[1] Letter in the *Irish Times*, 6 Nov. 1885.

[2] Introduced at the Wicklow Convention (see p. 128, n. 3). The most important rule was that relating to the party pledge (see § 4 (*a*), below).

[3] T. P. O'Connor, op. cit., ii. 15. This episode occurred in Jan. 1885. William O'Brien (*Evening Memories*, p. 66) recalls that the party man was 'rejected in the fury of a local war-dance' and that Parnell 'summoned a second convention to reconsider the decision'. The R.I.C. were professionally impressed by the 'discipline' shown in this episode (R. E. Beckerson to Lord Carnarvon, Report on the Progress of the Irish National League, Jan.–June 1885, 5 July 1885, among unindexed papers in S.P.O., Dublin Castle).

[4] For the selection of candidates after 1885 see Chap. VIII, § 3 (*a*).

[5] The American Land League followed suit; a convention at Philadelphia in Apr. 1883 turned the organization into the National League of America (Davitt, op. cit., p. 390).

[6] For its secondary purpose of 'land law reform' its branches, which were probably mostly revived branches of the Land League, seem to have shown undue zeal. See Chap. VI, p. 165, n. 1.

league' and commented on the 'effectiveness of the county convention system as illustrated in recent by-elections'.[1] But at that time the number of working league branches in existence was only 818:[1] by 1 January 1886 the police returns listed 1,261, and by 1 July 1886 there were 1,285 of them.[2] Even if we allow for the probability that many of the branches newly formed for electioneering purposes may have been small in membership, these figures are still remarkable.[3] The Land League, by its founder's estimate, had not had more than 1,000 branches at the height of its power.[4] The foundation of the National League had, in effect, turned the active home rule movement from a loose conglomeration of independent and sometimes discrepant elements into a well-knit political party of a modern type, existing at four levels—the local branch, the county convention, the organizing committee, and the parliamentary party —and effectively monopolizing the political expression of national sentiment.

### 3. Party Finance

The financial effect of the 'Kilmainham treaty' was a double one: first, it caused an immediate sharp falling-off in the revenue of the 'national movement' (i.e. the associated organizations of the New Departure), and, second, it put what remained, and the disposal of future revenue, under the complete control of the party, or rather of Parnell and two colleagues. These two phenomena are best examined separately.

### (a) The revenue of the movement

It had been one of the fears of the Land League that a too overt association with a parliamentarian movement would cause a slump in American enthusiasm and therefore a decline in revenue. The effect of the parliamentary 'counter-

[1] Beckerson Report, as above, p. 132, n. 3.
[2] Ibid. ii. Jan.–June 1886.
[3] The secretary of the National League stated in an interview with Press representatives in Dec. 1885, that there were then 1,600 National League branches in Ireland, with an average branch membership of 300 (*F.J.*, 17 Dec. 1885). This estimate may have been exaggerated.
[4] Davitt, *Fall of Feudalism*, p. 301.

revolution'[1] of May 1882 proved that these fears were not unjustified, as the following figures[2] show:

### TABLE 6

*Gross Receipts of National Organizations*
(*excluding* Parliamentary Fund Receipts beginning in 1885)

| Financial year | | Receipts | |
|---|---|---|---|
| (part year) 1879–80 | . . . . | £55,327 | Total receipts of |
| (full year) 1880–1 | . . . . | £67,690 | 'Land League' |
| „ 1881–2 | . . . . | £110,403 | period—£233,420 |
| „ 1882–3 | . . . . | £34,000 | |
| „ 1883–4 | . . . . | £17,918 | Receipts of four |
| „ 1884–5 | . . . . | £11,686 | 'National League' |
| „ 1885–6 | . . . . | £47,275 | years—£109,734 |
| „ 1886–7 | . . . . | £32,855 | |

Unhappily the 'disappearance'[3] of the Land League books deprives us of full and reliable figures as to the exact proportion of American subscriptions in league receipts, but it is clear that such subscriptions formed the great bulk of the funds. We know that in the first months of the league's existence (November 1879–30 June 1880), 95 per cent. of its receipts came from America (total receipts, £69,000; American contributions £66,000),[4] and there is no reason to suppose that this proportion altered to any substantial

[1] The phrase is Davitt's (*Fall of Feudalism*, p. 377).

[2] *Special Comm. Proc.* vi. 345 (Hardcastle's evidence). The receipts for the 'interregnal' year 1882–3 were made up of £28,000 for the Land League and £6,000 for the National League. The 'Land League period' receipts include the receipts of the Land League and Ladies' Land League, both for relief and organization, but do not include the state trials defence fund. The 'National League' receipts include the parliamentary fund and parliamentary expenses fund, in their initial stages (see p. 138, n. 4).

[3] Most of the Land League books were not available for inspection by the Parnell Commission in 1888. Counsel for *The Times* insinuated that they were deliberately held back or had been destroyed (*Special Comm. Proc.* i. 165). The Parnellites stated that they did not know what had become of them. Dr. J. E. Kenny swore that on the suppression of the Land League the books had passed into the possession of W. F. Moloney, and that he knew nothing further (ibid.). Parnell believed that Patrick Egan might have taken some of them with him to America, but could give no definite information (ibid. vii. 250). Biggar professed complete ignorance of the whole subject (ibid. 387).

[4] Ibid. vi. 280. From 1 July 1880 the relevant lodgement slips were not available.

extent throughout the Land League period. Davitt[1] estimated that the amount contributed by America in the period
November 1879–October 1882 was about £250,000, which
would put the 95 per cent. calculation on the conservative
side. The first full year (ended 31 December 1883) of the
National League, however, yielded only £2,129 from
America out of £11,068 collected for the league, and the
next year (ended 31 December 1884) was not much better
(£3,101 out of £11,508).[2]

The proportion of American help had dwindled from
over 95 per cent. to under 30 per cent. in the immediate
aftermath of the Kilmainham treaty. Parnell had taken the
calculated risk of alienating the American supporters who
had financed the national movement.[3] This support did not
return until the home rule crisis of 1885–6.

In taking this risk Parnell had been fortified by the knowledge that the years of agitation had left a considerable cash
residue, in the shape of Land League funds invested, mostly
in American securities, through a Paris bank (Munroe &
Co.), in the names of Parnell, Biggar, McCarthy, Egan, and
Davitt. Shortly after the Kilmainham treaty Parnell and his
parliamentary colleagues took care to protect these funds
against alienation by their 'extreme' co-trustees.[4] In October
1882 the funds, usually known as the Paris funds, and
amounting to over £30,000, passed entirely into Parnellite
control, Egan announcing his resignation as treasurer of the
Land League.[5] It is significant that the funds were not
handed over to the National League, as successor body to
the Land League; they were not even handed over to the

---

[1] *Fall of Feudalism*, p. 713. He is probably including contributions to the
defence fund.

[2] *Special Comm. Proc.* vi. 326.

[3] J. L. Hammond ascribes Parnell's intransigence in the autumn of 1881
to the political influence of American money, and observes pertinently that
'the funds that English parties could raise for their needs were subscribed
secretly by private persons but Parnell had to depend on the open support of
poor Irishmen on both sides of the Atlantic' (*Gladstone and the Irish Nation*,
p. 243).

[4] In June 1882 Biggar, McCarthy, and Parnell instructed Messrs. Munroe
not to part with the bonds except on their signatures, in addition to those of
Egan and Davitt. Previously any two signatures had sufficed (reference in letter
dated 31 Mar. 1890 from Messrs. Munroe to Parnell; N.L.I., Harrington MSS.).

[5] *F.J.*, 18 Oct. 1882; Davitt, *Fall of Feudalism*, p. 573.

parliamentary party, but were kept under the direct control of Parnell with two senior parliamentary colleagues.[1] The disappearance of the Land League, therefore, was made to contribute in a very natural way to an increase in Parnell's power.

## (b) *The party budget*

The rejection by Isaac Butt of Mitchell Henry's suggestion that the Home Rule League should raise and distribute election funds left the home rule party without any financial organization whatever, other than what was required to pay for headquarters' rooms and note-paper. This was financed by a subscription of £2. 2s., payable by each home rule M.P. after election.[2] As regards electioneering, the theory, and, in 1874, the practice, was that candidates were substantial people capable of defraying their own expenses. The Parnellite programme of 1880, rendering it necessary to draw some candidates from outside that class, made the creation of some sort of election fund unavoidable. The machinery for raising such a fund not being in existence, the amount obtained was very small. Parnell was at that time in an equivocal position, being leader of a national movement but not of his own party, and this circumstance made it difficult for him to make what would have been a purely factional appeal to the country for funds. His position as chairman of the Land League (which, as an organization, was holding ostentatiously aloof from the elections) and the general distress of the country finally ruled out the possibility of a national appeal. In the circumstances, the Parnellites were unable to collect more than £2,300[3] made up as follows :

[1] See below, p. 268. Harrington, on behalf of the National League, had often to assure inquirers that 'the funds of the National League are altogether distinct from the funds of any previous organization' and that 'the balance of the Land League funds was never placed at our disposal' (N.L.I., Harrington MSS.; National League correspondence; see, for example, letter of 10 Nov. 1883 to Fr. Gilhooly, letter of 27 Dec. 1883 to J. Clarke).

[2] *F.J.*, 4 Mar. 1874.

[3] T. P. O'Connor (*Parnell Movement*, p. 312) gives the amount as £1,250: £1,000 of which he obtained as a personal loan, £100 sent from Liverpool and £150 (from tory funds). M. M. O'Hara (*Chief and Tribune*, p. 127) makes it £1,350, computed in the same way but making the tory contribution £250. Neither adverts to the Land League's contribution, but I am assuming that the 'personal loan' is a veiled, and inaccurate, reference to this.

| | |
|---|---|
| Advanced by Land League[1] .   .   .   . | £2,000 |
| Contributed by a priest in Liverpool   .   . | £100 |
| Conservative Club, Cork[2]   .   .   .   . | £200 (approx.) |

According to the figures which we have for the expenses of candidates at the 1880 election, this sum would not cover the election of more than seven members.[3] The remaining Parnellites had to pay their own expenses. Some of them may have obtained small individual payments from the Land League[4] 'for services rendered', and some had part of their expenses defrayed by popular subscription in their own constituencies,[5] but it is safe to assume that most of them paid for their election out of their own private money —or lost by reason of inability to pay. The lack of parliamentary funds remained acute through the 'pre-Kilmainham' period. In September 1881, speaking at a Land League meeting and explaining the recent defeat of the nationalist candidate at a by-election, Parnell revealed that the party of which he was now head had 'spent no money upon the election. We did not hire a single agent. All our work was done by volunteer committees hastily formed. We did not hire a single car to bring in a single voter.'[6] He added with more dignity than truth: 'We act on principle in these matters.'[6] The party could not have afforded any other principle at this date, and the principle disappeared with the expansion of the party finances. The setting up of the National League under parliamentarian control provided a convenient means,

---

[1] See § 1 (a) above.

[2] *Special Comm. Proc.* vii, q. 54,485: 'I was indebted to the Conservative Club at Cork for the expenses of my own return' (Parnell). This tory contribution was made in the misguided belief that Parnell's candidature would split the liberal vote and let a tory in.

[3] The average returned expenditure of Parnellites was about £300 (figure based on *Return of election charges, etc., 1880*, H.C. 1880 (382)).

[4] We know that T. M. Healy received £290 under this heading from the Land League during 1880 (*Letters and Leaders*, pp. 95, 100).

[5] In Meath, for example, Bishop Nulty instituted a collection at all the churches to defray Parnell's expenses (Redpath's interview with Parnell, *Nation*, 2 Oct. 1880). In Clare the Farmers' Club advocated 'voluntary contributions towards the expenses of the home rule candidates' (*F.J.*, 19 Mar. 1880). Counties Waterford and Wexford had 'pay the members' funds, which they later turned into collections for the parliamentary fund (ibid., 21 Jan. 1887 and 23 July 1890). These arrangements were, however, exceptional.

[6] Ibid., 19 Sept. 1881.

*inter alia*, of financing by-elections. The books of the National League, as examined on behalf of the Special Commission, revealed that the new machinery went into operation without delay. In the calendar year 1883 the new league paid out a total of £1,267 on by-election expenses,[1] or rather more than half what had been extorted from the old league for the general election. The current income of the National League[2] was not such, however, as to be able to support the heavy expense of a general election under the reformed franchise and, as the election approached, it became necessary to set up a special parliamentary fund, for which money was collected through the league. A special account for this collection was opened in March 1885, and, in the favourable circumstances of the time, the fund proved a great success.[3] £17,950 is known to have been collected by the end of 1885 and, of that, £14,610 is known to have been disbursed, probably all in connexion with the general election, leaving a balance in the fund, as on 1 January 1886, of £3,340.[4]

[1] *Special Comm. Proc.* vi. 325 ff. (Hardcastle's evidence). There were six by-elections during this period. Total expenditure for parliamentary purposes from National League funds before the general election of 1885 was only £2,325. (N.L.I., Harrington MSS., Harrington affidavit, 16,292.) Parnell, of course, had also in reserve the Paris funds, not under National League control.

[2] £11,068 in 1883; £11,508 in 1884; £12,014 in 1885 (*Special Comm. Proc.* vi. 326).

[3] Parnell estimated that remittances first came 'to any extent' from America for the fund in June 1885 (ibid. x. 319). A parliamentary collection had been going on in America since the Philadelphian convention (8 Apr. 1883), but apparently met with little success (ibid. xi. 559). The earlier remittances were presumably sent to the National League.

[4] *Irish Parliamentary Fund—Receipts, etc.* from 'Parliamentary Cash Book' among the J. F. X. O'Brien Papers in the National Library of Ireland. The receipts were made up mainly of £8,000 from the Irish National League of America and nearly £6,000 transferred on 21 Nov. from the National League (and probably also representing American subscriptions). The account referred to here runs from the date of this transfer, which would appear to mark the handing over of control of the fund from the league to the party trustees. There were probably previous disbursements from the fund while it was in the hands of the league, but these are not likely to have been substantial. According to Timothy Harrington (interview—*F.J.*, 17 Dec. 1885) the campaign of 1885 cost 'about £15,000'—an estimate which agrees with the £14,610 of the 'Parliamentary Cash Book'. The 'Cash Book' gives particulars of expenditure on 40 contests, totalling £8,141—or an average of about £200 per contest; taking this average as general, the figure of 'about £15,000' would have sufficed for 75 contests, which is about right. (The total number of contested seats was 80; a few candidates are understood to have paid their

The problem of election expenses was now largely solved, but there remained throughout the Parnellite period a natural inclination on the part of the party managers to spare the party funds by choosing, other things being equal, candidates rich enough to pay for the cost of their own return.[1] This consideration had all the more force, when it was realized that candidates unable to pay their own election expenses would also have to be supported while in parliament. In the early years the latter expense had perforce been avoided.[2] A high percentage of the new Parnellites of 1880 were Londoners, able to keep themselves. This system continued throughout the first National League years, with the modification that the former resources of the Land League now constituted a fund, under Parnellite control, out of which, *inter alia*, grants might be made to necessitous members.[3] It was not until after the setting-up of the

own expenses.) Of the 40 individual entries in the 'Cash Book', 12 are of exactly £200; the others range from £25 (in such safe constituencies as North and South Mayo) to £475 in what was expected to be a close contest in East Donegal.

[1] The late Henry Harrison, in a letter to the writer (29 June 1943) stated that his own nomination (May 1890) was agreed to by Parnell on condition that he was to be 'no charge on party funds', and that, generally speaking, he believed that someone 'rich as well as politically robust' would be preferred if such a person could be found.

[2] Parnell's evidence before the special commission is informative as regards the Land League's role:

*Attorney general*: When did members first begin to be paid as a class?

*Parnell*: The end of 1885 after the general election . . . I should think there were very small casual payments made from the beginning, from 1880. Mr. Egan perhaps would have made some very small payments but they were very small payments, because the Land League had deliberately adopted the policy of starving us all out.

He added that he thought any such allowances 'would have been in the nature of travelling expenses' (*Special Comm. Proc.* x. 319).

[3] It appears that the yield of these 'Paris funds' was used for 'the current expenses of the National League and of the parliamentary party' (ibid. x. 302—Parnell's evidence). T. M. Healy in an affidavit sworn after Parnell's death, when the control of these funds was disputed, said that the funds were 'drawn on jointly for the parliamentary party and to assist the National League as the objects of both were akin . . . Mr. Parnell from 1882 to 1890 drew the income of the No. 1 funds [as distinct from the parliamentary fund set up in 1885] from which he made grants to the League or to a member establishing a claim for parliamentary expenses' (N.L.I., Harrington MSS.: Healy's affidavit, 26 Apr. 1892). Healy states that the members who drew expenses in this way were only a very few. From Healy's statement that Parnell himself drew and made grants from the income of the funds it seems that

parliamentary fund and the return of a large body of party members at the end of 1885 that the payment of members really began. The parliamentary fund, like the residue of the Land League funds, was controlled not by the party itself, but by Parnell himself with the same two co-trustees, Biggar and McCarthy.[1]

### 4. *Party Discipline*

#### (a) *The party pledge*

At the great Rotunda Home Rule Conference of 1873, which marked the beginning of home rule as a large-scale national movement, it had been one of the first cares of Isaac Butt to deprecate any 'pledging' of parliamentary candidates. 'Select honest men as your representatives', he advised, 'send them into parliament and leave it to them to act when the time comes as their conscience and duty tells them and have, outside parliament, as I hope you will have to-day, a strong and influential national organization, sustaining them if right and controlling and rebuking them if wrong. . . . Pledges, after all, imply doubts.'[2] A very vaguely worded resolution, in the sense of this declaration, received the approval of the conference, and an amendment, backed by Biggar,[3] recommending that home rulers should 'always

the payments made from Parnell's personal account to eight members—(*Special Comm. Proc.* vii. 273) derived ultimately from the Paris funds and that John Howard Parnell's statement that his brother 'had in many cases actually to keep' members (*Charles Stewart Parnell*, p. 286) was an error, understandable if based on these transactions. The account given in the present writer's article 'The Machinery of the Irish Parliamentary Party' (*I.H.S.*, Mar. 1946, p. 73, n. 2) errs in attributing probability to J. H. Parnell's statement. The eight members referred to at the Special Commission were T. P. O'Connor, Matt Harris, Justin McCarthy, J. J. O'Kelly, William O'Brien, Sexton, J. E. Redmond, and Biggar, and the payments made to them—probably subsidies, except in the cases of McCarthy, O'Brien, and Biggar—averaged £100 each.

[1] See chap. VIII, § 3 (*c*), for party finances after 1885, and the working of the parliamentary fund.

[2] *F.J.*, 19 Nov. 1873. It is ironical that the only 'strong, national organization' capable of playing the role envisaged, turned out to be not Butt's Home Rule League, but Davitt's Land League.

[3] The text of the amendment was: 'We recommend that the Irish members shall, after the general election, form themselves into a permanent committee for the public discussion of every ministerial or other proposal which may affect the interests of Ireland; that no individual representative shall introduce any bill or give notice of any motion of importance unless his proceeding

vote in a body' was rejected. In the course of the discussion Biggar mentioned his belief that there should be a clause calling upon candidates to 'give written pledges'[1] of subordination to the home rule majority, but he clearly regarded the whole matter as so far outside the bounds of practical politics that he did not formally propose the incorporation of such a clause. After the general election of 1874, when the elected home rulers met for the first time, they adopted three resolutions which, taken together, formed a sort of pledge, of a very elastic nature. These resolutions, which came to be regarded as the 'constitution' of the home rule party, are sufficiently important to be quoted:

(i) That in the opinion of this conference the time has arrived when the Irish members who have been elected to represent the national demand for home rule ought to form a separate and distinct party in the House of Commons united on the principle of obtaining self-government for Ireland as defined in the [1873] resolutions.

(ii) That while our future action must depend on the course of events and the occasions that may arise, it is essential . . . that we should individually and collectively hold ourselves aloof from and independent of all party combinations, whether of the ministerialists or of the opposition.

(iii) That deeply impressed with the importance of unity of action upon all matters that can affect the home rule cause, we engage . . . to obtain that unity by taking counsel together, by making all reasonable concessions to the opinion of each other, by avoiding as far as possible isolated action, and by sustaining and supporting each other. . . .[2]

These resolutions were endorsed by those present, and all other home rulers were required to sign them before becoming members of the party, so that, from its inception, the home rule party was a pledge-bound body. The bonds were not, however, very tight, as the many qualifications in the wording of the resolutions could be invoked to justify almost any course of action. There was one important restriction, however: no one could assent to resolution (ii)

shall be sanctioned and supported by such committees; and finally that the Irish members shall always vote in a body or abstain from voting in all party divisions as the majority shall direct' (*F.J.*, 22 Nov. 1873).

[1] Ibid.                                                    [2] Ibid., 4 Mar. 1874.

and then take office under the crown without a resounding breach of faith. The 'constitution of 1874' remained in force throughout the Butt and Shaw periods, and was duly endorsed by the first meeting of home rule members after the general election of 1880.[1]

It was not until some months after Parnell's election to the chairmanship that a new pledge, introducing the principle of obedience to majority rule, was adopted. A meeting of the party in the City Hall, Dublin, on 26 December 1880 resolved that '. . . we pledge ourselves to . . . consult on all questions of importance and to abide by the decisions of the majority, based on the principles upon which we were elected, as to the action to be taken'.[2] The importance of the qualification was illustrated not long afterwards by the action of a member who, wishing to disobey the party decision to abstain from voting on the second reading of Gladstone's Land Bill, justified himself with the allegation that the party decision had not been 'based' on the resolutions of 1873.[3] The party was still not tightly pledge-bound, nor was anything done to make it so until well after the Kilmainham treaty, which, for reasons indicated above, did not involve any immediate tightening of discipline within the party itself. It was not until August 1884, when the prospect of a general election under the reformed franchise was already becoming distinct, that a really watertight pledge was introduced. It is perhaps significant that the new pledge was not, like the previous ones, first introduced at a plenary session of the party (although it was afterwards ratified by the party), but was drafted at a county convention by the presiding M.P., a leading member of the party 'caucus', and assented to, before nomination, by the approved candidate.[4] This pledge, in a perfected form, was

[1] *F.J.*, 27 Apr. 1880.        [2] Ibid., 28 Dec. 1880; *Nation*, 1 Jan. 1881.
[3] Ibid., 14 May 1881. The member who did this (E. D. Gray) had been responsible for the insertion of the 'loophole' clause in the pledge. He finally bowed to the will of the majority.
[4] 'I attended the Dungarvan convention [in August 1884] to select a member in the room of Blake. Here I drew up what became known as the "Party Pledge". P. J. Power took it and was chosen. In 1885 I improved the wording, and it became the standard test for nationalists at all elections' (T. M. Healy, *Letters and Leaders*, i. 205). Parnell had, however, forecast this pledge, almost in its perfected wording, months before (*U.I.*, 29 Mar. 1884).

required in principle of all nationalist candidates in the general election of 1885 and, with some exceptions, thereafter.[1] It was completely devoid of the pious hopes, conscientious reservations, and qualifications of all kinds that had adorned earlier pledges.

I . . . pledge myself that in the event of my election to parliament I will sit, act and vote with the Irish parliamentary party and if at a meeting of the party convened upon due notice specially to consider the question, it be decided by a resolution supported by a majority of the entire parliamentary party that I have not fulfilled the above pledge I hereby undertake forthwith to resign my seat.[2]

The main point which distinguished this pledge from all previous ones was the time at which it had to be taken. The home rule parties of 1874 and 1880 were pledge-bound by voluntary act, made after they had already been elected; the men of 1885 were forced to sign the pledge—or, if absent, to have undertaken to sign it—as a condition of election, and the 'resignation' proviso made their mandate a qualified one.

[1] At the Wicklow Convention, the first in the general election campaign of 1885, Timothy Harrington read a code of rules of which the following was the sixth: 'If the person proposed to be adopted as a candidate is in attendance upon the convention, or is within immediate reach, he shall be asked to subscribe, in presence of the convention, the pledge required by the Irish party. If he is not present and cannot be communicated with at once his proposer shall notify whether he has undertaken to give the pledge in question. In case the pledge is not subscribed in the presence of the convention, or a positive undertaking on behalf of the candidate is not given by the proposer, the motion shall not be put' (*F.J.*, 6 Oct. 1885). This implemented a resolution passed at a meeting of the Irish party on 25 Aug. 1885 (*U.I.*, 29 Aug. 1885). The rules were accepted and enforced by the conventions. For the history of the pledge after 1885 see Chap. VIII, § 3 (*b*).

[2] This standard form of the pledge was that in use at the conventions of 1885 and subsequently—as the numerous signed printed pledge-forms among the Harrington papers in the National Library show. It differs slightly from the form quoted in Curtis and McDowell (*Irish Historical Documents*, p. 281) which omits the words 'entire' and 'forthwith' and appears to be an earlier version. In the Committee Room 15 debates, Healy quoted the relevant part of the pledge in the form 'if it should appear by a majority of *two-thirds* of the whole party etc.' (*F.J.*, 5 Dec. 1890). The pledges actually signed by most of the party—more than 80 of which are among the Harrington Papers—were in the form quoted in the text above, with no mention of a two-thirds majority.

## (b) *Committee and caucus*

The first meeting of the home rule party had set up a party machinery of a very rudimentary kind. A parliamentary committee, consisting of nine members, including two honorary secretaries, was elected for the session and empowered to convene party meetings, summon members to attend the House, and collect subscriptions.[1] No chairman was elected, Butt's leadership being apparently allowed to rest on his moral authority and prestige as founder of the home rule movement. The death of Butt and the lack of an immediate successor of similar standing led to the introduction of the office of sessional chairman. The office of vice-chairman was introduced in December 1880 by a party meeting in the City Hall, the committee being then made up as follows:[2] 1 sessional chairman, 1 sessional vice-chairman, 2 honorary secretaries, 2 whips, 1 treasurer, 9 other members of committee.

Up to this time the functions of the committee had remained the modest ones originally assigned to it, but this meeting, consisting, of course, almost entirely of Parnellites, agreed to confer further powers on it. A resolution, proposed by Parnell, was passed, to the effect that 'the parliamentary committee, acting as a cabinet of the party, shall have the power to shape and direct the policy of the party in any emergency or in any particular measure or proposal in reference to which the party has not already met and decided and to arrange the details for carrying out the general policy decided upon by the party'. The importance of this resolution was not so much the powers conferred, which are not very precisely defined, as the claim that a committee originally set up as an organizational convenience was now 'acting as a cabinet'. It is noteworthy that this very considerable accession of prestige coincides closely with the entrance of T. M. Healy into parliament and that Healy, although a member of little more than a month's standing, was placed on the parliamentary committee in the office of joint honorary secretary. As Parnell's private secretary, Healy, according to his own account[3] (which there is here

[1] *F.J.*, 4 Mar. 1874.          [2] Ibid., 28 Dec. 1880.
[3] T. M. Healy, *Letters and Leaders*, i. 72.

no reason to doubt), had played a considerable part, even while outside the party, in shaping 'party decisions', and his new position not merely within the party but in office in what was now described as the 'cabinet of the party' was of strategic importance for a young man of ambition. At this date, however, and for some time afterwards, there was no question in anyone's mind of a 'cabinet minister' or group of 'ministers' ruling the party in Parnell's name. The powers conferred on the 'cabinet' were a result of the new situation, i.e. that a group of members had been elected as supporters of a national leader. They now went through the formality of submitting themselves in advance to such direction as the leader might choose to give them.

In fact, the parliamentary committee never really functioned as a 'cabinet' at all. The first 'emergency decision' radically affecting party policy (the Kilmainham treaty) was made—like subsequent decisions—not by the parliamentary committee, but by Parnell himself after discussion with such members as he chose to consult.[1] But the form of the resolution had recognized the leadership-principle not merely as regards the chief but as regards his lieutenants. Long before the formation of a unified parliamentary party, and while the daily workings of the parliamentary machine were still very erratic—the two party whips, for example, were sitting on opposite sides of the House and it was not unknown for them to 'whip' home rule members into opposing lobbies— even then the existence of an *élite* was recognized within the party. Up to 1883, the *élite* recognized was proportionately a broad one; the sixteen members of the parliamentary committee made up about half the effective strength of the party.[2] Succeeding sessional elections, with the monotonous re-election of Parnell as chairman and Justin McCarthy as vice-chairman, tended increasingly to re-elect also the previous officers.

[1] Years later, during the split, Parnell described his system. 'Parnell', says William O'Brien, 'especially cautioned Dillon against having a committee associated with him in the management of the party.' 'Get the advice', he said, 'of everybody whose advice is worth having—they are very few—and then do what you think best yourself' (William O'Brien, *An Olive Branch in Ireland and its History*, p. 47).

[2] At the first sessional meeting after the Kilmainham treaty, on 19 Feb. 1883, the officers were re-elected but the general committee lapsed (*Irish Times*, 15 Feb. 1883).

This body was too cumbrous for the effective manipulation of power, and there was a tendency for an informal inner managerial clique to grow up consisting of 'the lieutenants' as they were called, that is, men who were politically close to Parnell and trusted by him (and who were not necessarily officers of the party). This group consisted initially of Healy, Sexton, and J. J. O'Kelly; later elections added Dr. J. E. Kenny, Timothy Harrington, and William O'Brien.[1] These men, although able, were not necessarily the men of highest standing in the 1880–5 party—Biggar, McCarthy, Dillon, and Gray, were all at least as respected figures—but collectively, with their capacity for hard work and conformity to the party line, they were much more formidable than any agglomeration of semi-individualists, however brilliant. It was not until after October 1882, however, that these men really came into their own, and that for three reasons. First,

---

[1] 'The committee who met at Morrison's Hotel to select candidates for the 1885 election consisted generally of Parnell, Gray, Kenny, Sexton, O'Brien, O'Kelly, Harrington, Healy, Biggar and John Redmond' (Healy, op. cit., i. 230). T. P. O'Connor also attended when in Dublin (*Memoirs of an Old Parliamentarian*, ii. 14). All these were members of the caucus in a sense, but Biggar as an individualist, Redmond as a comparative stripling, and O'Connor and Gray, whose outside interests left them little time for party manœuvres, were not quite in the inner ring. Similar considerations apply to Dillon and McCarthy, at this period, although Henry Harrison, in the letter from which I have quoted, gave 'O'Brien, Healy, Dillon and Sexton' as the principal managers of the constituencies for the period 1882–90. The following figures, based on reports in the *Freeman's Journal* for Oct. and Nov. 1885, show the ten members who showed most activity in the crucial campaign of that time, with the number of county conventions attended by each:

| | | | | | | |
|---|---|---|---|---|---|---|
| O'Kelly | . | . | . | 14 | Harrington. . . | 6 |
| Sexton | . | . | . | 10 | T. D. Sullivan . . | 6 |
| Healy | . | . | . | 9 | Wm. O'Brien . . | 4 |
| Biggar | . | . | . | 9 | Dillon . . . | 4 |
| Parnell | . | . | . | 6 | John Redmond . . | 4 |

The list corresponds as to eight names with the 'Morrison's Hotel committee' as given by Healy. The two mentioned by Healy who do not figure on the list —Kenny and Gray—attended, respectively, three conventions and one convention. Sullivan and Dillon, who figure in the list, but are omitted by Healy, may well have been more active in the open campaign than in the committee work. Sullivan's reputation was that of a hard and loyal worker rather than a leader, and in any case it is not likely that if he had been a member of the inner ring his name would have been omitted by Healy, his close relative and friend. As for Dillon, who had just returned to public life after an absence of over three years, it is probable that he was still in some degree suspect for his earlier tendency to pursue an independent policy.

the Kilmainham treaty had greatly strengthened the Parnellite power in the national movement. Second, Parnell himself withdrew to a great extent from active politics in the years 1883–4.[1] Third, the creation of the National League provided them for the first time with a real political machine. It was now they, and particularly Healy and Harrington, who had the picking of the new members, and they tended, with the natural instinct of party managers, to pick 'yes-men'.[2] It is notable that not one of the fifty-odd new members of the Irish party returned in the 1885–6 elections, under the National League system of managed conventions, ever rose to any sort of leadership in the party, although many of them had very long parliamentary careers. By their selection the 'lieutenants' ensured not merely the provision of a solid block of votes for any Parnellite policy, but their own continued predominance in the councils of the party. They, rather than the parliamentary committee, constituted the 'cabinet' of the party, but it was a 'cabinet' in the American rather than in the British sense; its members derived their powers from a leader who did not share his responsibility with them.[3]

## 5. Policy and Implements

The lamentations of men like F. H. O'Donnell about the rising power of the machine were futile. A united party was essential if anything practical was to be achieved, and a

[1] Cf. R. Barry O'Brien, op. cit., pp. 317, 415.

[2] Healy, especially, did this with gusto (cf. op. cit., i. 232). There was even some suspicion that he was collecting personal rather than Parnellite 'yes-men' (T. P. O'Connor, Memoirs of an Old Parliamentarian, ii. 105). From very early on he had tended to exalt Parnell's prestige for reasons of 'power-politics' ('I regard it as almost a calamity that our political interests compel us to idolize this man in public'—letter of Dec. 1879 quoted ibid., i. 78). He later looked back nostalgically to the power he had wielded in Parnell's name when the latter was in Kilmainham ('The discipline of the Irish party at this date was perfect. Everyone spoke or moved according to plan', ibid., i. 152). The use by 'the lieutenants' of Parnell's name as an instrumentum regni is commented on by Davitt (op. cit., p. 467). During the 1885 conventions Davitt named 'Healy, Harrington, O'Brien and Biggar' as having 'the full control of member making' (Davitt MSS.: McGhee correspondence: letter of 23 Sept. 1885).

[3] See Chap. VIII, § 2, p. 248, for the activities and powers of 'the lieutenants' after 1885.

united party was necessarily a disciplined one and therefore machine-controlled. The sacrifices involved—including often the rejection of individuals of high integrity and ability in favour of pliant henchmen[1]—had to be accepted if political effectiveness was to be secured. Similarly, it is not necessary to cite Michels's 'iron law of oligarchy' in order to show that the rise of some sort of party directorate, intermediate between the leader and the rank-and-file, is bound to come with any high degree of organization.

Throughout the United Kingdom, as the application of democracy widened, party politics required more machinery.

Ostrogorski's full and detailed analysis (*Democracy and the Organization of Political Parties*) of the development of party machinery in England shows that the liberal party in the great cities had become highly mechanized by the mid-seventies, on the model of the Schnadhorst–Chamberlain organization in Birmingham. The National Liberal Federation, based on such organizations, was not founded until 1877, i.e. four years after the foundation of the Home Rule Confederation of Great Britain, so that Irishmen in England were, to say the least of it, not backward in this type of political mechanism. The type of machine finally adopted in Ireland seems to have been more powerful in its limited sphere than the liberal one. There were a number of 'checks and balances' against the power of the liberal executive in the seventies and early eighties, e.g. the conflict between radical and whig, and especially the great power and prestige of some of the local organizations themselves. No Irish 'county convention' could stand up to Parnellite dictation in the way the liberal association of, say, Bradford or Liverpool could, if necessary, resist the liberal executive. Ostrogorski regarded it as a rare occurrence for the liberal central organization to bring 'regular pressure to bear' on a local association in favour of a candidate. The party pledge and the payment of the majority of members out of party funds also conferred powers on the Irish machine which were lacking in the English counterpart. Similarly in America,

---

[1] At an early stage a leader in *The Nation* had put the matter brutally: 'Ireland cannot afford to have representatives of the "independent" pattern' (July 1881).

although party machinery had become very complex by this date, and considerable power was wielded by the congressional campaign committees of the major parties, conditions did not permit of anything like the Irish degree of centralization. On the whole the comment of the *Irish Times* (2 Oct. 1885) on the working of the convention system seems justified: 'This process of finding a parliamentary representation is unique. There has not been anything like it.'

The special political significance of the installation of political machinery in Ireland resided in the period at which it occurred. In April 1880 Shaw had had no organization with which either to attempt to keep Parnell's followers out of parliament or to discipline them when they got there. By the next general election, at the end of 1885, an organization existed, such that it was impossible to return on the home rule ticket any potential opponent of Parnellite policy. The new members, as we have seen, were hand-picked, pledge-bound, and paid out of party funds. The 'policy of the party' came down to them from above, from the leader and his lieutenants, and they had no choice but to obey. But the party policy was still, in essentials, the Kilmainham policy, i.e. a strictly constitutional anti-revolutionary policy, which could probably only have been framed at a period when the social make-up of the party was relatively upper class, and its political make-up contained large conservative elements. That it was possible to continue this policy smoothly through and after the general election of 1885 with the greatly widened suffrage and consequent choice of more plebeian representatives, was due in a large measure to the development of the party machine in the years between the Kilmainham treaty and the general election. Throughout that period the Healys and the Harringtons, the engineers of the party, had been hard at work, so that, when the flood of mass-democracy rose, it did not sweep away the Kilmainham edifice, but was held in new and solid dykes.

# V

## THE NEW PARTY, 1885

Mr. Gladstone continued to say that one could not doubt the opinion of Ireland when eighty-six members were returned by the Irish people in favour of it [Home Rule]. I observed that these were mostly low, disreputable men, who were elected by order of Parnell, and did not genuinely represent the whole country.      QUEEN VICTORIA, *Journals*,[1] 1 Feb. 1886

THE elections of 1885 proved, as had been expected, a great victory for Parnell's party in Ireland. Outside eastern Ulster (and Trinity College), no candidates other than pledge-bound party members succeeded in winning a seat. The tories, who started contests in all constituencies in order to test the demand for home rule, were humiliated by the huge majorities against them.[2] As for the liberals, they were not able to return a member for any constituency in the whole of Ireland.

The strength of the party as returned in the general election was 86 (as against 61 in 1880). But these figures do not give anything like a true picture of the extent of the gain. The effective home rule party returned in 1880, Parnell's supporters, had been about 20, subsequently increased to about 30. Now, however, the success of the National League system and the pledge ensured that the effective strength of the party, united under one leadership, was the same as its strength on paper.

As was also expected, the post-election party was more 'democratic', i.e. lacking in upper-class elements, than the party of the 1880 parliament had been; a fact ascribed to the extension of the franchise to agricultural labourers by the franchise act of 1884[3] and to the elimination of the old

---

[1] 3rd ser., i. 36.

[2] In the 49 contested elections outside Ulster the approximate average majority of the home rule candidate over his nearest opponent was 4,250–635. The most spectacular majorities were those obtained by Jeremiah Sheehan in East Kerry (3,069–30) and by J. F. X. O'Brien in South Mayo (4,953–75).

[3] The Franchise Bill had been attacked by most of the tories because it would further democratize the Irish representation, already intolerably democratic. By its effect in the 'border' constituencies of Ulster it certainly increased

whiggish elements. The elimination of the 'whigs' itself was, it is clear, not due to the extension of the franchise to agricultural labourers, or to the machine-politics of the National League, but to the popular feeling against them which had first become clear early in 1880, and subsequently hardened into definite rejection. Since the general election of 1880, only one 'whiggish Home Ruler' (A. H. Bellingham) had won a by-election, and even that small victory had occurred as far back as the summer of 1880. The fifteen other by-elections at which home rulers had been successful over the period 1880–5 had all brought in declared supporters of Parnell.

The following table (Table 7, p. 152), based on the same principles as Table 3 in Chapter I, is an attempt at an analysis of the membership of the new party and should give a rough idea of the degree of 'declassing' which had taken place. As in Table 3, and for the same reason, figures for a recent Dáil are included.

On these figures the home rulers of 1885 were only 50 per cent. upper group, as against 79 per cent. in 1880. It is clear, however, that this 'declassing' took place not so much through a decrease in the 'upper group' as through an increase in the 'lower group' of the expanded party. In other words, most of the newly elected members belonged to the 'lower group'. The line of a class-division in the party now tended to fall, not along the old political cleavage between 'whig' and Parnellite, but between the 'old party', i.e. those who had taken their seats in parliament in (at latest) 1880, and the members returned later than the general election of 1880. This is clearly illustrated by Table 8 on p. 152.

Thus of the 44 'lower group' members no less than 38 had been returned for the first time later than the elections of 1880,

the strength of the Irish party but its effect on the party's class-composition is doubtful. The figures in Table 7 (below) seem to indicate that there was no very clear class-distinction between the type of member returned in the by-elections of 1880–5 and the type returned in the general elections after the Franchise and Redistribution Acts. The effect of the Franchise Bill on Irish politics has often been overstated; the by-election returns show that Parnellism had a firm hold on the Irish electorate (outside Ulster) even before the franchise was extended. It made a difference of about ten seats, according to separate estimates by Chamberlain and Parnell (above, Chap. III, p. 87). The statement in the Cambridge Modern History (xii. 41) that nationalist influence in British politics was enormously increased by Ireland's inclusion in this measure is an exaggeration.

## TABLE 7[1]

| (1) Group | (2) Class | (3) Home rulers of 1880 (61) | (4) Home rulers of 1885 (86) | (5) Tenth Dáil (138 T.D.s) |
|---|---|---|---|---|
| 'A' Upper group | 1. Landowners (over 1,000 acres) | 8 | 5 | 0 |
| | 2. Merchants, industrialists, bankers, rentiers, &c. | 19 | 15 | 9 |
| | 3. Higher professions | 21 | 22 | 35 |
| | Total group 'A' | 48 | 42 | 44 |
| 'B' Lower group | 1. Lower professions | 8 | 19 | 22 |
| | 2. Farmers, shopkeepers, wage-earners, &c. | 2 | 22 | 57 |
| | 3. Undefined occupations | 3 | 3 | 15 |
| | Total group 'B' | 13 | 44 | 94 |

## TABLE 8

| (1) Group | (2) Class | (3) Members previously returned in 1880 | (4) Members returned at subsequent by-elections | (5) Members elected in 1885 for first time |
|---|---|---|---|---|
| 'A' Upper group | 1. Landowners | 3 | 1 | 1 |
| | 2. Merchants, &c. | 8 | 1 | 6 |
| | 3. Higher professions | 9 | 3 | 10 |
| | Total group 'A' | 20 | 5 | 17 |
| 'B' Lower group | 1. Lower professions | 5 | 3 | 11 |
| | 2. Farmers, &c. | 1 | 2 | 19 |
| | 3. Unidentified occupations | 0 | 3 | 0 |
| | Total group 'B' | 6 | 8 | 30 |

[1] I have included the results of the 'consequential' by-elections in the aggregate of the 'Home Rulers of 1885', but have excluded these from the 'Home Rulers of 1880'. The reason for this is that, in the rapidly changing situation of 1880, the 'by-election' members returned after the election of Parnell as leader of the party could not properly be included with those returned while Shaw was still nominally leader. The tables in Chapter I were therefore prepared on a basis of a 61-member party. In 1885, of course, no such consideration applied, and the 'by-election members' are included with the others. The differentiation is of very little significance for the purposes of the table.

while of the 42 'upper group' members 20 had been returned
at those elections. This differentiation had no direct political
significance; it may, however, have played its part in maintaining the prestige of Parnell's 'lieutenants' in the 1880
parliament (see Chapter III). F. H. O'Donnell[1] points out
that the party 'lieutenants', like Healy or T. P. O'Connor,
rose in social status and reputation during the Parnellite
decade, and asserts that this fact made it easier for them in
the end to turn against their leader. Similarly, the relatively
high social standing of the 'old guard' may have helped to
preserve its ascendancy over the party's approved recruits.[2]

Unlike the elections of 1880, those of 1885 were not
fought on the issue of the land. There was, as so often, a
land crisis, caused this time not mainly by crop failure but
by falling agricultural prices: many tenants, especially in
the west, had fallen into arrears with their rent, even where
these were 'fair rents' fixed by the Land Courts under the
Act of 1881; evictions, accompanied often by scenes of
horror, were rising sharply in number. But the National
League, in the period of the 'tory alliance' especially, had
been concerned to keep land agitation within bounds, and
to persuade the people that home rule, now within reach,
would solve the land problem. Home rule, having moved
out of academic into practical politics, had become the question of the hour; furthermore, the landlord interest had been
driven out of nationalist politics by the events of the Land
League period. In these circumstances it would be waste of
time to go into the same detail on land held by the 1885
members as was done in Chapter I for the 1880 members. It
is sufficient to note that of the members newly returned in
1885, only one is known to have owned land, and he was a
declared supporter of land league principles.[3]

But these new members, although they resembled the new
Parnellites of 1880 in their landless position and compara-

[1] Op. cit., ii. 298–9.
[2] M. J. F. McCarthy, who knew the Irish members well, says that the 'old
members' held aloof from the recruits and that the two sections 'did not drink
or dine or converse together' (*The Irish Revolution*, p. 461).
[3] The gentleman concerned, Thomas Grattan Esmonde, was a leading
Catholic landowner—he owned over 8,000 acres of land in Ireland—but he
was strong in his denunciations of landlordism, and his candidature was
endorsed by Michael Davitt.

tively low social standing, were remote from them in other ways. The outstanding difference was that, unlike the Parnellites of 1880, most of the new men had their homes in Ireland. Very few of the 1880 Parnellites lived in their constituencies; almost half of them lived in England. The figures for the new men of 1885 present quite a different picture:

Resident in constituency . . . . 20
Resident in Ireland, but outside constituency. 21
Resident in England . . . . . 6

Most of these men were farmers, small tradesmen, provincial journalists, and the like, and it is probably safe to presume that few of them had previously moved much out of their own parishes. They were undoubtedly a more representative cross-section of Irish life than the 'carpet-baggers' of 1880 (who now belonged to the 'old guard' of the party) had been, but they were at a disadvantage in experience of the world and perhaps in talent. Disregarding altogether the copious sneers directed at them by the unionist press, one may gather even from nationalist comment that some of them were very raw men indeed. A bishop recommending one of them to a convention had to choose his words with full episcopal care. 'You can afford to devote your whole time to parliamentary work', he wrote, addressing the candidate; 'your talents and abilities will, with culture, training and experience soon ripen into the intellectual gifts and acquirements that will, I believe, enable you to become a practical and useful parliamentary representative.'[1] The same tone of temperate eulogy was adopted by the *Freeman's Journal* in describing another successful candidate simply as 'one of those silent workers to whom the country owes so much'.[2] Biggar, as usual, was more candid: 'If they had only men like Mr.—— and himself they would not have a good party. They should also have ready and fluent men who would talk well.'[3]

[1] Extract from a letter by Dr. Nulty, Bishop of Meath, recommending James Tuite to the Westmeath Convention of the National League; quoted in *F.J.*, 15 Oct. 1885.        [2] Ibid., 14 Nov. 1885.
[3] Ibid., 20 Oct. 1885. The social deficiencies of several of the new members are heavily stressed by M. J. F. McCarthy (*Irish Revolution*, p. 459). They seem, however, to have adapted themselves rapidly. Sir Henry Lucy was running out of material for badinage by 1888 and wrote of 'the garment of commonplace decorum which Irish members now wear' (*Salisbury Parliament*, p. 85).

Such particulars as are available regarding the education of these men tend to confirm the view of them as, on the whole, lower-class and parochially minded. The following table gives some indication of the difference in type between the new members and the old:

TABLE 9[1]

| Type of education | Members elected before the 1885 general elections | Members newly elected in 1885 general elections |
|---|---|---|
| Primary . . | 7 | 18 |
| Secondary . . | 22 | 19 |
| University . . | 18 | 9 |

Clearly this was no mere social difference of the type illustrated in the contrast in Chapter I between the classes of universities attended by different political sections. The new members of 1885 were on the whole not merely socially below the old Parnellites, but distinctly inferior in degree of education. Roughly half of them had been able to go no farther in pursuit of knowledge than their local national or Christian Brothers school, and not all of these schools could boast the success of those Munster schools which trained the minds of T. M. Healy and the brothers Sullivan.

But what these men may have lacked in articulateness, knowledge, and experience of the world they more than made up for, politically, in other ways. Most of them were

[1] In making this table I have equated 'unknown' with 'primary', i.e. where I can obtain no evidence as to a member's education, and have no reason to believe that he had any superior degree of instruction, I have put him down as 'primary'. Among the 'secondary' group I include three ex-seminarians. The 'university' group may be subdivided as follows:

| Type of university | Pre-1885 members | 1885 members |
|---|---|---|
| Oxford or Cambridge . . | 3 | 0 |
| Dublin . . . . | 7 | 2 |
| English-provincial and foreign | 3 | 1 |
| Queen's University or Catholic University . . . | 5 | 6 |
| | 18 | 9 |

Compare Table 4, Chap. I.

'veterans' of the land-war, and several had served sentences under coercion in 1881. Some, like J. F. X. O'Brien, Donal Sullivan, Matthew Harris, and James Gilhooly, had national records reaching back beyond that to the fenian days,[1] and there was even one link, in the person of Kevin Izod O'Doherty, with the rising of 1848. With a few exceptions —mostly rich self-made men, selected presumably because of their largesse to party funds[2]—the new members of 1885 were tested nationalists, who had been active in the movement before they could have had any thought of achieving prominence, let alone profit, by its means. They became useful M.P.s because of their regular attendance and disciplined voting. Unionist commentators attributed their attention to duty to the party whip and the party treasurer, and certain Sinn Féin speakers were later to adapt this gibe to their own purposes. But a study of their record, both before their election and especially afterwards during the harsh struggles of the Plan of Campaign, convinces that what stimulated most of them was not whips or pledges or treasurers or parliamentarian vanity but their devotion to the idea of Irish freedom. A party composed of such men as these would, if it had existed in 1881–2, have made the evolution into constitutionalism decidedly more difficult.

And yet the Kilmainham policy not merely imposed itself on them; it had played its part in selecting them. For these men represented the devoted workers of the land move-

[1] J. F. X. O'Brien had of course been a leader in the 1867 rising—and had been sentenced to be hanged, drawn, and quartered—but he does not seem to have played any active part in 'extremist' politics subsequently. An R.I.C. report on him, dated 19 Feb. 1879, mentions that he 'is not now observed to mix much with suspected fenians' (S.P.O., Miscellaneous 'Fenian Papers' unnumbered and unindexed). James Gilhooly was believed by the R.I.C. to have been 'Head centre' for Bantry in 67 (S.P.O. 'Fenian Papers', 7192–271). D. Sullivan was described as an 'active agent' by the police and 'suspected of propagating fenianism' at election times (S.P.O., Irish Crimes Records, 1862–5). Matthew Harris, who later gained some notoriety with a picturesque remark about 'shooting the landlords down like partridges in September' acted, according to the R.I.C., as 'chief organiser, head centre and clansman' for the I.R.B. in Ballinasloe. They added, as if anticipating his famous phrase, that he 'has a game licence and roves about the country with his gun' (S.P.O., 'Fenian Papers', F. 4027).

[2] William Martin Murphy, Laurence Connolly of New Brighton, P. J. Foley of the Pearl Assurance Co., London, and, perhaps, Patrick O'Brien of Liverpool belong to this group of men of substance.

ment, not its directing brains. Davitt and Egan, Louden and Brennan all remained outside parliament, in exile or in the wilderness.[1] The subordination of the land question to home rule was now expressed in the composition of the party, the leaders were mostly the men responsible for the Kilmainham policy, and the rank and file was composed in large part of simple ex-land-leaguers. The new members were not just voting robots, and if given a lead, as in the Plan of Campaign, they could show plenty of spirit. But they had passed through the ingenious sieve of the National League convention system with its double 'screen' of clergy and party managers. The clergy had, under the rules of the National League, a voice in their selection and there is evidence that clerical participation was not always merely a formal one. Biggar, speaking in support of the official— and successful—candidate in Leitrim, declared with his usual frankness that 'he was not the nominee of the Irish party, he was the nominee of the Reverend Doctor Maguire'.[2] And, in the letter to Devoy from which we have quoted on p. 90, J. J. O'Kelly, having alluded to 'the enormous power of the Church party', wrote: 'Already there is a tendency to put men into the parliamentary party whom we certainly would not have chosen had we been free to consult only our own wishes.'[3] There is, however, no real evidence of a conflict of interest or policy between the clergy and the party managers at this date. Rather the pattern seems to have been that the party managers, in the many cases where they had no candidate of their own in view, asked the local clergy, if sympathetic—as was now generally the case—to name someone who was 'nationally sound', and not likely to 'fly off the

[1] Of these Louden alone had sought nomination, but had been rejected by a convention which he claimed was 'manipulated' (see Chap. IV).

[2] *F.J.*, 28 Oct. 1885.

[3] *Devoy's Postbag*, ii. 265 (letter of 17 Sept. 1885). Allowance must be made for some degree of exaggeration in O'Kelly's descriptions of the influence of the clergy. The general trend of his discourse to Devoy was to show that Parnell and he were still fenians at heart; and so it was convenient to throw the responsibility for the obviously non-fenian tendency of party policy on the shoulders of the clergy. The clergy, for their part, wished to make it clear that the responsibility for moderation rested squarely on the Parnellites. Archbishop Walsh told the press about this time that this same J. J. O'Kelly (who was representing himself to Devoy as a separatist) had told him that the Parnellites 'did not want any power as an independent nation at all. That was

handle'—the phrase then current for what is now called deviation. This system would not have elicited the names of a T. P. O'Connor, or a J. J. O'Kelly, or a Lysaght Finigan, any more than that of Parnell himself; furthermore if, in 1885, the party managers had wished—which they did not —to put forward 'radical' candidates, such as these men had been in 1880, they probably could not have done so, because of clerical opposition within the league. In the nature of the case, the influence of the clergy would have been stronger in keeping out 'undesirable' candidates than in imposing, as O'Kelly improbably suggests, their own candidates against the will of the leadership. But, even supposing some degree of tension between the lay leaders and the clergy, the tendency was to produce, by cancellation or accommodation, the sort of candidate who had no awkward corners, individualism, or heterodox opinion.[1] It was the beginning, in an individualistic country—too often betrayed by picturesque individualists—of the sombre age of the *parteimensch*. The members chosen by this system impressed observers by their virtue and resolution. W. S. Blunt, an intelligent and not uncritical English sympathizer, wrote that, excluding Parnell, and perhaps four others, they were 'an almost complete army of pious and virtuous men, including three or four real saints, the Irish members.'[2] The new party, according to William O'Brien, 'gave us . . . dozens of Spartan comrades, eager to go anywhere and obey any orders.'[3] But in private, even William O'Brien was scathing about the abilities of some of his 'Spartan comrades'. 'Parnell has no objection that a good many of our men should be run in this winter. Many of them are fit for nothing else.'[4]

As long as a clear-cut policy and a decisive leadership existed—as they did up to 1890—these were good men to have in the party. But they were not men, when need arose, to provide a new leader or a new policy.

to say they did not want an independent army or navy or any power outside their own country. What they wanted was to rule Ireland as Canada and Australia ruled themselves within the Empire' (*F.J.*, 28 Sept. 1885).

[1] This did not apply to Protestantism. Protestants were welcomed in the Parnellite movement by both priests and laity.

[2] *Land War in Ireland*, p. 447.      [3] *Evening Memories*, p. 162.

[4] Dillon MSS. 11: undated 1888.

# VI

## THE PARTY AND THE
## HOME RULE CRISIS (1885–6)

When full expression is given to Irish opinion, there will be declared to the
world in larger print what we all know to be the case: that we hold Ireland
*by force and by force alone* as much to-day as in the days of Cromwell, only that
we are obliged to hold it by a force ten times larger than he found necessary.[1]
> HARCOURT tO GLADSTONE (28 Dec. 1883)

Suppose Parnell to come back eighty or ninety strong, to keep them together,
to bring forward a plan which shall contain in your opinion adequate securities for the union of the Empire and to press this plan . . . do you think no
Government should be formed to promote such a plan?[2]
> GLADSTONE tO CHAMBERLAIN (28 Sept. 1885)

### 1. *The Situation after the General Election of* 1885

THE results of the general election of 1885 made home
rule for Ireland a burning English problem. Parnell's
party had 86 seats, the liberals 334, the tories 250. It
was, therefore, impossible for either of the great English
parties to govern without Parnell's assent. For the tories—
still the government—it would be virtually impossible to
continue in power, even with his assent, since the combined
majority of a tory-Parnellite alliance against the liberals
would be of two votes only; and it was hardly thinkable
that the whole tory party, including the members from
Ulster and Trinity College, would go over to home rule.
This parliament, as an eminent English historian has remarked, 'is noticeable as being the first since 1832 in which
the British two-party system was broken up by the appearance of a permanent Third Party, allied to neither of the
others and strong enough to prevent either from having a
working majority'.[3]
This was a situation which Gladstone had foreseen and
tried to avoid. Asking for a majority independent of the

---

[1] Letter quoted in Gardiner, *Harcourt*, i. 497.
[2] Letter quoted in Gwynn and Tuckwell, *Dilke*, ii. 188.
[3] R. C. K. Ensor, *England 1870–1914*, p. 99.

Irish vote, he had declared in a speech at Midlothian, before the polling, that nothing 'could be more dangerous to the public weal than that [Irish affairs] should be handled in a parliament where there was no party strong enough to direct its action according to judgment and conscience without being liable to be seduced from the right path by the temptations which might be offered to it by the votes of the Irish members'.[1]

Yet, if the eighty-six Irish votes represented a parliamentary temptation—to purchase power by assenting to home rule—did they not also, to the liberal mind, represent a moral force, the deliberate voice of the majority of the Irish people, for the first time unequivocally expressed, in favour of home rule? This idea also was present to Gladstone's mind, as a hypothesis, before the general election; he asked his chief associates in that autumn of 1885 : should not the liberals be prepared to act, if Ireland both declares for home rule and stands by her declaration?[2] Once the results, in their main outline, were known, Gladstone prepared, in his majestic way, to draw the necessary conclusion.

If it becomes requisite [he wrote to Grosvenor on 6 December] to be assured of the position of the Irish party, probably this could be got at by some public explanation from me—but here is matter for reflection and there is time. In any case the principle that the ministers must have the confidence of the House of Commons is now the root-principle of our institutions . . . and this would therefore be the question of questions on the day of the Queen's speech, anterior in order even to the question of Ireland.[3]

The Irish party, then, represents, for English politicians, a disturbing combination of parliamentary force, moral force, and 'seductive temptations'. There will be, of course, those—the Queen herself, Lord Hartington, later the tory party—who will fail to discern any moral force behind the great popular vote for home rule, who will see the Parnellites only as 'low disreputable men' emerging from a fog of

---

[1] *The Times*, &c., 23 Nov. 1885.
[2] Letters of 6 Aug. 1885 to Derby (Morley, *Gladstone*, iii. 216); of 3 Sept. to Hartington (Holland, *Devonshire*, ii. 79); of 28 Sept. to Chamberlain (Gwynn and Tuckwell, loc. cit.).
[3] B.M., Gladstone Papers, 44316.

intrigue and intimidation.[1] Yet even some of those who
failed to hear—or were indifferent if they did hear—the
voice of a people in this vote, saw in it a portent that Ireland
was no longer governable. Lord Spencer, from his experience as viceroy, thought that coercion would no longer
work, and the only alternative was home rule.[2] Harcourt—
who as home secretary had had to deal with Irish-American
dynamiters in England—tried to explain to Hartington the
ultimate implications of ignoring so unmistakable a popular
demand:

> In former Irish rebellions the Irish were *in Ireland*. We could
> reach their forces, cut off their resources in men and money, and
> then to subjugate was comparatively easy. Now there is an Irish
> nation in the United States, equally hostile, with plenty of money,
> absolutely beyond our reach and yet within ten days sail of our
> shores. . . . No government could carry on such a war with a
> divided opinion in Britain. . . . The tory government struck the
> fatal blow at any prospect of a really patriotic union on this ques-
> tion when they played for the Parnellite vote last summer.[3]

However one looked at it, whether on the plane of democratic morality, or of parliamentary tactics, or of the highest
political strategy, the Parnellites were at this moment in a
strong position: the strongest the constitutional movement
ever held. Parnell did not, naturally—although pressed to
do so—declare his hand, and say how little home rule he
would be prepared to accept. It was known that home rule

---

[1] The best statement of this attitude was made, in the form of a query, by
Lord Hartington at the Eighty Club, when Gladstone's 'conversion' to home
rule was already known: 'I ask now whether under the circumstances in which
this late election has been conducted by an inexperienced electorate under an
influence, not to say an intimidation, as widespread, as severe, and far more
subtle than was ever exercised by the landlord influence in Ireland, the
opinion of the people of Ireland is to be taken as conclusively proved by this
election?' (*The Times*, 6 Mar. 1886). He went on to say that even if it were
conclusively proved, he would still oppose home rule. No one produced any
evidence of intimidation or improper influence at the elections of 1885. As
for the 'inexperienced electorate', it went on voting for home rule at every
election up to 1918, when it started voting for a republic.
[2] Gardiner, *Harcourt*, i. 553–4. Spencer was a very reluctant convert to
home rule: 'how odious (and maybe wicked) it is to think that Parnell and
his crew are to govern Ireland' (letter of 30 Dec. 1885 to Rosebery, in Crewe,
*Rosebery*, i. 255).
[3] Letter of 24 Dec. 1885, in Gardiner, *Harcourt*, i. 553.

meant a parliament in Dublin and that it did not mean complete separation from Britain,[1] or a separate army, navy, and
foreign service; but that was all that was known, except that
the Irish would naturally try to obtain for their parliament
as many powers as possible, including, if Parnell could,
Protection. Gladstone himself admitted 'great ignorance' of
'the interior mind' of the Irish party.[2] There were, indeed,
some very disturbing rumours as to Parnell's intentions. 'I
hear on reliable authority', wrote Grosvenor to Gladstone
early in January 1886, 'that Parnell is going to move a
definite resolution in favour of a separate parliament for
Ireland and when this is refused to withdraw with all his
men *en bloc*. In consequence of his having made this arrangement with the fenians he is getting any quantity of money
now.'[3] Gladstone was disturbed. 'I should regard the withdrawal *en bloc* as by far the most formidable thing that can
happen', he replied. 'It will be followed by an assembly in
Dublin, which brings into view very violent aberrations. If
Parnell is wise he will keep to the game he has been upon
heretofore, viz. the ejecting of Governments. . . . I am not
quite certain how far we ought to persist in the system of
making no spontaneous communication to Parnell: this is
matter for consideration.'[4] These were speculations in the
dark and there is no evidence on the Irish side that the idea
of secession was ever seriously considered, at least since the
beginning of 1881. But from Parnell's point of view the
ignorance of the liberals and their fears were all to the good:
let the approach once be made by the liberals and it would
become a liberal interest, as well as an Irish interest, to see
that the home rule scheme they propounded would be
sufficiently far-reaching not to be rejected by the Irish.

[1] 'Home rule as described by the Irish parliamentary party was a strictly
constitutional movement. The Irish did not want separation from England,
but what they really wanted was an Irish parliament'—J. J. O'Kelly at York
(*F.J.*, 3 Oct. 1885). O'Kelly was the closest associate of Parnell in the party.
The election speeches in Ireland itself were more swashbuckling in tone but
meant the same thing.
[2] Letter to Rosebery, 13 Nov. 1885 (in Morley, *Gladstone*, iii. 259).
[3] B.M., Gladstone Papers, 44316, f. 164. Grosvenor's letter is undated, but
Gladstone's reply is dated 7 Jan. Grosvenor's 'reliable authority' may have
been Samuel Walker, a Dublin liberal with whom he was in correspondence
at this time.                                          [4] Ibid., f. 165.

Also, while any conceivable detailed scheme which the Irish could put forward would be either rejected in England, or regarded as treachery in Ireland, an offer from the liberals would stand, at least in Ireland, a better chance of being examined on its merits.[1]

It was of course clear to the Irish leaders, in the light of the election results, that the only real hope lay in the liberals. When Parnell was asked by an American correspondent from what party he expected the settlement of the Irish question he replied plainly: 'I expect the settlement to come from the liberals.'[2] Whatever hopes had been entertained— and we have seen that they were not necessarily high hopes —that the tories might take up home rule, had now to be dropped.[3] And from the liberal side, very soon after Parnell's prediction, a signal went up, in the form of a report, universally believed to be inspired, that Gladstone would take office 'with a view to the creation of an Irish parliament to be entrusted with the entire management of all legislative and administrative affairs, securities being taken for the representation of minorities and for an equitable partition of all imperial charges'.[4] We know what heart-searching this famous 'Hawarden kite', 'unauthorized' as it was later declared to be, caused among the liberals. On the Irish side, the only fear was that Gladstone might be forced to make

[1] In a letter to E. D. Gray (24 Dec. 1885) Parnell said that 'public discussion on our side about details is mischievous, as it supplies too many points for criticism to the English mind before the latter has accustomed itself to considering the principle' (published by T. W. Moody in *I.H.S.*, Mar. 1955).

[2] Interview with correspondent of the *Boston Herald*, quoted in *F.J.*, 7 Dec. 1885. He added that the tories, in approaching the problem, would be embarrassed by their Irish supporters. He could have added, but did not, that the liberals were saved this embarrassment by the fact that they had no Irish supporters; the elections of 1885 had not left a single liberal in the Irish representation, which now consisted of 86 Parnellites and 17 tories. Hitherto, of course, the liberals—in the guise of 'home rule whigs' or otherwise—had always held a substantial share of the Irish representation in the parliament of the United Kingdom.

[3] The last to drop them was *United Ireland* which as late as 2 Jan. thought editorially that the tories were likely to take up home rule. This, however, was just part of a general outburst of exuberance; home rule was irresistible and Chamberlain and Hartington, as well as the tories, were supposed to be rallying to it.

[4] *Leeds Mercury and Standard*, 16 Dec. 1885, quoted in Garvin, *Chamberlain*, ii. 135.

such concessions to reluctant followers—to Hartington and his whig landlords, and to Chamberlain, that disgruntled 'friend of Ireland'—that his bill might not be acceptable in Ireland. The special parliamentary correspondent of the *Freeman's Journal*—probably Healy—found it necessary to 'drop the hint' on 11 January that 'the reasons ought to be overwhelming which will induce the Irish party to help the perfidious whigs into office without declarations and pledges from them which even their skilled and eel-like powers of evasion will not enable them to depart from'.[1]

The reasons *were* overwhelming. At the opening of the new parliament on 21 January, the Queen's speech indicated that the Salisbury government not merely did not intend to introduce home rule, but actually was thinking of reintroducing what it itself had dropped in the previous parliament —a measure of coercion for Ireland. Gladstone opposed the suggestion of coercion, and showed, though without committing himself to anything precise, sympathy for Ireland's claim. Parnell found that Gladstone had 'approached the question to-night in a manner worthy of the traditions which attach to his name'.[2] The whole trend of Parnell's speech was one of moderation, aimed not at attacking the tories—a task which now could safely be left to the division lobbies—but at conciliating Gladstone's doubtful followers, and making the path smoother for a liberal Home Rule Bill. Home rule, instead of increasing, would 'very largely diminish', the chances of separation. As far as the land movement was concerned, the Irish party had exercised 'repressing and restraining influences' on a land agitation which had sprung up spontaneously among the people themselves. Specifically, the party had 'refrained from making any expenditure whatever in aid of the movement for the reduction of rents'.[3] He drew the distinction between the present unorganized land agitation on certain estates and the great organized Land League movement of 1879–82 on which £250,000 had been spent. In short, his picture was of a national movement which, whatever it had been in the past, was now thoroughly constitutional in aim and law-abiding in method. This pic-

[1] *F.J.*, 12 Jan. 1886.
[2] *Hansard*, 302. 151 sqq.          [3] Ibid., 302. 156.

ture was substantially accurate and, in any event, reality—
in the few cases where there was a discrepancy—could be
made to conform. Parnell, within a week of this speech,
privately informed Gladstone, through Mrs. O'Shea, that any
National League branches which would not 'keep within
bounds' would be dissolved.[1]

In touch, through Mrs. O'Shea, with Gladstone, Parnell
was also still in touch, through Captain O'Shea, with Gladstone's most important, and most doubtful, lieutenant,
Chamberlain. Chamberlain was not anxious for the tory
government to fall for the moment, but since it had to fall
—and its coercion threat made this inevitable—he desired,
in his own interest and that of the continued unity of the
liberal party, that it should at least not fall on an Irish issue.
'If it be out of the question', he wrote to Parnell through
O'Shea, 'to maintain them [the tories] in power, it would
seem to be desirable, in the interests of a fair solution of the
Irish question, that the defeat should be brought about on
some other issue. . . .'[2] The 'other issue'—an English agricultural amendment to the address, proposed by Chamberlain's faithful follower Jesse Collings—was suggested by
Chamberlain and taken up by Parnell; the government was
defeated on it on 26 January, by a margin of 79 votes. 'The
country', wrote the *Freeman's Journal*, 'will not fail to note
that the majority represents almost exactly the strength of
the Irish vote, which, we need scarcely add, was given solid
against the ministry.'[3]

On 28 January Lord Salisbury's government resigned;
on 1 February Gladstone saw the Queen, accepted office,
and made known to the Queen his intention of introducing
a measure of home rule. On 4 February he made, but in
cautious words, a public pronouncement with the same

---

[1] 'It may interest you to learn that some days since Mr. Parnell sent Mr.
Harrington to Ireland with directions to overhaul the doings of the branches
of the National League and with power to dissolve any that will not keep
within bounds' (memorandum of 29 Jan. 1886 in Katherine O'Shea, *Parnell*,
ii. 33). The letter-book of the National League contains during the spring of
1886 many letters from headquarters severely rebuking branches for violent
language and threatening expulsion (N.L.I., Harrington MSS.).
[2] Memorandum of 22 Jan. 1886 in Garvin, *Chamberlain*, ii. 167.
[3] *F.J.*, 27 Jan. 1886. Seventy-three Parnellites voted in this division; two
more were present but had not yet been sworn.

tendency: 'the hope and purpose of the new government in taking office is to examine carefully whether it is practicable to try some other method [than coercion] of meeting the present case of Ireland'.[1]

A liberal government, depending on Irish votes, and generally believed to be intending a measure of home rule, was now in office. It had not, however, yet publicly pledged itself even to the principle of home rule, much less to the details of a measure. It was at this, still crucial, moment that a singular episode occurred which looked for a few days likely to destroy the Irish party and with it the prospect of the adoption by the liberal party of the home rule cause. It will be remembered that Gladstone's hypothetical preconditions, in his letter to Chamberlain,[2] to the promotion of a home rule plan, had included not only the return of a strong Irish party, but Parnell's ability 'to keep them together'. 'I wish', he had written about the same time to that other doubtful starter, Lord Hartington, 'there were good hopes of effecting a disintegration [of the Irish party] in the new parliament like that of 1880.'[3] At the time, and even more after the general election of 1885, there seemed to be very small hopes of disintegration. But now, in the first weeks of February 1886, it seemed as if the candidature of Captain O'Shea in a by-election at Galway City might make it impossible for Parnell any longer 'to keep them together'. This Galway election, the only serious internal crisis in the Irish party between the Kilmainham treaty and the split of 1890, is worth examining in a little detail.

## 2. *The Galway Election*

At the general election one Parnellite candidate, T. P. O'Connor, was elected for two constituencies: Liverpool (Scotland Division) and Galway City. He elected to sit for Liverpool, and the Galway seat, a safe seat for a nationalist candidate, was therefore vacant. At the same time, Captain O'Shea, M.P. for Clare in the last parliament, was now without a seat. On 6 February the *Freeman's Journal*, acting as

---

[1] *F.J.*, 5 Feb. 1886.        [2] Gwynn and Tuckwell, *Dilke*, ii. 188.
[3] Letter of 3 Sept. 1885 in Holland, *Devonshire*, ii. 79.

Parnell's mouthpiece, announced editorially that 'Captain O'Shea is about to proceed to Galway immediately to seek the representation of that constituency with the approval and support of Mr. Parnell.'

To understand the disarray into which this candidature—and Parnell's support for it—threw the nationalist leaders, it is necessary to dwell for a little on the career of Captain O'Shea, and of his wife. O'Shea was a small Irish landlord and ex-hussar officer; ambitious, with a small, but sufficiently disastrous, talent for political intrigue. Although by social type and general outlook a 'whig', he voted, in the fateful party meeting of May 1880, for Parnell, not for Shaw. Shortly afterwards he introduced Parnell to his wife, an attractive English lady, born Katherine Wood, a sister of Field Marshal Sir Evelyn Wood. The O'Sheas do not appear, even then, to have been living together, but this is not altogether clear.[1] Parnell and Mrs. O'Shea fell in love and the liaison between them began at some time in 1880. How soon O'Shea learned of the liaison is a matter of conjecture—he had strong reason at least to suspect it as early as 1881[2]—but he certainly knew, early on, of his wife's influence with Parnell, and was prepared to use it to further his own ambitions. Both he and his wife acted, as we have seen, rather frequently as intermediaries between Parnell and English politicians: O'Shea dealing with Chamberlain—with whom he had a fairly close political association—and Mrs. O'Shea taking messages in a more straightforward way to Gladstone or Lord Richard Grosvenor, the liberal whip. Both had a considerable part in the negotiation, and implementation, of the Kilmainham treaty; O'Shea had fatally fumbled the negotiations with Chamberlain over the local government proposals; both O'Sheas were busy in the negotiations with the liberals over the coming Home Rule Bill—O'Shea as usual with Chamberlain and Mrs. O'Shea with Gladstone.

The liberal government had known as early as May 1882,

---

[1] Henry Harrison, in *Parnell Vindicated*, rejects certain implications to the contrary effect in Katherine O'Shea's *Parnell*, which he holds to have been written under O'Shea family influence.

[2] Harrison, *Parnell Vindicated*, pp. 261–2.

on the information of home secretary Harcourt, that O'Shea, the negotiator of the Kilmainham treaty, was also 'the husband of Parnell's mistress'.[1] This naturally became more widely known in liberal circles and also among at least the inner circle of the Irish party:[2] their actions and words in the Galway election crisis show that at least Healy, Biggar, T. P. O'Connor, Dillon, and William O'Brien were among those who knew of—or at least suspected—the existence of the liaison. Even if they had not known of it, they would have been bound to object strongly to O'Shea's candidature, for political reasons of which O'Shea was well aware. 'O'Brien, Sullivan, Biggar and others', O'Shea had written to Dilke (then a member of the liberal government), 'detest me more than any other member of the House, on account of the restraining influences which I have so long exercised over Parnell and the support direct and indirect which I have given the government. I am for certain reasons rather more dangerous to attack than any other Irish member sitting on our side of the House.'[3] 'Our side of the House' was the liberal government side, where O'Shea sat with the old 'whiggish home rulers', although he never formally seceded from the home rule party.[4] But apart altogether from per-

[1] Gwynn and Tuckwell, *Dilke*, i. 445.

[2] Rosebery, hardly yet in the liberal inner circle, learned of it in Feb. 1885 (Crewe, *Rosebery*, i. 224; note dated 25 Feb. 1885). Labouchere reported to Chamberlain in the autumn of 1885 that the liaison was the reason why the Irish party would not accept O'Shea as a candidate at the general elections: 'I found out from "the boys" that the difficulty was in their knowledge of the love-affair and in their not seeing why on account of it he was to be treated better than others who had given a half support to Parnell' (letter quoted in C. H. D. Howard's article on the Central Board Scheme, *I.H.S.*, Sept. 1953). Healy was Labouchere's informant on such matters.

[3] Letter of 26 Oct. 1884, No. 1283/41228 among the Campbell-Bannerman MSS. (on microfilm in National Library, Dublin). The 'certain reasons', as advanced by O'Shea, were his own alleged 'fenian' and clerical supporters. Dilke and chief secretary Campbell-Bannerman—to whom Dilke sent the letter—may well, in the light of what the government had learned from Harcourt, have put a different interpretation on the remark. Lord Spencer, then lord lieutenant, believed in 'humouring' O'Shea but that 'any serious work with him will probably be dangerous' (letter of Campbell-Bannerman of 29 Oct. 1884: same no.). In the event Spencer did not 'humour' O'Shea, even to the extent of the piece of local patronage in question, because he 'did not think it right'. The only English politician who made serious use of O'Shea was Chamberlain.

[4] For a time, early in 1881, he seems to have obeyed, unlike the whigs,

sonal and political unpopularity, and his wife's relations with Parnell, there was a specific reason making O'Shea an 'impossible' candidate. As we have seen, the party pledge had been introduced for all nationalist candidates, and this O'Shea had refused to take; this was why he had had to retire from the representation of Clare. At the Ennis Convention O'Shea—so Parnell wrote to Mrs. O'Shea—'informed O'Kelly he would not take the pledge, when O'Kelly informed him at once that it was not in the power of any mortal man to get him in for any national constituency without it, and that even I could not do it'.[1] O'Shea's reluctance to take the pledge was due to his position as a follower of Chamberlain. On that same day (23 October) Mrs. O'Shea, on Parnell's behalf, made a curious proposal to the liberals.

> Opposition to Mr. O'Shea in the county Clare [she wrote to Lord Richard Grosvenor] is *very* great—so great that I do not feel justified in asking Mr. Parnell to re-elect him for Clare. . . . It seems that Messrs. Davitt, Healy, O'Brien and others have for many months past been organising an opposition to Mr. O'Shea— I believe for various reasons which I need not trouble you with under the circumstances. Mr. Parnell promises that if Mr. O'Shea is adopted as the liberal candidate for Mid-Armagh, where the Catholic voters are within 600 of the Episcopalians and Presbyterians combined, Mr. Parnell will get him the whole of the former (Catholic) vote and will, moreover, give his votes for East Down, North Antrim, North Armagh and North Derry to the liberal candidates. He will also secure the Irish vote in Wolverhampton to Mr. H. Fowler, who seems desponding about the effects of its being cast against him. The arrangement will certainly cause a gain of three seats to the liberal party, being East Down, North Derry and Mid-Armagh, which can only be won by such a combination.[2]

the party decision to sit in opposition, but he was among the members who, in May 1881, disobeyed the party decision to abstain from voting on Gladstone's Land Bill. The other members who 'ratted on the land bill' had all by now been driven, or had withdrawn, from home rule politics (see above, Chap. III, p. 56, n. 4; p. 57, n. 1; p. 67, n. 6.

[1] Letter of 23 Oct. 1885 in Katherine O'Shea, *Parnell*, ii. 86. Mrs. O'Shea goes on to remark that O'Shea did not know Parnell's 'true reason' for pressing his candidature. This does—in the light of O'Shea's previous suspicions—read like one of those 'O'Shea family' points which Harrison infers.

[2] B.M., Gladstone Papers, 43316, f. 63. Grosvenor told Gladstone a few days later that he had met O'Shea 'who told me very much what he and *she*

The liberals seem, naturally enough, to have been attracted by such a bargain, although they attempted unsuccessfully to improve on it by annexing a constituency with a nationalist majority, South Tyrone.[1] The scheme fell through in the end, not through any lack of willingness on the part of either Parnell or the liberals, but because O'Shea himself estimated, correctly, that the tories would, in any case, win the seat.[2] He then, with Chamberlain's support, got the liberal nomination for a Liverpool division. Parnell, who was a home rule candidate for the same division, withdrew and campaigned on O'Shea's behalf among the Irish population of the city. 'His return to parliament this time', wrote Mrs. O'Shea to Grosvenor, 'is a matter of the greatest importance to me for reasons I need not trouble you with— they are not those given in the ill-advised address.'[3] O'Shea had claimed, in his election address, that if elected he would assist in laying 'the foundation of a great work which while retaining the unity of the empire [would] remove the rancour of centuries'.[4] O'Shea's campaign in Liverpool ended in defeat, by a narrow margin.

The announcement of this man's candidature for a nationalist constituency, with Parnell's approval and after having previously campaigned as a liberal, was certain to be greeted with abhorrence and alarm by the Irish party. But before considering the effect of the candidature, we may ask a question as to its cause: why did Parnell, in February 1886, undertake a task which had seemed, in the previous October, beyond 'the power of any mortal man'?

The immediate answer is that Chamberlain pressed him to do so. On 22 January—the day after the opening of the new parliament with its indications of a Gladstone–Parnell alliance—Chamberlain gave definite support to O'Shea's ambitions for an Irish seat.

[sic] have written to you' (Grosvenor to Gladstone, 26 Oct. 1885; Gladstone Papers, 43316, f. 72).

[1] B.M., Gladstone Papers, 44316, f. 70. Captain O'Shea to Lord Richard Grosvenor, 25 Oct. 1885. After this, the possibility of running him as a liberal candidate in Belfast was briefly explored and dropped (Gladstone Papers, 44316, ff. 82–84).

[2] Ibid., f. 70. Letter dated 4 Dec. 1885.

[3] B.M., Gladstone Papers, 44316, f. 128.

[4] *Liverpool Mercury*, 24 Nov. 1885.

In the present condition of affairs [he wrote to O'Shea] it is more than ever unfortunate that you have not found a seat. Is there any chance of your standing for one of those now vacant by double election in Ireland? Surely it must be to the interest of the Irish party to keep open channels of communication with the liberal leaders? Can you not get Mr. Parnell's *exequatur* for one of the vacant seats? It is really the least he can do for you, after all you have done for him.[1]

Well before this intervention of Chamberlain's, however, O'Shea had been making use of Chamberlain's name to secure the Galway nomination. Parnell seems to have hoped, at first, that the nomination might be obtained for O'Shea on political grounds without his personal intervention. In reply to a letter from E. D. Gray, who seems to have acted as political intermediary between Parnell and O'Shea at this date, Parnell wrote as follows:

With regard to O'Shea, I consider that I have done everything that I possibly could be expected to do for him to satisfy the claims of personal friendship, having regard to my public duty and my public position. I could not possibly have recommended him to any national constituency during the general election, unless he had consented to subscribe to the undertaking required from all candidates. Such action on my part would have thrown discredit upon the proceedings of all other conventions and would have been productive of disunion and grave injury to the national cause. I do not see even now, when the situation is very materially changed, and when these evils could not result, how I could undertake the responsibility of recommending his candidature to Galway unpledged in any respect even as regards his vote.

You inform me, however, that Chamberlain is very adversely disposed towards the plan of Irish self-government attributed to Mr. Gladstone, and that you fear his opposition may be fatal to the settlement and the absence of his good-will may render it extremely difficult. You seem to intimate that O'Shea's influence

---

[1] Letter of 22 Jan. 1886 in Garvin, *Chamberlain*, ii. 382. The final reference is presumably to the Kilmainham treaty negotiations. The ambiguity of the phrase is odd, however, in the light of what Chamberlain knew, through Harcourt and through Labouchere; so indeed is the request itself. It is interesting and, I believe, significant, that Chamberlain's own retrospective account, otherwise so detailed, of his Irish transactions of this period contains not a word about this letter to O'Shea or indeed about the whole important episode of the Galway election (Chamberlain, *A Political Memoir*).

upon Chamberlain, if it were exercised, might be of service, and I do not know how far I correctly interpret your letter in supposing it to suggest that, if some hope of Galway were held out to the former, this influence might be exercised. Under these circumstances do you think I should be justified in saying to you that, if you can induce the leading members of the party to tolerate O'Shea's unpledged candidature for Galway, neither would I oppose it? If you think so, it would be well for you to see O'Shea yourself soon, and try to restore his good-humour before his visit to C[hamberlain].[1]

Gray, however, declined this rather obvious gambit: 'there is only one way of doing it in my opinion—for you openly to take the responsibility.' At the same time he reiterated O'Shea's political message: 'According to O'Shea the whole attitude of the radical leaders depends upon him —get him a seat and all things are possible—don't get him a seat and nothing is possible.' Gray seems to have been rather sceptical about O'Shea's claims, and conscious of the danger to Parnell: 'I do not ignore the fact that to espouse him would involve a certain amount of risk even to you.'[2]

Was 'the Chamberlain argument' an adequate explanation for Parnell's putting forward of Captain O'Shea? One of Parnell's supporters, writing after the split of 1890, recalled that during the Galway election Parnell had 'explained to his followers that he had only adopted Captain O'Shea as candidate for Galway at the special request of Mr. Chamberlain, stating at the same time that under the circumstances he did not think he was justified in stating so publicly'.[3] There is, however, good evidence, which may be accepted as contemporary, that what Parnell told his followers was something rather different. Healy in his reminiscences gives

[1] Letter of 24 Dec. 1885, published by T. W. Moody in I.H.S., Mar. 1955.
[2] Ibid., letter of 30 Dec. 1885. In this corrected copy letter—from among the Gray Papers—two deleted passages seem significant. The first is: 'He, however, maintains that you are personally pledged to him. Of that of course I can know nothing.' The second is: 'I am only telling you what our friend says. You know him infinitely better than I do and'—the following words are not deleted—'you are much better able than I am to decide how much salt may be required (wholesomely) to digest his arguments.' These passages, and the deletions, suggest, at least to the present writer, that Gray was aware that O'Shea's case for nomination was not based entirely on political arguments.
[3] Letter of T. Harrington, M.P. (F.J., 29 Dec. 1890).

the text of a telegram, sent by Deasy, the party whip, to
Healy and other M.P.s when the 'revolt' against O'Shea's
candidature had begun: 'Parnell telegraphs following to
Gray: "Advise friends that I have promised that if certain person adopted his chief's views regarding Irish
government O'Shea should have my strongest support.
I consequently feel bound if not returned to resign my
seat." '[1]

There is no evidence at all in support of this claim that the
'certain person'—Chamberlain—ever gave Parnell to understand that he had 'adopted his chief's views' on home rule;
if he had done so, we should certainly have heard more of
the matter when Chamberlain later voted against the Home
Rule Bill. As we have seen, Chamberlain's support of O'Shea
took the form of a simple request, not of a bargain. Apparently Parnell, facing the indignation of his followers, did not
himself feel—whatever those loyal to him felt afterwards—
that Chamberlain's simple request was an adequate explanation for so extraordinary a candidature. The reaction of
Healy and Biggar to the use of Chamberlain's name was
contemptuous: 'We believe Parnell's wire instigated by
O'Shea and I [Healy] am well able to judge of O'Shea's
supposed influence with the cabinet.'[2] Parnell's previous
treatment of Chamberlain's overtures—at the time of the
local government proposals—does not suggest that he
would have run grave risks—as he did with the O'Shea
candidature—simply to conciliate Chamberlain. Indeed it
seems that O'Shea's intimacy with Chamberlain had for
some time been regarded as a disadvantage both from the
Irish and from the liberal point of view. Writing to Grosvenor on 4 October 1885—that is, before the Ennis Convention and no doubt foreseeing its outcome—Mrs. O'Shea,
vainly seeking a government appointment for her husband,
scornfully discounted his ostensible claim to political

---

[1] Quoted (but probably wrongly dated) in Healy, *Letters and Leaders of
My Day*, i. 243. There is no serious reason to doubt the authenticity of documents quoted by Healy, although there often is a great deal of reason to
doubt the accuracy of his own recollections. See p. 177, n. 2.
[2] Letter to Gray dated 6 Feb. (*I.H.S.*, Mar. 1955). See p. 177, n. 2 below.
Healy's 'inside information' about the cabinet came from Labouchere, who
was very close to Chamberlain at this time.

importance: 'I hope you will remember, lest his desire to pose as a mediator should stand in his way, that the Irish side dread it even more than you can and that it is natural for an Irishman who has some of the Chief Characteristics of his race *strongly* defined, to be ever ready to accept and even court the communications of a Minister who seems ever ready for negotiations of some sort—I need scarcely say I do not refer to Mr. Gladstone.'[1] As we have seen, O'Shea's 'mediation' was not altogether a 'pose', but neither was it an overwhelming argument in favour of his candidature.

The more obvious explanation of the Galway candidature and that which suggested itself to the minds of contemporaries, both in the party itself, and in the hostile press, was of course that of a kind of blackmail. Captain O'Shea was to get Galway in order to keep his mouth shut. Crude as this explanation is, it cannot be left out of account. Captain O'Shea had failed at Ennis and Parnell, despite Mrs. O'Shea's urging, could do nothing for him; the alternative scheme for mid-Armagh had also foundered; he failed again at Liverpool, although Parnell had campaigned for him among the Irish there, making this liberal candidate a conspicuous and incongruous exception to the rule of the 'vote tory manifesto'. Now an ambitious and twice-rejected Captain O'Shea, who had good reason at least to suspect that his wife was Parnell's mistress, was obviously most dangerous. The fact that he had, or thought he had, a political claim on Parnell, joined itself to the private peril; Chamberlain's letter, bolstering up O'Shea's political claim, inflated the man, and made it harder for Parnell to reject his claim.[2] It

---

[1] B.M., Gladstone Papers, 44316, ff. 128–35. Mrs. O'Shea's style, if not her character, has something in common with that of Queen Victoria.

[2] Henry Harrison indignantly rejected the suggestion that Parnell's private life had anything to do with the nomination of Captain O'Shea: 'The charge [made by Parnell's enemies] was, in one form or another, that Parnell had made Captain O'Shea member for nationalist Galway as the price of Mrs. O'Shea's honour. It was wholly false' (*Parnell Vindicated*, p. 362). The charge is really that the nomination was—probably by implication rather than by bargain—the price not of Mrs. O'Shea's honour but of Captain O'Shea's silence, and Harrison did not demonstrate its falsity. This is one of the rare occasions in Harrison's works where the loyalty of the old Parnellite triumphs over the objectivity of the historian.

also provided a reason which, in a somewhat embellished form, could be given to the party. Furthermore Parnell, now at the head of a party of 85 (many of them elected simply as 'his men'), and holding the balance of power in the House of Commons, with home rule now in his grasp, was in a better position to *impose* a candidate, even perhaps such a candidate as Captain O'Shea.

Perhaps. The doubt must also have been present to Chamberlain's mind. He knew of the liaison;[1] he knew, as everyone did, of O'Shea's bitter unpopularity with the members of the party; he knew, through Labouchere, that members of the party knew of the liaison.[2] He also knew, as few others did, that at least one important member of the party affected to despise Parnell, and claimed that the party was really ruled by an 'inner circle' which did not include him. Labouchere, in tortuous efforts to keep Chamberlain from breaking with Gladstone, and to persuade him of the essential reasonableness of the Irish party as distinct from Parnell, brought him tales of Healy's conversation: 'Parnell is half mad. We always act without him. He accepts this position; if he did not we should overlook him. Do not trouble yourself about him. Dillon, McCarthy, O'Brien and I settle everything. When we agree, no-one can disagree.'[3] Whether Chamberlain believed this account or not, he can hardly have failed to be interested in the potential 'two powers' within the Irish party: the party that was now in a position to dictate to the liberal party, and to make his own political future questionable. Already, in October, learning through O'Shea of alleged 'internecine conflicts' in the party— including a quarrel between Healy and Parnell's secretary, Campbell—he had expressed the hope to Gladstone that 'it may be possible to divide them. . . .'[4] When, therefore, he urged O'Shea's candidature on Parnell he was fully aware

---

[1] See p. 168, n. 2.    [2] See p. 168, n. 2.
[3] Letter from Labouchere to Chamberlain, 19 Dec. 1885, in Thorold, *Labouchere*, p. 251. Labouchere believed Healy and gave Chamberlain substantially the same assurances about the Irish party, in his own name, on 12 Jan. (ibid., p. 284). Labouchere is not necessarily a reliable witness, but his account of what Healy said may be accepted; it accords well with the tone of references to Parnell in the letters to Maurice Healy quoted in *Letters and Leaders*.    [4] B.M., Dilke Papers, 43931, f. 275.

that he was making an embarrassing position more embarrassing. If Parnell refused, what might O'Shea do? If Parnell accepted, what would Healy and the others do? Would they 'overlook him' and 'act without him'? And, if so, what might become of Gladstone's grand project, founded on the hypothesis of Parnell's ability 'to keep them together'?

It is possible that such questions did not suggest themselves to Chamberlain's mind; it is hardly likely, considering what he knew, what he hoped, and how he acted. At all events, whatever Chamberlain's motives—and even supposing that he acted from admiration of the Captain's diplomatic gifts and pity for his unrepresentative condition—the effect of his action was not altered; it was a severe and early laboratory test of the solidity and loyalty of the new Irish party.

Before the *Freeman's* announcement, T. P. O'Connor, as the elected member for Galway, was the first to learn of Parnell's intention to nominate O'Shea. From London, O'Connor wired the news to Healy in Dublin and declared, according to Healy's later account, that he would resign in protest if Healy would also resign; Healy agreed, but O'Connor shortly afterwards gave in to Parnell.[1] Biggar, however, also informed by O'Connor, and animated by a lifelong detestation of 'whigs', crossed to Dublin; then travelled to Galway with Healy, arriving on 6 February— the day of the *Freeman's* announcement—to oppose O'Shea's candidature. They were a rather formidable pair: Biggar, one of the most respected and courageous members of the party: Healy, one of the ablest and most feared, at the head of a little 'party within the party'.[2] Biggar, strangely enough, had been the most extreme exponent of Parnell's 'dictatorship'; he had said that the members of the party were 'simply machines in the hands of the director—of the man who directs the movement'.[3] Neither Biggar nor Healy was yet in open revolt against his leader—even at the height of

[1] Healy, *Letters and Leaders*, i. 239 sqq.
[2] T. D. Sullivan, Chance, William Murphy, Donal Sullivan, and Maurice Healy, all relatives—the 'Bantry band'. See M. J. F. McCarthy, *The Irish Revolution*, p. 452.
[3] At the central branch of the National League (*F.J.*, 21 Oct. 1885); Dillon strongly refuted Biggar's view.

the brief campaign Healy was still 'declining to believe' that 'our illustrious leader' was really supporting O'Shea—but the pretence of obedience was a very thin one.

In Galway, on 6 and 7 February, wires came thick and fast to Healy, urging him to withdraw; T. P. O'Connor, Gray, Leamy, Kenny, Deasy, William O'Brien, Harrington, all wired, several of them more than once; others followed.[1] How unhappy these loyal members felt about having to support O'Shea we know from—among other indications— an interesting letter dated 7 February from William O'Brien in Dublin to Dillon in Mayo; Dillon apparently had had some idea of going to Galway to support O'Shea. O'Brien said he agreed with Dillon in 'loathing' O'Shea and resenting Parnell's action, but

the question was, in the special circumstances of the moment, whether we should swallow O'Shea, or utterly destroy our movement and party at its brightest moment for a personal reason which we could not even explain. It was a most bitter and scandalous alternative, but it seemed to us an alternative between accepting an odious personality and chaos. We were all thoroughly in favour of terrorising Parnell by every means short of public scandal but when he committed himself [by the *Freeman* announcement] it became a question as to which if defeated by his own party it was impossible for him to continue leader. . . . T. P. agreed and wouldn't go, but Healy and Biggar persisted in going, knowing well Parnell's determination, and, I'm afraid, determined to pick a quarrel. They . . . insisted that Parnell was not with O'Shea. We begged them in vain to return. Even after getting Parnell's telegram[2] they sent an ultimatum to O'Shea treating Parnell's threats with scoffs. They relied on Parnell's helplessness. We pressed Parnell by all means short of open revolt but his

---

[1] Healy, *Letters and Leaders*, i. 240.
[2] Evidently Deasy's telegram, about 'a certain person' (above, p. 173). Healy dates that telegram 8 Feb., but that is probably a mistake. A letter from Biggar at Galway to Gray, dated 5 Feb., almost certainly refers to this telegram. 'Deasy's telegram just to hand. I cannot believe Parnell can have wired such rubbish. Surely he's not insane?' (*I.H.S.*, Mar. 1955). Unfortunately Biggar's date is also mistaken, as he did not arrive in Galway until 6 Feb. (Healy, *Letters and Leaders*, i. 240; *F.J.*, 8 Feb. 1886). A letter from Healy to Gray (*I.H.S.*, Mar. 1955) obviously written on the same day and dealing with the same telegram is dated 6 Feb., which we are justified in taking as the correct date for both letters and for the arrival of this important telegram. The 'threats' referred to by O'Brien are therefore threats of resignation.

answer was emphatic and he is plainly bound by some influence he cannot resist.[1]

This letter shows the extraordinary strain to which the O'Shea candidature subjected the party's loyalty; it also implies, although discreetly, that the personal motive was regarded as decisive. William O'Brien was in a position to know of, and to evaluate, the Chamberlain aspect, and the fact that he does not even find this worth mentioning to Dillon—whom he wished to persuade not to help Healy— is in itself significant. O'Brien and Dillon were, of course, generally recognized as two of the most disinterested leaders of the party and they are not open, as Healy was, to imputations of jealousy or personal ambition.

On this same Sunday, 7 February, a meeting of Galway nationalists, addressed by Healy and Biggar, selected a strong local candidate, Michael Lynch, to challenge O'Shea's candidature.[2] A Dublin tory paper asked a pertinent question: 'And why, may we ask, was not the ordinary procedure followed and a convention of the borough nationalists called before a candidate was selected?'[3] There were now two nationalist candidates and there had been no convention. The reasons were clear enough. No convention could be held to endorse Captain O'Shea because he would not take the pledge, which was an essential part of the convention machinery. A convention in the case of the 'rebel' candidate, Lynch, could have been declared null, since the National League committee, under Harrington's control, would have opposed it, and Healy and Biggar had no authority to represent the party. Even so, it might have been tried, but for the fact that the local clergy—also an essential part of the convention machinery—were not pre-

---

[1] Dillon MSS., This letter has now been published (*I.H.S.*, Mar. 1955). Dillon refused O'Brien's request to declare on Parnell's side and took up a neutral position: 'Regret deeply but cannot give my name. I shall say nothing unless Healy is attacked' (telegram marked 8 Feb.: N.L.I., Harrington MSS.). Other telegrams in the Harrington collection show that several other members—the two McCarthys, A. O'Connor, Hooper, Clancy, Sheil, Smithwick, Kenny—declared in favour of Parnell only with considerable misgivings, and deploring the O'Shea candidature.

[2] *F.J.*, 8 Feb. 1886.

[3] *Evening Mail*, 8 Feb. 1886.

pared to support the 'rebels'.[1] In their private conversations with leading Galway nationalists, Biggar frequently, and Healy at least once, made known what was, in their opinion, the real cause of the contest. ' "The candidate's wife is Parnell's mistress and there is nothing more to be said" were words frequently on [Biggar's] lips.'[2]

In public, Healy's line, apart from brisk invective against O'Shea—'a whig grub', a *chameleon militaire*', 'a miserable and incompetent marplot'—was mainly that O'Shea was not, and could not be, an official nationalist candidate. 'I asked Colonel Nolan'—who represented Parnell in Galway and nominated O'Shea—'whether Captain O'Shea intended to take the pledge of the Irish party to sit, act and vote with that party in the house of commons. I could get no information from Colonel Nolan. . . . Let me say if Captain O'Shea poses here as the representative or choice of the Irish party, I am here to say that the Irish party was never consulted.'[3]

Here was the crux: Healy's remarks were perfectly true, and yet if they were allowed to go unchallenged, if the party in fact did not now 'swallow' O'Shea, Parnell's leadership, and with it the prospects of home rule, would be seriously endangered. O'Brien and those with him acted promptly. On the day Healy's speech was published—8 February— they asked every member of the party—many of them by telegram—to support Parnell: 'Parnell has intimated to us his leadership at stake in Galway contest. Healy's speech has created impression that party generally is against Parnell. Will you authorize us attach your name with ours to

[1] Both the *Freeman's Journal* and the *Evening Mail* for 8 Feb. noted, as a significant fact, the absence of any member of the clergy from the Lynch meeting.
[2] Memorandum by John Muldoon, K.C., entitled 'The O'Shea election for Galway' in the writer's possession. Muldoon covered the election as a reporter for a local paper *The Galway Vindicator* and 'was privileged to attend all meetings and gatherings, and was in fact present at many secret conclaves about the election but it was only on the understanding that nothing would be then published as to what was taking place'. This memorandum, apparently written years later, is based, he states, on notes taken at the time. It has now been published by T. W. Moody (*I.H.S.*, Mar. 1955).
[3] Healy at the meeting of Lynch supporters on 7 Feb. (*F.J.*, 8 Feb. 1886). Healy here hinted publicly at the underlying scandal: 'The issue is knit. It is one about which I could say a great deal more than I choose to say here to-day' (*Evening Mail*, 8 Feb. 1886).

public declaration upholding Parnell.'[1] This appeal which carried, among other signatures, the names of four of the best-known members—Sexton, William O'Brien, T. P. O'Connor, and T. Harrington—had the desired effect. A declaration, signed by fifty members, called on the electors of Galway to 'uphold the authority of Mr. Parnell as leader of the Irish people'.[2] The remainder of the party could not, it was explained, be contacted in time; which was likely enough, parliament being in a short recess.[3] The *Freeman's Journal* in a powerful editorial drove home the message of the declaration. Galway should express its confidence in

Mr. Parnell the recognized leader of the nationalist party and of the nationalist cause ... vested as no other Irishman is or ever has been with the responsibility of speaking and of acting with the mandate of a united nation. . . . The issue is not between Captain O'Shea and Mr. Lynch but whether at the very moment of the crisis, when the question of home rule hangs in the balance, when Mr. Parnell almost holds it in the hollow of his hand, Galway will strike a blow at his prestige and his authority. . . . The power of Mr. Parnell has consisted, and must consist, in English statesmen recognizing that he is the personal embodiment of the Irish nation, delegated by them to speak and act on their behalf.

The mutineers were now on the defensive. They had against them not only the prestige of the national leader, but the majority of the party and the nationalist press, with the decisive, and just, argument that their action was endangering home rule. The clergy, though discreet, were also against them: on the day of the 'declaration' the local bishops 'begged' Healy to 'consider his position'.[4] Archbishop Walsh on 8 February advised Gray by telegram: 'Wire to Healy counselling abandonment of position.'[5] There was no hope now of forcing Parnell to disavow O'Shea; even a

---

[1] From a specimen addressed to Dillon among the Dillon MSS., V. The text as given in Healy, *Letters and Leaders*, i. 243, is identical. The telegram addressed to Dillon carried fifteen signatures, while that addressed to Murphy, and quoted by Healy, carried only seven. Presumably names were added as replies came in.

[2] *F.J.*, 9 Feb. 1886.

[3] A few members—T. D. Sullivan, Chance, Murphy, among them— refused to sign but the 'revolt' did not go beyond the limits of the immediate Healy connexion (*Letters and Leaders*, i. 239 sqq.).

[4] *Letters and Leaders*, i. 245.          [5] *I.H.S.*, Mar. 1955.

local victory in Galway could do no more than break a splinter off the party.

Following up his advantage, Parnell went down to Galway (9 February) accompanied by Sexton, T. P. O'Connor, J. J. O'Kelly, Deasy, and Campbell; William O'Brien had arrived the previous day. The Galway population, inflamed by Healy and Biggar, received them badly. 'No sooner did the engine enter the building', records a local paper, 'than a shout was raised unparalleled in the history of Galway station.'[1] The shouts—of 'Hie for Lynch!' and 'To hell with Parnell and whiggery!'—and 'a good deal of rough pushing' were checked by Healy and Colonel Nolan.[2] 'Mr. Healy', wrote a Dublin tory paper, 'could afford to be generous. He had made Mr. Parnell bite the dust.'[3]

Although the mutiny was really almost over, it now seemed to outside observers to be at its height. The fact that Parnell had had to travel to Galway at all, and especially his hostile reception when he got there, seemed to hopeful political opponents to mean the end of his power. 'Mr. Parnell's power', wrote the London correspondent of the *Evening Mail*, 'is more in tradition than in fact . . . there is plenty of gossip about the mere figurehead uses to which he is put by those over whom he is supposed to be omnipotent. . . .' The liberals also were attentive to possible implications as regards Gladstone and home rule. 'The split among the Parnellites', wrote the *Daily News*, 'is a very real thing and may prove to be of high import.'[4]

By the time those words appeared, Parnell's power was unchallenged and there was no longer any split among the Parnellites. After the arrival of Parnell's party, the M.P.s conferred together and Healy, though not Biggar, agreed to withdraw opposition to O'Shea. A private meeting 'of Mr. Lynch's supporters' was then held and was addressed by Parnell, Biggar, Healy, Sexton, T. P. O'Connor, and William O'Brien. Parnell's appeal was simply for unity under his

[1] *Galway Express*, 12 Feb. 1886.
[2] Ibid., same date; *F.J.*, 10 Feb. 1886.
[3] *Evening Mail*, 10 Feb. 1886. On the following day the same writer had to strike a different note: 'Mr. Healy has been beaten and has surrendered with shrunken words, for all his promises and boasts.'
[4] 10 Feb. 1886.

leadership: 'When was it so absolutely essential to uphold my authority as at this moment when I hold in my hand the measure that will secure peace and prosperity to this long neglected country. . . ?'[1] Biggar maintained his stand against O'Shea and was received with great cheering. Healy, however, withdrew: 'I retire from this contest and Captain O'Shea becomes, I suppose, the member for Galway. It is a bitter cup for you. God knows to me it is a cup of poison, but even so, let it be taken for the sake of the unity of the Party we love. . . .' But the decisive speech seems to have been that of William O'Brien, who made no case for Captain O'Shea, but told with eloquence the story of what Parnell had achieved and what was now in jeopardy. 'It was clear', writes John Muldoon, 'that he was making converts with every sentence and the simple truth is that he carried the day for Captain O'Shea. There was no dissent when O'Brien sat down. It was not really a speech; it was a thunderstorm.' The resolution was passed: 'That we the electors and non-electors of Galway and supporters of Mr. Lynch, having heard the statements of Mr. Parnell, Mr. Biggar and Mr. Healy do authorize Mr. Lynch our candidate to retire in favour of Mr. O'Shea in obedience to the advice of our leader and his colleagues of the Irish parliamentary party.'[2] The *Freeman's Journal* announced—and 'understood' that Parnell had informed the meeting—that O'Shea had 'taken the pledge to sit act and vote with the Irish party'. This, however, was false.[3] Lynch withdrew his candidature and O'Shea was elected.

The episode of the Galway election demonstrated, according to one observer, the weakness of Parnell's hold on the party:[4] it revealed according to another 'the strength of the disintegrating influences in the Parnellite ranks'.[5] These

---

[1] 'Muldoon Memorandum'. My whole account of this meeting is based on that memorandum.        [2] *F.J.*, 10 Feb. 1886.

[3] At a public meeting on the following day Parnell did not assert that O'Shea had taken the pledge, but claimed he had promised not to *sit* with the government. A subsequent controversy between Healy and O'Shea makes it clear that O'Shea never took the pledge and that he did not take his seat with the party (ibid., 13–18 May 1886).

[4] F. H. O'Donnell, *Irish Parliamentary Party*, ii. 167. This view is partly accounted for by another eccentric opinion of the author's, that 'O'Shea was an excellent candidate'.        [5] The London *Standard*, 10 Feb. 1886.

judgements seem strangely wide of the mark. What emerged most clearly from the Galway election, surely, was the power of Parnell, based on the desire of the party, and of the people, for unity, seen as the necessary pre-condition of home rule. For this, the party were prepared to accept the breaking of the rules by which all had bound themselves, and to accept also a personality whom they regarded as odious, both for private and political reasons: O'Brien's 'scandalous alternative'. If Chamberlain had really had a political experiment in mind, he had at least obtained a clear result: Parnell *could* 'keep them together', even under markedly unfavourable circumstances. More, the necessity for unity, and therefore blind acceptance of what the leader ordered, led to an increased exaltation, in public print, of Parnell's status and genius. He became a kind of Moses: 'the man whom [the Irish people] look upon as the Leader destined by Providence to carry them to the Goal of the National Aspirations'.[1]

It is true that the condition of the Parnellite movement, as revealed by the Galway election, was not an altogether healthy one. The seeds of danger in it did not, however, lie in the party so much as in the leadership; great as the public adulation was, those who were near to Parnell, and followed him loyally in this crisis, henceforward had a doubt of him: a doubt that was not diminished when O'Shea, home rule member for Galway, refused to vote for the Home Rule Bill. Parnell's relations with Mrs. O'Shea were being referred to publicly,[2] thus making O'Shea himself an enemy.[3]

---

[1] *F.J.*, 10 Feb. 1886. *United Ireland* (13 Feb. 1886) wrote to the same effect. *The Nation*, controlled by Healy's friend and relative, T. D. Sullivan, was very much more reserved, regarded the starting of Captain O'Shea as 'a deplorable mistake', hinted that no leader was indispensable and warned that every Irish patriot 'should be prepared to make sacrifices of personal feelings' (13 Feb. 1886). The influence of *The Nation* was insignificant at this period compared with that of the *Freeman's Journal* and *United Ireland*.

[2] The Dublin *Evening Mail* dropped a particularly heavy hint, mentioning 'a toast of some elderly wags—the family friendships of the O'Sheas and the Parnells. . . . It seems simple enough but there is more in it than politics apparently' (11 Feb. 1886).

[3] F. H. O'Donnell (op. cit., ii. 167) states that the taunts made during the Galway election roused O'Shea's suspicions. O'Shea's abstention on the Home Rule Bill is also said to have been motivated by these suspicions, confirmed by a later newspaper paragraph (*Pall Mall Gazette*, 24 May 1886)

The Galway election probably contributed to the over-confidence which proved disastrous to Parnell in 1890; it also sowed seeds of distrust among his followers, which germinated in that later crisis. The 'Chamberlain experiment' —if such there was—proved, in the long run, not altogether unsuccessful. For the immediate home rule crisis, however, the result obtained was negative: the party of 1885 was not going to 'disintegrate' like that of 1880.

### 3. The Home Rule Bill

It must have been with great relief that the Parnellites emerged from the internal torment of Galway to face, as a united party, the straightforward political struggle of the Home Rule Bill. This was something that divided English-men, not Irishmen: the Irish were united in their deter-mination to get as much home rule as could be got—and, on the whole, content to leave to Parnell the determination of how much that was. John Dillon—who still had the reputa-tion of being 'more extreme' than his leader—made it clear, on the day before parliament reassembled, that Parnell, and only Parnell, had authority to treat this matter. The English, he said, would have to be made to see that Parnell spoke 'as the accredited leader and ambassador of the Irish people'.[1]

Parnell's hand was further strengthened by the Irish bishops who now, for the first time, on 16 February, declared themselves in favour of home rule: '. . . it is our firm and conscientious conviction that [home rule] alone can satisfy . . . the legitimate aspirations of the Irish people. . . . These wishes and aspirations have been expressed with unmistake-able clearness by the constituencies of the four provinces of Ireland at the recent elections.'[2]

Parnell, meanwhile, was 'in free and constant communica-

showing that Parnell was living at Eltham with Mrs. O'Shea (Garvin, *Chamberlain*, ii. 382). Harrison (*Parnell Vindicated*, p. 273, &c.) showed that O'Shea had already had very strong reasons at least to suspect the liaison and puts forward, cogently, the view that he was now forced by publicity to take up an appropriate position.

[1] *F.J.*, 17 Feb. 1886. Dillon was speaking at a meeting of the central branch of the National League.

[2] *Addresses of the Most Reverend Dr. Walsh, Archbishop of Dublin*, app. B II, pp. 462–3.

tion' with the new chief secretary, John Morley, as Gladstone did not wish, as yet, to meet him himself.[1] Morley has recorded that Parnell, in these negotiations, showed himself 'acute, frank, patient, closely attentive and possessed of striking, though not rapid, insight'. These gifts were called for, since Parnell was dealing with the representative of a cabinet that was still divided on the fundamental issue of a parliament for Ireland. It was not until after Chamberlain's resignation (27 March) that Gladstone first publicly announced his intention to move for 'leave to bring in a bill to make provision for the future government of Ireland' (29 March). Very shortly afterwards (5 April) Gladstone and Parnell met privately, for the first time, with Morley; their conversation was confined mainly to 'the root of the matter': the financial, and especially the fiscal, aspects of home rule. Parnell was 'extraordinarily close, tenacious and sharp', according to Morley; he indicated he might 'break the bill in committee' on the question of the extent of Ireland's imperial contribution; he agreed, however, in view of the state of British public opinion, to drop the claim to customs.[2] It was only after this interview, and on the day before the introduction of the bill, that he took some of his colleagues into his confidence, and showed them a draft, supplied by Morley, of the main provisions of the bill.[3] The eight members thus consulted—McCarthy, O'Kelly, Sexton, O'Brien, Dillon, Gray, O'Connor, and Healy—had, by all accounts, nothing of value to offer, and the consultation at so late a date was no doubt, as O'Brien says, 'perfunctory'.

On 8 April Gladstone gave the House the outline of his bill. Ireland was to have her own parliament, with its own executive for the management of Irish affairs, reserving to the imperial parliament the crown, peace or war, the armed forces, foreign relations, and some other matters. The Irish parliament was specifically forbidden to endow any religion,

---

[1] Morley, *Gladstone*, iii. 304.
[2] Ibid., iii. 305; O'Brien, *Evening Memories*, p. 106.
[3] Healy, *Letters and Leaders*, i. 251; T. P. O'Connor, *Life of Parnell*, p. 182; O'Brien, *Evening Memories*, p. 111; Morley *Recollections*, i. 244. O'Brien states that Davitt was present, but this is denied by Healy. Morley notes with respect that although 'three of the men who saw it (the draft Home Rule Bill) were newspapermen, not a word came out'.

or restrain educational freedom, or deal with customs or excise. The Royal Irish Constabulary was to remain under imperial control for a time but eventually would be handed over to Ireland. Ireland was to contribute one-fifteenth of the imperial revenue. The Irish members were to be excluded from the imperial parliament. There were to be two houses or 'orders' in the Irish parliament, and the upper house—'first order'—would have power to hold up legislation.

Immediately after Gladstone's speech, a full meeting of the Irish party was held. 'General dissatisfaction was expressed by many members and also by the chairman [Parnell]' about four points: the customs; the imperial contribution; the constabulary; voting by orders. 'It was agreed that Mr. Parnell should take part in the debate to-night objecting to these four provisions and stating that, if it be amended in this respect in committee, it will be accepted by the party and the Irish people.'[1] This decision, which was no doubt mainly a ratification of Parnell's attitude, left the party free to give Gladstone the necessary support, on the first and second readings, while disclaiming responsibility for the aspects of the bill which were likely to be most unpopular in Ireland and in America.[2]

Parnell, therefore, with his party solidly behind him, gave the bill a cautious welcome, voicing the agreed criticisms. 'Whatever the fate of the measure', the cause of Irish autonomy would gain enormously.[3] Healy, speaking on the following day, was more exuberant. He could, he declared, 'go to the most extreme council of the most extreme orga-

[1] Dillon MSS.: Minutes, 8 Apr. 1886. Healy (*Letters and Leaders*, i. 251) refers to this meeting, but neither he nor any of the other memoir-writers makes it clear that the party's attitude to the bill was decided at a formal meeting. T. P. O'Connor (*Parnell*, p. 182) states that Parnell never consulted any of his colleagues 'except individually'—and at the caucus meeting on 7 Apr. —about the bill. The meeting of 8 Apr. was a very full one, eighty members being present.

[2] The objection to the customs provision was, however, almost certainly, peculiarly Parnell's. The party's position on this issue had been betrayed in advance by Healy, who had privately informed Labouchere that there was 'no fear of Protection. Parnell and some Belfast manufacturers are the only protectionists in Ireland' (Labouchere to Chamberlain, 19 Dec. 1885 in Thorold, *Labouchere*, p. 251). See above, Chap. III, pp. 109 sqq.

[3] *F.J.*, 9 Apr. 1886.

nization of extreme Irishmen at home and abroad', and gain their assent to Gladstone's bill.[1]

There must have been many who were rather more doubtful than Healy about the attitude of the 'extreme Irishmen', especially in America. The influential—and not very extreme—John Boyle O'Reilly wrote, in the *Boston Pilot*, on the day after Healy's speech, that the bill 'leaves Ireland with a chain around her neck like a wild beast'.[2] These were dangerous words, to a movement which depended so much on the Irish in America for moral and financial support. But there was no general breakaway. Patrick Egan, ex-treasurer of the Land League, and well known as an extremist and critic of Parnell, said that the bill would 'meet with the approbation of the Irish in America'.[2] Alexander Sullivan, one of the most influential and extreme of the Irish-Americans, thought the bill 'a great step in the right direction', and a justification of Parnell's policy; he criticized the same points as the party had singled out.[3] Generally, despite a few murmurs, the Irish in America supported the bill and praised Gladstone.

At home, of course, the national press and the people welcomed the bill; almost incredulously, indeed, so remote had seemed the possibility that a great English party might seriously propose to grant a measure of autonomy to Ireland. The nationalist bishops and clergy praised the bill and the author;[4] there were convincing signs that Gladstone's gesture, and the eloquence with which it was accompanied, had captured the imagination of the people generally.[5] Irish public opinion was concerned not with the imperfections of the bill, but with whether it could pass the Commons in the

[1] Ibid., 10 Apr. 1886.
[2] Quoted in ibid., 12 Apr. 1886.
[3] Interview with *Chicago Daily News*, quoted in *F.J.*, 24 Apr. 1886.
[4] Archbishop Croke and his clergy, for example, passed a formal resolution conveying to Gladstone an expression of their gratitude (ibid., 30 Apr. 1886).
[5] William O'Brien's biographer, Michael McDonogh, states that O'Brien's paper *United Ireland* 'which . . . had a steady sale of about 90,000 copies weekly reached its highest circulation, 125,000, the week it presented its readers with a coloured portrait of Gladstone'. The point is significant when it is remembered that the readers of *United Ireland* formed one of the most 'advanced' sections of Irish nationalism and that the paper itself had been bitterly hostile to Gladstone's 'coercion' administration of 1880–5.

form outlined by Gladstone.[1] The danger of a defeat on the second reading became plain; the opposition of Hartington and Chamberlain was known, and, with them, there would be defections from both the right and left wings of the liberal party.

When, on 10 May, Gladstone moved the second reading of the Home Rule Bill, Parnell and the party knew that they would have Ireland, and the whole Irish movement, behind them in giving Gladstone the fullest support. As each of the leading members of the party, in the following days of debate, rose to support the bill their speeches—unusually eloquent and moving—dwelt on one significant theme: the bill, if passed, would be a final settlement of the long strife between England and Ireland. Speakers on the other side dwelt, naturally, on Parnell's more seditious utterances in the past. Had he not said in America that he would not be satisfied 'till we have destroyed the last link that binds Ireland to England'?[2] Had he not, more recently and in Ireland, asserted the doctrine: 'No man has the right to set a boundary to the onward march of a nation. . . .'?[3] Whatever Parnell and others had said in the past, they were now explicit about the finality of their acceptance of Gladstonian home rule. Parnell replied plainly to a point-blank question:

> *Mr. E. Leatham*: Did the hon. member for Cork accept the bill as a final settlement of the question?
> *Mr. Parnell*: Yes.[4]

On the same day Dillon—whose speech, according to the *Freeman's Journal*, 'was looked forward to with the keenest anxiety' because of his reputation as 'one of the extreme men

---

[1] The parliamentary correspondent of the *Freeman's Journal* gave almost a daily bulletin on 'the chances'—hopeful in April, flickering into despondency after mid-May.

[2] Trevelyan made this point, referring to the New York paper *The Irish World* (23 Feb. 1880) as his source; Parnell said the statement was a 'calumny' and Healy asked, rather perfidiously, 'Is Ireland to be eternally condemned because of strong speeches by ephemeral representatives?' (*F.J.*, 26 May 1886).

[3] This point was raised by Chamberlain on 1 June; the remarks were quoted from ibid., 21 Jan. 1886. They are, of course, the words which now stand on Parnell's monument in O'Connell Street, Dublin.

[4] Ibid., 14 May 1886.

of the party'—spoke in the same sense: 'with the modifications suggested by [Parnell] we are honest in our intentions
to loyally accept this measure as a settlement of the Irish
question'.[1] The old fenian, J. F. X. O'Brien—sentenced in
May 1867 to be hanged, drawn, and quartered for treason—
said nationalist Ireland was ready to accept Gladstone's bill,
and end the strife of centuries. On the last day of the debate
Parnell formally reiterated his pledge: 'I accept this bill as a
final settlement of our national question and I believe the
Irish people will accept it.'[2] It was with reason that a liberal
leader, speaking to a meeting of his friends on the following
day, underlined the importance of this pledge: 'By running
the risk to his influence which such an announcement undoubtedly entails, Mr. Parnell gives us the very strongest
pledge that a man can. . . . We have never before seen an
Irish nationalist leader with Mr. Parnell's power and we
have never before had from an Irish leader such a pledge.'[3]

The eagerness of the nationalists to support Gladstone
was perhaps a measure of the opposition he was facing outside nationalist Ireland. Lord Randolph Churchill had
'played the Orange card'; the north-east of Ireland was in a
ferment;[4] the verdict of the English people—if a secession
from the liberals forced an election—seemed at best doubtful. Gladstone sounded possibilities of compromise. At a
meeting of all liberals favouring 'a legislative body in Dublin' he suggested two concessions: the reconsideration of
the clause excluding Irish members from Westminster, and

[1] Ibid.

[2] Ibid., 8 June 1886. These pledges were not the subject of a party decision
but could be taken as implementing the conditional acceptance agreed on at
the party meeting of 7 Apr.

[3] Ibid., 9 June 1886 (Morley). The pledge was afterwards criticized, but not
very seriously, by certain Irish leaders. Archbishop Walsh, in a published
interview, revealed that he was 'a little surprised' at the readiness with which
the pledge was given, and that he personally 'could not have been a party to
the giving of it' (ibid., 11 Aug. 1886). Michael Davitt about a year later said
that 'We have accepted, at least Mr. Parnell on behalf of Ireland has accepted,
Mr. Gladstone's home rule constitution although he and all the world knows
that many of us had cherished far higher ideals for the future of our country'
(ibid., 6 June 1887).

[4] On 13 May an advertisement appeared in the *Belfast News-Letter*:
'Wanted a few men thoroughly competent in military drill. . . . Apply . . .
Loyalist.'

the postponement, after the second reading, of further consideration of the bill until the autumn.[1]

The Irish were, on the whole, indifferent on the question
of 'retention' or 'exclusion' at Westminster[2]—which was a
debating point of Chamberlain's—but they were alarmed at
the idea of postponement. Parnell told Gladstone that he
might have to vote against the second reading, and confided
this also to William O'Brien: 'Parnell thinks the time is
come to call a meeting of the party to decide whether we
should not straightway throw out the bill.'[3] This seems,
however, to have been little more than a passing mood or
threat, for no meeting of the party was called until after the
defeat of the bill.[4] It is probable that the forces gathering
against Gladstone caused Parnell to drop the idea; if the bill
was to be wrecked in any case, it would be better not to
provide the excuse of 'Irish intransigence'.

On the day of the fateful division—7 June—Parnell made,
in support of Gladstone, 'one of the most masterly speeches
that ever fell from him'; a speech which, in Morley's
opinion, 'made even able disputants on either side look like
amateurs'.[5] Accepting Gladstone's bill, as we have seen, as
a final settlement, he said that Gladstonian home rule was
better practically, though not sentimentally, than Grattan's
parliament, since it provided for an executive responsible to
the Irish parliament. He insisted—for Chamberlain had put
out some ideas of partition—on the inclusion of Ulster: 'we
cannot give up a single Irishman.' The inclusion of Ulster
would lessen, not increase, the danger of religious discrimination. There were 'many liberal nationalists that do
not share the views of the Roman Catholic church in regard
to education', and, with Ulster in, there would be no risk of
the Catholic hierarchy using its power unfairly. A separate
legislature for Ulster—which Chamberlain and his friends
at one time envisaged—would leave 400,000 Protestants in

[1] Morley, *Gladstone*, iii. 334.
[2] Parnell disliked for practical reasons the idea of continued representation
at Westminster (Thorold, *Labouchere*, p. 301) but attached no theoretical importance to it, and indeed later accepted it.
[3] O'Brien's diary for 27 May 1886; *Evening Memories*, p. 125.
[4] Dillon MSS.: Minutes. The last meeting of the party during this session
was held on 14 May.          [5] Morley, *Gladstone*, iii. 337.

a minority in the rest of the country. It was doubtful whether Protestant unionists were in a majority in Ulster itself: the Ulster representation in parliament was, in majority, for home rule. If, on the other hand, the unionists took refuge in the north-east corner of Ulster, which Parnell defined as consisting of three counties, they would actually be abandoning a majority of Irish Protestants to their fate under a Dublin parliament.[1] A united Ireland would be a balanced one: 'The best form of government should be the resultant of what forces are in that country.' As regards Protection, he admitted that he hoped it could have been obtained as part of the tory home rule scheme. He knew there was no hope of obtaining it from the liberals, and he accepted the bill without it. He concluded by a glance at the alternative: 'there is no half-way house between the concession of legislative autonomy to Ireland and the disfranchisement of the country and her government as a crown colony'.

Eighty-five members—the whole Irish party with the exception of O'Shea—voted for the second reading, but liberal defections brought about its defeat, 341–311. Parliament dissolved on 25 June, and Britain faced, for the first time, a general election on the issue of home rule for Ireland.

Despite their disappointment at the defeat of the second reading, the nationalists had good reason to be satisfied with their progress. 'The bill', wrote the *Freeman's Journal* on the day after the division, 'is lost, but home rule triumphs.'[2] This was a little excessive, but it had a certain solid basis. The most famous Englishman of the day had taken up the cause of home rule, and had carried with him the bulk both of the

[1] Parnell's argument is, of course, here directed at English public opinion, which was believed to be anxious about the fate of Irish Protestants in general, rather than about Ulster in particular. Whether he fully understood the strong position of the Ulster unionists in their stronghold of north-east Ulster, and with their power to appeal to deep-rooted English emotions, may perhaps be doubted. He acted as if he believed that the status of Ireland could be decided by negotiation between the representatives of Irish and English majorities. This belief may, in the circumstances of the 1880's, have been right; it would be unsafe to say that an English majority led by Gladstone and an Irish majority led by Parnell could not—especially in the favourable climate of opinion created by the exposure, in 1889, of the forgeries published by *The Times* (below, Chap. VII)—have achieved a settlement which preserved Irish unity.      [2] *F.J.*, 8 June 1886.

prominent men and of the rank-and-file of his great party. The liberal party had then behind it a long record of success; the fact that it was now pledged to home rule seemed to augur the certain victory of that cause.

There was another implication of the liberal conversion which did not receive so much attention. This was that, if the liberals were pledged to home rule, the Irish home rule party was pledged to the liberals and its days of altogether independent action were over.

'Gladstone', wrote an historian quoted earlier, 'by embracing home rule, did at least restore the two-party system. In form and spirit the Irish remained a separate organisation, but in fact down to 1914 they were linked with the liberal party.'[1]

'For over a year', writes Chamberlain's biographer, in a retrospect from the defeat of the bill, 'in a manner almost unbelievable to-day—Salisbury and Churchill being Parnell's dependants first, Gladstone and Morley afterwards— the uncrowned king of Ireland had been a dictator in British politics. That phase was over.'[2]

[1] R. C. K. Ensor, *England 1870–1914*, p. 100.
[2] Garvin, *Chamberlain*, ii. 257.

# VII

## THE UNION OF HEARTS

She hears the ocean protesting against separation, but she hears the sea protesting against union. She follows therefore her physical destination when she protests against the two situations, both equally unnatural—separation and union.                                                    HENRY GRATTAN

### 1. *Foundations of the Liberal Alliance*

THE dissolution of parliament, following the defeat of Gladstone's bill, brought the question of home rule for Ireland before the British people for the first time. The Irish people had already given its verdict, and it was obvious that nothing had occurred to change it. The Parnellites were therefore free to devote most of their attention to helping the liberal party in England; they did this whole-heartedly. Gladstone, Ireland's saviour, was the subject of countless Irish speeches and articles, although few could match the incense of William O'Brien's phrase: 'a white old man with a face like a benediction and a voice like an Archangel's'.[1] Parnell himself, making his first appearances on English platforms, spoke again and again at liberal meetings, exalting the genius of 'the illustrious Englishman who towers head and shoulders over all living men . . . for whose equal as a statesman we have to search the pages of history in vain'.[2] The National League of Great Britain, branches of which had been, according to its president, T. P. O'Connor, 'committee rooms' for the tory candidates[3] in the general election of six months before, was now organizing the Irish voters for the liberal party. No manifesto was issued or needed—the Home Rule Bill itself was manifesto enough— but the executive instructed the branches, by circular, how best to help the liberal candidates.[4] It even appears that the

[1] *U.I.*, 12 June 1886.
[2] *F.J.*, 28 June 1886. In 1881 Gladstone had been, for Parnell, 'the masquerading knight errant'; in 1890 he was to be 'that unrivalled sophist'; such reversals are, however, the ordinary stuff of politics.
[3] Ibid., 4 June 1886.                              [4] Ibid., 17 June 1886.

Irish helped such candidates financially.[1] Throughout
Britain, Irish M.P.s, especially those whose own seats had
been uncontested, spoke on English platforms to allay English fears with assurances of the kind which Parnell himself
gave at Portsmouth in the first speech of this campaign:
'There is not the slightest risk or danger of separation.'[2]

England, however, chose to believe the contrary. The tory
party said that home rule meant separation[3] and England
voted tory in a strength which overwhelmed the liberal
majorities in Scotland and Wales and the home rule majority
in Ireland. The Irish vote, expected to turn the scales in
many English constituencies, failed to do so.[4] The final
result was that the unionists—tories and seceding liberals—
had 394; the liberals 191; the Irish party 85[5] making a
unionist majority of 118. Gladstone resigned on July 20
and Lord Salisbury again took office.

The new situation was a peculiarly trying one for the Irish
party. On the one hand, the liberal alliance, which alone
gave promise of an eventual victory of home rule, had to be
preserved; this pointed to a moderate policy, restraint of
language, and the curbing, as far as possible, of agrarian

[1] 'T. P. [O'Connor] has got a sum of £2000 he wants to spend on English
elections and asked me to arrange with Ashburnham that the sums given to
candidates should be given under cover of the British Home Rule Association': Diary of W. S. Blunt, 24 June 1886 (Blunt, *Land War in Ireland*, p. 155).

[2] *F.J.*, 26 June 1886.

[3] It was Lord Randolph Churchill in his election address on 19 June who
set the tone for the tory campaign against the bill: 'This design for the
separation of Ireland from Britain, this insane recurrence to heptarchical
arrangements, this trafficking with treason, this condonation of crime, this
exaltation of the disloyal, this abasement of the loyal, this desertion of our
Protestant co-religionists, this monstrous mixture of imbecility and extrava-
gance and political hysterics, better known as "the bill for the future government of Ireland".'

[4] 'The most remarkable fact of the struggle so far', wrote the London
correspondent of the *Freeman's Journal* on 4 July, 'has been the failure of the
Irish vote in the English constituencies.' If, as was generally believed, the
Irish vote, directed by the 'manifesto', had carried several English urban
constituencies for the tories in 1885, why should it not swing these constituencies back to the liberals in 1886? Certainly the Irish vote would have
been more solid for the party which it traditionally supported, and which
had now come out for home rule, than it ever could have been for the tories,
the traditional enemy. It seems probable, however, that in areas with a large
Irish vote there was also a large potential *anti-Irish* vote, which did not emerge
in 1885, when Ireland was not an issue, but declared itself in 1886.

[5] The strength of the party was later restored to 86.

violence. On the other hand, the prospect of about seven years of tory government, dashing the hope of immediate home rule, meant the removal, or at any rate enfeebling, of what had been the most effective check on the political and agrarian extremists. Political extremism was a less dangerous threat to the Parnellite compromise than agrarian extremism. In Ireland itself the political extremists were negligible, except as a latent force; two successive general elections had conclusively proved the ascendancy, in the whole area with nationalist traditions, of the party led by Parnell. But in America, source of almost all the financial strength of the movement, and of much of its importance in political strategy, the political dominance of Parnell was less certain. Had not American support dropped away after the Kilmainham treaty?[1] Might not the Irish-American activists again repudiate the parliamentary movement and demand violent action against British rule? Such a call to violence would be a blow in itself; if it were obeyed, it might be ruinous. Even a mere failure to support the Parnellite movement would be serious: if it could be said that 'Gladstone's home rule' was repudiated by the Irish Americans—of whom, in the tory mythology, Parnell was a mere puppet—there would be an argument that might keep Gladstone out of office indefinitely. The eyes of all political observers therefore turned anxiously to Chicago, where the annual convention of the Irish National League of America, due to open on 18 August, would show whether the Irish in America still followed Parnell. 'Without American support', wrote a contemporary, 'Mr. Parnell ceases to be a power and without the support of Mr. Parnell, Mr. Gladstone is helpless.'[2]

The Irish supporters of home rule sent a strong team to Chicago: three parliamentarians, led by one of the ablest, most loyal, and most eloquent of the Irish members, William O'Brien, and accompanied, as evidence of solidarity, by the best-known Irish leader outside parliament, Michael Davitt, famous and well loved among the Irish in America as the founder of the Land League.[3] From the moment the

---

[1] See Chap. IV, § 3.   [2] *The Globe* quoted in *I.T.*, 19 Aug. 1886.
[3] *Special Comm. Proc.*, v. 90; O'Brien, *Evening Memories*, pp. 140 sqq.; Davitt, *Fall of Feudalism*, p. 515.

proceedings were opened by Patrick Egan in a 'hall decorated with mottoes from Gladstone, Grattan and others', the issue was in no doubt.[1] The convention resolved: 'We heartily approve the course pursued by Mr. Parnell and his party associates in the House of Commons....' A telegram went to Parnell conveying 'the cordial endorsement of your policy by a united and harmonious convention'.[2] From such a body, this was a remarkable result, which seemed to justify the words of a Parnellite participant: 'Here was a great gathering of Irish-American citizens, men who had differences ... —but at the name of Parnell, those differences disappeared. . . . It is one of the most marvellous things which, I think, have occurred in the history of our country—the marvellous allegiance of the Irish race throughout the world to their leader.'[3]

This result, vital to the success of the constitutional movement, was not achieved by the Irish envoys without the aid of a certain element of ambiguity. At a private meeting before the public sessions, one of the Irish Americans had urged the advantages of terrorism as a weapon against tory rule. 'Even from the parliamentarian standpoint, it was adroitly suggested, worse might happen than extreme measures from an irresponsible left wing.'[4] O'Brien's reply

[1] Reuter dispatch in *I.T.*, 19 Aug. 1886.

[2] Ibid., 20 Aug. 1886.

[3] John Redmond, interviewed on his return to Dublin from Chicago (ibid., 4 Sept. 1886). It could be argued that there were other factors affecting the Chicago decision; that the Irish National League of America was of its nature a docile 'Kilmainhamite' body, and that the prestige of Gladstone, rather than that of Parnell, dominated the proceedings. It seems, however, that Irish-American opinion generally, including such indocile personalities as Alexander Sullivan, supported, no doubt with mental reservations, the Parnellite attitude on home rule. As for Gladstone's prestige, it is true that one observer recorded that his name, at this convention, received 'still louder and more prolonged cheering from the nationalists than they had accorded to their own leader' (ibid., 25 Aug.). There is no reason to doubt the genuineness of Gladstone's popularity among the Irish everywhere, but that popularity reposed in great part upon the fact that he was the author of a measure which the leader of the Irish people had declared to be acceptable. I believe that Redmond's interpretation, oratorically and rather ineptly expressed as it was, was basically the sound one.

[4] O'Brien, *Evening Memories*, pp. 141 sqq. Patrick Egan, Patrick Ford, and Alexander Sullivan were the Americans present at this talk. Davitt, O'Brien, and Redmond were the Irishmen present. It was Sullivan (who had a certain reputation as a practical terrorist) who made the suggestion recorded here.

—as he has recorded it—was that evictions would be re-sisted and that 'at any peril of our own liberties and lives the government of Ireland could and would be made impos-sible'. This firm but rather vague declaration satisfied Ford, and Davitt succeeded in persuading Sullivan and his friends to hold both their hands and their tongues. There were to be no more acts of Irish-American terrorism.[1]

The solidarity of the movement had been publicly and convincingly affirmed. Political extremism no longer repre-sented a direct threat to the projected Gladstonian settle-ment. But in averting the threat from the political extremists a guarantee had been given which intensified the agrarian threat. O'Brien's promise—which would hardly have been given by Parnell—was in effect a promise to carry on the land war, that permanent agrarian revolution which the parliamentarians had been trying, ever since 1882, to restrain.

Since the winter of 1885/6 the restraint imposed, although backed by the strong argument of imminent home rule, had been only partially successful. Resistance to eviction had broken out in many places, notably on the notoriously rack-rented Clanricarde estate in Galway. William O'Brien states that this resistance sprang up 'regardless of the earnest ex-postulations of the Irish party'.[2] We have seen[3] that Parnell not merely publicly disavowed this movement but took steps to discipline the National League branches which pub-licly associated themselves with it. There was naturally an undercurrent of discontent in the league itself. At a meeting of the central branch of the league as early as December 1885 a Mr. Roche of Woodford had raised the question of the Clanricarde evictions and Matt Harris, a Land League veteran, had confirmed that 'the most dreadful war was being carried on by the landlords against their tenantry all through the west'.[4] In January 1886 a meeting of the party, at which Parnell was not present, referred to an adjourned meeting the question of 'the deplorable state of Irish

---

[1] *Evening Memories*, loc. cit. The only voice publicly raised in 'extreme' criticism of the Gladstonian proposals was a relatively uninfluential one, that of John Finerty.

[2] *Evening Memories*, p. 157. O'Brien's account is confirmed by T. P. O'Con-nor (*Parnell Movement*, p. 298).

[3] Chap. VI, p. 165.    [4] *F.J.*, 23 Dec. 1885.

agriculture and the deplorable determination of the Irish landlords to enforce impossible rackrents by a system of wholesale eviction'; the adjourned meeting, however, with Parnel
in the chair, simply decided that 'members attending meetings in Ireland at present should be as guarded as possible ir
the language which they may use and that members shoulc
attend as few demonstrations as they can . . .'[1] In May
Davitt spoke to an English sympathizer about the 'great
dissatisfaction with the parliamentary party' about their
neglect of the land question, and in June Dillon informed
the same sympathizer that 'they' (apparently the party) 'had
thoroughly made up their minds not to postpone the land
question longer than for another six months. . . . In the case
of Salisbury's coming into office all were prepared for a new
land struggle.'[2] The general picture is one of a spontaneous
popular movement, temporarily held in check by its natural
leaders; the popular tory view that the subsequent agitation
was artificially worked up for political rather than agrarian
reasons will not stand examination.

Meanwhile, at home, weighty decisions were taken, which,
in effect, 'froze' Ireland's national demand into the form of
Gladstonian home rule. The 'new' Irish party—elected in
1886—at its first meeting, in the City Hall, Dublin, on
4 August, decided, on Dillon's proposal: 'That we reaffirm
the right of the Irish people to self-government and declare
that no measure offering less legislative or executive control
over Irish affairs than that contained in Mr. Gladstone's bill
can be accepted as a settlement of the Irish national question.'[3]

This resolution was, of course, essentially defensive of the
position gained, against criticism from Irish extremists and
encroachment from English liberals. The political unity of
the Irish people, from the extremists in America to the
bishops in Maynooth,[4] was a large and striking fact. This
unity, in support of the liberal alliance, had yet to meet a
severe test: the test of a winter on the land under a hostile
'landlord' government. Agricultural prices had fallen so

---

[1] Dillon MSS.: Minutes, 11 and 28 Jan. 1886. This caution was renewed in
April.                                    [2] Blunt, *Land War in Ireland*, pp. 96, 137.
[3] Dillon MSS.: Minutes.                 [4] Above, Chap. VI, p. 184.

sharply that (so the farmers held) even the judicial rents,
fixed by the land courts, could not be paid. The landlords
would get full support in evicting; the people, stiffened by
the Land League years, would certainly resist. What form
would the resistance take? Would it be led or opposed by
the constitutional leaders? And would not any form of
resistance be disruptive of the liberal alliance, and perhaps
of the very bases of the constitutional movement?

Such questions were in the air in the autumn of 1886. The
bishops themselves joined to a renewed declaration in favour
of home rule a demand for temporary measures to deal with
the land crisis, 'while awaiting permanent remedies in order
to prevent the outrages and disorders which they apprehend. . . .'[1] The question of the hour was no longer home
rule: it was again, as in 1880, the question of the land. But
the old question had to be answered in a new and unfamiliar
political context: a context of alliance with an English party
and respect for English public opinion.

## 2. *The Land Question Reopened*

Following the accustomed pattern, the first phase of the
organized land agitation was a parliamentary one. At its
first meeting on 4 August the new party passed a resolution
of its intention to warn the government of the impossibility
of paying the judicial rents;[2] this resolution was rightly seen
to be the opening of a new land campaign.[3]

Parnell himself was the rather reluctant leader in this
stage of the campaign. He told Morley that the rents could
not be paid and that 'if the country was to be kept quiet,
the Government would have to do something'. Morley
gathered that his wish for quiet was based on fear of successful coercion, and also of frightening away the liberals.
He wanted the next stage of the movement to be 'in the
largest sense political and not agrarian'.[4]

With the Woodford evictions, on the Clanricarde estate,
now in full swing,[5] there was little hope of evading the

[1] *I.T.*, 10 Sept. 1886.
[3] *I.T.*, 5 Aug. 1886.
[5] Above, p. 197.
[2] Dillon MSS.: Minutes.
[4] Morley, *Gladstone*, iii. 369.

agrarian question. Parnell's first action in the new session of parliament was to move an amendment to the Address,

> humbly to assure Her Majesty that we fear that owing to the heavy fall in prices of agricultural products, the greatest difficulty will be experienced during the coming winter by the Irish tenant farmers in the payment of their present rents and many will be unable to pay these rents: that numerous evictions, confiscating the rights vested in the tenants by the Land Act of 1881, causing widespread suffering and endangering the maintenance of social order, will be the result. . . . [1]

Parnell, introducing the amendment, was under no illusion as to its fate. 'We see what is coming', he said. 'We believe it will be coercion'. His speech was regarded even by hostile observers as 'striking and impressive';[2] its object, and the object of subsequent parliamentary action, was to make the land crisis known in England, and to prepare the minds of friendly Englishmen for the inevitable struggle of the winter. Meanwhile the preparations for the struggle itself were going on in Ireland.[3]

In the House, Parnell indicated the nature and the limitations of that coming struggle. 'Neither the Irish members nor the government had any control over the events which might occur in Ireland during the months of the winter.' He compared the existing situation with the crisis of the autumn of 1880, when the Compensation for Disturbance Bill had been rejected by the Lords, but—and it was an important qualification—'he desired that it should not be supposed that because he had done so, he was going again to lead such an agitation as took place in the winter of 1880'; he feared, however, a spontaneous movement. He asked for, and got,

---

[1] I.T., 25 Aug. 1886. The amendment also contained a clause objecting to any extension of land-purchase on the basis of the present rents.

[2] 'The House listened with profound attention and once or twice when the ministerialists laughed incredulously at his conclusions he, with a coolness and cleverness which were remarkable, turned the tables on them' (ibid., 25 Aug. 1886).

[3] 'The time had come', Harrington publicly informed the central branch of the National League on 24 Aug., 'when all the branches of the National League in the country should reorganize themselves and be ready to fight the battle of the tenants' (ibid., 26 Aug. 1886). This was of course a new departure; see above, p. 165, n 1.

time to discuss a measure of his own for staying evictions.[1] The essence of this measure, which was shown in draft to the liberal leaders[2] and which was supported by Gladstone,[3] was that the land court should have power to suspend eviction proceedings on payment of half the rent.[4] The defeat of the bill was, in a conservative House of Commons, inevitable, but it served its purpose as, on the part of the Irish leaders, a declaration of emergency.

After the end, on 24 September, of the parliamentary session, preparations for a winter land campaign were made, publicly and in terms designed to reassure, as far as possible, the new English friends of the Irish movement. Parnell wrote to the president of the Irish National League of America asking support for an anti-eviction fund, seeing 'the imminence of a trouble and peril which has seldom been equalled even in the troubled history of Ireland'; aid from America would 'assist in preserving for our movement that peaceable character which has enabled it to win the most recent and almost crowning triumph'.[5] This appeal was promptly answered. The similar appeal which was made concurrently in Ireland made it clear that what was intended was a fighting fund, not just a relief fund. 'The Irish subscriptions', Harrington explained to a meeting of the central branch of the National League, 'would be devoted to the evicted tenants in those localities where the tenants made the best fight.'[6]

### 3. The Plan of Campaign

There could be no longer any doubt that an organized land struggle was impending, and that this struggle would have to be sufficiently determined to command the support of the tenantry and sufficiently constitutional not to cause excessive alarm to the liberals. On 23 October *United Ireland*

[1] Ibid., 4 Sept. 1886. The government concession in allowing time for discussion was given, as Churchill made clear, in order to minimize obstruction on the estimates.

[2] Ibid., 11 Sept. 1886.     [3] Ibid., 21 Sept. 1886.

[4] There were two other clauses, one giving the court power to vary the judicial rent, and one admitting leaseholders to the benefits of the act, but the vital clause was that suspending evictions.

[5] Ibid., 28 Sept. 1886.     [6] Ibid., 29 Sept. 1886.

published a bold and ingenious plan which, despite many and severe trials, was to succeed well enough, over the next four years, in satisfying these difficult and conflicting conditions. The article, entitled 'A Plan of Campaign', was written, though not signed, by Timothy Harrington,[1] the secretary of the National League. Tenants on each estate were 'to consult together and decide by resolution on the amount of abatement they will demand'; should that abatement be refused, the proferred rent was to be handed over to a managing committee elected by the tenants themselves and used for the benefit of the evicted. National League branches might co-operate in bringing the tenants on each estate together, and the league itself should guarantee the Estate Fund, but the actual struggle was to be carried out not by the league but by the tenants on each estate. This procedure would make it more difficult, under the Coercion Act, which was now foreseen, to suppress the league. At the same time it gave the new movement an unofficial character, which should be helpful to the leadership of the parliamentary party in its dealings with the liberals.

Among the party leaders, Dillon and O'Brien, probably the most influential members after Parnell, put themselves at the head of the new campaign; they were followed by most of the newly elected members and by a few relatively senior members, notably T. D. Sullivan, the brothers Redmond, and—in the early period of the Plan—Sexton. Other leading members, notably Healy and Biggar, stood more aloof from the struggle as, for different reasons, did Davitt. Parnell's own position, at this date, was somewhat equivocal. He later publicly stated that he had not been consulted about it, and would not have approved it if he had been. 'One behind the scenes'—probably Harrington himself—informed R. Barry O'Brien that 'Parnell was dead against it . . . he meant to keep the movement on national as opposed to agrarian lines.'[2] This account is confirmed by the recollec-

---

[1] Davitt, *Fall of Feudalism*, p. 516; O'Brien, *Evening Memories*, p. 163. A recent, and otherwise admirable, biography of Gladstone contains a very misleading description of the well-organized movement which issued from this manifesto, as consisting of 'unauthorized associations of ignorant and desperate peasants' (Sir Philip Magnus, *Gladstone*, p. 367).

[2] *Parnell*, p. 416.

tions of Healy[1] and of Davitt, who states that Parnell 'severely criticized the tactical wisdom of the whole proceedings'.[2] William O'Brien, on the other hand, states that he informed Parnell of his plans and that Parnell, while himself unwilling to take part in any such agitation, indicated that he was 'in absolute agreement with the men who might be prepared to suffer the penalties, provided always that crime or any extreme courses that would paralyse Gladstone in his crusade in Britain could be avoided'.[3]

Wherever the truth may lie in this conflict of testimony, it is clear that Parnell did support the principle of an organized agrarian movement—his appeal for funds from America can have no other significance—and that he left the shaping of that movement to others, whose actions he kept himself free to criticize. There were no doubt subjective reasons for this attitude—ill-health, personal dislike of agrarian agitation, the influence of Mrs. O'Shea—but there were also objective political reasons in its favour. A basic contradiction existed between Irish public opinion and even friendly English public opinion on many matters, and notably on the Irish land system. English opinion regarded that system as an integral, although apparently not very satisfactory, part of the structure of laws which Englishmen venerated and upheld. It was permissible, in the English view, for Irishmen to seek from parliament changes in the land system; it was not permissible, however, for them to resist, or interfere with the working of, the existing laws, however much they might dislike them. Irishmen on the other hand—those Irishmen who had elected the eighty-six Parnellite members—regarded the land system as something altogether odious and immoral, imposed on them by force, and to be resisted and made null by almost any means that

[1] *Letters and Leaders*, i. 266. Healy's testimony should be treated with reserve. He says that Sexton urged him not to support the Plan, as Parnell had not been consulted. Sexton, however, publicly endorsed the Plan at meetings in Nov. 1886 (see, for example, *F.J.*, 29 Nov. 1886).

[2] *Fall of Feudalism*, pp. 517 sqq. Blunt, *Land war in Ireland*, p. 292, casts doubt on Davitt's account also and says 'I certainly never heard from Dillon or O'Brien or Davitt or anyone in Ireland a hint of Parnell's disapproval of the Plan till I read his speech at the Eighty Club in 1888.'

[3] *Evening Memories*, pp. 156–7. O'Brien's recollections are, at several points, the only source for a relatively 'extreme' position of Parnell.

might prove expedient. This contradiction made Irish co-operation with an English party a matter of peculiar difficulty. It was perhaps almost involuntarily, and in obedience to the gravitational pull of great political forces, that one section of the party drew towards Irish opinion, and the leadership of an agrarian movement, while the other kept in touch with the leaders of English opinion.[1]

Parnell himself certainly attached more value to the victory of home rule, and therefore to the liberal alliance, than he did to any agrarian successes. He also knew, however, from previous experience that a land crisis could not simply be shelved while home rule was being awaited. In short, the formula of a constitutionally minded leader with turbulent followers was one which admirably suited the general situation, from whatever elements of myth and reality that formula was compounded. In fact, as might be expected, the balance of these elements shifted with the development of the general situation itself.

The Plan rapidly gained the confidence of the people. Throughout the country, in the autumn and winter of 1886/7, mass-meetings, such as had not been seen in Ireland since the semi-revolutionary period of 1880–2, heard members of parliament explain the technique of the Plan. The mass-meetings were, of course, themselves part of the technique; their objects were to give the tenants a sense of their collective strength, to overawe potential land-grabbers, and to impress landlords with the wisdom of accepting a reasonable offer rather than face a long and costly struggle. The estates on which the Plan was actually 'put into operation' by the funding of the rent always remained few; the most famous at this period was that of Clanricarde, where the rents were 'collected' by three M.P.s—Dillon, Harris, and Sheehy.[2] Each such estate was a costly agrarian battlefield, in which the interests of both landlord and tenant suffered. Its benefits, from the tenant's point of view, were felt not on the actual

[1] The contrast is by no means a perfect one; Dillon, for example, was active both in the land movement and in the liberal campaign in England. His activities in England were, however, at a later stage, when tory coercion, Gladstone's eloquence, and the warming of the party spirit had created among Englishmen a greater sympathy with Ireland than ever existed before or since.
[2] *F.J.*, 29 Nov. 1886.

'rent-funded' estate but throughout the country, as landlords reflected on the consequences of pushing tenants too far.

The demonstrations increased in number, size, and enthusiasm throughout November—the month when the half-yearly rents became due. By the beginning of December the *Freeman's Journal* which in the beginning, in the absence of a sign from Parnell, had been cautious—'It may be workable or it may not'[1]—recognized the existence of a mass-movement: 'The Plan of Campaign advances rapidly. A few days ago it was a little driblet. To-day it is a great stream.'[2] By this time, still without any signal from their leader, more than a score of members had taken part—some of them several times—in Plan demonstrations.

It is certain that Parnell now—whatever his attitude had originally been—began to be concerned about the effect of the Plan, and of the fighting language of Plan demonstrations, on the liberal alliance. He asked John Morley on 7 December for his views and Morley told him: 'In England the effect is wholly bad.' Parnell explained that he had been very ill and had taken no part in the agitation. 'He was anxious to have it fully understood that the fixed point in his tactics is to maintain the alliance with the English liberals: He would send for a lieutenant and press for an immediate cessation of the violent speeches.'[3] The 'lieutenant'—William O'Brien—came and had an interview with his chief in a somewhat melodramatic setting, behind Greenwich Observatory. Parnell criticized the threatening language which had been used, especially by Dillon, and the tendency to widen the scope of the agitation. He pointed out that neither Irish priests—who were liable to rebuke from Rome—nor English nonconformists could be relied on to support the Plan. He stressed also the financial difficulties of a long-drawn-out struggle.[4] According to O'Brien, the result of

[1] 23 Oct. 1886. This editorial summarized the *United Ireland* scheme and stressed its legality.

[2] Ibid., 3 Dec. 1886. The growth of the movement was not quite so sudden as the phrase 'a few days' suggests.

[3] Morley, *Gladstone*, iii. 370. About the same time (9 Dec.) Morley wrote direct to Dillon cautioning him about the effect of some reckless language he had used at a demonstration in Castlerea (Dillon MSS. 10).

[4] O'Brien, *Evening Memories*, p. 183. O'Brien does not give the date of this conversation, but Morley's account places it between 7 and 12 Dec.

the conversation was that (except under extreme provocation) the campaign should be limited to those estates where
it was already in operation.[1] The agitation continued, un-
diminished in volume and supported by parliamentarians in
no less strength than before, up to the opening of parliament on 28 January 1887. In parliament Parnell exerted
himself to regain whatever might have been lost in liberal
support: a moderately worded amendment to the Address—
asserting that the remedy for Irish ills lay not in coercion but
in reform, and pointing out that landlords who had granted
reasonable abatements had not been troubled—was, though
defeated, yet successful in its object. The division on 11
February—352 against the amendment, 246 for it—showed
that the liberals had not been detached, by tory taunts or
Irish lawlessness, from their alliance with the Irish. Parnell
took advantage of the occasion to reveal to the House that
he himself was 'in no sense responsible for the Plan of
Campaign' and at the same time to ascribe to it, almost
certainly with justice, the reduction in the quarterly eviction
rate from 1,100 to 666.

So far, the Parnellites had succeeded remarkably well in
their new task of spanning the great gulf between Irish and
English public opinion. A new and great land agitation had
been set successfully in motion and kept free from crime—
unless boycotting was to be counted a crime—and the
liberal alliance had been preserved intact. A groan or two
from John Morley was a small price to pay for a movement
which almost halved evictions, kept rents down, and preserved the solidarity of the Irish people behind the constitutional leaders. The liberals were continuing not merely to
support the Irish party on Irish issues in parliament, but to
ask for the assistance of Irish members at by-elections in
England.[2] Despite marked internal contradictions, the home
rule movement was holding together very successfully in
the two islands.

---

[1] *Evening Memories*, p. 183. Morley states, however, that Parnell informed
him, on 12 Dec., that the understanding was, 'the meetings should be
dropped and the movement calmed as much as could be' (*Gladstone*, iii. 370).
Certainly the meetings were not dropped, and it is hardly likely that Parnell
gave such an undertaking, for which Morley had not asked.
[2] Minutes, 11 Mar. 1887 (by-election at St. Austell, Cornwall).

The tory government, hitherto on the defensive, now went over to the attack against the Plan. After the ritual preliminary of State trials and acquittals[1]—'demonstrating the inadequacy of the ordinary law'—the long-awaited Crimes Bill was introduced, on 28 March. The main clause of this measure empowered the lord lieutenant to suppress any associations and combinations 'illegal in their intent and operation': reflecting the general tory view that all Irish disorder was caused by the National League and its paid organizers. The effect of this measure was to consolidate, rather than divide, the home rule movement. To attack tory coercion was a congenial theme for the eloquence of Gladstone, Morley, and the other liberal leaders; Irish speakers—'especially men who had been in jail'[2]—were more than ever in demand at English liberal meetings. But the tories, led on this question by Arthur Balfour, their new chief secretary for Ireland, were not deterred by this consideration. The bill was forced through, with plentiful use of the closure; O'Brien was arrested on 15 April, Dillon 17 April; on 18 April *The Times* published a facsimile (later to become notorious) of a letter, purporting to be written by Parnell, condoning the murder of Under-secretary Burke in the Phoenix Park in May 1882. Parnell immediately denounced this as a 'felonious and bare-faced forgery', which *The Times* had produced to influence the coercion division.[3] This contention was perfectly correct, but it took two years to prove it; meanwhile the Crimes Bill was successfully passed, and the confidence of many liberal supporters must have been severely shaken.

The liberal leaders, however, with their superior knowledge of what Parnellism really represented, were not deceived by the forgeries. On 20 July, just as the Coercion Act was coming into force in Ireland, the liberal–Irish alliance was ostentatiously reaffirmed at a banquet in the National Liberal Club, attended by eighty liberal and fifty Irish members including Parnell. At this banquet—'one of the great historical landmarks of the home rule movement', according

---

[1] The members prosecuted this time on charges of intimidation, were William O'Brien, Dillon, Crilly, and Sheehy (*F.J.*, 9 Feb. 1887).

[2] Ibid., 5 Apr. 1887.　　　　　　　　　　　[3] Ibid., 19 Apr. 1887.

to the leading nationalist organ,[1] Parnell described the achievement of Gladstone: 'To bring two nations together, to stop agrarian crime and outrage, to banish feelings of revenge, to bring the Irish people to look to the law of the constitution and to parliamentary methods for the redress of their grievances, is a great gain and a great reward.' He urged upon the Irish people restraint in the face of coercion: 'they would be fools if by any word or by any acts or by any programme or any policies they were to endanger the position—I won't say endanger the position because that would be impossible—but to retard the progress of the great liberal party in their path of justice to Ireland'.[1]

In parliament Parnell had acted in the same spirit of moderation. The government's new Land Bill, introduced and passed in the Lords, came before the Commons on 11 July. It was a constructive measure, complementing the Coercion Bill on the usual pattern of 'coercion followed by conciliation.' It conceded a long-standing nationalist demand by bringing leaseholders within the benefits of the Act of 1881, and it gave county court judges power to grant stays of eviction, either spreading the tenant's debt or allowing him to go into bankruptcy. Dillon, in Parnell's absence, rejected the bill—except for the leaseholder clause —with 'contempt', but Parnell, speaking later, adopted a very different tone. As with previous land bills, his aim was not to obstruct the government, but to get the most workable possible measure: to quiet the country, not to inflame it. He urged the need for a provision for revising judicial rents and actually, by not dividing on the second reading, obtained a government amendment to that effect: no small thing to obtain from a party which believed, or affected to believe, that he was a revolutionary and the accomplice of murderers. He welcomed the amended bill as 'alleviating the present difficulty and troubles in Ireland'; and only regretted that, by not covering rent due in the following autumn, it would leave tenants to struggle 'under the Plan of Campaign and all other doubtful ways'.[2] Dillon, after his initial *écart*, followed his leader meekly enough, stressing that 'they were not anxious to prolong the agrarian contro-

[1] *F.J.*, 21 July 1887.                    [2] Ibid., 22 July 1887.

versy in Ireland', if only because they already found it hard to support the seven or eight hundred families dependent on Plan funds.[1]

With the passage of the Crimes Act, the initiative passed to the government, and the role of the Irish party became one of resistance and protest. Of protest above all, for the main effort both of liberals and Irish was now to make known in England both the brutality and the failure of tory rule in Ireland. The tory thesis was that 'resolute government', plus a progressive agrarian policy, would solve all Irish difficulties; the liberals were now committed to the proposition that only home rule would do so. As a pure theory, the tory proposition had some merit. Parnell himself is said to have admitted privately that 'it is a great mistake to suppose that Ireland cannot be governed by coercion'; at the same time giving the reason why coercion was not a practicable policy: '. . . under your English party system neither party can be trusted to make the policy continuous'.[2] In 1885 the tories had combined with the Parnellites against a liberal coercion measure. Now the liberals were to go to great lengths in attacking the principles and methods of tory coercion; liberal M.P.s were to join the suppressed National League, to attend at proclaimed meetings, to witness baton charges, and to lecture in England before audiences to which such themes were novel and rather shocking. Coercion, accompanied by such publicity, could hardly be successful. Neither the National League nor the Plan of Campaign was seriously damaged by Balfour's 'strong' administration; Balfour's biographer admits that in the winter of 1889/90— the last winter before the whole Parnellite movement fell asunder, for reasons which had nothing to do with coercion —'the Plan of Campaign was more formidably organized than ever'.[3] This was after two years of Balfour's administration.

From the point of view of long-term political strategy it would be hard to justify the tory coercion policy. Parnell,

---

[1] Ibid. This became an acute concern later on; see below, p. 228 (a).
[2] Asquith, *Fifty Years in Parliament*, i. 122. This conversation took place while Asquith was Parnell's Counsel before the Special Commission.
[3] Dugdale, *Balfour*, ii. 171.

indeed, claimed to see in that policy the workings of a far-sighted and sinister strategy of exasperation: 'You find [Ireland] peaceful and law-abiding . . .', he told the tories in the House. 'You are doing your best to drive her to despair.'[1] He feared that the aim of the tory strategy was to drive Ireland into rebellion, or sporadic violence, which would ruin the liberal alliance and the home rule movement. These words were probably intended as a caution to the Irish rather than as serious political analysis. The effect of coercion was not to destroy the constitutional movement, and open a path for terrorism, but, once again, to unite the people more solidly than ever behind the constitutional leaders whom the English government was persecuting. It is certain that a resounding Irish outrage would have been politically helpful to the tories, but their policy, of noisy and superficial repression, combined with agrarian conciliation, was not designed to elicit such events. It is hard, indeed, to see that the coercion policy did more than answer certain internal needs of the tory party. It satisfied those who feared a repetition of the 'Maamtrasna alliance' with the Irish rebels; it distracted attention from British domestic issues; it built up, at small expense, the personal reputation of Arthur Balfour as a strong man. It also—and this, as far as it goes, is its only long-term justification—made it possible to get the tory party as a whole in a suitable frame of mind to accept the large schemes of land purchase, which formed the real panacea of tory strategists on the Irish question.

On 19 July the lord lieutenant by his powers under the Crimes Act declared the National League to be a dangerous association 'which in parts of Ireland provokes and incites to acts of violence and intimidation'; on 24 July the clauses of the act, giving increased powers to resident magistrates and providing for prosecution in courts of summary jurisdiction in cases of intimidation and boycotting, were put into force in most areas of Ireland.

[1] *F.J.*, 14 Sept. 1887. The *Freeman's Journal*, some weeks later, editorially expressed a similar idea: 'They [the Government] have just three months of freedom from parliamentary control and in that brief period they must create in this country such a great outbreak of lawlessness as will enable them to appeal to British public opinion for support in their efforts to suppress disorder' (1 Nov. 1887).

There followed, and continued throughout our period, a cycle of defiant speeches, arrests, more speeches, more arrests, motions for the adjournment, liberal protests, tory sneers, proclaimed meetings, mob violence denied by the Parnellites, and police violence denied by the government. It would be unrewarding and unnecessary, as far as the history of the Irish party is concerned, to follow this conflict in detail. The party had two simple parts to play. Those members whose work had been mainly on what might be called 'the agrarian front' had to carry on their work as before, and be ready to go to jail. Those who had been mainly active on 'the liberal front' had to help the liberal party, in the House and in England, in the campaign of publicity against coercion. The second task presented no special difficulty; the first was more exacting. By the spring of 1889 twenty-four Irish members had served prison terms,[1] for such offences as attending at proclaimed meetings, advising tenants to resist eviction, publishing reports of meetings of suppressed league branches, &c. The sentences were mostly short—only O'Brien and Sheehy served sentences of longer than a year—but the conditions were severe; Balfour, unlike previous chief secretaries, long insisted that political prisoners should be treated as common criminals; they for their part refused to wear the prison clothing; the result, in winter, was punishing enough, especially on men who, like several of the Irish leaders, were of frail physique.[2]

The sufferings of the prisoners, although real, were not as great as Parnellite and liberal eloquence represented them to be. There was here an opportunity for ridicule, and ridicule, of which Balfour was considered a master, became the stock tory counter to the moral indignation of the liberals. A reference to 'William O'Brien's breeches' was considered a sufficient reply to any protest about prison conditions. The

[1] *Journal of the Home Rule Union*, 6 Mar. 1889. Only seven of those who served sentences were 'old'—pre-1885 members.

[2] The poor health—usually tuberculosis records—of several Irish leaders was at this time, for English politicians, a subject of inexhaustible amusement: public among the tories, private among the liberals. 'Patriotism does not seem to be a healthy occupation', wrote Harcourt to Morley in the autumn of 1887. 'What a lot they are!—Parnell, Dillon, O'Brien, Sexton—all interesting gentlemen in the last stages of debility; only T. P. O'Connor seems in rude health and he is not a patriot' (Gardiner, *Harcourt*, ii. 49).

tactics of certain members, in avoiding arrest as long as possible in order to prolong the agitation, aroused laughter both in Ireland and in England. One member, Pyne, cheered all hearts by enduring a siege in Lisfinny Castle, serenaded by his admiring constituents with brass-bands and fife-and-drum bands: 'Mr. Pyne who was lowered down by a rope and a pulley until he came within about fifteen or twenty feet of the ground, was received with tremendous cheers.'[1]

The coercion struggle had, however, a grimmer aspect. Very early on, the police fired on a crowd at Mitchelstown; three men were killed and a coroner's jury returned a verdict of wilful murder against the district inspector of the R.I.C. and five named policemen.[2] When Balfour refused an inquiry, Gladstone campaigned in England against the lawlessness of the Irish executive. Backed by such authority, 'Remember Mitchelstown' became a watchword to which Balfour's irony did not provide an effective answer. When John Mandeville, co-prisoner of William O'Brien in Tullamore Jail, was stripped of his clothes and left naked in his cell,[3] it was possible for the chief secretary to treat the matter in a light tone. But when Mandeville died within a few months of his release,[4] it was not so easy for the chief secretary, in the face of liberal indignation, to satisfy the middle-class conscience of England that the death had nothing to do with prison treatment.

In political terms, Balfour coercion was sufficiently severe to enable the liberal party to alarm a considerable sector of English public opinion, and not sufficiently severe either to stop the agitation in Ireland or to provoke violent counter-measures. It represented the kind of attack which the constitutional nationalist movement was best fitted to withstand and repel, and it made co-operation easier between Irish and liberals. When, early in 1888, Lord Ripon and John Morley arrived in Dublin as 'standard-bearers of the Great Old Chief',[5] and received the freedom of the city, the occasion was made a demonstration both of Ireland's friend-

---

[1] *F.J.*, 21 Sept. 1887. Davitt spoke contemptuously of the 'hide-and-go-seek policy' of attempting to avoid arrest (ibid., 21 Nov. 1887).
[2] Ibid., 13 Oct. 1887.                    [3] Ibid., 24 Nov. 1887.
[4] Ibid., 10 July 1888.                    [5] Ibid., 2 Feb. 1888.

ship for the liberals and of the thoroughly constitutional character of the nationalist movement; at the Mansion House banquet in honour of the new freemen the toast to the Queen was honoured. Shortly afterwards, in the House of Commons, Parnell summed up the progress which the Irish movement had made away from its revolutionary past. 'For one who favoured parliamentary agitation'—when he entered public life—'there were 9 or 10 who looked to violence and revolution as the true means of saving Ireland. . . . I think you may reverse those figures now.'[1]

The parliamentary flank of the movement now seemed well secured, and the agrarian flank could withstand indefinitely the assaults of Balfour's police; for police cannot break a boycott, and the boycott was the heart not merely of the Plan of Campaign but of the whole national-agrarian system. At this heart, from a not altogether unexpected quarter, a heavy blow was now aimed.

### 4. The Church and the Plan

When the Plan of Campaign had first come into operation, the two most influential churchmen in Ireland had considered its morality and decided in its favour. Archbishop Walsh, indeed, had at first some qualms and 'privately conveyed to Harrington his apprehension regarding its moral justification'.[2] He found on examination, however, and informed the press, that the Plan was morally justifiable, in view of the 'dual ownership' which existed in Irish land 'since the Land Act of 1881'.[3] At the same time he reminded his audience that the bishops were the custodians of the moral boundaries of the agitation, and a great latent political power: 'a single vigorous letter from the Archbishop of Cashel broke the back of the no-rent manifesto'.[4] Dr. Croke himself was not so queasy and thought it sufficient, in a letter to Dr. Walsh, to justify the Plan on the ground that

---

[1] *F.J.*, 14 Feb. 1888.     [2] Walsh, *Archbishop Walsh*, p. 237.
[3] Interview with *Pall Mall Gazette*, 2 Dec. 1886.
[4] Ibid. The reference to the manifesto was one of those edifying but slightly misleading historical retrospects to which both Dr. Walsh and Dr. Croke were addicted.

'the so-called law as expounded by Irish judges and enforced by British bayonets is simply no law at all'.[1] The
other Irish bishops were less vocal, but the general impression was that most of them either favoured the Plan or had
no views about it; those clergy—the great majority—who
were co-operating in the National League were usually
also active in the Plan.

There were, however, a few churchmen who, from the
start, strongly disapproved of the Plan. Pre-eminent among
these were Dr. Healy, then coadjutor-Bishop of Clonfert,
and Dr. O'Dwyer, Bishop of Limerick, widely regarded as
unionists or 'castle bishops'. When Archbishop Walsh had
declared in favour of the Plan, Dr. Healy wrote to Rome, to
the Prefect of Propaganda, denouncing both the Plan and
the archbishop and declaring that 'boycotting almost everywhere obtains, especially in the south and west and terrifies
everybody, even the bishops themselves and the priests who
hardly venture to absent themselves from the meetings of
the National League'.[2]

Moved apparently by such complaints, the Holy See
decided to send a representative, Mgr. Persico, to investigate the situation in Ireland.[3] His visit was embarrassing to
nationalists, and especially to nationalist bishops, from the
start. Archbishop Walsh had to deny the rumour that the
mission had been abandoned because of his opposition.
Knowing what he knew of the mission's object, he said, he
could not possibly oppose it; the rumours had been put out

[1] Walsh, *Archbishop Walsh*, p. 245. A few months later Dr. Croke caused
serious offence both in Rome and among the senior clergy in Ireland by
advocating or appearing to advocate a general strike against taxation. In
extricating himself from this position he incurred for a time a certain loss of
dignity and political prestige (ibid., pp. 269–74; *F.J.*, 8 Mar. 1887).

[2] Rev. P. J. Joyce, *John Healy, Archbishop of Tuam*, p. 139.

[3] Nationalists, remembering the Errington mission and the condemnation
of the Parnell tribute, used to assert that the Persico mission was brought
about by British government intrigue. In this connexion an unpublished
letter to John Dillon from an apparently well-informed Irish Franciscan
resident in Rome is of interest. The mission, wrote this correspondent, was
prompted *from Ireland*, by letters 'from some Irish bishops, many Irish
ecclesiastics and a great number of Irish Catholic laymen. As far as I know,
the government did not interfere directly . . .' (Dillon MSS. V, letter dated
14 July 1890, from Fr. David Fleming, O.S.F.). The word 'directly' is, of
course, important. It is not probable that the Irish administration was unaware of the action of the various 'castle bishops' and 'castle Catholics'.

'to shake the confidence of the Irish people in their Chief Pastor'.[1]

Persico came in July 1887 and heard both sides. Archbishop Walsh gave him the nationalist point of view under four heads: the political movement was 'not revolutionary but thoroughly constitutional'; the land movement was 'not communistic' but in favour of fair rents; there was a complete absence of crime; these satisfactory aspects were 'the result mainly of guidance of the movement by the bishops and priests'.[2] Persico, however, seems to have been more impressed by what he heard on the other side.[3] Even during his mission a number of Irish priests were requested, at his instance, 'to act with the greatest caution and moderation' and to keep themselves outside the reach of the Crimes Act.[4]

Persico returned to Rome and a few months afterwards the blow fell. The Congregation of the Holy Office addressed to the Irish bishops a circular, dated 20 April 1888, condemning both the Plan and boycotting:

In disputes between letters and holders of farms in Ireland, is it lawful to have recourse to those means known as the *Plan of Campaign* and Boycotting? . . . their Eminences having long and maturely weighed the matter unanimously replied: *In the negative.*

Our Holy Father confirmed and approved this reply on Wednesday the 18th of the present month.

Your lordship will therefore prudently but effectively admonish the clergy and people in reference to this matter.[5]

It was made known that this decision had been reached on three main grounds: that it was unlawful to break contracts freely entered into; that the land courts were available if

[1] *F.J.*, 28 June 1887. The rumours were put out by the Dublin *Evening Mail*, which took a mischievous interest in the mission from start to finish.

[2] Walsh to Manning, 8 July 1887 (Walsh, *Archbishop Walsh*, p. 290).

[3] At least one member of the junior clergy was critical of his seniors on this matter: 'The nationalist bishops, most of them, did not act as they might and ought have done. . . . They ought to have called in the most capable exponents of our views and *compelled* Persico to listen to them. But they did not. Dr. Walsh and Dr. Croke were almost *alone*' (Dillon MSS., V: letter dated 6 May 1888 from Fr. Kennedy, Newmarket, Co. Cork).

[4] Dillon MSS., V: copy letter of 29 Nov. 1887 from the secretary of the Bishop of Killaloe to a Fr. Glynn.

[5] Walsh, *Archbishop Walsh*, p. 331.

rents were unfair; that the Plan funds were extorted by boycotting, a means contrary to justice and charity.[1]

The Roman circular threw many nationalists into consternation. True, it was not the first time that Rome had intervened against the sense of the Irish nationalist-agrarian movement, but this intervention was far more serious than the last. The so-called 'De Parnellio' letter, fruit of the Errington mission,[2] forbade the clergy to participate in National League activities and in the Parnell tribute collection: matters not of vital importance. But the new circular was not a mere matter of ecclesiastical discipline: it was a pronouncement, approved by the pope himself, in the sphere of morals, where every Catholic, lay or clerical, accepted the papal authority as final. And it struck not at some minor aspect of the Irish movement, but at the whole current organization of the agrarian struggle—the Plan of Campaign—and at the one great principle, of the boycott, which gave the organized farmers all their power.

The first, and natural, instinct of some important nationalists was to drop the Plan of Campaign. The *Freeman's Journal* editorial on the day the news was published is full of preparations for retreat. The Plan was 'a mere incident in the agitation . . . no part of the programme of the National League . . . always an open question . . . a moot point'. As for boycotting it was 'diminishing'. However, it was for the bishops to give a lead: 'The Irish people will receive the decree of the Pope or the Propaganda with respect the most profound. They will await the propounding of it by the prelates whom they love and trust as ever heretofore with anxiety but with courage.' The editorial also expressed confidence in 'the great national movement led by Mr. Parnell and his fellows of the Irish parliamentary party' and ended with some not very appropriate remarks about nailing colours to the mast.[3]

The prelates whom the Irish people loved and trusted— and the *Freeman* was describing a class of prelates rather than defining an attribute of prelates generally—differed in their initial reaction to the circular. Dr. Walsh wrote to

[1] *F.J.*, 27 Apr. 1888.                    [2] Above, Chap. III, p. 185.
[3] *F.J.*, 27 Apr. 1888.

Dr. Croke 'advising that it should be quietly accepted and that as far as possible all public discussions, especially in newspapers, should be avoided'.[1] Dr. Croke, however, seems to have been made of sterner stuff. William O'Brien has left an eye-witness description of that great archbishop, at dinner—'his purple-edged biretta planted as usual at the top of the massive brow, like a banner above a rampart'— receiving and reading out, to his guest (the chief exponent of the Plan), the Roman circular. O'Brien asked whether he should not leave. The bishop took a pinch of snuff. '"Mike," he said with a solemnity worthy of the Day of General Judgment, "Mike, kill another pig!"'[2]

The archbishop's ingenuity was as remarkable as his fortitude, for he now inspired a remarkable article, which undoubtedly saved the national movement a great deal of internal strife. This article, which appeared in the Irish papers the day after the publication (on 30 April) of the text of the circular, looked to the bishops for 'an authentic interpretation of this highly technical document', but drew the distinction between authority on doctrine and authority on fact: Irish Catholics would accept the decision if they could accept as correct the assumptions of fact which it contained; it did, actually, contain an incorrect assumption of fact 'because most land tenure in Ireland was not based on a simple relationship between letter and holder (*locator* and *conductor*) but on dual ownership, as established by the Act of 1881.[3]

So far, the lay leaders had made no public statement. Both O'Brien and Dillon, the leaders of the Plan, had, however, been in close touch with Dr. Croke, and the line taken in the *Freeman* article was substantially agreed on in advance between Dillon and Dr. Croke.[4] Immediately after the publication of that article had formed a theological shelter-

---

[1] Walsh, *Archbishop Walsh*, p. 333.

[2] O'Brien, *Evening Memories*, pp. 349–50.

[3] *F.J.*, 1 May 1888. Walsh (*Archbishop Walsh*, pp. 334–8) says that these views seem to have been in substance the views of Dr. Croke.

[4] 'We agreed with each other fully and the course determined on was to agree with the Inquisitors in condemning the Plan and boycotting when they were or are attended with the conditions referred to in the so-called "Decree"' (Croke to Walsh, 2 May 1888, describing a conversation with Dillon on 28 Apr. 1888: *Walsh*, p. 338).

belt, political leaders prepared to emerge. Dillon and Dr. Kenny suggested to O'Brien that a meeting of the Catholic members of parliament should be convened by Sexton, then lord mayor of Dublin.[1] Parnell agreed and the meeting was summoned for 17 May, at the Mansion House, Dublin.

Parnell himself was not, of course, to be present at the Mansion House meeting, but it was very soon made known that he too intended to speak on the question of the hour. The *Freeman's Journal* on 4 May forecast that Parnell, at the dinner of the Eighty Club—an important gathering of the liberal *élite* at which he had been invited to speak—would make 'one of the most important pronouncements which the leader of the Irish parliamentary party and the Irish people has ever addressed to his sympathizers and followers'. 'We believe', wrote a special correspondent, 'that it is Mr. Parnell's opinion that the agrarian movement in Ireland may be conducted with sufficient effectiveness without collision with the religious feelings . . . of the Irish people.' The *Irish Times* the next day added its unfriendly gloss: 'Mr. Parnell was not the author of the Plan. . . . He has now an opportunity of throwing it over.' The pope's decree, according to the writer, had 'forced the parliamentary party from the old and forbidden on to an entirely new and less startling track'.

Parnell's speech, when it came, on 8 May, in London, was different in two important particulars from what friend and foe had expected. He did not bow in any way to the circular and he did not order the dropping of the Plan. Of the circular he said that it was bound to be 'a disastrous failure' but that it was not his business to interfere with any line which his Catholic colleagues might take on it. As far as the Plan was concerned, he pointed out that he had been very ill when it was started; he would have advised against it, because of its bad effects on English public opinion. By the beginning of 1887 when he could speak, Dillon and O'Brien had been

---

[1] O'Brien's telegram (2 May 1888) to Dillon agreeing to this proposal is among the Dillon Papers. O'Brien in his memoirs (*Evening Memories*, p. 354) states that Parnell's consent to the summoning of this meeting was obtained *after* his Eighty Club speech (8 May), but this is an error. The letter, signed by 66 Irish Catholic M.P.'s asking for the meeting to be convened, and the letter from Sexton convening it for 17 May were published in the *Freeman's Journal* on 7 May.

under arrest and it was too late for him to disavow it.[1] He had, however, stipulated that neither the league nor the party should be identified with it, that it should be restricted to the estates where it was then in operation, and that there should be moderation in speech and action. These conditions had been generally kept. He believed that the Plan would have to be gradually replaced by 'a method of agrarian organization' which he had for some time been engaged in maturing. 'But we shall now have to wait.' He concluded by advising his countrymen to rely for their release on 'the great liberal party of England . . . men who have never ultimately been beaten'.[2]

Parnell's speech to the Eighty Club was, in the literal sense, a masterly one. No leader who was not immensely sure of his own prestige could have made such a speech; the leader who could make it, and evoke no public protest, might be pardoned if he thought himself thereafter to be almost omnipotent. In the Parnellite movement, from the beginning, there had been a left wing, mainly agrarian in character, and a right wing, mainly clerical in composition and associations. For long, Parnell had had, as we have seen, to manœuvre carefully between these two groups, assuring himself of the support of one before doing anything that could offend the other. He now, however, with consummate self-confidence, reached out and knocked their heads together, lightly but firmly. The coolness with which he treated the circular as a political irrelevancy was made the more effective by the criticisms, of a purely political nature, which he directed against the agrarian movement. No rhetoric against the circular could possibly have been so effective as his mild implication that, because of it, his decision to 'replace' the Plan would have to be deferred. Conversely, no ecclesiastical denunciation of the Plan could have been so effective as the Irish leader's declaration against it on political grounds. The whole speech was a reminder to Irishmen that the grand object of their movement was home rule, and that he alone—and not agrarian agitators or

---

[1] This was not the whole truth. As we have seen, it was in Dec. 1886, and to O'Brien himself, that Parnell expressed his reserves about the Plan.
[2] *F.J.*, 9 May 1888.

ecclesiastical theorists—decided the strategy necessary to achieve that end. The setting in which he spoke—the Eighty Club—was a reminder of the victory which his strategy had achieved in 1886, and of the fact that the hope of final victory rested on the alliance which he then had won.

The Eighty Club speech gave, according to the *Freeman's Journal*, 'unqualified satisfaction to the home rule party'.[1] Such was, indeed, the public response of a well-disciplined movement, but at heart the leaders of the Plan were angry and dismayed. These feelings, indeed, very nearly became public. William O'Brien wrote for *United Ireland* an emotional article protesting, but not rebelling, against Parnell's speech:

> ... At this moment we shall say no more than that the originators of the Plan of Campaign little dream, ten thousand times less [*sic*] of weakening his authority as the unquestionable head of the universal Irish church [*sic*]. ... Mr. Parnell has come to the conclusion that the Plan is a mistake and has taken a solemn occasion to state that as his responsible opinion and advice. ... We cannot honestly endorse Mr. Parnell's reasoning: we loyally and finally bow to his authoritative judgment. He is the only man living who has the right and the power to wound the Plan of Campaign in a fatal spot.[2]

This article never saw the light of day; it was suppressed by Dillon and Harrington, who feared that it would ruin the movement.[2] The most curious thing about this abortive gesture of protest is that it was, at the same time, an act of submission and an elevation of the leader's authority to absurd heights. The fact that, even so, the two other 'Plan' leaders felt it too rebellious to print, is ample proof of Par-

---

[1] 10 May 1888. It gave qualified satisfaction to some opponents of home rule. The *Morning Post* produced on this occasion (9 May) a fine example of the grudging tribute: 'Nor are we prepared to say that the single-hearted patriotism by which his friends maintain that he is animated can be called absolutely mythical.'

[2] The proof of this article is among the Dillon Papers. The envelope containing it is marked in John Dillon's hand: 'Proof of article telegraphed from London to *United Ireland* by William O'Brien on Wednesday, 9 May 1888. This article was stopped by Tim Harrington and by me. Had it been published it would have utterly ruined our movement and driven me and others out of public life (John Dillon, Wednesday night, 9 May 1888).'

nell's complete ascendancy over his party at this period. His 'Eighty Club' speech imposed a strain on the loyalty of many of his followers, but he had not miscalculated the capacity of that loyalty to bear such a strain.

Meanwhile, the ground was being prepared for the meeting of Catholic members to consider the decree. Archbishop Croke on 4 May advised firmness in challenging the facts, but that there should be no protest against papal interference in politics.[1] From Rome on 5 May Archbishop Walsh gave to Harrington more cautious and detailed advice: the first resolution should be that 'any political organization would be out of place in a Catholic country such as Ireland which would fail to receive not only with respect'—the word used by the *Freeman's Journal*—'but with profound submission, the teaching of the Holy See on a point of morals'; second that '*as questions have been raised as to the precise meaning and extent of the decree*, you await whatever instructions may be issued regarding it by the bishops'; third, 'you should impress earnestly on all nationalists the necessity of not attacking the Pope'. The archbishop also advised that the Plan of Campaign should be dropped 'as quietly as possible': he assumed—this was before the Eighty Club speech—'that Mr. Parnell would in no way incur the responsibility of advising the continuance (of the Plan) in face of the new state of things'.[2]

When this advice was given, one of the leading Catholic members had already publicly taken a very different line. Dillon, at a Plan demonstration in Kilmurray on 4 May, made short work of the circular: 'That document is not binding on the conscience of any Irishman at all'; it was merely 'advice on temporal matters from a quarter whose advice has not always been wise advice'.[3] This language, repeated at other demonstrations, gave more pleasure to Irish Protestants and English liberals than it did to the Catholic hierarchy. 'The proceedings at Drogheda yesterday', wrote the Dublin *Evening Mail* after one Dillon demonstration, 'would have gladdened the heart of poor old Luther'.[4]

---

[1] Blunt, *Land War in Ireland*, p. 426.
[2] Walsh, *Archbishop Walsh*, pp. 342–3.    [3] *F.J.*, 5 May 1888.
[4] *Evening Mail*, 8 May 1888. As for the liberals, the *Journal of the Home Rule*

At a meeting of the Irish bishops on 9 May it appears that Archbishop Croke had 'difficulty in preventing a censure being passed on Dillon'; he feared that his own attitude would be disavowed by the other bishops, should the Irish members at their meeting pass a resolution against papal interference.[1] Cardinal Manning also advised against the inclusion of any such resolution.[2]

The meeting at the Mansion House was attended by forty-one members—a good attendance for any meeting held outside the parliamentary session—and eighteen others afterwards subscribed the resolutions which it had passed.[3] These resolutions were of a very different character from what the party's episcopal friends had advised. It was resolved that the 'allegations of fact' in the circular were unfounded; that it was regrettable that the Holy Office should be silent about the perversion of justice by the executive in Ireland; that this silence would be misused by enemies of our religious and of our national cause; that 'the demand of the Irish people for agrarian reform and political liberty was necessary and just and conducted by modes of action and methods of organization that were legal and constitutional'; and finally that 'while unreservedly acknowledging as Catholics the spiritual jurisdiction of the Holy See, we, as guardians in common with our brother Irish representatives of other creeds, of those civil liberties which our Catholic forefathers have resolutely defended, feel bound solemnly to reassert that Irish Catholics can recognize no right in the Holy See to interfere with the Irish people in the management of their political affairs'.[4]

*Union* (May 1888) dwelt on what a 'sweet revenge' the tory intrigues at the Vatican, and the Irish reaction to them, afforded for the tory election cries of 'No Popery'.

[1] Blunt, *Land War*, p. 432.

[2] Leslie, *Manning*, p. 93; Blunt, *Land War*, p. 435.

[3] The only Catholic members of any prominence who neither attended nor subscribed the resolutions were Justin McCarthy, T. P. O'Connor—both of whom had, however, signed the requisition for the convening of the meeting—and J. J. O'Kelly. Neither O'Connor nor O'Kelly would have been taken very seriously in Ireland as Catholic spokesmen, and it is possible that they effaced themselves for that reason. McCarthy, however, and a few others may well have kept aloof from prudential reasons.

[4] *F.J.*, 18 May 1888. The summary given in Walsh's *Life of Archbishop Walsh* (pp. 349–50) of these resolutions is not reliable. The last and most

It would be hard to imagine a more thorough-going re-buff, not only to the intervention of the Holy Office but also to the advice of those archbishops who had been best disposed to the national cause. Yet the ecclesiastical reply was remarkably mild. Meeting at Clonliffe on 30 May—after a series of public 'monster demonstrations' had been held throughout the country in support of the Irish party's attitude—the archbishops and bishops of Ireland resolved that the circular 'was intended to affect the domain of morals alone and in no way to interfere with politics as such in this country'; that the Holy Father wished, not 'to injure our national movement' but to remove obstacles to its success; that 'hasty or irreverent language should be avoided', and finally that 'while expressing our deep and lasting gratitude to the leaders of the national movement for the signal ser-vices they have rendered to religion and country, we deem it our duty, at the same time, to remind them and our flocks, as we most emphatically do, that the Roman Pontiff has an inalienable and divine right to speak with authority on all questions appertaining to faith and morals'.[1] The gentle tone and vague substance of the Clonliffe resolutions encouraged the nationalists and disgusted their enemies. For the *Freeman's Journal* the resolutions were 'the Magna Charta' of the Irish people; for the tory *Evening Mail* they were 'a four-jointed subterfuge'.[2] But no one had any doubt as to their meaning: that the bishops as a whole neither would nor could enforce the circular. One bishop, indeed, O'Dwyer of Limerick, did declare 'the decree' binding, warned his flock against the Plan and boycotting, and re-ferred scornfully to 'that curious body the *conciliabulum* of laymen that sat on the Pope in Dublin'.[3] But the Bishop of

important resolution is condensed in such a manner as to leave out all mention both of civil liberties and of the existence of Irish representatives of other creeds.                                                            [2] *F.J.*, 31 May 1888.

[3] *F.J.*, 12 June 1888. The Bishop of Limerick was of course generally regarded as a 'castle bishop' and one of the 'wire-pullers' who had instigated the circular. O'Brien had publicly attacked him as 'an arrogant ecclesiastical official' at a demonstration in his own cathedral city. In a demonstration in Kildare on the same day Dillon had quaintly defended him: 'No word of dis-respect shall be heard against him. He has a right to his opinions. He is the supporter and the champion of rackrenting and landgrabbing in Ireland' (ibid., 28 May 1888).

Limerick had no influence over popular opinion and could restrain only his own clergy. Even when Leo XIII himself intervened with an encyclical letter,[1] condemning the excited meetings, the questioning of the decree, and the 'forced interpretations' of it and reiterating that 'the entire method of action whose employment We have forbidden is forbidden as altogether unlawful', his commands seem to have fallen on ears which were, if not deaf, at least singularly selective. The *Freeman's Journal* fastened on one phrase in the encyclical—'Let your people seek to advance their lawful interests by lawful means'—and described this, with an imbecility that was perhaps partly feigned, as 'the Pope's Plan of Campaign for the Irish people'.[1] Archbishop Walsh, receiving an address from the corporation of Dublin, on the very day on which the encyclical was published, dwelt on what the Pope had *not* condemned—the cause of Irish nationality—rather than on the actual words of the encyclical, and took occasion to praise the resolutions of the Irish party as 'honest and accurate' in substance, whatever might be said about their form and phraseology.[2]

The Plan of Campaign itself continued, on the lines which had been agreed between Parnell and O'Brien in December 1886, that is, on existing 'Plan' estates. Priests, in general, now kept clear of it, but the efforts of nationalist prelates to ensure, not even indeed that the Plan and boycotting should be dropped, but that they 'should not be mentioned publicly any more' were unsuccessful.[3] The real effects of

---

[1] *F.J.*, 16 July 1888.

[2] Ibid., 18 July 1888; Walsh, *Archbishop Walsh*, p. 369.

[3] John Dillon's diary (Dillon MSS.) has some interesting notes on this: '10 *October* 1888.—Croke said bishops were very much vexed and disturbed —some of their own priests having advocated the Plan of Campaign—and asked me whether it could not be arranged that the Plan and boycotting should not be mentioned publicly any more. 11 *October*—Have just seen Dr. Croke—satisfactory—all right about Plan.' The Plan continued to be defended publicly throughout the period. There were few mentions, on the nationalist side, of boycotting, but that system had, for years, been so universally understood in Ireland, that it was now part of the atmosphere. For the same reason, spectacular instances of boycotting, such as occurred in the Land League period, are not reported during the Plan of Campaign. Cardinal Manning's biographer asserts that: 'The papal rescript nipped that evil [the Plan and boycotting] in the bud. And its successful results showed once more that the Catholics of Ireland are sound at heart and far more attached to the

the circular were felt not in the agrarian but in the political sphere. The Irish party had gained immensely in prestige, by taking the opportunity offered to assert its exclusive right to speak for the Irish people in political matters. The firmness and unity with which the members had acted; the popular support they had received; their attitude of inpendence towards ecclesiastical friends and determined outspokenness against ecclesiastical enemies—these attributes could not fail to impress those who remembered 'the old days' of less than ten years ago, when the political influence of the representatives of Irish Catholic constituencies had been recognized as subordinate to that of the bishops. The prestige and unity of the party was generally regarded as, in the main, the work of Parnell and, had it not been for the implicit backing of Parnell's immense influence, the party could hardly have adopted the tone it did. At the same time, Parnell himself stood, as we have seen, somewhat above the battle. If his party had 'sat on the Pope'—to use the Bishop of Limerick's phrase—he alone could 'sit on' his party. If his party, in vindicating the principle of lay control in politics, relied on the prestige of his name, at the same time the bishops, desiring to moderate the agrarian campaign, relied on the inner conservatism of his political strategy.[1] He was not, at this time, popular[2] either with bishops or with 'campaigners', but he was necessary to both. His belief—which later events were to reveal—that he was the indispensable and unassailable master of his country, independent of party or clergy, must certainly have been strengthened, if it was not first implanted, by the episode of the pope's intervention.

Holy See and obedient to its decrees than were their political leaders' (Purcell, *Manning*, pp. 624–5). This assertion, so far as the 'successful results' of the papal intervention are concerned, runs counter to the evidence.

[1] 'Parnell's advice', wrote Archbishop Walsh to Cardinal Logue after the Eighty Club speech, 'will probably relieve us of all trouble as regards the Plan of Campaign' (Walsh, *Archbishop Walsh*, p. 353).

[2] Blunt, who enjoyed the confidence both of the nationalist bishops and of the chief 'campaigners' says that both groups knew about the O'Shea relationship and mentioned Parnell's name 'with scant respect'. He dwells also on the resentment caused by Parnell's inactivity during 1887–8 and by his Eighty Club speech (*Land War in Ireland*, p. 431).

## 5. *The Flowing Tide*

The great political feature of the closing years of the eighties was the evident drift of the electorate back to liberalism, and consequently to home rule. Irishmen followed the results of English by-elections with an interest never recorded before or since.[1] The Gladstonian slogan, 'The flowing tide is with us', was as popular among nationalists as among liberals, and was the basic theme of all Parnell's speeches. Despite Morley's fears, the cycle of coercion, resistance, and protest, which the Plan of Campaign had set in motion, seemed to strengthen rather than strain the liberal alliance. 'Balfour's criminals', the released coercion prisoners William O'Brien and T. D. Sullivan, with the English sympathizers, W. S. Blunt and Lady Anne Blunt, were entertained at a public banquet in the Free Trade Hall, Manchester, by a number of prominent liberals. It is true that, at this period, the liberal front-benchers seem to have held somewhat aloof from such marked demonstrations of unity. The liberal members who formed the various delegations which the Home Rule Union sent to Ireland during the coercion period were back-benchers, mostly of a radical tinge. For this section indeed the trouble with the Irish was that they were not lawless enough. Labouchere's paper, *Truth*, noting the 'marvellous self-restraint under cruel provocation' of the Irish, asked for 'a little more devil'.[2] On the Irish side, the anti-radical bitterness of 1884–5 seems to have been completely forgotten. William O'Brien spoke with Davitt at a rally in Trafalgar Square demanding the release of John Burns[3] and the party got a whip to support the same cause in the house.[4] The party acted with the radicals in support of Scotch miners' claims to shorter working hours.[5] Many speakers proclaimed their confidence in

[1] The *Freeman's Journal* at this time gave at least one leading article to each such by-election. On 20 Apr. 1888 it carried an analysis of by-elections since the general election, showing that there had been ten liberal gains as against one tory gain. [2] Quoted in *F.J.*, 26 Apr. 1888.

[3] Ibid., 21 Feb. 1888. See also Moody, 'Michael Davitt and the British Labour Movement, 1882–1906', *Transactions of the Royal Historical Society*, 5th ser., vol. 3, 1953; also above, Chap. II, pp. 62 sqq. [4] *F.J.*, 29 Feb. 1888.

[5] A special meeting of the party was held to meet the representatives of the miners and assure them of support (Dillon MSS.: Minutes, 11 Feb. 1887).

'the British masses' who would show themselves 'the true Unionists' by bringing Mr. Gladstone back to office.

This close co-operation was criticized, publicly on the right, and more or less privately on the left. Parnell, Davitt explained to the faithful McGhee, 'is practically a part of the Liberal party'.[1] The *Irish Times* constantly harped on the theme of 'absorption', and used it to explain Parnell's attitude to the Roman circular: 'The double aim of the Irish leader is now declared to be the alienation of the influence of the Pope and the absorption of the nationalist party into the party led by Mr. Gladstone.'[2] The taunts from the tory camp were ignored, but when Davitt, in September 1888, brought his criticisms partly into the open, he had to be answered. 'Most of the evils inflicted upon us by tory rule since 1886', Davitt claimed, 'are on account of the alliance between Mr. Gladstone's following and that of Mr. Parnell'.[3] He complained of the failure of the liberals to give effective support against coercion. It was necessary for one of the party whips, Deasy, to reassert the party's independence: 'They were still an independent party and they were not going to be fused with the English radicals or any other section of English politicians. He wished to emphasize this because there seemed to be an idea growing up in the country that the Irish party had given themselves over body and soul to the Gladstonian party.'[4] When Dillon, at the central branch of the National League, indicated his continued support of the liberals,[5] the incident was closed. The

---

[1] Davitt MS.: letter of 13 Apr. 1887. For Davitt's personal position see Moody, 'Michael Davitt and the British Labour Movement', pp. 65–66. In Keir Hardie's unsuccessful struggle for Mid-Lanark (Mar.–Apr. 1888) as independent labour candidate, Davitt backed Hardie, while Parnell and his party backed the successful liberal.                    [2] 7 May 1888.

[3] Speech at Knockaroo, 9 Sept. 1888. This intervention of Davitt's is discussed, in a spirit of self-criticism, in the *Journal of the Home Rule Union* (Oct. 1888).

[4] *F.J.*, 24 Sept. 1888. Deasy was speaking at a demonstration in Tullow. A. O'Connor, speaking on the same day at Maryborough, took rather the same line as Davitt: 'if they did not do their fighting for themselves the English liberal party would not do their fighting for them (hear, hear). It was nonsense to talk about embarrassing the liberal party (cheers).' O'Connor's remarks represented nothing more than a personal view; I know of no other case where a member of the party, at this time, spoke in such a way about the liberals.                    [5] *Nation*, 29 Sept. 1888.

question of the liberal alliance did not become a controversial issue in Ireland again until the final crisis of the Parnellite movement.

A memorandum of Gladstone's of a conversation with Parnell about this time (10 March 1888) sheds an interesting light on relations between the liberals and the Irish and also between the tories and the Irish. Gladstone suggested that the Irish tactic should be: 'To keep the administration of the coercion act in its details before the eyes of the country and of parliament by speeches and by statistics.' This point Parnell 'noted'. Gladstone then put the point that the Irish should 'remain detached and in a condition to accept a settlement from the tories'; to this Parnell replied that he 'expected nothing from the tories as long as they should feel that they could get on without concessions'. 'What course', asked Gladstone, 'should be taken if the [tory] government offers measures good in themselves but insufficient for a settlement? Accept without prejudice?' Parnell thought that 'the turning point lay in a Dublin parliament. He did not see what could be done short of this that would be worth taking, whereas if this could be had, even with insufficient powers it might be accepted.' 'I understood him', Gladstone noted, 'to mean "might be accepted as a beginning"'. To Gladstone's next suggestion, that the government's non-Irish legislation should not, in general, be opposed by the Irish, Parnell agreed, and he also agreed with Gladstone's idea, that 'the American Union' might be considered as a constitutional 'groundwork' for an eventual settlement. Parnell did not 'wholly repel even the idea of [Imperial] parliamentary intervention to stop extreme and violent proceedings in Dublin [after home rule]'. On the whole Parnell was 'extremely moderate and reasonable', 'very conservative', and Gladstone even feared that his political energies 'were somewhat abated by his physical condition'.[1]

The 'liberal' flank of the movement was still secure, but the agrarian flank was now again causing some concern to the leaders. The Plan of Campaign was in difficulties, not for religious but for financial reasons. Expenditure on maintaining evicted tenants was running at about £20,000 a

[1] B.M., Gladstone Papers, 44773, ff. 48–49.

year; existing funds—in the autumn of 1888—were sufficient to maintain that rate of expenditure for not more than
a year and, without the sanction of Parnell's name, it was
thought to be impossible to raise new funds on a sufficient
scale.[1] Failure to maintain the evicted 'Plan' tenants, would
of course be ruinous, not only to the Plan, but to the whole
movement. This dangerous situation came to a crisis in the
summer of 1889, when the Irish landlords formed themselves into a syndicate, headed by Smith-Barry of Cork, to
share the expense of evictions on 'Plan estates'. O'Brien
pointed out to Parnell that the strength of the landlords'
position was the result of Parnell's own insistence on limit-
ing the 'Plan', which was now in operation in only about
twenty estates, the tenants on which could easily be ruined
by the new syndicate.[2] Parnell agreed, in effect, to take over
the Plan of Campaign, to the extent of organizing the defence of the Plan tenants: 'to meet the new landlords'
combination by a counter-combination embracing the entire
strength of the Irish people and their representatives'.[3]

The announcement that such a combination—the Tenants'
League—would be formed, was welcomed both on the left
and on the right of the movement. The liberal *Daily News*
was pleased that the movement would be under Parnell's
guidance.[4] Davitt, in an interview, revealed that he was
partly responsible for this new start. The new organization
was set up by a unanimous resolution of the parliamentary
party: 'That the members of the Irish parliamentary party
declare that it is imperatively necessary that the tenant farmers of Ireland should be invited to combine themselves
against their attempted extermination by the landlord

---

[1] Dillon MSS.: Dillon's diary, 28 Oct. 1888: 'Received from Ginnell this morning summary of Plan expenditure to 26 October. Shows that we have now 312 tenants and 92 labourers in our grant-list. The monthly expenditure in grants alone is £1,261.2.0. That means an expenditure of over £20,000 a year—all items included.' 5 Nov.: 'We [William O'Brien and himself] both agreed that if Parnell maintains attitude he has—for the last year—we could not see how it would be possible to maintain the fight over another year.' Dillon himself went to Australia at the beginning of 1889, partly in order to raise funds for the Plan (O'Brien, *Evening Memories*, p. 422).

[2] Ibid.; *F.J.*, 19 June 1889 (for the number of estates then involved in the Plan).

[3] *Evening Memories*, p. 422.      [4] 12 July 1889.

conspiracy'.[1] A committee of the party, under Parnell's
guidance, drew up the draft constitution of the new league,[2]
and the party itself, at a special public meeting in the Mansion
House, ratified the constitution, formally established the
Tenants' Defence Association, as it was now called, and
elected a council, consisting of fourteen members of the
party and Davitt.[3] The objects of the new association were
defined by Parnell in an open letter to Sexton. They were:
to protect tenants 'threatened by the landlord conspiracy';
to assert the principle of freedom of speech and public
meeting and also the freedom of 'combination and organization as possessed by English trade unions'. The last two
objects were little more than declarations symptomatic of
the greater concern for liberal and radical opinion which
Parnell, no doubt with Davitt's approval, was now import-
ing into the agrarian side of the movement. The serious aim
was to raise funds to provide for the tenants already evicted
and the many more who were now likely to be evicted.

The association—or rather the drive for funds—was
launched by a series of county conventions, each attended
by several—usually four or five—members of the party,
many clergy, representatives of local bodies, and the local
branches of the National League. Each convention resolved
on a levy of threepence in the pound on the poor law valuation of each member and appointed 'the priests and delegates in this convention' as 'secretaries and treasurers to the
Defence Association in their respective areas'.[4] The first of
these conventions was held at Thurles on 28 October, and
the series continued throughout November and December
and well into January. All the conventions—except those
in the unionist north-east—seem to have been well attended
and well organized. The association was immensely successful in providing a formula within which priests,
'campaigners', and orthodox Parnellites could work together
—with the entire approval of the English liberals—for the

[1] Minutes, 15 July 1889.                    [2] Ibid., 22 July 1889.
[3] I.T., 25 Oct. 1889. The draft constitution itself provided that the council
should be elected by the members; apparently the party as founder-members
were able to ratify the constitution and elect the first council.
[4] Report of the Wexford Convention; F.J., 6 Nov. 1889. The resolution
became a stock one.

benefit of the tenants. The financial results of the conventions are an index of the soundness of the idea which had
prompted it. When the fund was closed, in May 1890, it
stood at £61,000,[1] a very substantial figure for a national
collection in the Ireland of those days, and one which provided over a reasonable period to come for the needs of the
tenants already evicted. It was true that many new burdens
were to be added; the 'landlords' syndicate' was a formidable
foe, and eviction notices rained down on the Smith-Barry
and Ponsonby tenants. The shop-keepers of Tipperary refused to pay their rents to the 'leader of the eviction syndicate' and a new shopping centre, the famous town of 'New
Tipperary' was built for them and solemnly opened, on
13 April 1890, in the presence of twenty-five members of the
Irish party.[2] This campaign was inevitably costly and it
became necessary to reopen the fund. The new fund had
been open for only a few weeks and had realized less than
£6,000,[3] when, at the end of November 1890, the divorce
crisis and the debate on Parnell's leadership tore asunder
both the political and the agrarian movements and utterly
destroyed that framework of unity which was the essential
structure of the 'tenants' defence' idea.

'Tenants' defence' was, indeed, Parnell's last contribution
—and might have proved one of the most important—to the
strange and effective political system which had evolved,
with his aid, from Davitt's 'new departure'. The two basic
elements in that system—the agrarian and political demands
—still remained, but the balance between them, and the
methods of relating them, had widely altered. In the Land
League days the agrarian element had been dominant; with
the National League, the political element had acquired a
definite predominance, but under forms which did not posit
a dictatorship of the parliamentary party. Now, however, it

---

[1] Ibid., 26 May 1890.
[2] Ibid., 14 Apr. 1890. O'Brien (*Evening Memories*, p. 431 sqq.) says that this
development, which he rightly describes as a most remarkable early case of
the 'sympathetic strike', was a spontaneous movement of the local people
themselves. He, however, made himself its chief propagandist and it is generally associated with his name.
[3] It stood at £5,600 on 29 Nov. (*F.J.*). The fund had been re-opened by
resolution of the party, on 6 Oct. (Minutes; ibid., 7 Oct. 1890).

was 'the party' which dictated the form which the agrarian organization should take, which drafted its constitution, and which elected, from the party itself, its directing body. The fact that Davitt, though not a member of the party, accepted election to such a directing body, stresses rather than mitigates the dictatorship of the party. The founder of the Land League was accepting a necessarily subordinate position within a movement entirely controlled by the parliamentarians whom he had long distrusted and disliked. He was forced to recognize the fact that they, under Parnell's supreme command, were masters of nationalist Ireland.

Both the success of the 'tenants' defence' movement and its unqualified and undisguised 'parliamentarian' character reflect not alone the shrewd political judgement of Parnell, but the decisive influence of his prestige; a prestige which now, for extraneous reasons, had reached a new great peak. *The Times* charges had recoiled on the tory party. The forger, Richard Pigott, had been unmasked, in February 1889, before the Special Commission[1] which parliament—refusing Parnell's request for a select committee of the House to investigate the specific charge of condoning murder—had established to examine the whole case made by *The Times*, in its series of articles 'Parnellism and Crime'. The dramatic collapse of Pigott in the witness-box, once Parnell's counsel had elicited from him, in spelling a series of words, the fatal spelling mistake, 'hesitency', which had occurred in one of the forged Parnell letters; Pigott's flight to Madrid; his suicide there—these were events which not merely cleared Parnell's name, but did so with the greatest possible fanfare of publicity, and the maximum effect upon public opinion.[1] Parnell was not merely cleared, but exalted by the tide of popular emotion. It was, unusually, a tide that swept in the same direction through both countries. For the Irish—many of whom would certainly have thought little the worse of him if he had been proved to be the author of the letters— Parnell appeared now as the symbol of their country, slandered by Englishmen before the world. For the English

---

[1] *F.J.*, 2 Mar. 1889, &c. The story of the Special Commission and the Pigott forgeries has been so often told that I have not felt it necessary to cite sources in the narrative of the public events.

liberals, who had long had to bear taunts about 'associating with murderers', it was another 'sweet revenge' to be able to talk, more unanswerably, about 'the forger and his pay-masters'. When Parnell first appeared in the House, after the collapse of Pigott, the entire opposition, including Gladstone and all the ex-ministers, rose to their feet and cheered him for some minutes: a demonstration of feeling which he characteristically ignored. Even those liberals who had been most chary about the 'Parnell alliance' now began to see it as a political asset rather than a liability. 'There need now be no further difficulty', wrote Harcourt to Gladstone, 'on the public recognition of our *solidarité* with Parnell in the interest of Home Rule.'[1] The public was given no chance to forget Pigott. The memory of that unhappy man was kept alive by the long-drawn-out anti-climactic proceedings of the Special Commission; by Parnell's action against *The Times*, which *The Times* settled with a payment of £5,000[2] and by the publication on 13 February 1890 of the Com-mission's report. The tories made the most of the Commis-sion's findings about the complicity of the Parnellites in illegal aspects—intimidation and boycotting—of the agra-rian struggle of 1880–2, but the general public in both countries had, all along, been interested only in the letters. The commission found that all the facsimile letters published by *The Times* were forgeries.

We have seen how Parnell, in this atmosphere of vindica-tion and enhanced prestige, was able to use the power of his name—without himself attending any meetings in Ire-land—to bring together the whole of nationalist Ireland, with the approval of liberal England, in one great and effective agrarian movement.

In the purely political sphere, he used this brighter nimbus of authority to make still more sacred and untouchable the principle of home rule, as defined in Gladstone's bill: neither more nor less. This was his theme, both for England and for Ireland. For Ireland—perhaps under the effect of per-sonal preoccupation—he made it sound almost revolutionary:

If our constitutional movement were to fail, if it became evident that we could not, by parliamentary action and continued

---

[1] Letter of 9 Mar. 1889: Gardiner, *Harcourt*, ii. 75.     [2] *F.J.*, 4 Feb. 1890.

representation at Westminster restore to Ireland the high privilege of self-government.... I for one would not continue to remain for 24 hours longer in the House of Commons at Westminster. ... The most advanced section of Irishmen as well as the least advanced have always understood that the parliamentary policy was to be a trial and that we did not ourselves believe in the possibility of maintaining for all time an incorruptible and independent Irish representation at Westminster.[1]

For English audiences the 'constitutional' aspect of the same policy was stressed in a formula closely resembling the classical doctrine of Mitchell Henry and the whigs. 'And if the armed hand of rebellion', Parnell assured the people of Edinburgh, 'after the concession of this great measure, were to be lifted against the authority of the Queen in Ireland, you could stamp out that rebellion as remorselessly with your power as you would a rebellion in the heart of Edinburgh. And you would be justified, in the measures you took, by the public opinion of the world.'[2]

[1] *F.J.*, 24 May 1889. Parnell was here accepting an address from the municipal bodies of Ireland. The speech is remarkably unlike any other of Parnell's utterances of this period; it was also the only important political speech he addressed to an Irish audience. He avoided all political or agrarian meetings in Ireland during this period and, on the rare occasions when he returned there, shut himself up in his house at Avondale. His political speeches were made either in the House or at liberal rallies in England and Scotland. Remarks about the difficulty of maintaining an independent and incorruptible party had not been heard for a long time—three years at least; they were, however, to become the war-cry of Parnell's supporters in the debates on the leadership (see Chap. IX). A tempting conjecture is that when, in May 1889, Parnell made these remarks—not specially called for by the occasion—he already knew that the divorce proceedings, long threatened, were at last going ahead. In support of this conjecture is the fact that on 19 May 1889—a few days before this speech—Mrs. Benjamin Wood, Mrs. O'Shea's wealthy aunt, had died. According to Mrs. O'Shea's own account (which there is no reason here to doubt) it was this lady's life, and Captain O'Shea's money benefits from it, which alone stood between him and the starting of divorce proceedings: 'There would have been no divorce case only that my poor aunt died' (Harrison, *Parnell Vindicated*, p. 127). The case itself was started at the end of 1889. I believe that the parts of this speech which concerned the Irish representation at Westminster reflected not so much anxiety about the 'corruption' of the Irish representatives by the liberals, as anxiety about the effect of the divorce on Parnell's own leadership, He was preparing a possible line of counter-attack in advance. In any case, however, his speech on such an occasion would have been 'stronger' than his usual addresses to the 'corrupting' English liberals, which continued on the usual lines.

[2] *F.J.*, 22 July 1889. Parnell had just received the freedom of the city of Edinburgh,

In a private discussion with Gladstone at Hawarden not long afterwards, Parnell dispassionately considered possible modifications in an eventual home rule settlement on the land question; the question of inhibiting the Irish legislature from voting a law against contracts; the question of supremacy—a possible clause reserving the supremacy of the imperial parliament over Ireland in common with the rest of the empire; the question of delegation—should it be the imperial questions or the delegated powers which should be enumerated; judicial appointments—'for seven or ten years [after home rule] judges to be appointed from London'; Irish representation at Westminster to be retained in some form if public opinion should require it; finally, the distribution of the financial burden should be assessed by a commission.

Nothing could be more satisfactory [wrote Gladstone] than Parnell's conversation; full as I thought of good sense from beginning to end. . . . I did not press him to positive conclusions but learned pretty well the bearing of his mind and ascertained that, so far as I could judge, nothing like a crotchet or an irrational demand from his side was likely to interfere with the freedom of our deliberations when the proposition comes for practical steps. . . . We were quite agreed in thinking the main difficulty lies in determining the particular form in which Irish representation may have to be retained at Westminster.[1]

There could be no surer index of the overwhelming character of Parnell's authority than that speeches like that in Edinburgh—and he made several such speeches about this time—should have been accepted without a murmur by the nationalists of Ireland; just as the warnings about the dangers of corruption by the English liberal atmosphere had been accepted. Under so unquestioned a leadership, it seemed that the unity of the home rule movement could stand any degree of political strain.

This proposition was tested by the tories with two well-

[1] B.M., Gladstone Papers, 44773, f. 170, memoranda dated 18 Dec. 1889 (with the points to be discussed with Parnell) and 23 Dec. 1889 with the note of the actual discussion. This Hawarden conversation became a matter of acute controversy after the 'split', and Parnell's recollection of it—as made public by him—does not tally with Gladstone's account here. See below, Chap. IX, p. 307.

worn political devices: a conciliatory approach to Catholic education, and a 'good' Land Bill. Of the two the 'education' gesture was the more successful in producing symptoms of strain. At the end of August 1889 Balfour, replying to a question from Sexton, said that 'something ought to be done to give Roman Catholics higher education in Ireland'.[1] This was generally taken to be a cautiously worded promise of the Catholic university in Dublin, for which the Irish bishops were asking. Nothing could have been better calculated to cause friction between liberals and Parnellites. The radicals, who were now the closest allies of the Irish party, and even of the 'campaigners', were the traditional enemies of 'denominational education'; the Irish party, on the other hand, was, since 1884, the official mouthpiece of the Irish Catholic hierarchy's demands, which were, of course, for 'denominational education' in an uncompromising sense.[2] Parnell dealt firmly and sensibly with this difficulty. 'The radicals', he told a press correspondent, 'are perfectly entitled to object to it [a Catholic University Bill] and to defeat it if they can, but they are not entitled to expect us to refuse it'.[3] The radicals immediately became uneasy and there was talk of a new 'Carnarvon treaty' between tories and Parnellites.[4] The *Freeman's Journal*, speaking for the Irish party, found it necessary to refute these rumours: 'The liberals of Great Britain may rest assured that there is an end of overtures to the tories. Broken promises and deluded hopes— these have been the fruits of every tory and Irish alliance. . . . Every tie of gratitude, of mutual goodwill and mutual interest, binds us irrevocably to the liberal party, so long as they remain firm upon the principle of home rule.'[5] Members of the party were active behind the scenes in reassuring the liberal leaders.[6] But within the party itself there were

---

[1] *F.J.*, 29 Aug. 1889.
[2] Above, Chap. III, p. 116.     [3] *F.J.*, 29 Aug. 89.
[4] 'There is no doubt that a certain amount of friction had taken place between the Irish parliamentary party and the English radicals in the House of Commons . . . there was a suspicion that Mr. Parnell had made a bargain with Mr. Balfour' (*Journal of the Home Rule Union*, Oct. 1889). The *Journal* instances other actions of the Irish party which had alarmed radicals, but the education question was undoubtedly the main source of disquiet.     [5] *F.J.*, 6 Sept. 1889.
[6] The *Journal of the Home Rule Union*, in the article already quoted, mentions a series of interviews, involving Sexton, Harrington, Davitt, radical leaders,

now some signs of alarm and dissension. An Irish tory observer commented that '. . . if the Government did make this endeavour, it would infallibly breed a difference between the two sections of home rulers, the pious men and those mere politicians who don't care a snap of their fingers for Holy Church . . .'.[1] Events proceeded to justify this shrewd, although polemically expressed, opinion. T. D. Sullivan— certainly one of 'the pious men'—explained to the National League that he would support a Catholic University Bill, but found it necessary to add that 'if he saw a chance of defeating the tory government upon a question connected with a Catholic university he would vote against it (applause)'.[2] One of the most anti-clerical of the 'mere politicians', the veteran land leaguer Matt Harris, rebuked Sullivan for welcoming Balfour's overture in any way and objected to 'the secret and sinister manner in which this great measure of Catholic education had been introduced'.[3]

As a means of sowing dissension among the home rulers, the 'Catholic university' looked, at this stage, decidedly promising. Unfortunately for Balfour, however, the idea put as much strain upon the tories as it did upon their opponents. It alarmed the 'No Popery' section, to whom the victory of 1886 was, in large part, attributed. Balfour capitulated, and explained, in a letter to the secretary of the Scottish Protestant Alliance, that he had never really meant to propose a Catholic university.[4] Healy expressed the feelings of that section of the party which was—at this time—most friendly with the radicals: 'I trust that those with whom the Government have been bargaining in high places will consider themselves sold. . . . [The Irish party will resist] every attempt to govern Ireland through Rome.'[5]

and, finally, Gladstone and Parnell, and states that these interviews cleared away all the doubts of the liberals.

[1] *Evening Mail*, 10 Sept. 1889.            [2] *F.J.*, 11 Sept. 1889.
[3] Ibid., 16 Sept. 1889. William O'Brien (*Evening Memories*, p. 355), recalls that, at the meeting of the Catholic members of the party, to consider the pope's condemnation of the Plan of Campaign and boycotting, it was Matt Harris who, when others hesitated, opened the proceedings with the words: 'Well, Mr Chairman, I suppose we have nothing to do here but to pass two resolutions—one to endorse the Plan of Campaign and one to endorse boycotting.'        [4] *Evening Mail*, 24 Sept. 1889.
[5] *F.J.*, 25 Sept. 1889. Healy was probably referring to the Bishop of

With his Land Bill, Balfour was, from the point of view of political tactics, no more fortunate. Introduced on 24 March 1890, it was a large measure of land purchase, providing for advances up to a total of £33 million, and decorated with attractive provisions for the relief of the 'congested districts' in the west, and for labourers' cottages. Parnell described it immediately as 'absurd and objectionable',[1] intended to induce the tenants to buy out their holdings at a price based on the current excessive rents; he revealed that his decision to oppose it had been taken after consultation with the liberal leaders.[2] In opposing it, on the second reading (21 April), his basic case was that a revision of judicial rents, downwards by 30 per cent., should precede any measure of land purchase.[3] The second reading passed—3 May—with the Irish and liberals voting against it, but the bill was withdrawn shortly afterwards—10 July—with the promise that it would be reintroduced in the autumn. After its withdrawal, Parnell made it clear that an improved measure would have his support, although he knew that his friends 'would prefer to fight it out'. He would protect the Plan tenants to the end but believed that suggestions for 'terminating this turmoil' on the Plan estates[4] would be welcome. Balfour congratulated him on the 'moderation' of these remarks, but might have been less happy about them had he been aware that they gave equal satisfaction to the left, or 'Plan', wing of the nationalist party, because of their public pledge to protect the Plan tenants.[5]

Between the general election of 1886 and the autumn of 1890, the Irish party, and the whole movement under its leadership, had successfully encountered a remarkable series of threats, and had emerged stronger than ever from each

Limerick. Archbishop Walsh later denied the 'painful suggestion' of a 'barter' to which 'the only conceivable parties' would be the Irish bishops (*F.J.*, 6 Dec. 1889).                                    [1] Ibid., 25 Mar. 1890.
[2] Agency interview in ibid., 15 Apr. 1890.
[3] He also used the argument—almost comically insincere, coming from him—that the measure was unfair to the British taxpayer (ibid., 22 Apr. 1890).
[4] Ibid., 12 July 1890.
[5] 'On the whole I like it better than any other [speech] he has delivered on the subject of the Plan of Campaign. He has distinctly accepted responsibility for the present position [*sic*] of the tenants' (Dillon MSS.: Diary, 10 July 1890).

encounter. It had survived, successively, the dangers of American defection and agrarian unrest, of liberal qualms and tory coercion, of calumny and forgery, of papal condemnation and landlord syndicates, and, finally, of tory overtures. The party was united; the leader's supremacy was unquestioned; the liberal alliance seemed secure, and the liberals themselves were in the ascendant in England. It has been said that, if a dissolution had taken place in the first half of 1890 there can be little doubt that Gladstone would have been returned to power with an overwhelming home rule majority.[1] It seemed that T. D. Sullivan spoke justly when he said, at the birthday banquet which the party gave in Parnell's honour: 'our leader is on the very verge of accomplishing all he ever promised us.'[2]

But the leadership, on which both unity and effective alliance depended, was already open to question. In the last days of 1889 Captain O'Shea had filed a divorce suit against his wife Katherine and had named Parnell as co-respondent.

---

[1] R. C. K. Ensor, *England*, p. 182.       [2] *F.J.*, 30 June 1890.

# VIII

## THE LEADERSHIP AND THE MACHINE
### (1886–90)

*La hardiesse de l'esprit, qui est ce que l'on a nommé résolution, est plus nécessaire pour les grandes actions; et y a-t-il une action plus grande au monde que la conduite d'un parti? Celle d'une armée a, sans comparaison, moins de ressorts, celle d'un état en a davantage; mais les ressorts n'en sont, à beaucoup près, ni si fragiles ni si délicats.*    CARDINAL DE RETZ

### 1. *Leadership*

THE general elections of 1885 and 1886 had a dual effect on the political leadership of the Irish people. They enhanced the already very great prestige of Parnell and they created a new centre of prestige, and potential leadership, in the united party of which Parnell was the chairman. Parnell's chairmanship of the party dated from May 1880; his claim to the less tangible status of leader of the Irish people dated farther back, to the day when he had ousted Isaac Butt from the chairmanship of the Home Rule Confederation of Great Britain. Until the general election of 1885, Parnell's status as chairman of the Irish party had seemed clearly secondary to his status as national leader or 'uncrowned king'. The party itself had been divided, and, because of the fairly large whiggish or landlord element which remained even after the secession of Shaw's immediate following, it had had, as a party, little appeal to the Irish people. The test for each individual had been: for or against Parnell?

This, of course, was also the basic though unformulated test applied in the selection of the candidates who afterwards became the Irish parliamentary parties of 1885–6 and 1886–90. But, once these men had been selected and had taken the pledge to 'sit, act and vote' together, the situation became subtly different. The whig and landlord representatives had gone, and the average member of the party was now much nearer to the people not merely than the whigs had been but than Parnell himself was. It was permissible for the people to take pride—as well as in the achievements of their aristocratic champion—in the discipline, unity, courage, and often talent of men who spoke with accents like their own. This was a latent political force, the development of which must have been favoured both by the Galway election crisis and, much more, by the initiation of the Plan of Campaign. 'The party', it seemed, was now more advanced than Parnell on the land question, not more conservative as it had been before. It would have been surprising if 'the party' had not made an advance, also, in the people's affections.

Independently of the people's affections, however, it was almost a political necessity that those who were launching the Plan of Campaign should exalt the prestige of the party. Only with caution could they use Parnell's name, since the leader's attitude to the Plan was, at best, equivocal. They could not use, as a rallying cry, the names of the Plan's real leaders, O'Brien, Harrington, and Dillon, for to do so would create jealousy, suspicion, and dissension. But to stress 'the party' was a reassuring sign of unity and loyalty, and was justified, in appearance at least, by the number of members of the party on Plan demonstration platforms. The fact that the party, as such, had not taken up any position on the Plan of Campaign was probably known to relatively few.

The resolutions passed at these Plan demonstrations always mentioned Parnell—for it was necessary to be clear that there was no question of another Galway 'rebellion'— but they hardly ever failed to associate the party with his name. The most common formula was one which mentioned the leader first and then the party, but even within this formula there was a range of implicit difference. In 1886 the difference between the wording: 'confidence in our illustrious leader Charles Stewart Parnell and in the Irish parliamentary party',[1] and the wording 'confidence in the leadership of Mr. Parnell and the Irish parliamentary party'[2] cannot have seemed very important. Its importance was seen after the split of 1890, when Parnellites asserted that the position

---

[1] *F.J.*, 8 Nov. 1886. This meeting was at Cranford, Co. Wexford, and was attended by John Redmond.

[2] Ibid., 9 Nov. 1886. Meeting at Monasterevan, attended by Esmonde, Carew, and Leahy.

of the national leader was independent of the party and anti-Parnellites asserted that the party could 'depose' the leader. On the whole, the Plan resolutions—and the similar resolutions passed at popular demonstrations during the period 1886–90—tend, by a small margin, to support the 'constitutional' or later 'anti-Parnellite' view. In a spot-check of 26 early Plan meetings which passed 'confidence' resolutions, I find 11 resolutions tending to support the 'absolutist' or later Parnellite theory. Of these, 5 mention Parnell alone and the other 6, while mentioning the party, refer to Parnell as 'our leader' or 'the leader of the Irish people'. The remaining 17 resolutions are of confidence in 'Mr. Parnell and the party' or in 'the party led by Mr. Parnell'.[1]

The tendency for 'the party' to play an increasingly important part was accentuated by Parnell's frequent and prolonged spells of inactivity and inaccessibility, from the defeat of the Home Rule Bill up to the Special Commission hearings in 1889. Parnell's absences were in part due to ill-health; in part also they were, as we have seen, favoured by the double demands of the political situation. Unfortunately, there was a third factor: the O'Shea influence. Those politically close to Parnell explained, in public, his absence by ill-health but in private they spoke bitterly of 'the O'Sheas'. To the English sympathizer, W. S. Blunt, Davitt spoke of Parnell as 'a mere *laissez-faire* leader . . . idling at Captain O'Shea's', and added: 'it will go hard with him some day, for we are all getting very tired'.[2] Again and again the nationalist newspapers refer to his delicate health, his recent indisposition, or his convalescence.[3] The unionist press

[1] The considerable variety in the wording of these resolutions suggests that they were framed locally, in which case they would usually have been drafted by, or for, a clerical chairman. It is not improbable that many of the clergy, alarmed by the Galway election, would have wished to emphasize the importance of the united party, rather than the prestige of the national leader.

[2] Blunt, *Land War in Ireland*, p. 153: extract from diary for 24 June 1886. A few months later Davitt had a concrete instance of Parnell's *laissez-faire* to report to Dillon: 'I have come over [to London, before his American journey] on a fool's errand. Parnell wired me from *Hastings* yesterday: "Regret unable to go to London to-day". The business in America is not worth the trouble of a journey of 50 miles!. . . How long can this sort of thing be tolerated?' (Dillon MSS., 12: the letter is undated, but relates to the end of 1886).

[3] See, for example, *F.J.*, 2 May 1887, 14 May 1887, 11 June 1887—denying

hinted that there was really nothing very much the matter with his health[1] and *The Times* must have shaken nationalist circles considerably by the revelation that their leader was living at No. 112 Tressilian Road, Brackley, under the name of Mr. C. Preston.[2] His mysterious absences at unknown addresses distressed and alarmed his subordinates for whom it can have been small comfort to know that letters addressed to the leader at Avondale would 'always reach me in due course'.[3] Even the most loyal members of the inner circle were deeply dismayed. 'I am dreadfully afraid', wrote Harrington to Dillon 'that this condition of things will end in something very unpleasant.'[4]

If, among the inner circle, from 1886 to 1889, Parnell's prestige was considerably lessened by irritation and suspicion at his absences, it is inevitable that it should have been affected also, though to a much lesser extent, throughout the party as a whole. When, as often happened, the leader reprimanded members for slack attendance, they would hardly have been human if they had not reflected that their attendance was, at any rate, better than his. At a party meeting, during the Coercion Bill period, a proposal was made which, if passed, might have resulted in leadership by a committee—set up to 'discuss amendments' on the Coercion Bill.[5] Harrington opposed this suggestion 'in the absence of

a report that he was about to relinquish the leadership—11 Jan. 1888, 10 Feb. 1888, 14 Dec. 1889, 24 Feb. 1890.

[1] See, for example, *I.T.*, 21 Nov. 1887.

[2] The *Freeman's Journal* carried *The Times* report (26 Nov. 1887). *The Times* suggested that Parnell adopted the alias to hide from 'the extreme men' —a rather absurd idea which may have been suggested by Captain O'Shea.

[3] A letter from Parnell to Dillon, dated 11 Jan. 1888, acknowledges one from Dillon of 21 Dec. but states he did not receive an earlier letter: 'Where did you address it to? Letters sent to Avondale, also House of Commons, at any time during the year always reach me in due course' (Dillon MSS., 13).

[4] Ibid.: letter of 14 Jan. 1888. Harrington's comment arose from a wire he had sent Parnell asking to see him 'on very pressing business'— the financial condition of the Plan. Parnell had wired back: 'Better write as I am not much at home'. This comment is particularly interesting, since Harrington was the only member of the 'inner circle' who followed Parnell when the 'split'—the 'something very unpleasant' of his fears—actually occurred.

[5] Minutes, 3 May 1887: 'Mr. McCarthy (in chair) said the discussion was to consider the carrying on of the debates on the coercion bill to the greatest advantage without bringing on the closure. He suggested that the House should not be left during the discussion of the amendments to the coercion

Mr. Parnell' and no resolution was put to the meeting; no such proposal was ever made again during the Parnell period. The dissatisfaction which undoubtedly existed in the party at Parnell's *laissez-faire* did not find a voice until the crisis of 1890.

In the country generally, Parnell's prestige was enormous, and probably only slightly affected by his relative inaction during this period and by the growing importance of 'the party'. He had behind him the great achievement of the 'conversion' of Gladstone, and it was firmly believed, and proclaimed by all nationalist newspapers and orators, that, after the next general election, he and Gladstone together would win home rule for Ireland. Compared with that great fact and that great hope, it was a small matter that his voice was now seldom heard in the House of Commons and never —during this period—in Ireland. The people had heard something, during the Galway campaign, of an O'Shea scandal, but it does not appear that they believed in it, or connected it with his political inactivity. Rather, the danger was that they should ascribe his political inactivity to a

bill without the presence of one or two of the principal men of the party. A discussion then ensued, in which Mr. Chance, Mr. T. D. Sullivan, Mr. T. M. Healy, Mr. Dillon and Mr. A. O'Connor [joined] as to whether a committee should be appointed of the legal members of the party to draw up amendments and to leave the discussion of these technical amendments in their hands. Mr. T. Harrington said it would not be advisable to come to any fixed resolution to form a committee for the discussion of these amendments in the absence of Mr. Parnell. He thought the discussion which had taken place together with the remarks made by the chairman and Mr. Dillon were sufficient. No resolution was put to the meeting. Mr. Dillon finally suggested that, in the absence of Mr. Parnell, the vice-chairman arrange with two senior members of the party in the house to direct the debates whether they should be carried on [*sc.* by obstruction] or dropped after a certain amount of discussion.' These proceedings show something, I think, both of the extent and of the limits of the dissatisfaction with Parnell's leadership. It is clear that 'the party' as a whole would not have been consulted on such a matter of political tactics if there had not been not merely uneasiness but also dissensions among the inner circle. The names of those reported as joining in the discussion are significant: Healy had led the Galway rebellion, and Chance and Sullivan, his relatives, had supported him; Dillon had refused to support Parnell. Of these five speakers only A. O'Connor had been among the large majority which rallied to Parnell in the Galway crisis. The proposed 'legal committee' would have been dominated by Healy and his relatives, and the proceedings generally suggest that the 'Galway group' were trying to assert themselves again. But it was sufficient for one man to speak in Parnell's name and their manœuvre was so effectively stopped that they did not even put a resolution to the meeting.

political reason: his desire to put a brake on all further agrarian agitation. It would have been disastrous if the people had come to share Michael Davitt's view that 'Parnell does not want *any* energetic policy adopted. He is practically a part of the liberal party.'[1]

This danger might have become acute if Parnell had set his face firmly against any renewal of the land agitation. In fact, as we have seen, his 'inactivity' in the early months of the Plan of Campaign proved sound policy, and when he did act, with the Eighty Club speech, and later in establishing the Tenants' Defence Association, he acted as a master. A certain repose and economy characterized his leadership: when he spoke there was a weight of silence behind his words. He acted, in his sparse way, as one who knew that a leader does not just shape events: he must watch, often for long periods, to see how they would shape themselves if left alone. When he dealt, at the Eighty Club, with the agrarian agitation and also with the clerical opposition to it, he was able to be firm in security, for he was dealing with forces of which he had taken the measure. At the beginning of his career, in the semi-revolutionary days of the Land League, great events had followed closely, clashing against one another, and he had, as it were, to slip through brief interstices between them. Then, too, he had used inaction——or pseudo-action as in his famous 'Paris visit' of February 1881—as an historical vantage-point and then, too, he had interpreted events correctly enough to influence them successfully. His success had a momentum of its own; his political influence was now far greater than that of any agrarian leader, far greater even—in normal circumstances—than that of the clergy; the nationalist press was entirely his; he was the unquestioned leader of a great united party. The whole political complex of nationalist Ireland—the complex in which he had once so cautiously threaded his way—now seemed dominated by him. It was a domination which depended on a correct understanding of its own limits: in certain conditions some of the forces which made up Parnellism were not controllable. So Parnell, in watching rather than trying to hold back the great wave of agrarian

---

[1] Davitt MSS.: Davitt to McGhee, 13 Apr. 1887.

unrest that broke in the autumn of 1886, was certainly right. If, in the winter of 1890, he had been able to measure, with the same dispassionateness—and with the same opportunities of temporary neutrality—the forces then massed for his destruction, he would never have tried to hold the leadership and there would never have been a split.

Parnell was as unlike as possible to those politicians who believe in keeping 'in the public eye'. He was therefore apt to be regarded as a man of mystery: a condition which, for a political leader, has its advantages. But, more than that, it seems that the secretive life he was now leading, and perhaps his health, had made mystery, for him, something more than a political cloak. William O'Brien has left a record of his meeting with Parnell in December 1886, when he was sent for in order to impose limitations on the Plan of Campaign. They met by arrangement behind Greenwich Observatory in, as it happened, a fog:

After groping around helplessly . . . I suddenly came upon Parnell's figure emerging from the gloom in a guise so strange and with a face so ghastly that the effect could scarcely have been more startling if it was his ghost I met wandering in the eternal shades. He wore a gigantic fur cap, a shooting-jacket of rough tweed, a knitted woollen vest of bright scarlet and a pair of shooting or wading boots reaching to the thighs—a costume that could not well have looked more bizarre in a dreary London park if the object had been to attract and not to escape attention. But the overpowering fascination lay in the unearthly half-extinguished eyes flickering mournfully out of their deep caverns, the complexion of dead clay, the overgrown fair beard and the locks rolling down behind almost to his shoulders. It was the apparition of a poet plunged in some divine anguish or a mad scientist mourning over the fate of some forlorn invention.[1]

Even allowing for O'Brien's excitable imagination the description is sufficiently strange, and not easy to relate to other descriptions of Parnell, which stress his impassivity and formality. The present study is not a biography but an essay in political history and it might be thought that, in such an essay, O'Brien's colourful description should have no place. Yet the description, *whether it is true or not*, has

[1] W. O'Brien, *The Parnell of Real Life*, p. 125.

political significance. The apparition which O'Brien saw with 'overpowering fascination' was that of a romantic hero. To what extent the attributes of the hero were worn by Parnell, and to what extent they were supplied by the imagination of his lieutenant, is not, politically, very material. The point is that history had turned Parnell, in his own eyes and those of his followers, into a man of destiny. The figure that appeared to O'Brien in the fog behind the observatory was an incarnate myth.[1]

The false charges made by *The Times* against Parnell, and their dramatic collapse,[2] completed Parnell's stature as a romantic, semi-mythical, symbol of a wronged and fighting people. If the party itself had risen in prestige, and if it had in the past been partly doubtful of Parnell, there was nothing for it to do now but to put aside its doubts and lay its prestige at Parnell's feet:

*Resolving*: that we the Party look to the skill, courage and integrity of Mr. Parnell to be the great means in the future, as they have been in the past, to assist them in obtaining their rights. . . . Congratulating our leader Mr. Parnell upon the providential exposure of the plot for his destruction, a plot the most cowardly and nefarious ever formed against a political leader in the history of British political life. . . . Finally we once more reiterate in the name of our party and the united Irish race our ever-increasing confidence in the wisdom, honour and integrity of our great leader and our lasting gratitude for his priceless services to the Irish race and his imperishable part in Mr. Gladstone's great work of reconciliation between the two peoples.[3]

He had never seemed higher or more unshakeable than then, within nine months of utter ruin.

[1] That the 'Parnell legend' was a contemporary phenomenon, not merely a result of the final tragedy, is shown by an editorial which appeared in the nationalist daily some months before the split: 'There is no doubt that Mr. Parnell's mysterious appearances and disappearances have added to the popularity and even the parliamentary interest and gravity attaching to all that he says and does. . . . Mr. Parnell is one of those men with that strange atmosphere, that indefinable fascination, the nimbus by which those beings are surrounded that have the mighty force of will to control the minds of multitudes of their fellow men' (*F.J.*, 21 July 1890). The use of the quasi-magical word, 'fascination', in both this and O'Brien's narrative is interesting.

[2] Above, Chap. VII, p. 232.

[3] Minutes, 11 Feb. 1890. All these resolutions were passed unanimously amid loud and prolonged cheering.

## 2. *The Lieutenants*

We have seen[1] that in the period 1882–5 an informal 'caucus' grew up which controlled, in some important ways, the administration of the party, and that the members who figured in this group in 1885 were Healy, Sexton, J. J. O'Kelly, Dr. Kenny, Harrington, and William O'Brien. After the general election of 1885, and especially after that of 1886, this situation no longer held good, and that for several reasons, both political and personal. First the 'dual strategy', with one face to parliament and the other to the Plan of Campaign, led inevitably to a certain separation of functions. Harrington's time was now almost entirely devoted to the Plan and the National League; O'Brien was mainly taken up with the Plan and so was Dillon (who did not figure in the original group). Neither J. J. O'Kelly nor Dr. Kenny was as active as before, perhaps for personal reasons. As for Healy, Parnell, inevitably, disliked and distrusted him from the time of the Galway election, and probably from before that, and Parnell seems also to have distrusted Dillon.[2] Finally, both Healy and O'Brien were defeated in the general election of 1886 (as a result of being selected to fight marginal constituencies in Ulster) and did not find a seat again for several months.[3]

Now, instead of a relatively compact central group, we find two groups, rather loosely related. The leaders of the land agitation, and therefore the leaders who, next to Parnell, were the most prominent throughout the period, were Dillon and O'Brien. As a result of their efforts, and of the extent to which they were singled out for punishment by the authorities, their status rose, until in fame and popular esteem they were at least as far above their other colleagues (except Healy) as they were below Parnell.

On the purely parliamentary side, there were, first, two set committees. The less important of the two was now that

---

[1] Above, Chap. IV, § 4 (*b*).

[2] O'Brien (*Evening Memories*, p. 183) refers to two members of whom Parnell was then (Dec. 1886) 'beginning to entertain a settled distrust'. Although he does not name the members, his description of them makes it clear that they were Dillon and Healy.

[3] Healy in Feb. 1887 and O'Brien in July 1887.

consisting of the party's officers. With the exception of the chairman (Parnell) and vice-chairman (McCarthy) and of Biggar, the officers did not become in any sense, the leaders of the party—the 'cabinet' as was at one time expected—but remained its executive servants, diminishing in real importance after 1885.[1] However, their routine duties naturally increased with the great expansion of the party, and the number of whips and secretaries was increased from two to four of each. More important, from the beginning of 1886 onward, was the small group of trustees, consisting of Parnell, Biggar and McCarthy, which controlled the parliamentary fund and, hence, the payment of members' salaries. This group, as such, was not elected by, or responsible to, the party.[2] Neither it nor the group of 'officers' could be said to correspond to a cabinet, even as closely as the 'caucus' of 1882–5 had done. But a rather amorphous group did exist, out of which the members available at any time did form a sort of cabinet, or, more exactly, a committee of elders. Those who belonged to this, leaving Parnell aside, were: McCarthy and Biggar (trustees of the fund), Dillon, O'Brien, and Harrington (National League and Plan), and also Sexton, Healy, T. P. O'Connor, A. O'Connor, and Gray. When, as occasionally happened, it was necessary to select a committee to deputize for Parnell, in order to select a candidate or convene a meeting of the party, it was from this group that the committee was formed. But such powers were exercised with caution, not to say timidity; the candidate selected was 'subject to approval, or disapproval by Mr. Parnell' and the meeting was likely to adjourn until the leader could be present.[3]

In general, it may be said that, although the party itself,

[1] See above, Chap. IV, p. 144.
[2] N.L.I., Harrington MSS.: affidavits of Justin McCarthy, J. F. X. O'Brien, Timothy Harrington, and others. See below, p. 265.
[3] A meeting of the party was convened in June 1887 by Dillon, Biggar, Healy, and Sexton to decide, in Parnell's absence, on the course to adopt in the Coercion Bill debates. The matter was 'left open for consultation with Mr. Parnell' (Minutes, 17 June 1887). A candidate, Webb, was selected for Waterford, in Parnell's absence, and subject to his approval, by a committee consisting of McCarthy, O'Brien, Sexton, and T. P. O'Connor, with Condon and Carew (N.L.I., Harrington MSS., Miscellaneous; Clancy to Harrington, 21 Feb. 1890).

as a corporate entity, had risen in prestige, and although two of its members, Dillon and O'Brien, greatly increased their fame and popularity, yet the personal authority of the leader remained uncontested. The influential inner circle which functioned before the general election of 1885 failed to develop in coherence or responsibility, although the leader's frequent absences might have been expected to favour such a development. One reason for this is certainly the dispersal of the 'cabinet-rank' personalities between England and Ireland; another reason may be that Parnell himself took care to disperse subordinate authority—it is noticeable that no member of the group which we have defined as the 'inner circle' of 1882–5 was either an officer of the party (after 1885) or a trustee of the parliamentary fund. But a reason may also be found in the character of the 'lieutenants' themselves. Most of these, whether because of other interests—Gray, T. P. O'Connor, McCarthy—or peculiarities of character—Sexton and Biggar—were ineligible, even if their abilities were sufficient, for effective leadership. Three members only—Dillon, O'Brien, and Healy—had qualities of political leadership, but two of them would not, and the other could not, establish a position as deputy and successor of Parnell. It is worth while to glance briefly at the characters of these three men.

Of the three, and of all the followers of Parnell, John Dillon had the greatest qualifications for leadership. He was the son of the 1848 patriot, John Blake Dillon; he had played an important part in the land war; he was—a rather rare qualification—respected both in the House of Commons and in Ireland.[1] He was friendly with the leading nationalist clergy, but he was more outspoken than any other national leader in rejecting ecclesiastical attempts to hamper the popular movement. Fearlessness, extreme candour, and a deep consistent devotion to the Irish people—these were acknowledged to be his qualities. His abilities were more open to question: he had not the shrewdness of Healy, or Sexton's eloquence, or O'Brien's popular touch. But he had

[1] That class-conscious observer, Sir Henry Lucy, noted that Dillon was 'free by birth and social surroundings from the noisy vulgarity that made some of his colleagues insufferable' (*Diary of Eight Parliaments*, p. 315).

an independence, an originality of mind, that they had not. During the land war period it was Dillon, as we have seen, who on several occasions set a pace faster than Parnell desired. No other member of the party ever took the initiative away from Parnell as Dillon did in that period, and it is probable that Parnell did not easily forget it. He told William O'Brien of his distrust of Dillon,[1] and he seems also to have been concerned to block the possibility of Dillon becoming vice-chairman of the party.[2] Dillon's attitude towards the Kilmainham treaty and his neutrality in the Galway crisis must certainly have been main factors in Parnell's distrust of him. This distrust seems to have been particularly acute in the summer of 1887, when Parnell was recovering from one of his more serious bouts of illness. It was at this time that Parnell persuaded McCarthy to hold on to the vice-chairmanship and at this time also that Parnell publicly, though in veiled language, disavowed the lead which Dillon had been giving, in his absence, in obstructing the Coercion Bill.[3] Parnell's suspicions were probably strengthened by Dillon's initiative in having a meeting of the party summoned in his absence, to discuss this very question of parliamentary tactics on the Coercion Bill.[4]

Yet, in so far as Parnell distrusted Dillon he was confusing—as it is natural for leaders to do—independence with intrigue. Dillon's closest political associate was O'Brien, whose loyalty to Parnell was undoubted; he does not appear

[1] Above, p. 248, n. 2.

[2] In the summer of 1887, Parnell dissuaded McCarthy from resigning as vice-chairman, because of the effect of such a resignation on English public opinion, and because 'at this crisis . . . the party would be sure to elect as vice-chairman some extreme man' (Justin McCarthy to Mrs. Campbell Praed, July 1887: Campbell and Praed, *Our Book of Memories*, p. 115). The 'extreme man' whose candidature Parnell feared was almost certainly Dillon. O'Brien would have been the only other possibility, but Parnell regarded him with affection rather than suspicion.

[3] He expressed the hope that 'my honourable friends who have conducted the opposition to this bill up to the present moment with such skill, judgment, and ability . . . should select the points they wish to discuss' (*F.J.*, 8 June 1887). The London *Standard* commented, with some justice, that: 'The first act of the leader on his return to the field is to reverse publicly the course which was such a miracle of craft and cleverness.' In view of Parnell's well-known policy of exerting his moderate influence by private advice and not by public rebukes, these remarks seem to have been a deliberate humiliation of Dillon.                              [4] Above, p. 243, n. 5.

to have had, as Healy had, any faction of his own in the party at this time, or to have been interested in forming one. When, in May 1888, a potential crisis arose, as a result of Parnell's Eighty Club speech, it was O'Brien who half-revolted, and Dillon who, with Harrington, upheld Parnell's authority by suppressing O'Brien's editorial.[1] Dillon's melancholy, scrupulous, introspective temperament was neither that of a born leader nor that of a born henchman. He sometimes questioned the wisdom of Parnell's policies, sometimes refrained from following them, but he never systematically undermined them in order to set up his own. He saw, indeed, very clearly that he himself was 'lacking in intensity and continuity of purpose', and also that 'it is the possession of that in great degree which makes Parnell so thoroughly the master'.[2]

For much of the period we are considering, William O'Brien was the most popular leader in Ireland. Under the strain of Balfour coercion, as so often before, the Irish needed, in one man, an incarnate symbol of their resistance. Parnell, at this time, was quiescent and absent from Ireland; it took *The Times* and Pigott to restore to him his full value as a symbol. O'Brien, the most spirited of fighting journalists, the fieriest of popular orators, was the soul of the Plan of Campaign. His imprisonments and his vigorous and well-publicized fight for 'political' status in prison made much of the 'news' in the Plan struggle. His daring innovations in politics, from his 'invasion of Canada' to inform the Canadians of the Irish misdeeds of their viceroy, Lord Lansdowne, to the foundation of 'New Tipperary', struck all imaginations, although not with uniform emotions. His kindly but ebullient personality, and his great range of apparently impromptu eloquence, so sensitive in its oscillation from invective to pathos, so free and happy in its play of fantasy, leaped out to meet what was most generous in Irish minds. The cold mastery of Parnell, the dogged exhortations of Dillon, seemed foreign beside this archetype of the traditional Irish qualities and virtues. He really had them, as I think no Irish politician since his day has had them, and his audiences had at least enough sense of them

---

[1] Above, Chap. VII, p. 220.    [2] Dillon MSS.: Diary, 15 July 1890.

to warm to his fire. If the Irish had been choosing a leader simply to please themselves, it might well have been not Parnell and not Dillon, but O'Brien. In reality, however, the people chose a leader who could speak for them, and work for them, in England. The leader of the Irish, at that time, had to be a kind of plebiscitary ambassador, representing not a government but a nation which was sovereign only by volition. He was 'accredited' not to a court, but to the English House of Commons and his success depended in great part on a correct understanding and manipulation of the forces that moved that House. Not even William O'Brien's greatest admirers could imagine him in such a role. He did not possess the calculating mind, the 'instinct of combinations' of which Pareto speaks, which was essential for effective parliamentary leadership; nor, it must be said, did he possess the formal dignity which was necessary to sustain the quasi-ambassadorial character. He hated the House of Commons—those 'detestable precincts'[1]—and although his oratory in time impressed the House,[2] he never seems to have been treated with the respect that was given to Dillon and even Healy, not to speak of Parnell. The favourite tory joke during the Balfour period was 'William O'Brien's breeches'—a way of referring to his refusal to wear the prison dress. One who could, however unjustly, be treated as a butt, was not qualified to lead the Irish representation in parliament. William O'Brien seems to have recognized this himself and to have been content with his peculiar position as leader of the agitation in Ireland, subordinate to Parnell in the movement as a whole. He was more trusted, and it seems better liked, by Parnell, than any of the other really prominent members of the party, and Parnell enjoyed a considerable personal influence over him, which he sometimes put severely to the test.[3]

[1] He used the phrase in an open letter asking to be excused for a time from further parliamentary service (*F.J.*, 5 Feb. 1887).

[2] 'Mr. O'Brien is one of the large body of members, chiefly Irish, who have taught themselves parliamentary oratory at the expense of the House of Commons. When he took his seat for Mallow little more than five years ago [i.e. in 1883] he was even repulsively uncouth' (Lucy, *Salisbury Parliament*, p. 135). Lucy places him, in 1888, among 'the four orators in the house'.

[3] Notably in the Galway crisis and with the Eighty Club speech.

Of the leaders of the 'parliamentary', as distinct from the 'agrarian', wing of the party, by far the ablest and most eminent was T. M. Healy. He was the best debater, though not the best orator; the best legal mind; the best calculator of parliamentary chances. The 'instinct of combinations', in which O'Brien was so deficient, was to him the breath of life, and yet, like O'Brien, he had a popular touch. At the National League, as well as in political trials and in parliament, he drew eager listeners. His speech was always racy, often witty, sometimes scurrilous—as in the Galway campaign; he was moved as easily to tears as he was to some terrible and unforgivable gibe. Like O'Brien he had his share of traditional national characteristics, the supposed 'celtic' qualities. He surpassed Dillon in this respect as much as he surpassed O'Brien in parliamentary capacity, and he surpassed both of them in intellectual energy and in his grasp of political strategy. One other important qualification for leadership, which they both lacked, was his: the desire for power. His letters—especially his letters to his brother —are redolent of his feeling that he, being cleverer than Parnell, had a better right to be leader. It cannot be proved that in the crisis of 1885–6 he was aiming at ousting Parnell from power, or establishing himself in a dominant position, nominally subordinate to Parnell, but his line of action is hard to explain except on some such hypothesis. It is true that Biggar, as well as Healy, defied Parnell at Galway, and that no one suspects Biggar of aiming at personal power; but the cases are hardly comparable. Biggar was an unsophisticated person with strong and simple prejudices; he thought O'Shea an impossible candidate, who had to be stopped; there is no reason to believe that he was aware of the extent of the danger to home rule which was involved in his Galway foray. Healy, on the other hand, was a subtle tactician who thought of himself as the party's masterplanner at this time: he had given a friend in the liberal party to understand that Parnell was already no more than a nominal leader, who could be 'overlooked' by an inner circle of which he himself was one.[1] In his speeches at Galway he attempted to set up 'the party' as against Parnell's

[1] Above, Chap. VI, p. 175.

personal choice.[1] To hostile outside observers it seemed, at one point, as if Healy had scored a personal triumph over Parnell[2] and it is a fact that, if the O'Shea candidature had been dropped, it would have been a personal triumph for Healy. The principle vindicated would have been the supremacy of 'the party'; the beneficiaries of the principle would have been the 'inner circle'; and the dominant member of the inner circle would have been the victorious Healy, the tamer of Parnell. It is not to be supposed that these considerations escaped Healy's attention.

In the event, Healy was beaten, but it would be a mistake to believe that he never had a serious chance of success. If Dillon and O'Brien had followed his lead, it is hard to imagine how even Parnell's prestige, even the need for unity, could have carried the day. Dillon had, in fact, enough sympathy with Healy's point of view to refrain from rallying to Parnell, and it seems likely that, had it not been for O'Brien's frantic appeals, he might actually have followed Healy's example. The tone of the responses from many of those who did, at O'Brien's request, support Parnell, suggests that they might equally well have followed an O'Brien lead *against* Parnell. And even O'Brien himself, whose arguments rallied the majority of the party, felt it 'a bitter and scandalous alternative' that he should have to support the candidature of O'Shea. If O'Brien had been more interested in 'the party' and less concerned for the party's object—home rule—the Healy revolt might well have had a different result.

As it was, Healy, having tried his strength and failed, fell back to a less influential position than he had occupied in the period before the general election of 1885. He distinguished himself, as he could hardly fail to do, in the debates on the Home Rule Bill',[3] but then, in the general

---

[1] Above, Chap. VI, p. 179.      [2] Above, Chap. VI, p. 181.

[3] In an attack on Chamberlain during those debates he made a curious reference to his own leader: 'I do not know if ever I shall rise to the dignity of being a minister in an Irish parliament. But if I should happen to have a position of this kind under my honourable friend the member for the city of Cork [Parnell] and if I should want when I am leaving him to give him a very deadly stab I will take good care to imitate as closely as possible the action of the member for Birmingham' (*F.J.*, 10 Apr. 1886). Modern psychologists

election of 1886, a new misfortune befell him: he lost his seat in south Derry. It took several months and two resolutions of the party[1] before he managed to get another seat (north Longford, February 1887) and the months which intervened were decisively formative. O'Brien, who had also lost his seat, was devoting himself to the Plan of Campaign, but Healy had never been particularly interested in the purely agrarian side of the movement, and in any event can have felt little inclination to play second fiddle to the man who, at Galway, had done so much to defeat him.[2] His humiliation was emphasized by some of those who had exaggerated his influence in the Galway days. The *Irish Times*, foreseeing his return for some other constituency, foresaw also diminished influence: 'Mr. Healy will probably not occupy as peculiar a position as was expected, when he shall directly owe his seat to the special interference of Mr. Parnell on his behalf.'[3]

Shortly after his return to parliament and during Parnell's illness, he seems to have made, with some support from Dillon and others, an effort to reassert himself and build up again the power of an 'inner circle'.[4] The party, however, did not respond favourably and Healy does not seem to have sought any further trial of strength. Between 1887 and 1890 he was active in parliament and at the meetings of the central branch of the National League in Dublin, and, more rarely, at Plan meetings, but—since the main struggle was agrarian—he was much less prominent than O'Brien or

might well see in this language—so extraordinarily tactless within two months of the Galway 'stab'—the revelation of a badly suppressed wish.

[1] On 4 Aug. 1886 the party resolved unanimously, on Dillon's proposal, seconded by Dr. Kenny: 'That we earnestly trust that our colleagues Messrs. O'Brien and Healy will allow themselves to be placed in nomination for the first available vacancy, as we consider that the presence of both these gentlemen in parliament is absolutely indispensable in the present juncture, and that our chairman be requested to make the necessary arrangements' (Minutes). A similar resolution, but this time omitting mention of the chairman, was proposed by Gray and seconded by Chance on the eve of the by-elections of Feb. 1887 (Minutes, 27 Jan. 1887).

[2] Very shortly after the Galway election, Healy informed O'Brien 'that I could no longer write for *United Ireland*. . . . I persisted in my refusal and left him with a feeling of a broken friendship. No two men had worked in closer relations' (*Letters and Leaders*, i. 249).

[3] 20 July 1886.                    [4] Above, p. 243, n. 5.

Dillon, while, in parliament and in the party, he suffered from being in the shadow of Parnell's displeasure. One slight he resented bitterly, because it denied him the greatest possible occasion of displaying his peculiar combination of abilities: this was his exclusion from the ranks of counsel for Parnell at the Special Commission inquiry into *The Times* charges.[1]

Healy's 'fall' was not a great one. His real influence in the party was probably only slightly—though perceptibly—less in the years 1887–90 than it had been in the years 1882–5. He was still one of the four principal men in the party; he still figured on all important committees. But his influence was enormously shrunken compared with what he had imagined it to be. There was no question now of a puppet-Parnell being manipulated by the unseen Healy and his friends; no question even of rule by a 'cabinet' which included Parnell. It is interesting to conjecture how far the intellectual arrogance, which had led Healy to exaggerate his own influence, was itself responsible for the decline of that influence. That arrogance was both aggressive and articulate, and it cannot have been pleasing to the simple men who made up the majority of the party. The fact that no one, except relatives and cronies like Chance and the Sullivans, was ready to follow Healy's lead is significant not only of Parnell's dominance, but also of Healy's own lack of appeal to the party. A revolt led by Dillon or O'Brien would probably have split the party; a revolt led by the two of them together might, even then, have carried with it a majority; the revolt of Healy and Biggar failed to produce even a splinter. One can scarcely doubt that the party's decision was right, not only in the judgement of the immediate issue—the overriding necessity of unity—but in the

[1] R. Barry O'Brien asserts that Healy was excluded not at Parnell's wish but at Davitt's (O'Brien, *Parnell*, p. 538). Davitt asserts that he pressed strongly for Healy's employment 'but Mr. Parnell's recollection of the Galway election incident intervened' (*Fall of Feudalism*, p. 543). Healy himself believed that the decision was Parnell's and that it was motivated by speeches he had made supporting the Plan of Campaign (*Letters and Leaders*, i. 290–1). We may assume that it would have taken very little to quicken Parnell's distrust of Healy; the fillip which participation in the Commission's proceedings might give to Healy's prestige would have inclined Parnell to seek a reason to exclude him.

instinct that rejected the bid for leadership of a man so dazzled by his own great talents.

With the single exception of the Galway episode, Parnell's ascendancy over his party remained unchallenged, often with little exertion on his part, over the years of his chairmanship. That this was so was due in part to the characters of his principal lieutenants: characters which had been formed, politically, under his leadership, as specialists and therefore as subordinates. The success of the movement depended, in part, on both agitators and parliamentarians, but its leader could not be classed as either. His speciality was simply to be leader; his lieutenants had not distinguished themselves by their talents in that direction, but by complementary qualities, useful in subordinates. Their characters, and their relative incapacity for leadership—an incapacity which eventually threw the way open for a new movement of an entirely different kind—were symptoms of the basic tendency of institutions to 'run down', extinguishing the creative spirit under the weight of organizational necessity. As long as Parnell was in control of the movement he had formed it still possessed direction, flexibility, and coherence. But there was no provision, in the 'inner circle' of the party, for the perpetuation of these qualities.[1] The central organization was admirably apt for a 'short sharp struggle' of up to ten or fifteen years. That, however, was not what was in store for the party.

### 3. The Machine

#### (a) Selection of candidates

The system of county conventions[2] which had, at least nominally, selected all the candidates in the election of 1885 fell thereafter into general disuse. Conventions were not held at the consequential by-elections following the 'double returns' in some constituencies, nor were they held in the

---

[1] Even so severe a critic of Parnell as Michael Davitt thought apprehensively about the succession: 'I shrink with horror from the spectacle which Irish movements would present to Gods and men if once Parnell was replaced by Dillons, Healys and O'Connors at the heads of cliques and factions' (Davitt MSS.: McGhee correspondence; letter of 21 May 1888).

[2] Above, Chap. IV, § 2.

elections of 1886, even for those constituencies where a new candidate was needed, nor yet (as a general rule) in the by-elections during the period 1886–90.[1] The decay of the convention system may perhaps have been accelerated by the Galway crisis—in which neither side could summon a convention[2]—and by Parnell's subsequent distrust of some of his subordinates.[3] It is probable, however, that the convention system would, in any case, have tended to fall into disuse outside general election periods. The assembly of a county convention was cumbrous and inconvenient and it was natural enough to leave it to 'the party' to fill up the vacancies that arose, during the life of parliament, in its own ranks.

After the split, Healy was to maintain that 'for the last five years he [Parnell] filled up vacancies in the Irish representation without consulting either his party or the constituencies'.[4] This was literally true, but misleading. The constituencies were not consulted—except on one or two occasions—and neither was the party as a whole, but the 'inner circle' of the party was consulted.[5] Indeed the approved name was often suggested by one of the 'inner

---

[1] A partial exception was the Kilkenny convention of 28 Nov. 1890, on the eve of the split. It is significant, however, that this convention was not summoned to select a candidate but 'for the purpose of hearing an address from Sir John Pope Hennessy, the candidate approved of by the Irish parliamentary party . . . and of adopting a resolution in favour of his candidature' (*F.J.*, 28 Nov. 1890). A convention was held earlier in the same year in Cavan to select a successor to Biggar. Clancy, M.P., representing the Irish party, 'hoped some resolution would be passed that day recommending Mr. Vesey Knox to the constituency' (ibid., 19 Mar. 1890). The resolution was passed.

[2] Parnell, because his candidate, O'Shea, would not take the party pledge, and Healy because he could neither speak for 'the party' as a whole, nor obtain the support of the local clergy.

[3] M. J. F. McCarthy (*The Irish Revolution*, p. 489) says of the general elections of 1886: 'This time Mr. Parnell did not summon any conventions for the selection of candidates, fearing lest the claims of rival aspirants should provoke dissensions beyond even his power to control.' It is not clear why that should be, unless such dissensions were to be fanned, to Parnell's detriment, by an influential lieutenant.

[4] 'The Rise and Fall of Mr. Parnell'; article in *The New Review*, Mar. 1891.

[5] Sometimes (as in Healy's own case) reference was publicly made to such consultation: 'After consultation with my principal colleagues', wrote Parnell in a letter published on the eve of nomination day, 'it has been decided to ask Mr. Swift McNeill and Mr. T. M. Healy to offer themselves to the constituencies of south Donegal and north Longford' (*F.J.*, 24 Jan. 1887). Here the reference to 'principal colleagues' was a partial understatement as

circle'[1]—which is natural enough when one considers that Parnell, during this period, was never in contact with the constituencies and had no opportunity to survey rising political talent. It is admitted by other anti-Parnellite writers that Parnell did not pick personal henchmen.[2] We know that on at least one occasion, a choice, made nominally by Parnell, was in fact made by a group of the 'inner circle', subject to Parnell's later approval, which was given.[3]

The machinery for the selection of candidates during the period 1886–90 was, in appearance, very different from that in use in 1885, since it substituted the personal authority of Parnell for the convention system. The underlying reality, however, the control of selection by an 'inner circle', was little changed, although the 'inner circle' was a more amorphous group than the Morrison's Hotel caucus of 1885. It now consisted, in normal practice, of those whom Parnell chose to consult: a category which did not include Healy.

There was one potentially significant factor involved in the decay of the convention system. This was the lessening of direct ecclesiastical participation in the selection of candidates. The clergy were not altogether excluded from any say

Healy's nomination (and that of O'Brien) had been—quite exceptionally—the subject of resolutions of the whole party. On other occasions, however, candidates were recommended as the choice of the Irish party : 'Mr. O'Keeffe, mayor of Limerick, to-day received a letter from Mr. Parnell stating that the Irish party warmly approved of his candidature' (*F.J.*, 13 Apr. 1888); 'Mr. Parnell and the Irish party have decided to recommend Mr. John Roche of Woodford to the electorate of east Galway' (ibid., 6 May 1890). The minutes of the party, however, give no indication that the party was consulted about either of those candidates; it was probably the 'principal colleagues' who had in fact approved. Normally, however, the selection was in Parnell's name only (selection of O'Mara, ibid., 5 Feb. 1886; Dickson, ibid., 4 May 1888; Dr. Fitzgerald, ibid., 12 June 1888; Harrison, ibid., 16 May 1890; Dalton, ibid., 31 May 1890).

[1] R. Barry O'Brien, *Parnell*, p. 537; William O'Brien, *Evening Memories*, p. 67.

[2] '[Parnell] was quite right in suggesting [after the split] that with more trouble and more assistance he could have created a party which would have been . . . so partisan . . . that he would never have been rejected by a majority' (T. P. O'Connor, *Memoirs of an Old Parliamentarian*, ii. 16).

[3] Letter of Clancy to Harrington, 21 Feb. 1890 (N.L.I., Harrington MSS.: Miscellaneous). The candidate selected was Webb for west Waterford and the group who picked him consisted of McCarthy, O'Brien, Sexton, T. P. O'Connor, Condon, and Carew.

in the selection of candidates,[1] but they no longer had all
the power which their votes and influence could command
under the convention system. Up to the beginning of 1890,
however, the character of the representatives selected—with
the exception of O'Shea—was similar to that of those who,
in 1885, had passed through the 'sieve' of the conventions[2]
—and probably as acceptable to the clergy. The candidates
selected and elected (and in one case approved by a convention) in 1890 present the peculiarity that four out of six of
them were Protestants. It is true that Protestants already
formed a considerably higher proportion of the parliamentary party than they did of the population of nationalist
Ireland, and that the Catholic clergy acquiesced in this situation. But the proportion of Protestants nominated in this
year is probably higher than could have been attained under
a fully working convention system in predominantly Catholic constituencies. The reason for the selection of so many
Protestants was, of course, to help the liberals in England
by allaying English fears about the treatment of Protestants
under a home rule parliament.[3] The fact that it was possible
to impose this policy on Irish constituencies without any
demur, either from ecclesiastics or lay zealots, or from local
nationalists who were passed over, is one more demonstration of the dominance which Parnell, working the policy of
the liberal alliance, held at this time over Irish opinion.[4]

[1] Parnell consulted the Archbishop of Cashel about the vacancy for mid-
Tipperary (Apr.–May 1890) and, when the archbishop had no candidate to
suggest, selected Henry Harrison on William O'Brien's advice (O'Brien,
*Evening Memories*, p. 67). After his election the chairman of the 'victory'
meeting, Fr. Rafferty, stated that 'Mr. Harrison has come amongst us as the
choice of Mr. Parnell, the leader of the Irish people, and . . . with the approval
of His Grace the Archbishop of Cashel' (*F.J.*, 16 May 1890).

[2] There was a higher proportion of business and professional men among
them, as we would expect with a party which had now shed all vestiges of its
semi-revolutionary past.

[3] At the Cavan Convention, Clancy recommended that Vesey Knox should
be selected immediately so that he could help the liberals at the Ayr Burghs
by-election as an 'example of the tolerance of the Irish people' (*F.J.*, 19
Mar. 1890).

[4] 'Some of Parnell's later appointments to the representation of Irish constituencies had been viewed with grave displeasure by the very persons who
soon jumped at the chance of removing him from leadership' (O'Donnell,
*Irish Parliamentary Party*, ii. 281). The context makes it clear that O'Donnell
is thinking of the agrarian wing of the party and not, as his language might

## (b) The pledge and discipline

The party pledge had developed as part of the convention system of selecting candidates; candidates were required to accept the pledge before being recommended by the convention to the constituency. It might have been expected therefore that the pledging of candidates would lapse along with the convention system. In fact, however, the pledge, the element in the system that was important to the party leadership, showed more vitality than the 'democratic' element, the convention itself. Yet the abandoning of the convention system made the difference—superficially an important one—that the pledge was now generally taken *after* election instead of before even nomination. At the first meeting of the party after the elections of 1886, it was resolved: 'that we take this opportunity of renewing and declaring our adhesion to the pledge given by the members of the Irish parliamentary party of last session to the conventions which selected them'.[1] Similarly, some at least of the members returned at by-elections after 1886 took the pledge after they had been returned; some never formally took it at all.[2]

Despite a certain laxity in administering it, however, the

lead one to suppose, of the bishops. The 'agrarians' were, in O'Donnell's interpretation, offended not by the religious outlook but by the social standing and conservative affiliations of some of these later choices. Neither clergy nor agrarians, however, made any public objection.

[1] Minutes, 4 Aug. 1886. The resolution was proposed by Gray and seconded by P. J. Power. The wording 'renewing and declaring' is intended, of course, to cover both the bulk of the party, who had already been pledged and elected in 1885, and the new members.

[2] A large collection of signed pledges forms part of the Harrington MSS. in the National Library of Ireland. It shows, for example, that Patrick O'Brien, who was sworn as a member of parliament on 1 Mar. 1886, signed the pledge on 3 Mar. 1886; Swift McNeill, sworn on 10 Feb. 1887, did not take the pledge until 25 June 1887. Many of the pledges are undated. No pledges later than early 1888 are in this collection; it is quite possible that the formal pledging of candidates (or members) lapsed altogether between 1888 and the split. O'Shea—contrary to a general belief—was certainly not the only member who never formally signed the pledge. Parnell never signed it himself: 'I believe I personally did not subscribe to it [the pledge] but considered myself equally bound by it with the other M.P.s' (speech at Leinster Hall meeting; *F.J.*, 24 July 1891). Another member who did not sign was T. A. Dickson, a former liberal, who did not wish to sign, on grounds of conscience, and whose candidature seems to have been accepted as a mark of respect to Gladstone (ibid., 4 May 1888).

pledge remained effectively in force. Apart from two peculiar cases—O'Shea and Dickson—no one who refused to
take the pledge was accepted as a nationalist candidate, nor
did any nationalist member, elected without having signed
the pledge, afterwards refuse to sign it. The force of the
pledge was moral rather than quasi-legal; the general pledge-
taking at the conventions of 1885 served as a demonstration
and notice to the Irish people that the Irish party was now a
disciplined one, pledged to act in unison. Thereafter the
nationalist candidate was assumed to be willing to bind
himself in this way, unless—like Dickson—he made a public
statement to the contrary effect. Thus the tendency, after
1885, to drop the formal requirement of 'pledge before
election' in no way implied a return to the old system of a
'voluntary' pledge, freely entered into by the elected members. On the contrary, it was now so well understood that
the Irish party was a pledge-bound party that the actual
ritual of signing a pledge had become of secondary importance. When the split came, no member on any side declared
himself not bound by the pledge; each side maintained,
with good show of reason, that it had not violated the
pledge by which all members admitted that they were bound.

From the introduction of the Home Rule Bill up to the
Parnell divorce crisis this pledge-bound party did show a
front of almost perfect unity to its adversaries.[1] In a few
cases, on matters of no immediate political importance, the
party granted some freedom of action to its members,[2] but

[1] O'Shea's defection on the Home Rule Bill itself is not really an exception
to this rule as he had not taken the pledge. There was only one exception: the
case of Sir Joseph McKenna. McKenna was a landlord, and one of five ex-
whigs who had voted for Shaw as chairman in 1880 but later made their
peace with Parnell, signed the party pledge, and were re-elected in 1885 or
1886 (the others were Blake, Gray, R. Power, and Smithwick). His tenants
adopted the Plan of Campaign (*F.J.*, 19 Feb. 1887) and he seems to have been
driven into difficulties which resulted in unwillingness to hamper the passage
of tory Land Purchase Bills. The *Freeman's Journal* commented unfavourably
on his action in abstaining on a Parnell amendment to one such bill: 'This is
not the first time that Sir Joseph McKenna has thought fit to dissociate
himself from the party with which he pledged himself to act and vote' (*F.J.*,
5 May 1890). It is a remarkable tribute to the discipline of the party that such
a comment did not become necessary in the case of any other member.

[2] The party took a vote on 2 Apr. 1886, as to what its attitude should be
if a Women's Suffrage Bill was introduced. The voting was 14 in favour and
25 against such a bill, and it was agreed that the minority in favour should

normally the *consigne* was one of strenuous and undeviating aid to the liberal party in the division lobbies. This policy met with no political resistance; the only difficulty was the ordinary parliamentary one of keeping attendance up to the required pitch. Again and again over the years of the union of hearts, the party passed resolutions urging better attendance, naming offenders, and requiring the chairman to admonish them; sometimes comment to similar effect was inspired in the nationalist press.[1] These resolutions and editorials should probably be read, however, not as the admissions of laxity which in form they were, but as simple disciplinary assertions, necessary to keep an excellent machine

abstain while those against should vote (Minutes). This division is of some interest as a 'pointer' to the proportions of radicalism and social conservatism in the party at this time.

[1] The vice-chairman rebuked members of the party for bad attendance during the coercion debates (Minutes, 2 May 1887). About a year later Parnell called a meeting on the same subject: '. . . in the early days of the session he asked the business-men to attend only on important divisions. But latterly these gentlemen did not attend on these divisions. He said the liberal party complained also of the bad attendance of the Irish members . . . we could not expect the liberal party to support us if we did not support them . . . there was no excuse for pairing' (Minutes, 14 June 1885). This meeting resolved to authorize Parnell to write to the absentees, so that the party, having considered their replies, could decide 'whether it will be necessary to take any further action on this subject'. The whips were also empowered to cause a list of members voting in, and absent from, each division on the local government bill to be supplied to the Irish papers. A hostile newspaper reported on the immediate effect of these measures: 'The sharp rap over the knuckles administered by Mr. Parnell to his followers appears to have had the desired effect. The Parnellites are now attending the House of Commons in their full numbers' (*Evening Mail*, 15 June 1888). A little more than a year later, Parnell had again to admonish his party for their 'indifferent attendance . . . on important occasions during the session'; on the Royal Titles Bill division 15 to 20 members of the Irish party had been absent when their attendance would have been sufficient to defeat the government; 'If in former times the small parliamentary party then existing . . . had acted in their time as the present party had acted during this session there would be no parliamentary party worthy of the name now in existence' (Minutes, 12 Aug. 1889). On the following day an inspired editorial in the *Freeman's Journal* deplored parliamentary absenteeism. Six months later, Parnell renewed his admonitions to the party (Minutes, 11 Feb. 1890) and shortly afterwards he accepted the resignation of one of the most persistent offenders, J. E. O'Doherty (*F.J.*, 27 Mar. 1890). After this, it seems to have been felt that the 'drive' against absentees could be moderated. Parnell informed the public that his strictures applied only to a few members and that 'the attendance of the party as a whole was better in proportion to membership than that of either the liberals or the conservatives' (ibid., 18 June 1890). This theme was elaborated by T. D. Sullivan in a letter some days later (ibid., 27 June 1890).

working with full efficiency. It was important, in Parnell's strategy, that the liberals should rely heavily and steadily on the voting strength of the Irish party, even on English questions. This policy imposed a much more continuous strain on the party than had the 'alliance-free' policy in the years 1882–5 and it was necessary that the 'whip' should be not only used but publicly brandished. The almost complete lack of any 'deviations' on policy left the leader of the party free to concentrate his disciplinary efforts on ensuring regular attendance. It was a singularly happy condition of things, as long as the party merely had to function as an essential and well-oiled piece of machinery in the Parnell–Gladstone alliance.

### (c) The parliamentary fund

One of the features which most clearly distinguished the 'new'—post-1885—Irish party both from the two great English parties and from any previous Irish parties at Westminster was the fact that many of its members received a salary out of funds controlled by the party leadership.

Certain contemporaries saw in the payment of members out of party funds a sinister phenomenon, portending the extinction of independence of conscience and judgement in parliamentary representatives.[1] Now that the payment of members of parliament out of *public* funds is generally accepted, these fears seem somewhat unreal; most important modern political parties, in parliamentary democracies of the British type, could be no more responsive to the party whip if they were actually paid out of party instead of out of public funds. In the case of the Irish party, we should, I believe, attach less importance, in matter of direct discipline, to the payment of members than to the pledging system and to the almost unchallengeable prestige of the leader. Yet the innovation of the parliamentary fund has its importance, if only as means of drawing on a wider class, yielding an adequate supply of members both amenable to discipline

---

[1] The publications of the *Irish Loyal and Patriotic Union*, the columns of the unionist press for the period, and the writings of F. H. O'Donnell abound in this sense.

and devoted to the principles associated with the name of Parnell.

As we have seen,[1] subscriptions to the parliamentary fund, opened in March 1885, were sufficient to cover the general election of that year, leaving over at the beginning of 1886 a small balance of slightly over £3,000. By the end of 1886, under the impetus of the great home rule crisis, receipts had reached the impressive peak of almost £100,000.[2] In later years the receipts were naturally very much smaller; by the end of 1889 total receipts stood at £125,654.[3] Almost all of this represented contributions from outside Ireland and England: £102,000 from the United States, £11,500 from Australasia, £2,000 from Canada.[4]

---

[1] Above, Chap. IV, § 3.

[2] It was after the defeat of Gladstone's bill that receipts notably accelerated. On 1 Jan. 1886 they stood at £3,340. Thereafter their movement, as we know it, was as follows:

|  | £ |  | £ |
|---|---|---|---|
| by 17 Mar. 1886 | 10,175 | by 4 Aug. 1886 | 73,826 |
| „ 12 May 1886 | 17,757 | „ 31 Aug. 1886 | 90,581 |
| „ 23 June 1886 | 52,930 | „ 19 Nov. 1886 | 97,967 |
| „ 26 July 1886 | 66,420 | „ 31 Dec. 1886 | 99,302 |

(N.L.I., J. F. X. O'Brien MSS.: Account Book of the Irish Parliamentary Fund, Jan. 1886 to Feb. 1890; later abbreviated as O'Brien Accounts).

[3] Annual receipts were as follows: 1887, £10,762; 1888, £9,377; 1889, £6,213 (O'Brien Accounts). Balfour's police were interested in what they could ascertain, without intensive sleuthing, about the progress of the parliamentary fund. In a half-yearly report on the National League (and allied matters) in Jan. 1888 a senior police official, Thynne, asserted, on the basis of newspaper acknowledgements, that fund receipts had 'dropped from £71,760 in 1886 to £3,860 as a total for 1887'. The under-secretary was rightly sceptical about this information: 'If I might venture an *opinion* on the decrease in the parliamentary fund I would say it is not so great as that. I would not place too much dependence on the non-appearance of receipts for that fund. Mr. Biggar is an old parliamentary hand, you must remember, and is greatly trusted' (S.P.O., Irish National League: Proceedings, 1883–91). The decline was not so sharp as the crimes branch imagined, but even if it had been, the fact would not necessarily have reflected a decline in the national movement. The year 1886 was the *annus mirabilis* of the home rule movement, as well as being one of a crucial general election; it was not to be expected that receipts for the parliamentary fund would be on anything like the same scale in subsequent years.

[4] O'Brien Accounts. The American subscriptions were mainly through the Irish National League of America (£59,000) and the New York Parliamentary Fund (£22,000). The remainder was accounted for by miscellaneous subscriptions sent direct to Ireland. Cecil Rhodes was understood to have presented £10,000 to the fund on the understanding that the party would not

Considerable as it was in relation to the poverty of Ireland and her exiles, this sum needed to be carefully eked out, if it was to carry the party through even to the next general election which, it was confidently hoped, would bring another flood of subscriptions, followed by a liberal–Parnellite victory, a Home Rule Act, an Irish parliament, and no further need for a full Irish party at Westminster. There was no question of living on the income from the 1886 receipts. The balance sheet of the fund,[1] as it stood when the split occurred, shows the following general picture of expenditure over the period:

|                                                                          | £       |
|--------------------------------------------------------------------------|---------|
| Registration expenses . . . . . . .                                      | 11,500  |
| Irish election expenses (including 1886 general election) .              | 25,000  |
| 'Election expenses' (English by-elections?) . . .                        | 3,500   |
| National League of Great Britain (elections and registration)           | 2,000   |
| Irish Press Agency (propaganda in Britain) . . .                         | 13,000  |
| Transferred to Dillon for evicted tenants . . . .                        | 7,000   |
| Special Commission . . . . . . .                                         | 1,500   |
| Travelling expenses, &c. . . . . . .                                     | 3,000   |
| Miscellaneous . . . . . . . .                                            | 2,000   |
| Salaries of members . . . . . . .                                        | 48,000  |
| Total working expenditure . . . . .                                      | £116,500 |

The balance sheet shows also a payment of £52,293 to Messrs. Munroe and Co., the investment bankers in Paris with whom Parnell and his co-trustees, for security reasons, invested the funds under their control.

oppose retention of the Irish members at Westminster. This was arranged in June 1888 (J. G. Swift MacNeill, *What I Have Seen and Heard*, pp. 264–6). The accounts of the fund do not make it clear when and how this large subscription—the announcement of which received wide publicity—was actually paid over. It is curious that neither in 1888 nor in 1889 did the *total* receipts of the fund amount to as much as £10,000 (above, p. 266, n. 3). The bulk payment of £5,000 marked 'source unknown' in the balance sheet (p. 268 below) may perhaps represent a partial payment of the promised subscription.

[1] N.L.I., J. F. X. O'Brien MSS.: Draft Balance-sheet of the Irish Parliamentary fund, 11 Jan. 1886 to 30 Nov. 1890: figures corrected to the nearest £500. The balance sheet runs to the end of 1890 but the account book shows receipts only to the end of 1889. The main expenditure heads in this draft balance sheet are confirmed in a summary of principal heads of expenditure in J. F. X. O'Brien's affidavit of 27 Apr. 1892 (in connexion with the control of the 'Paris funds') which, however, does not include the rather large figure (actually £3,336) given as 'election expenses' (third item in text) (N.L.I., Harrington MSS.: O'Brien affidavit).

The receipts side of the balance sheet is as follows:

|  | £ |
|---|---|
| Cash received for Irish parliamentary fund . . . | 124,769 |
| Irish National League, Dublin, temporary assistance . . | 4,300 |
| Sundry petty receipts, interest, &c. . . . . | 54 |
| Source unknown (Cecil Rhodes?) . . . . . | 5,000 |
| Received from Munroe & Co. (sale of securities) . . | 34,569 |
|  | £168,692 |

It appears from these figures that the trustees still had investments (made through Messrs. Munroe) amounting to about £18,000 in the autumn of 1890.[1] Against this should be set the debt of over £4,000 to the National League, so that the *net* resources of the fund, by the end of 1890, amounted to less than £14,000. At the rate of expenditure shown in the balance sheet this would have been insufficient to defray even one year's expenditure. Parnell therefore decided in the autumn of 1890 to send a collecting mission to the United States, consisting of Dillon, O'Brien, Harrington, T. P. O'Connor, T. D. Sullivan, and T. P. Gill. This mission was meeting with great success,[2] when the split brought subscriptions virtually to an end.

The parliamentary fund was controlled neither by the party nor by the National League but by three trustees— Parnell, Biggar, and McCarthy—who held it in trust for the party, but without any direct responsibility to the party for the manner of its use.[3] Given Parnell's prestige, which

[1] This £18,000 formed part of the 'Paris funds', control of which was disputed after the split. The Paris funds included, as well as the parliamentary fund securities, the reserve dating from Land League days and invested in the name of the same trustees (above, Chap. IV, p. 140). This reserve had amounted at the end of 1882 to over £30,000. Parnell had used the income, or some of it, for parliamentary and perhaps for National League purposes, but the capital seems to have been kept intact. The Paris funds at the time of the split totalled about £50,000 (Lyons, *Irish Parliamentary Party, 1890–1910*, p. 23, n. 2).

[2] Harrington, for example, records in his diary that a New York meeting on 10 Nov. yielded $30,000 (N.L.I., Harrington MSS.: American diary, 4 Nov. 1890 to 19 Dec. 1890).

[3] This is a summary of what appears from the affidavits in the Harrington collection (above, Chap. IV, p. 138, n. 4). Harrington's second affidavit (16 June 1892) makes the points that neither McCarthy nor Biggar was ever treasurer *of the party* and that the fund itself was 'never controlled by the party in any way'. These points are corroborated—the first explicitly and the second tacitly—by the minutes of the party. McCarthy, supported by J. F. X.

dwarfed that of his two fellow trustees, this situation certainly strengthened Parnell's authority and perhaps his conception of himself as autocrat rather than merely chairman of the party.[1] In so far as the payment of a salary implies additional control, this additional control applied to roughly half the party. Forty-four members received repeated payments, as a salary, in the period 1886 to 1890.[2] The basic salary was £200 a year, usually paid quarterly—a few members received extra payments for special services such as drafting bills, attendance in the recess, &c. Sixteen other members received payments from time to time to cover travelling expenses, as professional fees (as in the case of Dr. Kenny, physician to the party), or in special circumstances, as after a long illness, or simply to tide a member through a lean period.

Of the 44 members who received a regular salary, 39 already belonged to the party in 1885.[3] The fact that only 5 salaried members were recruited thereafter (up to 1890) confirms the view that a wealthier type of member was being recruited after 1885.[4] In general, the members who received salaries were the rank and file of the party, but there were a few prominent members among them—notably J. J. O'Kelly, Sexton, and T. D. Sullivan. Other prominent

O'Brien, denied in his second affidavit (10 May 1892) that the fund was in any way subject to the authority of the Irish National League and stated that Parnell, Biggar, and himself had 'absolute and uncontrolled discretion' in handling this fund for the purpose for which it was subscribed. These statements may also be unreservedly accepted.

[1] It might perhaps have been expected that Biggar, who did not stand in awe of Parnell, might have made himself a focus of opposition among the trustees. Two entries in the accounts of the fund are, however, significant in this respect: '25.2.'86—Galway election and meeting £19; 3.5.'86—Galway election expenses £57'. We may take it that, if Biggar as co-treasurer could have held out against Parnell on anything, he would have held out against any payment in connexion with the return of Captain O'Shea.

[2] O'Brien Accounts; sums paid to each member. In the article 'The Machinery of the Irish Parliamentary Party, 1880–85' (*I.H.S.*, Mar. 1946) the present writer stated (p. 84) that 38 members received a regular salary (after the 1885 elections). I am here taking a slightly less rigorous view of a regular salary than I did then (regular annual payments in 3 successive years instead of 4), thus admitting later entrants to parliament.

[3] Twelve of these salaried members belonged to the party before 1885; 27 were recruited at the general election of 1885; 2 at the general election of 1886, and only 3 out of the 21 by-elections 1886–91.

[4] Above, Chap. IV, § 3 (*b*); also p. 261, n. 4.

members, who were not paid salaries, received cash payments from time to time; these include Dillon, T. P. O'Connor, and Healy.[1]

The extent to which the fund was directly used for disciplinary purposes was slight. A few members were docked a payment for 'bad attendance'; no doubt others were threatened with the same fate. There is no evidence—and little likelihood—that it was used as a means of stifling conscientious scruples or checking incipient 'deviations'. Intangibly it may have helped to maintain an atmosphere of obedience, in a party already disposed to the practice of that virtue. In particular, those leading members who obtained Parnell's *fiat* for personal payments to them out of the fund would have been to some extent psychologically handicapped if they wished to oppose his political judgement. But it is only fair to the men concerned to say that such considerations can have played, at most, a secondary role, and that the parliamentary stipend—small even by the monetary values, and the Irish standards, of those days—was rightly regarded as compensation for the long displacements and heavy duties of parliamentary life.[2]

[1] Dillon received £450 'sundry expenses to date' in 1887 (probably in connexion with the Plan) and £25 per annum travelling expenses in the three years 1886–9. Healy received £300 in 1886 and £200 in 1887, apparently as personal remuneration. F. S. L. Lyons (op. cit., p. 206, n. 1) accepts Healy's own account that he 'never drew an indemnity from party funds'; this is no doubt correct from 1888 on (including the period with which Dr. Lyons is concerned). In general, the memoirs of leading members such as T. P. O'Connor and Healy give an impression that only the rank and file received payments from the party fund. The books of the fund do not wholly corroborate this. It may be worth remarking that Michael Davitt also (though not a member of the party and critical of it) accepted expenses from the fund totalling £350 (probably for his work in connexion with the Special Commission), during this period (balance sheet).

[2] For some members with businesses of their own, the 'compensation' of the parliamentary stipend was quite insufficient. The Dillon Papers include an interesting letter from a member, a butter merchant in Cork, who said that his business had been bringing him in from £1,000 to £2,000 a year. When he joined the party (1885) he had had 'a few thousand' saved; these savings were now (Nov. 1887) exhausted; one division alone had cost him £800. Biggar, he said, believed that, if he could get rid of him 'he can get a better bargain in some man who has no business to divide his attention. From Biggar's point of view he is quite right. Business men are unwanted in the party'. Biggar had offered him £200 a year to stay in London during the session, which he had refused (Dillon MSS.: letter from W. J. Lane, 11 Nov. 1887).

Contemporaries were interested not only in the power which the fund gave to the leader over the rank and file, but in the power which it was believed to give the American subscribers—'Parnell's American paymasters'—over the movement as a whole. There was little foundation for this belief. Since the Chicago Convention of 1886—if not earlier —the Irish National League of America, by far the most powerful organization supporting the Irish movement, had virtually ceded to Parnell and the party all say in political direction and had resigned itself to the role of a collecting agent. It is true that the party itself suspected the 'American league' of some ambition to dictate policy,[1] but Parnell was in such unchallengeable command of Irish national politics that he could impose his will on the American supporters.[2]

Parnell was no less firm in dealing with financial demands from the agrarian side of the movement than he was in quelling the political aspirations of the American subscribers. His principle was that the parliamentary fund, plus the Paris 'No. 1' fund (the Land League residue) must be held for purely parliamentary purposes, and that the agrarian movement must meet its heavier demands by its own exertions. He was prepared to sponsor appeals for the evicted tenants,[3] but not to contribute to any significant extent from

[1] O'Brien in a letter to Dillon on 14 July 1888 spoke of 'the renewed and menacing claim of the National League of America [through its executive] to be the only medium of American collections' (Dillon MSS. V).

[2] Parnell, in briefing Dillon before his departure on his American tour in the autumn of 1890, laid down a very firm line: 'You are to let both sides [in a dispute within the I.N.L.A.] understand that we will not again recognize any central authority in America or tolerate any more conventions or recriminations and that the branches must communicate and remit direct to Dublin' (Dillon MSS. V: letter of 10 Sept. 1890). In fact the most important part of this programme had already been carried out; in the previous month the treasurer of the I.N.L.A. at Parnell's request had circularized all branches instructing them to remit in future direct to Dublin (N.L.I., Harrington MSS.: Miscellaneous Correspondence: letter of 9 Aug. 1890). A league convention summoned for Detroit early in 1890 had been 'indefinitely postponed', when Parnell publicly expressed his 'disapproval' (F.J., 3 Feb. 1890; 27 Feb. 1890). The president of the I.N.L.A., John Fitzgerald, protested to Parnell about the 'mistaken decision' on direct remittances which 'practically wipes out a central American executive' (Harrington MSS.: Miscellaneous Correspondence: letter of 29 Sept. 1890). That, of course, is precisely what Parnell intended.

[3] See, for example, F.J., 13 Oct. 1886.

the funds under his own control.[1] In this respect, as in others, the situation of the Land League years was reversed.

## (d) The National League

The National League continued to function as, in Healy's phrase, 'an auxiliary of the party'.[2] There were no important changes in its organization, unless the suppression under the Crimes Act of a number of branches can be so described. This suppression seems, in some cases at least, to have been nominal only; in February 1888 Dr. Kenny informed a league meeting in Dublin that the suppressed branches 'were as good working branches as they were before'.[3] There was probably an element of defiant exaggeration in this claim, and there is some evidence that, even apart from suppression, the number of active branches was falling.[4]

In general, the importance of the National League was less than it had been in the earlier part of our period. One reason for this was the decay of the convention system which, at its apogee in 1885, had been such a striking—and in some eyes a sinister—proof of the country's adherence to the league. But 'the power of the league'—a phrase frequent in the unionist press—had been in part an illusion, springing from a recollection of the real power of the Land League— for unionists usually affected to be unable to distinguish between the two bodies—and in part a loose statement, standing for something real and strong, the power of Parnell. The National League, Parnell's creation, had in reality only what power Parnell chose to vest in it. This is strikingly demonstrated by the league's meek acquiescence in the series of personal nominations by Parnell to so many vacant seats in 1886–90.

The decline in the political importance of the league was

---

[1] Harrington explained publicly that it would be 'an abuse' of the parliamentary fund to use it for evicted tenants (F.J., 24 Nov. 1886). Such payments were made, however, to a small extent. The fund's balance sheet (above, p. 267) shows a total expenditure of £7,000 over five years on evicted tenants.

[2] Harrington MSS.: affidavit of 26 Apr. 1892.

[3] F.J., 15 Feb. 1888.

[4] 'On 1 January 1886 there were 1261 working branches returned by the police. On 1 January 1887 this . . . had fallen to 1243 and on 1 January 1888 to 1031' (S.P.O., Beckerson Report, 7 Jan. 1888).

paralleled by a decline in its importance in the agrarian struggle. From the end of 1886 on, that struggle was concentrated in the Plan of Campaign, and the National League had no say in the organization of the Plan.[1] True, Plan demonstrations probably consisted almost entirely of league members, and no doubt the organizers in each district were the most active members of the local branch of the league. But it would be a mistake to regard the separation between league and Plan as merely nominal. The league had no say in such matters of policy as the extension or narrowing of the Plan's operation, and therefore no real say in the most important phase of agrarian policy—the phase in which the league's ideas would have been most likely to come into conflict with those of Parnell. It is noteworthy that the separation between the league and the Plan was a principle laid down by Parnell himself.

Limited in both its political and its agrarian functions, the league, as such, now did little more than produce propaganda and demonstrations of solidarity. The fortnightly meeting of the league's central branch in Dublin—held after the private meetings of the organizing committee—was usually attended by several M.P.s and became, during the parliamentary recess, a convenient platform, especially for speakers such as Healy, who were not particularly active in the Plan. Occasionally, county conventions were held not now, usually, in order to select a parliamentary candidate, but as a demonstration of strength and to pass resolutions condemning land-grabbing, evictions, &c.[2]

The financial crisis of the Plan of Campaign and the consequent setting up of the Tenants' Defence Association[3] in the autumn of 1889, revealed more clearly the true position of the National League. The National League provided

[1] 'The National League should not *as the National League* have anything to say to the Plan of Campaign . . . this office has nothing to do with the Plan and any instructions or information you require about it can be had on application to Mr. Dillon or Mr. William O'Brien' (N.L.I., Harrington MSS.: National League letter-book; letter of 15 Jan. 1887 to McKeague, Kilconnell (presumably a branch secretary)). Harrington himself was, of course, one of the originators of the Plan and continued to be active in its business.

[2] Conventions took place at Waterford (*F.J.*, 21 Jan. 1887), Kildare (ibid., 10 Jan. 1889), and Wexford (ibid., 24 July 1890). Most counties held no conventions during the period.　　　　　　　　　[3] Chap. VII, p. 230.

the basic structure of the new association: each county convention of the association was attended by all the local branches of the league. But the organization of the new association and even the detailed programme of each convention had been laid down in advance by the parliamentary party. The function of both league and association was not to take part in the formation of a policy but to carry out the policies decided on by the parliamentary party.[1]

## (e) Working with the liberals

The atmosphere of the years 1886–90 was propitious to the growth of the Irish National League of Great Britain. In 1884 the league had had 127 branches in Britain with a total membership of 4,600 and an income of only £391. In 1890 it had 630 branches with a membership of 40,985 and an income of £3,744.[2]

The functions of the league were to see that the Irish vote got on the electoral register in the British cities and that the Irish electors voted for the liberals.[3] In this work the league

[1] 'We shall probably not be far astray', said the *Irish Times* editorially, 'if we take the Defence League rather than the National League as likely to prove the heart and substance of the Parnellite party for some time to come' (20 Nov. 1889). In reality the Defence Association, being purely a collecting organization, could hardly have ousted the National League. The new association is best conceived, indeed, as an instrument of the party for imposing a particular policy and method on both the National League and the Plan of Campaign.

[2] The full figures are as follows:

| Year | Branches | Income | Card-holding members |
|------|----------|--------|----------------------|
| 1883 | 52 | (unknown) | (unknown) |
| 1884 | 127 | £391 | 4,600 |
| 1885 | 240 | £1,162 | 13,000 |
| 1886 | 423 | £2,326 | 23,000 |
| 1887 | 524 | £2,351 | 26,920 |
| 1888 | 595 | £2,798 | 32,747 |
| 1889 | 623 | £3,954 | 34,117 |
| 1890 | 630 | £3,744 | 40,985 |

(Reports for Birmingham Convention—*F.J.*, 27 Aug. 1888—and Edinburgh Convention—ibid., 18 Sept. 1890.)

[3] Great importance was attached to the registration work. During the summer recess of 1890 the party assigned twelve M.P.s to help the league with a series of registration meetings in England and Scotland (*F.J.*, 18 Aug.

co-operated with the party's propaganda organization, the Irish Press Agency, and with the liberal Home Rule Union.

The Irish Press Agency was set up in 1886 for the distribution of literature in England on the Irish question.[1] It was under the control of J. J. Clancy, M.P., an able and energetic controversialist, assisted by two other M.P.s, Carew and Crilly. Its pamphlets were designed to inform, and where necessary to reassure, liberal opinion on such matters as the land question, the Ulster question, and the theoretical case for home rule. The party thought this work sufficiently important to spend on it, in the period 1886–90, the sum of £13,000, a considerable sum in relation to its total budget.[2]

The literature prepared by the Irish Press Agency was distributed mainly through the Home Rule Union, a very active division of the liberal party, with, in 1888, more than sixty liberal associations affiliated to it.[3] This body sent literature and lecturers throughout Great Britain and arranged for the reception of Irish M.P.s: Clancy as head of the Irish Press Agency was 'in almost daily contact with the union'.[4] 'Home rule vans', by 1889, were bringing speakers and literature into the more remote constituencies.[4] By the halcyon period of 1889–90 the union was able to report that 'at every by-election the constituency is flooded with Parnellite M.P.s who talk of nothing but Ireland and who form the chief attraction at the meetings'.[5] Further, the requests for Parnellite M.P.s in constituencies where there was no election were increasing monthly and 'the Irish Press Agency is at its wit's end to satisfy the demands that are made upon it.'[5]

The liberal alliance involved not only public speeches by

1890). The league made no bones about identifying itself with the liberals. When in 1886 the Kennington branch of the league dissolved and reorganized itself as the 'W. E. Gladstone branch', the *Irish Times* commented: 'There is a theory that the managers of the Irish National League of Great Britain are rendering these tributes in order to identify liberal home rule statesmanship with their movement and with the object of binding it to their interests. And it is a shrewd policy, moreover, although a somewhat risky one' (17 Aug. 1886).

[1] *F.J.*, 2 Oct. 1886.　　　　　　　　　[2] Above, § 3 (*c*), p. 267.
[3] *Journal of the Home Rule Union*, No. 1 (Mar. 1888).
[4] Ibid. (July 1889).
[5] Ibid. (Jan. 1890).

leading men on both sides, but close day-to-day functional co-operation, between the Irish Press Agency and the Home Rule Union, and between the National League (G.B.) branches and the liberal associations in the constituencies. The general impression one derives from the press reports and the reports of the Home Rule Union is of a co-operation which was achieved at first only with difficulty, but which warmed into an effective, and even enthusiastic, fighting alliance; an alliance which seemed, up to the autumn of 1890, to have great and growing prospects of success.

# IX

## THE SPLIT (1890)

The Bishops and the Party
That tragic story made . . .
W. B. YEATS

### *Chronology of Principal Events*

#### 1889

| | |
|---|---|
| *24 December.* | Divorce petition filed by Captain O'Shea, citing Parnell as co-respondent. |

#### 1890

| | |
|---|---|
| *4–31 January.* | Resolutions by almost all Irish public bodies, expressing unaltered confidence in Parnell's leadership. |
| *15* (Saturday) and and *17* (Monday) *November.* | Trial of O'Shea case; suit undefended; verdict against Mrs. O'Shea and Parnell. |
| *18 November.* | Central branch of National League re-affirms confidence in Parnell. |
| *20 November.* | Public meeting in Leinster Hall, attended by principal members of party, reaffirms confidence in Parnell. Reading of telegram from American delegates (O'Brien, Dillon, Harrington, T. P. O'Connor, and T. P. Gill) upholding Parnell's leadership. Resolutions of many Irish public bodies upholding Parnell. Davitt in *Labour World* calls for Parnell's retirement. |
| *21 November.* | Cardinal Manning urges Gladstone to repudiate Parnell. |
| *22 November.* | Harcourt reports to Gladstone the feeling of a liberal convention at Sheffield that co-operation between Parnell and the English liberals is now impossible. |

| | |
|---|---|
| *23 November.* | Gladstone asks Harcourt to send for McCarthy to ascertain Parnell's intentions; Rev. Hugh Price Hughes states publicly that nonconformists will not tolerate co-operation with a party led by Parnell. |
| *24 November.* | Gladstone sees McCarthy and tells him that Parnell's continuance as leader would be disastrous. He also writes to Morley a letter (intended to be shown to Parnell and McCarthy) asserting that Parnell's continuance as leader would render his own advocacy of home rule 'almost a nullity'. |
| *25 November.* | Sessional meeting of Irish party : Parnell re-elected chairman; Gladstone's views not communicated by McCarthy, who was unaware of the 'almost a nullity' letter to Morley. |
| *26 November.* | Gladstone's letter to Morley published; special meeting of Irish party held on requisition signed by 31 members; Parnell asked to 're-consider his position' and declines to do so. |
| *27 November.* | Second article from Davitt, complaining of hierarchy's silence on the moral issue. |
| *28 November.* | Special meeting of standing committee of Irish hierarchy convened for Wednesday, 3 December. |
| *29 November.* | Publication of Parnell's manifesto to the Irish people, attacking Gladstone and a section of the Irish party. |
| *30 November.* | Manifesto issued by American delegates (O'Brien, Dillon, T. P. O'Connor, T. P. Gill, T. D. Sullivan) asking Irish party to repudiate Parnell. |
| *1 December.* | Committee Room 15 debate on leadership opens. Telegram read from Archbishop Walsh calling on the party to act manfully. |

*2 December.*      Central branch of National League again votes confidence in Parnell.

In Committee Room 15 Col. Nolan's resolution (pro-Parnell in tactic) defeated 44–29.

*3 December.*      Standing committee of the hierarchy calls on Catholic people of Ireland to reject Parnell as its leader.

Compromise attempts in Committee Room 15.

*4 December.*      Compromise attempts continue in Committee Room 15.

*5 December.*      Party seeks guarantees from Gladstone of satisfactory home rule measure if Parnell is to retire. Gladstone refuses 'to open a discussion in connection with the question of leadership'.

*6 December.*      The majority of the party—45 members, led by McCarthy—withdraws from Committee Room 15 leaving Parnell with 28 followers.

1. *The Divorce Case*

On 24 December 1889 Captain O'Shea filed his petition for divorce, naming Parnell as co-respondent. This fact became known in Ireland, through the *Freeman's Journal*, on 30 December. The *Freeman's* correspondent at the same time gave nationalist Ireland a cue which it proved only too willing to take: the divorce proceedings were 'a weak and puny resort', set in motion by the tories to drown the effect of the failure of *The Times* charges. 'With regard to Mr. Parnell', said the *Freeman*, 'Ireland trusts implicitly what he says.'[1]

What Parnell said, however, was ambiguous. To Davitt he gave assurances which amounted, in Davitt's recollection, to saying that 'he would emerge from the whole trouble without a stain on his reputation'; this assurance

[1] F.J., 30 Dec. 1889.

Davitt was to convey to others.[1] This statement seems to have reassured Davitt, although it would hardly have reassured those who, like Healy and Biggar, had realized as early as 1886, at the time of the Galway election, how matters stood between Parnell and the O'Sheas.[2] The ambiguity here was that to Davitt, as to other Catholic Irishmen, the statement conveyed that the charge of adultery was false; Parnell, however, seems to have meant to say no more than that he had not infringed the code of honour of a gentleman, and that Captain O'Shea had not been deceived[3]—matters of indifference to most of Catholic Ireland, which was interested only in the truth or falsity of the adultery charge. About the same time, Parnell told William O'Brien: 'If this case is ever fully gone into, a matter which is exceedingly doubtful, you may rest assured that it will be shown that the dishonour and discredit have not been upon my side.'[4] This statement O'Brien rightly regarded as ominous rather than reassuring.[5] In a public interview, Parnell said that O'Shea had been threatening proceedings since 1886 and that the present proceedings had been launched on the instigation of E. C. Houston—a prominent figure in the Pigott case—in the interest of The Times to diminish damages in the libel action which Parnell was taking against them. As regards the burthen of the charges, he made a curious statement: 'Captain O'Shea was always aware that he [Parnell] was constantly there [Mrs. O'Shea's house at Eltham] in his absence from 1880 to 1886 and since 1886 he has known that Mr. Parnell constantly resided there from 1880 to 1886.'[6] Such a statement, carrying a fairly clear implication that Parnell, over a period of years—1880–6—had been

[1] Fall of Feudalism, p. 657. Davitt's recollection became an issue during the campaign of the split, and Parnell denied that he had used the words which Davitt remembered. According to his own recollection, Parnell had simply denied certain specific 'false statements' which Davitt reported to him (New York World, 12 Dec. 1890). [2] See above, Chap. VI, pp. 168 sqq.
[3] This is the argument, and the meaning of the title, of Henry Harrison's Parnell Vindicated.
[4] Letter of 14 Jan. 1890, reproduced in O'Brien, Evening Memories, p. 466.
[5] O'Brien said later that this letter gave him 'the first authentic glimpse of how much reality there was in the rumours which had long been the sport of the scandal-mongers' (ibid., pp. 465–6).
[6] F.J., 30 Dec. 1889. This very significant statement seems to have been ignored by all writers on Parnell and the divorce crisis.

living with Mrs. O'Shea in her husband's absence and *without* his knowledge at the time, would not normally have been received in nationalist Ireland with any high degree of approbation. But a year had not elapsed since the discomfiture of Pigott, and Irish opinion would not question any act or saying of Parnell's. During the month of January one public body after another passed resolutions of unaltered confidence in Parnell's leadership and denounced the 'infamous intrigues' and 'unscrupulous machinations of his enemies'.[1] In England there were signs that the liberal allies were unhappy about the proceedings,[2] but in Ireland the people were solid behind Parnell. Not only did they 'trust implicitly' what Parnell said, but they, or their spokesmen, seemed careful not to examine too closely exactly what it was that he did say.

The blind faith of the people in Parnell is not remarkable. What is remarkable is the fact that Parnell's lieutenants, few if any of whom can have 'trusted implicitly' that the adultery charge was unfounded, took no steps to prepare for two very foreseeable contingencies: first, that O'Shea would win his suit and, second, that the liberals would then refuse to co-operate with a party led by Parnell. O'Brien and Dillon expressed their fears in correspondence, but do not seem to have taken any action, or made any plans; when the crisis actually broke, both of them, threatened with arrest in Ireland, were in America.[3] Healy announced that he 'took

---

[1] Ibid., 4 Jan. 1890 to 30 Jan. 1890.

[2] 'A party whose chief is a prospective co-respondent is rather like a water-logged ship. But charges can be brought against any man' (*Pall Mall Gazette*, 30 Dec. 1889).

[3] Among the Dillon Papers are two letters from O'Brien to Dillon on this subject: 'T. D. Sullivan wrote me from London that he fears it is the O'S [deleted] case that is weighing on Parnell's mind and says he is really anxious for his own sake to come to Ireland, but why the devil does he not?' (undated, probably early August). 'The news about Parnell's return to England is serious. I will be very anxious to hear whether he has sent you any definite message. If he continues to shirk it we have only one alternative but he knows that and I cannot believe he is capable of such folly' (16 Aug. 1890; Dillon MSS.). It is clear also that up to mid-August they had been content to wait for a move from Parnell. Shortly afterwards Balfour relieved them of responsibility by having warrants issued for the arrest of both of them, in connexion with the Plan of Campaign. They made their escape to France, and then took part in the fund-raising tour in America, where they were at the date of the divorce verdict and during the subsequent crisis.

Mr. Parnell's word,'[1] although as to what, he did not make quite clear. No preparations were made to attempt to carry on the work of a united party in the event, already highly probable, of a personal disaster to Parnell. The liberals, observing the attitude of the principal members of the Irish party, formed the opinion that Parnell's position was un-shakeable.[2] Parnell himself believed that, at this period, the higher clergy were already beginning to 'intrigue against him',[3] but there does not appear to be any evidence that they were doing so; their subsequent actions do not suggest the existence of any well-laid plan. The months between the filing of the divorce petition and the verdict do not seem to have been used by the principal nationalists, clerical or lay, either for 'intrigue' or constructive preparation. The nationalist movement as a whole simply drifted towards the catastrophe, with a dumb confidence in its leader's ambiguous assurances, and a dumb expectation of 'another Pigott'.

On 17 November, after a two-day hearing, the divorce court delivered its verdict against Mrs. O'Shea and Parnell, the suit being undefended.

Henry Harrison, in *Parnell Vindicated*, has shown that the version accepted by the divorce court was almost certainly false, and that O'Shea had probably long been aware of his wife's relations with Parnell. He also suggests (appendix C) that the divorce proceedings were instigated by Chamberlain. This is not conclusively proved but no one who candidly studies the evidence which Harrison assembled, and considers it in relation to Chamberlain's role in the matter of O'Shea's nomination for Galway in 1886,[4] will regard Harrison's conclusion as inherently improbable. O'Shea, however, probably stood little in need of instigation by the latter half of 1889; up to then he had been restrained from

[1] *F.J.*, 30 Jan. 1890.
[2] 'I regard it as certain', wrote Morley to Harcourt on 10 Nov. 1890—a week before the hearing—'that the Irish will not throw him over in any case and if they don't, nobody else can' (Gardiner, *Harcourt*, ii. 82).
[3] John Morley recorded a conversation with Parnell at Brighton on 10 Nov.—the day on which he wrote to Harcourt (above, n. 2): '[Parnell] spoke of priests; is sure the clergy or the prelates at any rate . . . are beginning to intrigue against him; but has no fear of them' (Morley, *Recollections*, i. 255).
[4] Above, Chap. VI, pp. 170 sqq.

proceeding by the continued existence and subsidies of his wife's rich aunt, Mrs. Benjamin Wood.[1] Parnell himself believed that the proceedings were politically instigated but he mentioned not Chamberlain, but E. C. Houston and *The Times*.[2] The only form of instigation of which O'Shea may well have stood in need is that of guaranteeing his legal costs; he was always short of money.

## 2. *After the Verdict*

The week after the verdict was a period of astonishment, anguish, and indecision. On the home rule side, only a few people knew their own minds clearly, and of these the most conspicuous was Parnell, who had decided to treat the divorce proceedings as politically irrelevant and to retain the leadership. On 17 November—the very day of the verdict— the Irish papers carried a letter from him, reminding the Irish party of the necessity of attending at Westminster on 25 November, the opening day of the new session, 'as it is unquestionable that the coming session will be one of combat from first to last, and that great issues depend upon its course'.[3] The tone of this communication was more eloquent than its content: the leader intended to be leader still.

It looked, at first, as if he would be successful, for the forces which were to destroy him were slow in massing. Archbishop Croke thought that Parnell's disappearance from Irish politics at least for a while would seem to be a matter of course,[4] and did not think any effort on his part would be needed. Gladstone, on the other hand, was inclined to look to the Irish hierarchy, as well as to the Irish party, for decisive action. 'I own to some surprise', he wrote to Morley, as early as 18 November, 'at the apparent facility with which the Roman Catholic bishops and clergy

---

[1] Above, Chap. vii, p. 234, n. 1.
[2] Above, p. 280.                 [3] *F.J.*, 17 Nov. 1890.
[4] Davitt MSS.: Croke to Davitt, 17 Nov. 1890. The archbishop added: 'A leader is one who leads—and Parnell has not led for the last half dozen years.' O'Brien, not long after, gave the archbishop his frank opinion of such ideas: 'The stuff talked of Parnell's being a sham leader sucking the brains of his chief men is the most pitiful rubbish' (*Evening Memories*, p. 480).

appear to take the continued leadership, but they may have tried the ground and found it would not *bear*. It is the Irish parliamentary party, and that alone, to which we have to look.'[1]

While the liberals and the hierarchy hesitated, the *Freeman's Journal*, politically by far the most important newspaper in Ireland, came to Parnell's aid. Parnell had told its London correspondent that he had no intention of giving up the leadership 'either permanently or temporarily', and the newspaper at once supported this decision editorially. On 18 November, in the first of a series of impassioned and eloquent editorials in favour of Parnell, the *Freeman's Journal* produced what were to be the two basic arguments of Parnell's supporters in the split. First, the question of the leadership was a political one, not moral or religious; second, it was one which should be decided by the Irish people, not by the English people. With these were joined other arguments which were also to be heard again and again: England had not worried about the moral character of many of her leaders—Nelson, Wellington, Melbourne, Palmerston, and (an unhappy example) Dilke; Parnell was 'a member of a different church' and should not be judged as a Catholic would be judged;[2] the full story had not been told at the divorce court and 'if all were known' Parnell would appear in a different light. Finally, the *Freeman* gave a clear and ringing slogan: 'He is Leader and he shall remain Leader.'

On the day when this powerful and influential article appeared, the central branch of the National League held its fortnightly meeting in Dublin. The meeting was important, because it fell on the day after the verdict, and because it was the first opportunity that a representative nationalist body had of making a declaration about the leadership.

---

[1] Morley, *Gladstone*, iii. 430. In this letter Gladstone also said: 'I think it plain that we have nothing to do in the matter. The [Irish] party is as distinct from us as that of Smith or Hartington.'

[2] This argument was very widely used, no doubt for its popular appeal, and greatly resented by Irish Protestants. Most of the Protestants in the Irish party became anti-Parnellites, and it is not unlikely that their decisions may have been affected by this tactless argument with its implication, sometimes clearly expressed, that 'Protestants can't be expected to have any morals.'

Several members of the party attended—more than was normal for such a meeting—and there was a disproportion-ately high attendance of those members who later became known as the 'Parnellite' group in the party. John Redmond was in the chair, and other future 'Parnellites' present were Dr. Kenny, Leamy, W. A. Macdonald, Clancy, and W. Redmond. The much larger 'anti-Parnellite' group (of the future) was represented only by T. M. Healy—who came late—Swift McNeill, and a minor member of the 'Bantry band', D. Sullivan.[1] The 'Parnellite' group took command of the proceedings from the start. John Redmond declared from the chair that, 'The Irish party are bound to their leader by ties of absolute confidence and unquestioning loyalty. If he was thinking of quitting, the Irish people would come as one man and entreat him not to desert them, but thank God no such danger ever existed.'[2] Leamy said that 'no-one should come between the Irish people and the Irish leader . . . they should never abandon their leader at the threat of any party'. This was significant, for the liberal party, to which Leamy clearly referred, had as yet neither intervened nor 'threatened'; Parnell's supporters apparently foresaw such intervention, although the party as a whole did not do so.[3] Dr. Kenny, Macdonald, W. Redmond, and Clancy followed along the same lines, and Clancy branded anyone who would desert Parnell as 'a traitor'. The members who were later to be anti-Parnellites spoke at the end and followed the lead so energetically given by Redmond and his friends. Swift McNeill promised 'unswerving allegiance'; D. Sullivan said he would 'fight on by the side of his great leader'; Healy, the last member to speak, declared, rather ambiguously, that he had 'as much trust [in Parnell] to-day as in 1880'.

It does not seem likely that the attendance at this meeting of so high a proportion of Parnell's reliable supporters was

[1] There was also a member, Leahy, who did not vote in the leadership crisis. D. Sullivan later wrote a useful, but very partisan, history of the split (*The Story of Room 15*) in which he referred to this meeting, and to Redmond's speech, but failed to mention his own contribution.
[2] This account follows the report in the *Freeman's Journal* (19 Nov. 1890).
[3] This is clear from the disarray into which Gladstone's letter threw the party after Parnell's re-election.

fortuitous. It is a safe assumption that these men were sent
by him to guide this crucial meeting; their success was
absolute. The advantage of the Parnellites in these days was
that they still had a leader, and that their leader had a clear
policy: to hold power. The amorphous group which was
later to coalesce against him had at this time no leader and
no policy. Dillon and O'Brien, the natural leaders in default
of Parnell, were in America, as was T. P. O'Connor;
McCarthy, the vice-chairman, was a political figurehead;
Sexton was an orator rather than a man of decision; Biggar,
who would not have hesitated to fight Parnell, had died a
few months before; other key members of the party, Dr.
Kenny, John Redmond, and Timothy Harrington (who was
in America) supported Parnell's continued leadership. The
only prominent member available to give a lead was Healy,
and Healy, after all, had once before, at Galway, given a
lead which had not been followed.[1] For the present he went
with the general drift of the party, and the drift was towards
Parnell's re-election.

There were two men who were making strenuous efforts
to stop this drift, but neither of them belonged to the party.
Cardinal Manning sought to move both the Irish hierarchy
and the liberal party to a public condemnation of Parnell.
To Archbishop Walsh he held out what he assumed to be
the tempting baits of restored ecclesiastical supremacy in
Irish politics and restored Irish influence in Rome: '. . . if
ten years ago the bishops and priests had spoken and acted
together, the movement would not have fallen into the
hands of laymen. There is now both in Ireland and in Rome
the opportunity of your regaining the lead and direction.'[2]
To Gladstone he reported his efforts with Archbishop
Walsh, and made a momentous suggestion and a false pro-
phecy: 'But it rests more with you than with any man. If
you say "Do not fetter my freedom of action and take away
my strength". . . . , Mr. Parnell would retire from leadership

---

[1] In an interview after the split, Healy said that he had hesitated to oppose
Parnell at this early stage because, in view of the Galway election and his
exclusion from the Special Commission, he felt that 'I should examine my
conscience more keenly' (*Pall Mall Gazette*, 'Story of the Parnell Crisis',
p. 90).
[2] Letter of 19 Nov. 1890, in Walsh, *Archbishop Walsh*, p. 409.

and still give all aid as before to the Irish cause.'[1] But, for the present, neither Archbishop Walsh nor Gladstone spoke, and the first voice to be heard, from the home rule side, against Parnell's leadership came not from the ecclesiastical or liberal 'right' of the movement, but from the left, from Michael Davitt's *Labour World*. Davitt urged Parnell's retirement on the ground that Gladstone's followers in Britain would not tolerate Parnell's continued leadership. He put forward what was to become the basic argument of the anti-Parnellites: 'The question for Mr. Parnell is—is he going to put the loyalty of the Irish people to a test which will disintegrate the forces behind the home rule cause in Britain?'[2]

That Davitt's editorial, breaking the extraordinary harmony of the days immediately after the verdict, was a severe blow to Parnell's supporters is evident from the tone of the *Freeman* editorial commenting on it. Although Davitt's attack was political rather than moral, the *Freeman* writer is more concerned with the forces of moral reprobation which he obviously fears will be let loose by any dissension among the political leaders, and he produces some of those absurd arguments and analogies with which Parnellite speakers were later to cover their embarrassment about 'the moral issue': 'It is living in England which has contaminated Mr. Parnell and were he living at home in Ireland he would never have fallen in with the O'Sheas. But we have no more right to pry into his private affairs than we have to interfere with him as a Protestant if he chooses not to go to church on Sunday or to eat meat on Friday.'[3] As a reply to Davitt this was not very effective, particularly since it was becoming increasingly clear that Davitt was right in his estimate of the effect of Parnell's continued leadership on the home rule cause in Britain. The Irish could, to some extent at least, safely ignore the sneers in the English tory press, but the increasing signs of uneasiness among liberal supporters were another matter. Unfortunately for those who shared Davitt's

---

[1] Letter of 21 Nov. 1890 in Leslie, *Cardinal Manning*, p. 437.
[2] *The Labour World*, 2 Nov. 1890.
[3] *F.J.*, 21 Nov. 1890. The 'contamination' idea was particularly absurd from the *Freeman* which, when the divorce suit was filed, had said of Parnell that he 'stood before fair and honourable England, a Bayard without fear and without reproach' (ibid., 30 Dec. 1889).

views, however, some of the English nonconformist leaders who sought Parnell's retirement did so in terms which were not merely tactless but grossly offensive to Irish national feeling. The London correspondent of the *Freeman's Journal* knew that he was rendering a good service to the Parnellite cause when he told Irish readers of the comment, made in *The Methodist Times* by the celebrated preacher the Rev. Hugh Price Hughes, that if the Irish people continued to follow Parnell they would brand themselves as 'an obscene race utterly unfit for anything except a military despotism'; to which the *Freeman* correspondent made the spirited reply that 'if the Irish people abandoned Mr. Parnell to follow the Reverend Hugh Price Hughes, a military despotism would be 10,000 times too good for them'.[1] To get the debate on to this plane was very helpful, in Ireland, to the cause of Parnell's continued leadership; it was hardly helpful, however, to the continuance of that great alliance which had been the main fruit of Parnell's policy. One of the saddest and most striking features of the split was that, even in this incipient phase, immediately after the verdict, it destroyed the atmosphere of increasingly genuine cordiality that prevailed, in the late eighties, between Irishmen and a large section of Englishmen. The 'union of hearts' was probably never as unreserved as platform speakers claimed, but it was the happiest phase through which Anglo-Irish relations have passed in modern times.

In Ireland, despite Davitt, Parnell's supporters continued to hold the initiative. A great public meeting held in the Leinster Hall on 20 November to uphold Parnell's leadership was attended by twenty-four members of the party.[2] Unlike the National League meeting of two days before, the

[1] *F.J.*, 21 Nov. 1890.
[2] The account of this meeting is condensed from the lengthy report in ibid., 21 Nov. 1890. The members present were Justin McCarthy, Webb, Dr. Kenny, Leamy, John Redmond, W. Redmond, Jordan, McCartan, W. A. McDonald, T. M. Healy, Fox, Pinkerton, Condon, James Nolan, P. J. O'Brien, D. Sullivan, Fitzgerald, W. Murphy, Mahony, Col. Nolan, Esmonde, Clancy, Deasy, and Chance. D. Sullivan (*The Story of Room 15*) asserts that the Leinster Hall meeting had previously been summoned to support the evicted tenants, had been abandoned because of the divorce crisis, and was then 'diverted at the instigation of Mr. Redmond and Dr. Kenny, M.P. into one in sustainment of Mr. Parnell'.

Leinster Hall meeting was in no sense a packed one; a size-able majority (15) of the members present were later to vote against Parnell's leadership; the secretaries to the meeting, however, were leading Parnellites, Clancy and Dr. Kenny. The public lead at this meeting was given not by the little group of Parnell's committed supporters, but, much more influentially, by the 'American delegation' (led by Dillon and O'Brien) in a message read by the chairman, McCarthy. The message was a strong one:

> We stand firmly by the leadership of the man who has brought the Irish people through unparalleled difficulties and dangers, from servitude and despair to the very threshold of emancipation, with a genius, courage and success unequalled in our story. We do so, not only on the ground of gratitude for these imperishable services in the past, but in the profound conviction that Parnell's statesmanship and matchless qualities as a leader are essential to the safety of our cause.

The message was signed by Dillon, O'Brien, T. P. O'Connor, Gill, and Timothy Harrington—all the American delegates except T. D. Sullivan, a severe moralist. This message is surprising, especially in the light of O'Brien's ominous remarks to Dillon, *before* the verdict, about having 'no alternative' if Parnell continued to 'shirk it'.[1] But here again, as at the National League meeting, it was determined leadership which had been decisive. Two of Parnell's committed supporters, John Redmond and Dr. Kenny, acting no doubt on Parnell's instructions, had cabled to Dillon and O'Brien urging them to come out in favour of Parnell's leadership.[2] The future anti-Parnellites, however, were not only leaderless but in no position to send messages; the only authority which could be set against that of Parnell was 'the party' and the party had not yet met; Parnell was still chairman of the party, at least until the party meeting on 25 November.

After the message from the delegates, there could be no doubt of the success of the Leinster Hall meeting as a rally

---

[1] Above, p. 281, n. 3.

[2] O'Brien, *An Olive Branch in Ireland*, p. 12. 'The two men', says O'Brien, 'were our own *fidei commissi* in the direction of the movement in Ireland as well as devoted followers of Parnell.' O'Brien argues that he and Dillon would have prevented this meeting from being held at all, if they had been able to get together in time.

in favour of Parnell. It was proposed by McCarthy, and resolved: 'That this meeting, interpreting the sentiment of the Irish people that no side issues shall be permitted to obstruct the progress of the great cause of home rule for Ireland, declares that in all political matters Mr. Parnell possesses the confidence of the Irish nation, and rejoices at the determination of the Irish parliamentary party to stand by their leader.' The party, it may be noted, had not yet had the opportunity of meeting to express any such determination.

After McCarthy, Healy spoke, with an eloquence which he was later to regret. The leader should not be abandoned 'within sight of the Promised Land'; 'of all questions this is a domestic question'—the very core of the Parnellite case. Healy referred to the denunciations of people like Hughes and Stead (whose *Pall Mall Gazette* had been calling, ever since the verdict, for Parnell's resignation): 'If we joined with this howling pack', he said, in an image which Parnell was later to use, 'would that be a noble spectacle before the nations?' But Healy hinted strongly at something which was probably in the hearts of all the 'anti-Parnellites' of a week later: the hope that Parnell would end their trouble by a voluntary resignation. 'We have stood by Mr. Parnell', he said, 'Mr. Parnell must stand by us. As we have to consider our position, let him consider his.' Yet he closed with words more in accord with the spirit of the meeting, words that were often to be repeated: 'You are requested not to speak to the man at the wheel.'

The second resolution of the meeting, proposed by Redmond, was tactical in character, and designed to soothe the minds of those who had been disturbed by Davitt's criticisms. It referred to the 'generous sentiments of the masses of the people of Great Britain' and assured these of 'the gratitude of Ireland' and the determination of the Irish representatives to continue to fight the tories. But, in proposing this 'pro-liberal' resolution, Redmond envisaged, as other speakers did not, the possibility of a liberal defection. The Irish party's past victories had been due, he said, to 'absolute self-reliance', and only by self-reliance could its position be maintained. Both speech and resolution were

ably designed to mask the inner contradiction in the Parnell-
lite case: the emerging conflict between the continuance of
Parnell's leadership and the continuance of Parnell's policy,
the liberal alliance.

The triumph of Parnell's supporters at the Leinster Hall
meeting was enhanced by resolutions in favour of Parnell,
passed by public bodies all over the country, no doubt also
under the influence of the views of Dillon and O'Brien
which had become known in Ireland on the morning of
20 November. The bishops were dismayed. Archbishop
Croke, to whom Archbishop Walsh had communicated
Cardinal Manning's views, would not altogether agree that
Parnell's continuance as leader would mean ruin for the
national cause but he agreed it would mean serious damage.
He expressed his disgust with Parnell personally and with
his party:

I have flung him away from me forever. His bust which for
some time has held a prominent place in my hall I threw out
yesterday. And as for 'the party' generally, I go with you entirely
in thinking that they make small, or no, account of the bishops
and priests now, as independent agents, and only value them as
money gatherers and useful auxiliaries in the agitation. This I have
noticed for a considerable time past and I believe we shall have to
let them see and feel unmistakably that, without us, they would
be simply nowhere and nobodies.[1]

At the same time he made it clear that this strong attitude
was not suitable to the present crisis. 'But now'—since the
Leinster Hall meeting—'I fear things must be allowed to
take the direction given them by the Irish members—come
what may.'[1] To Davitt, who was urging him to speak out,
Archbishop Croke made his decision against intervention
more explicit:

The attitude of the Irish members and their pronouncement on
Thursday last [i.e. at the Leinster Hall] in favour of Parnell's continued leadership prevent me and others from making a move on
this matter. . . . They have apparently nailed their colours to the
mast and any attempt made now to tear them down, or to oblige
others to do it, would only end in two hostile camps and in a

[1] Letter of 22 Nov. 1890 in Walsh, *Archbishop Walsh*, p. 409.

weakening, if not a disruption of the party. Things must now take their course.[1]

Archbishop Walsh seems to have shared Archbishop Croke's views on the impossibility of a public statement, but, like Healy, he had not renounced the hope that Parnell might voluntarily retire. On 23 November he urged this view on Dr. Kenny, and on the following day he wrote to Kenny: 'All that has been done by the members up to now is excellent. It puts an end forever to the stories of disunion. But *above all*, it makes it easy for [Parnell] to do the right thing.'[2] This approach was without effect, as could have been foreseen, for Parnell had made no secret of his intention to hold the leadership.

While, in Ireland, the bishops were helpless to deal with a situation which they detested, the fate of the Irish leader was being decided in England. Ever since the verdict of the divorce court it had been plain that liberal opinion in England was at least uneasy about co-operation with Parnell, and some leading liberal journalists and preachers had been vehement against him. At first, however, no one could tell how widespread or how strong this feeling was, and Gladstone, as we have seen, thought that 'we have nothing to do in the matter'.[3] The liberal leaders, on the day after the Leinster Hall meeting, made known to a prominent Irish member, Justin McCarthy, their feeling 'that Parnell should give up the leadership for the time being', and they asked 'whether a letter of advice from Gladstone would have the effect if it could be got to Parnell in time'.[4] McCarthy made the not very helpful reply that 'a letter from Gladstone would have more effect on Parnell than a million of letters from the world in general'. He added, however, what was more to the point, 'that we, the Irish party, cannot throw Parnell over, but if the wish to withdraw for the present should come from him, that would be quite a different

---

[1] Davitt MSS.: undated letter from Croke to Davitt: written between the Leinster Hall meeting (20 Nov.) and the sessional meeting of the party (25 Nov.).

[2] Walsh, *Archbishop Walsh*, p. 410.                    [3] Above, p. 284, n. 1.

[4] Letter from McCarthy to Mrs. Campbell Praed, 21 Nov. 1890 (in McCarthy and Praed, *Our Book of Memories*, p. 256). Harcourt and Morley had sent Labouchere to sound out McCarthy.

thing'.[1] Over the week-end, 22–23 November, the direction and force of liberal feeling became unmistakable. Harcourt, who attended an important convention of the National Liberal Federation in Sheffield on Saturday, 22 November, reported to Gladstone from the meeting that:

the opinion was absolutely unanimous *and extremely strong* that, if Parnell is allowed to remain as the leader of the Irish party, all further co-operation between them and the English liberals must be at an end. . . . Whether it means a severance from the Irish party I know not but any other course will certainly involve the alienation of the greater and better portion of the liberal party of Great Britain—which after all is that which we have mainly to consider.[2]

On the Sunday, according to *The Times*, 'the "non-conformist conscience" spoke from a hundred chapels'.[3] Gladstone decided that he would have to intervene, before the meeting of the Irish party on 25 November. On his instructions, Harcourt sent for McCarthy, who came on 24 November.[4] Gladstone, who had just returned to London, saw him, learned that he bore no message from Parnell, and told him 'that notwithstanding the splendid services rendered by Mr. Parnell to his country, his continuance at the present moment in the leadership would be productive of consequences disastrous in the highest degree to the cause of Ireland'.[5] McCarthy was to tell Parnell of this, and, if Parnell refused to retire, was to tell his colleagues generally, at or before the party meeting.[6] That same day, Gladstone embodied his conclusions in a letter to Morley, intended to be shown to Parnell and McCarthy, and expanded them, by the momentous phrase: 'the continuance of Mr. Parnell at the present moment in the leadership of the Irish party . . . would render my retention of the leadership of the liberal party, based as it has been mainly upon the prosecution of the Irish cause, almost a nullity'.[6] Morley, at whose instigation this phrase had been inserted, records that Spencer—who as a former

[1] Ibid.
[2] Gardiner, *Harcourt*, ii. 83.
[3] *The Parnell Split* (1891), published by *The Times*.
[4] Gardiner, *Harcourt*, ii. 83.
[5] Morley, *Gladstone*, iii. 436–7; McCarthy and Praed, op. cit., pp. 258–9.
[6] Morley, *Gladstone*, loc. cit.

lord lieutenant knew more about Ireland than any of the other liberal leaders—was the only leader present at the drafting of the letter who doubted the wisdom of 'putting any screw at all upon Parnell . . . the only man who could drive the Irish team'.[1] On which Morley himself comments: 'Most true if only there were no English electors to be thought of. . . .'[1] The liberal leaders were later to be reproached in Ireland with hypocrisy,[2] as well as with a desire to ruin Parnell, but these reproaches are unfounded. Gladstone and his colleagues could have had no desire to destroy Parnell, who was their valued ally, until the news, most unwelcome to them, of the divorce-court verdict. Nor did they pretend that it was their reprobation of Parnell's adultery— about which they had known for eight years—which moved them to seek his retirement. Their action was based solely on the movement of English public opinion; they bowed before the moral indignation of the lower middle class, a force which hardly anyone in Victorian England, and certainly not the liberal party, could withstand for long. Home rule was not, in England, so popular a cause that its advocates could insult popular emotions about sexual morality.[3] To leave no doubt on the matter, a large nonconformist meeting was held at St. James's Hall on 23 November, at which the Reverend Hugh Price Hughes said that nonconformists would never tolerate Parnell and that 'unless he retired, the liberals would be absolutely defeated at the next general election'.[4]

McCarthy did not succeed in finding Parnell and delivering his fateful message until just before the sessional meeting on 25 November. Parnell refused to retire, and McCarthy, whether through timidity or regard for Parnell, or expectation that Parnell himself would make the position plain, did not inform the party of Gladstone's message. It is true that both he and Parnell seem to have been unaware of the letter

[1] Morley, *Recollections*, i. 261.
[2] This charge was made not only by Parnellites but, much later, by some anti-Parnellites, notably William O'Brien (*Evening Memories*, p. 467, n.).
[3] The Parnellite addiction to the *tu quoque* would not have helped the cause much either. In a London church when a clergyman at this time condemned Parnell's moral lapse, an interrupter loudly asked: 'What about the Prince of Wales?'                                                        [4] *F.J.*, 24 Nov. 1890.

to Morley, with its important 'amost a nullity' expansion.[1]
By his silence, the liberal scheme to influence the party to
elect a new chairman fell to the ground. The party, following the line of the National League and Leinster Hall
meetings, proceeded, as it had done at every sessional
meeting for the last ten years, to re-elect Parnell, with
acclamation, as its chairman for the session, on the proposal
of Sexton seconded by Colonel Nolan.[2] It has been claimed
that the party, in re-electing Parnell, was influenced by a
story, put out by his lieutenants, that Parnell would resign
after re-election.[3] Such a story, in itself—although some
members may well have believed it—could hardly have
decisively influenced the more experienced members, for
Parnell, as we have seen, had told the press, immediately
after the verdict, that he had no intention of retiring 'either
permanently or temporarily'. His whole comportment from
the beginning of the crisis was that of a leader who intended
to hold his power. Any confusion that prevailed among
the senior members is more likely to have concerned, in the
first place, Gladstone's intentions rather than Parnell's. The
*Freeman's Journal* of that morning, editorially urging Parnell's re-election, had said, with a high degree of ambiguity:
'The opinion of Mr. Gladstone has been, no doubt, taken,
and Mr. Parnell, it is certain, will be greatly influenced by the

---

[1] McCarthy and Praed, op. cit., pp. 258–9. Harcourt's biographer suggests
that McCarthy may have been 'affected by panic or timidity' (Gardiner,
*Harcourt*, ii. 86). According to R. Barry O'Brien (*Parnell*, p. 473) McCarthy
told him at some unspecified date 'that Gladstone did not at our meeting
ask me to convey anything to Parnell and besides I should not have done it
at his bidding'. This account conflicts with other evidence and is probably
not candid. McCarthy, whom Parnell later called 'a nice old gentleman for
a quiet tea-party', would not have found it easy to defy the chief whom he
had obeyed so long.

[2] One member, Jordan, apparently requested Parnell to retire, but his
intervention was brushed aside (D. Sullivan, *The Story of Room 15*; Healy,
*Letters and Leaders*, i. 322–3).

[3] D. Sullivan (op. cit.) states that these rumours were put out by Henry
Campbell, Parnell's secretary and the London correspondent of the *Freeman's
Journal*, Tuohy. In a letter to T. M. Healy immediately after the meeting
Sullivan wrote that: 'Up to a minute before Parnell finished his address I
thought he would conclude by announcing his resignation. We all expected
it' (Healy, *Letters and Leaders*, i. 322). A Press Association message after the
re-election and after the publication of Gladstone's letter stated that an idea
had got abroad that Parnell's re-election would be taken merely as a vote of
confidence, followed by retirement (*F.J.*, 27 Nov. 1890).

judgment of the statesman, the name and fame of whose
later years are almost as closely bound up with the success
of the home rule cause as are Mr. Parnell's own.' In the
excitable and over-hopeful atmosphere of these days, members may well have read this as an inspired assurance that
Parnell would not be standing for re-election without having
consulted Gladstone. The corollary that Parnell on Gladstone's suggestion, had agreed on re-election followed by
resignation might thus have found some credence, despite
the general tenor of Parnell's actions. Certainly only a body
of men anxious at almost any cost to avoid facing a hateful
alternative could have clutched at so shadowy an 'assurance'.

Parnell, after re-election, and having returned thanks,
made a brief reference to the divorce proceedings—a reference in the same vein as the statements he had already made
to Davitt and to O'Brien: 'He asked his friends and colleagues to keep their lips sealed as his were on the subject,
until the time came when he could freely speak on that topic.
When that time came they would find their confidence in
him was not misplaced. He would not further allude to the
matter beyond once more asking them to keep their lips
closed in reference to that topic.'[1] He said, naturally, nothing
about resignation or about talks with Gladstone.

Up to this point, Parnell's success in 'carrying off' the
divorce court's verdict seems to us now nothing short of
astounding. Ireland today is one of the most 'puritanical'

[1] Dillon MSS.: Minutes, 25 Nov. 1890. This account of Parnell's words is
probably considerably condensed. In the minute book, these words are
pasted on, over other matter (now illegible) on two facing sheets. These
minutes like all those from 11 Aug. to 6 Dec., are signed 'Justin McCarthy,
Chairman, 12 February 1891'. Two of the three secretaries—A. O'Connor
and D. Sullivan—were anti-Parnellites and took the minute books with them
into the McCarthy camp. D. Sullivan, in The Story of Room 15, gives a more
detailed account, which, although suspect for anti-Parnellite bias, is corroborated to some extent by the Parnellite historian, Harrison (Parnell Vindicated,
p. 10). Parnell, it seems, 'lifting aside a corner of the curtain' revealed that
'O'Shea was never my friend nor did I abuse his hospitality': he himself
'would rather appear to be dishonourable than be so'. Sullivan records the
'amazement and dismay' with which he and his friends listened to this
language, and their 'sickening feeling' that Parnell was concerned with the
social code rather than with morality. Sullivan gave a similar account to
Healy immediately after the meeting (Healy, Letters and Leaders, i. 323).

countries in the world; it is certainly far more puritanical
than England. In late-Victorian times, when English public
opinion was itself extremely severe in sexual matters, the
contrast between the two countries in this respect was
naturally much less marked, but it did exist. W. S. Blunt, an
intelligent observer who knew the tone of several levels of
society in both countries, felt that conduct was more in
line with precept on such matters in Ireland than in most
classes in Great Britain, and he was impressed in particular
by the austerity of the type of men who made up the Irish
party.[1] Yet this Ireland, and these severe and unimaginative
men, rallied to the support of a 'convicted adulterer' in a
manner which is impossible to imagine either in modern
Ireland or in Victorian England—which, in a much more
doubtful case, had destroyed, four years before, the promising career of Dilke.[2] As long as the divorce court verdict
and the 'moral issue' of whether an adulterer could be
accepted as leader formed the whole burden of 'the case
against Parnell', Ireland held to him, and her representatives
reaffirmed his leadership. The bishops, though deeply dis-
pleased, felt they could do nothing; in all nationalist Ireland
only one voice, that of Michael Davitt, was raised against
him. The view which has now become traditional, the view
of James Joyce's Mr. Casey speaking of how 'the priests and
the priests' pawns broke Parnell's heart,' the view implicit
in Yeats's lines:

> The Bishops and the Party
> That tragic story made . . .

is that Parnell's followers deserted him at the command of
the Catholic bishops, because of the divorce verdict. When
one follows the story of the crisis in detail, it becomes plain
that this view is misleading and that indeed the unity of
Parnell's followers, in the face of the divorce-court verdict,
was so impressive that the Catholic bishops felt they had
better 'let events take their course'. This situation, unthink-
able in respect of any other Irish elected leader, is one more
index of Parnell's extraordinary ascendancy over his people.

[1] *Land War in Ireland*, p. 447.
[2] Morley, *Gladstone*, iii. 438.

### 3. *After Gladstone's Intervention*

Gladstone, believing that the Irish party had decided to ignore his letter to Morley—of the existence of which it had not in fact been aware—released that letter to the press on the evening of 25 November, after the party meeting. Rumours of the letter reached the Irish members before they dispersed, and finally Professor Stuart, a radical member prominent in the Home Rule Union, procured a copy of the letter from the Press Association that same evening and read it to a group of the Irish members.[1] McCarthy, a little later, told of Gladstone's communication to him, and said that he had informed Parnell of its substance. A section of the party, led by John Barry and Arthur O'Connor now came to feel that they had been tricked into re-electing Parnell. They determined to reopen the whole question, but this was not easy. First Lane and then, 'very reluctantly', Sexton and McCarthy, asked Parnell to summon a new meeting. He refused.[2] It was, however, possible for a number of members to convene a meeting by requisition. This course was now adopted.

The decision to convene a meeting by requisition is the decisive event of the split. It marks the first revolt in the party against Parnell; the moment at which Parnell's enemies wrest the initiative from his friends. It was, if one does not allow for the excitement of the time, a rather surprising decision. The party had, after all, elected its chairman

---

[1] Sullivan, *The Story of Room 15*, p. 8. Sullivan asserts that, even before the contents of the letter were known, discontent at Parnell's re-election had been strong and that A. O'Connor had collected nineteen signatures to a round robin calling for a new meeting. Sullivan, however, writing as an anti-Parnellite when the fight was at its hottest (1891), has an interest in showing that the party did not, as the Parnellites claimed, reverse its position on Gladstone's dictation. His account on such a point as this is therefore open to question, particularly as some members seem to have learned the substance of Gladstone's letter before Professor Stuart obtained the text. It is significant that Sullivan in his *contemporary* account, written immediately after the meeting to Healy, states that 'I hear just as I write this that he [Gladstone] is going to resign' (Healy, *Letters and Leaders*, i. 323). He says nothing about A. O'Connor's round robin. It is interesting, however, that, a little later, Archbishop Walsh, writing to Cardinal Manning, refers to a rumour that the cardinal 'acting through Arthur O'Connor was the real author of the revolt against Parnell' (letter of 14 Dec. 1890 in Walsh, *Archbishop Walsh*, p. 425).                              [2] Healy, *Letters and Leaders*, i. 323.

for the session, and it could, with propriety, have asserted that with that decision (whether it had been based on inadequate information or not) the matter was closed for the session. At the next sessional meeting a new chairman could (if necessary) have been quietly elected. This course would have involved a short period of strained relations with the liberals, but might have avoided, and would certainly have minimized, the split in the Irish party itself. Yet this course, which seems in retrospect the most prudent, was never even considered; it was immediately rendered impossible by the decision, taken in haste and excitement on the evening of the re-election, to convene a meeting by requisition, thus reopening the whole question of the leadership. The requisition was signed by thirty-one members of the party, including McCarthy, Sexton, Barry, Maurice Healy, and William Martin Murphy. The signatories also included two inexperienced members—Mahony and Dalton—who were later to support Parnell, but they did not include any of the 'hard core' of Parnell's supporters, the men—like the Redmonds, Dr. Kenny, and Clancy—who had organized the series of Parnell's tactical victories in the days between the verdict and Gladstone's letter.[1] The bulk of the signatories were rank-and-file members, who later voted against Parnell's leadership.

The moving spirit in organizing this decisive requisition was John Barry. 'If it had not been for John Barry', wrote his friend Healy a few days later, 'Parnell might have tricked the party.'[2] Barry was a senior member of the party, an ex-fenian and an important figure in the New Departure of 1879–80. In 1880 he had been one of the small group of members who had decided that Parnell's name should be put forward for the chairmanship, in opposition to Shaw.

[1] The signatories, as recorded in the minutes (26 November) were: Justin McCarthy, Sexton, Molloy, Commins, McCartan, M. Kenny, Flynn, Dalton, Knox, Barry, Sheehy, M. Healy, Tanner, Mahony, Murphy, J. H. McCarthy, Deasy, P. McDonald, Crilly, Reynolds, J. F. X. O'Brien, Jordan, Esmonde, Roche, Lane, Stack, Sheehan, Kilbride, P. J. O'Brien, Fox, and Condon. One of the 'Parnellite' signatories (Mahony) later told Barry O'Brien that, at this stage, 'a number of us wrote a letter to Parnell saying that we thought it might be judicious for him to retire for a time but that whatever he did we would stick by him' (O'Brien, *Parnell*, p. 476).
[2] *Letters and Leaders*, i. 329.

Earlier still, as a founding member of the Home Rule Confederation of Great Britain, he had played a chief part in the
'deposition' of Isaac Butt in favour of Parnell. Despite his
part in these important events, he was not one of the party's
inner circle, and had not come into any prominence since
1880, probably because he devoted more time to his business
than to politics.[1] In 1888 he had been one of a small group
of members rebuked by the party for bad attendance.[2] Long
resident in England, he seems to have been more impressed
than were his colleagues by the feeling in England—
strongest among the nonconformist shopkeepers whom he
knew well through his business—against Parnell's leadership. He was now to show himself Parnell's most implacable
opponent in the party.

Once the political division had opened, it was obvious
that the anti-Parnellite side, as it now was, would invoke
clerical aid. William Martin Murphy, a relative of Healy's,
wired to Archbishop Walsh: 'Parnell determined to hold on
and no-one here strong enough to avert catastrophe. If you
think your interference called for you might wire Sexton.'[3]
The archbishop wired back his discreet but clear advice:
'Dr. Kenny knows my view by private letter. It is unchange-
able. Manifestly members hold no mandate from the country
to wreck the national movement. Take time. There never
was a case more clearly requiring calm and full deliberation.'[3]

At the requisitioned meeting, Barry, seconded by Commins—who had also seconded, in 1877, his motion deposing
Isaac Butt—moved: 'That a full meeting of the party be
held on Friday [28 November] to give Mr. Parnell an opportunity to reconsider his position.' Parnell refused to reconsider anything; he had been unanimously re-elected by the
party the day before, and if the party wished to make any
change, the responsibility should rest upon them. In the
rather tentative debate that followed, Sexton, Lane, Sheehy,
Dickson, and Webb urged Parnell to retire, in view of
Gladstone's letter. The main burden of their argument was

[1] In 1880 Barry was a commercial traveller for a linoleum firm in the
north of England. By 1890 he was a manufacturer on his own account.
[2] Dillon MSS.: Minutes, 14 June 1888.
[3] Walsh, *Archbishop Walsh*, p. 412.

that, unless he did so, 'the cause in England was lost.'
Sheehy put forward a corollary to this, which was to have
great weight with Dillon and O'Brien, and, through them,
with the country: 'the position of the evicted tenants would
be disastrous if the next general election went against
Mr. Gladstone and he . . . feared it would if the chairman
retained his present position'. Several of Parnell's supporters—of whom the most prominent was Colonel Nolan—
urged him to remain as leader; their arguments, if any, are
not recorded in the minutes. Finally, it was agreed on the
motion of Richard Power, seconded by Clancy—both supporters of Parnell—to adjourn the meeting until Monday
(1 December) and cable the American group informing them
of the situation.[1]

Inconclusive as were its proceedings, this meeting was
none the less a heavy blow to Parnell's power. Not merely
did it reopen the question of the leadership but it showed
that there was a large group in the party—probably a
majority—which would not support Parnell, if his retention
should mean the loss of the liberal alliance. It showed also
that this group included an important agrarian, 'Plan of
Campaign', section—a section which, being particularly re-
sistant to clerical pressure, and on the whole remote from
English liberal influence, might have been expected to hold
out against the forces which worked for Parnell's removal.
Finally, the speed with which the 'anti-Parnellites' reacted
to Gladstone's letter showed that, in John Barry, they had
found a leader who could act with resolution and dispatch.
From the time of the requisitioned meeting, Parnell must
have foreseen the defection of the majority of the party.
Certainly his subsequent actions suggest that, from this
time, he was addressing himself to the country rather than
to the party.

The publication of Gladstone's letter caused the greatest
excitement outside as well as inside the party. 'The conservatives and liberal unionists', cabled the Press Association,
'are jubilant at an event which they are confident will rend
the home rule alliance to its core.'[2] The London correspondent of the *Freeman's Journal* reported 'nothing short of

[1] Minutes, 26 Nov. 1890.          [2] *F.J.*, 26 Nov. 1890.

consternation' among the members of the party in London. But, editorially, that newspaper stood like a rock for Parnell. It reviewed the achievements of the leader who had created a party which was 'a model of disciplined organization and a tower of representative strength, proof against cajolery, or bribery or assault'. It recalled the libels of *The Times*, the period when Parnell had been 'hunted and hounded down with hellish malignity'; it recalled also that Gladstone and his party had not embraced home rule of their own accord, but that Parnell had 'compelled them to seek terms'. It reminded its readers of the Leinster Hall meeting, of the votes by local representative bodies, of Parnell's re-election, and asserted: 'Ireland has with one voice pronounced her wish that this man should continue to guide her progress from servitude to home rule.' Gladstone's letter, proceeding on 'the assumption that the Irish party is part of the liberal party', 'violated the principle of independent opposition— the hinge upon which the Irish party turns'. The liberals, concluded the *Freeman*, had a right to say their say but 'if Mr. Parnell remained at the head of a loyal and homogeneous party of 85 he could compel Mr. Gladstone, or any other liberal leader, to submit'.[1]

This fighting editorial, so prompt upon the crisis, and putting the Parnellite case so much more cogently than anyone had yet put the case of Parnell's opponents, must have done much to muffle the direct effect in Ireland of Gladstone's letter. But it was not in Ireland, at this stage of the conflict, that the critical decisions had to be taken, but in England and in America. In America the delegates read the text of Gladstone's letter, and received, on the same day a telegram from Dr. Kenny and Clancy, notifying them that the party, when re-electing Parnell, had not known of Gladstone's letter. They asked whether this 'altered the situation'.[2] O'Brien wired back recommending the party to open negotiations with Gladstone; Dillon wired asking that Parnell's opinion should be sought as to the effect of Gladstone's letter.[2] Harrington, who was with Dillon, noted that 'Dillon regarded it [Gladstone's letter] as a most important and

---

[1] *F.J.*, 26 Nov. 1890.
[2] Harrington MSS.: Harrington's diary, 26 Nov. 1890.

momentous one and I could see that his view of the present position of Irish politics is very much altered by it.'[1] Harrington himself, although determined not to desert Parnell, hoped he would voluntarily retire: 'Dillon asked me how far I would go and I declared that my intention was to join him and the others in a private expression of opinion to Parnell suggesting his temporary retirement but that on no account would I be a party to placing any public pressure on him.'[2] It would seem that at this stage—after the publication of Gladstone's letter and before the publication of Parnell's counter-manifesto—the opinion of the delegates as a group was tending against Parnell, but was less advanced in this respect than that of the principal signatories to the requisition. But the publication of the delegates' majority view—and O'Brien's telegram to Kenny and Clancy was immediately released in America to the press—was of great, and probably decisive, assistance to the anti-Parnellites in London. 'In view of our obligation to Mr. Gladstone', wired O'Brien, 'the interests of our cause and the responsibility we are under to the Irish tenantry on the faith of the general election which was fought in cordial alliance with the liberals we earnestly recommend the party to immediately open negotiations with Mr. Gladstone.'[3] Considering what Gladstone had said, 'negotiations' with him could hardly mean anything other than Parnell's retirement, although not necessarily his immediate or permanent retirement. It is hard to see that the publication of this message—as distinct from its dispatch—did anything but render the split, which O'Brien especially dreaded, all the more likely.

At home the tension steadily grew. Healy crossed to London on 27 November to strengthen the anti-Parnellite group,[4] and immediately joined with thirty-six colleagues in

---

[1] Ibid.

[2] Ibid. 27 Nov. 1890. Harrington refused, however, on the following day to sign a 'private telegram' to Parnell, sent by the other delegates, urging retirement. His refusal was on the grounds of the likelihood of a leakage in using the telegraph system (ibid., 28 Nov. 1890).

[3] Reuter dispatch from Cincinnati; in *F.J.*, 27 Nov. 1890, &c.

[4] 'It is better now Mr. Healy has come over, for he is a tower of strength' (Sir Henry Lucy, *Salisbury Parliament*, diary entry for 27 Nov. 1890).

requisitioning another meeting, for the following day, to
consider the following draft resolution: 'That any member
of this party who by speech or public declaration attempts
to influence or overawe the deliberations of the party, pending the adjourned meeting on Monday next, acts in breach
of the understanding as to the specific purpose for which the
adjournment was taken, viz. to afford opportunity for communication with absent colleagues, and we hereby declare
that the provocation and public controversy by members of
the party pledged to act and vote with the majority with
reference to the subject of the adjourned meeting is [*sic*]
against good policy and to be condemned accordingly.'[1]
This was an attempt to check the efforts which Dr. Kenny
had been successfully making to get the National League
machine working, pumping out branch resolutions in support of Parnell.[2] The meeting was probably also designed to
ward off the effect of an expected manifesto from Parnell—
a manifesto which had been 'called for' in a *Freeman* editorial
of 27 November.[3] The Press Association, reporting the requisition as signed by thirty-eight members, added that
thirty-eight members were 'pledged if necessary to insist on
Parnell's retirement'.[4] The meeting, without reaching a
decision, was adjourned until later, and the later meeting
fell through. It left behind it an impression of a mounting
opposition to Parnell, and an increasing self-confidence of
'the party', as distinct from its leader.

In Ireland Davitt's *Labour World* renewed its attack on
Parnell, and this time attacked the Irish clergy also for their
dilatoriness on 'the moral issue': 'The bishops and priests
of Ireland have left it to the sturdy dissenters of Great
Britain to make their protest.'[5] In fact, however, the clergy,
now that the party was divided, were beginning to exert
their influence. On 27 November a convention of the
National League was held in Kilkenny to adopt the candida-

---

[1] Minutes, 28 Nov. 1890.          [2] Sullivan, *Story of Room 15*, p. 11.

[3] In the same editorial, the *Freeman*, its infinitives already ravaged by the
split, called for a solution 'which the country may be able to honourably
accept and to unanimously fiat'.

[4] *F.J.*, 27 Nov. 1890. In fact, four of the thirty-eight signatories—Dalton,
Harrison, Hayden, and Quinn—remained with Parnell in the final division.

[5] *The Labour World*, 27 Nov. 1890.

ture of Sir John Pope-Hennessy, the candidate who, before
the crisis, had been approved by Parnell, and who was to
finish his campaign fighting as an anti-Parnellite. The convention, however, took place under truce conditions; the
party sent down a representative of each section, John
Redmond for the Parnellites, and Chance for the anti-
Parnellites. Sir John himself looked forward to the day
when Parnell would be prime minister in an independent
Ireland;[1] it seems, however, that, at the same time, he gave
assurances to the clergy of Kilkenny that he would act in
conformity with the wishes of the Catholic hierarchy. Afterwards, when the split was an accomplished fact, he sent a
telegram to the priests of Co. Kilkenny: 'I adhere to the
public declaration on which the Kilkenny convention unanimously adopted me, that is, to act with the majority of
the Irish party and in support of the Irish prelates.'[2] Archbishop Croke wished the candidate 'God-speed'. It was
left, however, to the greater diplomatic gifts of Archbishop
Walsh to handle the delicate and dangerous mission of
declaring the church's interest in the ending of Parnell's
leadership. On 28 November the archbishop released to the
press a carefully worded declaration, designed to influence
the party against Parnell, at its adjourned meeting on
1 December:

It is easy to conceive that the decision then come to by our
parliamentary representatives may have the effect of opening up
a new phase of the national movement and that the situation resulting from the decision may be one that will put upon the bishops
of Ireland, collectively as well as individually, a very grave duty—
the duty of considering whether, or how far, it will be in our
power to continue in future to place in the Irish parliamentary
party that confidence which, as a body, we felt justified in placing
in it in the past.[3]

The archbishop kept open a line of retreat, stating that a
'final judgment' on the divorce case was not possible, in

[1] F.J., 28 Nov. 1890.
[2] Ibid., 10 Dec. 1890. The latter part of this 'public declaration' was not
published at the time.
[3] Walsh, *Archbishop Walsh*, p. 413. This declaration was in the form of an
'answer' to the editor of the *Irish Catholic*, but was released to the press
generally. It appeared in the *Freeman's Journal* on 29 Nov.

view of the means used by Parnell's enemies in the Pigott case. The liberals and anti-Parnellites were hoping for something stronger than this. They hoped, according to the Press Association, that, before the adjourned meeting, the hierarchy would make 'a formal pronouncement' against Parnell which would bring out 'nearly the whole of the Irish parliamentary party' to oppose his retention of the leadership.[1] Archbishop Walsh, however, a subtler strategist than these, had a sounder idea. He informed Cardinal Manning (who, like Davitt, called for swift action) that he had called a meeting of the standing committee of the Irish episcopacy, but *not* in advance of the party meeting. 'I have called it', he wrote, 'for next Wednesday [December 3]. This will exercise a strong influence on Monday's proceedings [at the party meeting] and in a form that no politician can object to.'[2]

The state of mind of thoughtful nationalists generally about this time is probably best reflected in an editorial which appeared (a little later) in *The Nation*.[3] *The Nation* saw Gladstone's letter as 'a grave cloud upon the prospects of our cause'. It was neither pleasant nor 'over-safe' to abandon Parnell, 'the first leader since the Union who has succeeded in forming an independent Irish party in the House of Commons, and in maintaining it in efficiency and influence, and in surrendering him in response to an outcry [in England] that is to a large extent generated by the very services he has rendered to Ireland'. The only reason strong enough to end the present leadership would be 'the incompatibility of its continuance with the success of the Irish movement'. *The Nation* thought that Parnell's holding to the leadership was

---

[1] Press Association dispatch in *F.J.*, &c., 28 Nov. 1890.
[2] Letter of 28 Nov. 1890 in Leslie, *Manning*, p. 438.
[3] This editorial appeared in the issue of the weekly *Nation* for 29 Nov., by which date, however, events had moved beyond it with the publication, on the morning of that day, of Parnell's manifesto. In the history of the split this editorial properly belongs to the phase between Gladstone's letter and Parnell's manifesto, and it is so dealt with here. Owned by the Sullivan family, *The Nation* had always been cooler in its Parnellism than the *Freeman's Journal* or *United Ireland*, and it was also more sensitive to ecclesiastical opinion. It continued to express approbation for the ideals of its own Young Ireland founders, but by now it contained almost as much Catholic devotional reading as it did patriotic appeals.

due to his judgement of the interests of the cause. If, how-ever, his continued leadership meant 'the indefinite post-ponement of home rule', it became 'the guarantee of disaster', and duty pointed to Parnell's 'temporary retire-ment'. The danger of disunion, however, was greater than that of losing either Parnell or the liberal alliance. 'Let us stand together and act together for the sake of Ireland and for Ireland's sake alone.'

Parnell's position was now visibly crumbling. The Eng-lish liberals were openly against him; so was a large section, probably the majority, of his own party; Dillon and O'Brien, whose influence might be decisive with moderate people, were for negotiations with the liberals—negotiations which could only end in Parnell's dismissal or resignation. Now the Irish hierarchy was exerting a tactful but relentless pressure on those who had followed him so far. In this position, for Parnell to remain inactive would have been virtually to abandon the leadership. He could retire or he could fight back; no other choice was open to him. He chose to fight, and to fight by appealing to the country, over the heads of the party. *The Nation's* hope of pre-serving national unity was destroyed on the very day it was expressed.

Parnell's 'manifesto to the Irish people', published in the daily newspapers on 29 November, was, in the main, an appeal to certain basic, historically formed, national emo-tions—fear of treachery, suspicion of England—which he himself, since 1882, and especially since 1886, had been doing his best to calm. The manifesto began: 'The integrity and independence of a section of the Irish parliamentary party having been apparently sapped and destroyed by the wire-pullers of the English liberal party, it has been neces-sary for me, as the leader of the Irish nation, to take counsel with you.' Gladstone's letter, Parnell declared, had been the immediate cause of the disturbance in the party, but the independence of her members had been Ireland's 'only safe-guard within the constitution'. He went on to make 'revela-tions' about his visit to Hawarden in December 1889, when, he said, Gladstone had confided to him the details of the home rule proposals which the next liberal administration

would introduce.[1] These included—according to Parnell—
the reduction of the Irish representation in the imperial
parliament from 103 to 32; reservation to the imperial parliament of power to deal with the land question; constabulary to be kept under imperial control for an indefinite
period, judges for ten to twelve years. With so much reserved to the imperial parliament it would be 'the height of
madness for any Irish leader to imitate Grattan's example'
and consent to 'disband the army which had cleared the way
to victory' (i.e. to consent to a reduction in the Irish representation at Westminster). Parnell had told Gladstone that
he would try to 'reconcile Irish public opinion' on the constabulary and the judges, but he dissented from the reduction of the representation and from the absence of a land
settlement. The manifesto went on to speak of Balfour's
Land Purchase Bill,[2] which Parnell said he had opposed at
Morley's request; this had been a false strategy adopted out
of regard to 'English prejudices and radical peculiarities'.
He added that Morley had offered him, or a member of his
party, the chief secretaryship for Ireland in the next liberal
administration, 'and a law office for a legal member of the
party'. Parnell could not agree 'to forfeit in any way the
independence of the party'. Morley had also told him that
the liberals could do nothing for the evicted Plan of Campaign tenants in Tipperary; he, Parnell, would, however,
'stand by' these tenants. He ended by again stressing the
necessity for independence. 'I believe that the party will
obtain home rule only provided it remains independent of
any English party.' Even if an 'independent' policy meant
the defeat of the liberals at the next general election, 'a post-

---

[1] For Gladstone's own, contemporary, account of the meeting see above,
Chap. VII, p. 235. Gladstone's account, which differs from Parnell's (e.g. in
making no mention of the constabulary) is to be preferred to Parnell's in that
it was made at the time and for a non-polemical purpose.

[2] According to D. Sullivan (*The Story of Room 15*, p. 15) Parnell, on the
evening the manifesto appeared, called together a number of members, mostly
Parnellites, but with a few moderate anti-Parnellites—McCarthy, Condon,
Abraham, and Deasy. When Condon raised the difficulty about the evicted
tenants, Parnell suggested that this could be got over '*by an arrangement with
Mr. Balfour to allow the Land Purchase Bill to pass unopposed*' (Sullivan's italics).
These references seem to suggest Parnell was toying with the idea—now a
desperate one—of reverting to the 'tory policy' of 1885.

ponement would be preferable to a compromise of our national rights by the acceptance of a measure which would not realize the aspirations of our race'.[1]

To men who, two years before, had been reprimanded by Parnell, at a gathering of English liberals,[2] precisely for endangering the liberal alliance and the prospects of a liberal victory at the general election, the language of the manifesto could hardly carry much conviction. The basic argument indeed—the necessity for an independent party—was accepted by all Irish nationalists, and many on the anti-Parnellite side were sensitive to the force of the charge that they were abandoning their own leader at the command of the leader of an English party. But the belated 'Hawarden revelations', rendering impossible any resumption, under Parnell's leadership, of the liberal alliance which had been his main achievement, were such as to encourage his opponents and to turn the waverers in the party against him. Whatever the rank and file of the party might think of Healy —at whom, of course, the shaft about the 'law office' was aimed—they were not likely to accept the idea that the mass of Parnell's opponents, who now included most of the 'Plan of Campaign' members, had had their independence 'sapped' by 'the wire-pullers of the English liberal party'. But Parnell's manifesto was addressed not to the party, but to the Irish people, many of whom, recalling the fate of previous movements, would find nothing surprising in the idea that their representatives had been 'got at' by the English liberals. The manifesto, in effect, told the party that, if they tried to put him out, he would do his formidable best to rouse Ireland against them and their liberal allies. It made it clear, at the same time, that, if they held to him, the liberal alliance would become unworkable, for how could Gladstone again negotiate with a man who had so resoundingly broken confidence with him? After the manifesto, the question was no longer one of whether the home rule movement would split, but of *where* it would split; whether the line of division would run between the English and the Irish sections of the movement—probably making home

---

[1] Text of the manifesto in *F.J.*, &c., 29 Nov. 1890.
[2] See above, Chap. VII, pp. 218 sqq.

rule a lost cause in England[1]—or whether the Irish movement would itself be torn asunder. In either case, home rule
had suffered a terrible, perhaps a mortal, blow. Only the
enemies of home rule could feel unqualified satisfaction on
reading Parnell's manifesto.

In America the delegates read the manifesto with strong
and conflicting emotions.

With intense pain [noted Harrington in his diary] I hear both
Dillon and O'Brien declare that on no account would they ever
serve again under the leadership of the man who would issue such
a manifesto. I see the old demon of Ireland's past misfortunes
again triumphant. We are, with our eyes fully open, again wrecking the only hope which Ireland has probably in the present century and we are rushing hastily, as if scrambling with one another
in our haste, to ensure that destiny. I find it quite impossible to
control myself, the tears rush to my eyes and I can take no further
part in the discussion.[2]

But even this loyal Parnellite felt 'that his [Parnell's] giving
way voluntarily would on the whole be the best way out of the
difficulty'.[3] It is curious that, having read the manifesto, he
could still have thought of Parnell's voluntary retirement as
in any way likely.

In Ireland Parnell's ecclesiastical opponents, encouraged
by the manifesto, became more definite in their language.
Archbishop Croke wired to McCarthy: 'All sorry for Parnell
but still in God's name let him retire quietly.' The reasons
he urged were primarily political: if Parnell remained, the
liberal alliance would be lost, the general election would be
lost, the party would be damaged, coercion perpetuated, the
evicted tenants crushed, and—bringing in the moral issue
almost as an afterthought—'the public conscience outraged'.[4]
Archbishop Walsh, always more correct and circumspect,
voiced his opposition not less firmly, but in a more suitable
form. In a press interview which he gave on the following

---

[1] The comment of the London *Daily Chronicle* on the manifesto was
apposite: '[Mr. Parnell] is in error if he imagines that by wrecking the
Gladstonian party he will materially improve the prospects of Ireland.'

[2] Harrington MSS.: Diary, 29 Nov. 1890.

[3] Ibid. For this reason, he did not act on his first impulse, which was to
send a telegram of support to Parnell.

[4] Walsh, *Archbishop Walsh*, p. 416.

day (Sunday, 30 November) he asked whether Parnell could confirm his earlier assurance to Davitt: 'If the Irish leader would not, or could not, give a public assurance that his honour was still unsullied, the party that takes him or retains him as its leader can no longer count on the support of the bishops of Ireland.' As for the manifesto, it was a political matter, which—with a tact unknown to Archbishop Croke—he left 'to be dealt with by those who are the accredited representatives of the Irish people in the political affairs of the country'. He added, however, that he considered the manifesto 'an act of political suicide'.[1] The Press Association reported that the 'spirit of bitterness' which was now beginning to appear in the controversy was increased by Parnellite resentment at 'private advices' by the clergy against the manifesto.[2] One such 'private advice' was given by Archbishop Walsh to Healy on this same Sunday: 'You can take it from me that the support of the Irish bishops will be given *to the party* and to the duly constituted *leader* or leaders as the case may be. We know in this matter no distinction between individuals so long as they are not disqualified for a part in public life.'[3]

Parnell seems to have had some hope that the manifesto, with its 'revelations' on the liberal attitude to the land question, might win him the support of the Plan of Campaign group in the party, which might in turn determine the majority decision. His hopes were disappointed. The five members principally identified with the Plan cabled (Saturday, 29 November) to the American delegates protesting against the manifesto.[4] Healy thought their protest would be 'decisive with Dillon and O'Brien', but, as we know from Harrington's diary, Dillon and O'Brien had made up

---

[1] Ibid. On the previous day Archbishop Walsh had had the benefit of Cardinal Manning's advice and encouragement: 'This is a supreme moment to convince Rome that you do not put politics before faith and morals' (ibid., p. 424).

[2] *F.J.*, &c., 29 Nov. 1890.    [3] Walsh, *Archbishop Walsh*, p. 417.

[4] '[Parnell] got facers from every one of them, especially Condon and Sheehy whom he tried to influence by entreaty. They afterwards joined a knot in another room and signed the cable with J. Roche, Kilbride and Lane [the three other Campaign members] to America protesting against his manifesto. This will be decisive with Dillon and O'Brien' (letter from Healy to his wife, 29 Nov. 1890, in *Letters and Leaders*, i. 328).

their minds on the strength of the manifesto itself. The reply of the American delegates—except Harrington—was sent to Justin McCarthy on the same Saturday, arriving late that night. It was uncompromising: 'We suspended judgment at Mr. Parnell's request pending the appearance of his manifesto. We have this morning read the manifesto with the deepest pain. It fully convinces us that Mr. Parnell's continued leadership is impossible.'[1] This statement was amplified on the following day in a long and argumentative manifesto defending Gladstone, asserting the integrity of the Irish party, deploring personal attacks on Parnell, but pointing out that the choice was now 'between the leader and the cause' and asking the party for 'a decisive vote'.[2] But the political importance of the messages from America did not lie in their argumentative content. It lay in the fact that Dillon and O'Brien, the two most important men in Parnell's party, had now declared against Parnell's leadership.

On Sunday (30 November) a conference of the anti-Parnellite members—except Healy who was ill—was held in A. O'Connor's chambers.[3] Fortified by the American messages, the anti-Parnellites decided that Abraham—one of the less prominent members of the party, selected on this occasion probably because he was a Protestant—should, at the party meeting on the following day, move a resolution declaring Parnell's tenure of the chairmanship terminated.

Meanwhile, Parnell and his supporters were fighting to improve his position on the eve of the party meeting. In Ireland many branches of the National League met, on that Sunday, and passed resolutions in support of Parnell.[3] In London Parnell actually persuaded the unhappy McCarthy to seek concessions from Gladstone.

I was with Mr. Gladstone, yesterday (Sunday) [wrote Harcourt to his wife] when he saw Justin McCarthy, who, poor man, was the bearer of a message from Parnell proposing that Mr. Gladstone, John Morley and I should sign a letter containing certain terms to

---

[1] Text in *Evening Mail*, &c., 1 Dec. 1890.

[2] Ibid. Harrington, who did not sign this manifesto, was reported as saying 'my judgment is against Parnell but my heart is with him' (*F.J.*, 2 Dec. 1890). His diary, however, suggests that he supported Parnell on grounds of policy as well as of sentiment.

[3] D. Sullivan, *The Story of Room 15*, pp. 16–17.

be binding on us in the final settlement of home rule which he, Parnell, undertook to keep an *inviolable* secret!!. . . You may imagine the answer which was given to this inconceivable proposal.[1]

This demand for guarantees from Gladstone was, as we shall see, to be the hinge of Parnell's strategy in his fight to hold if not the chairmanship of the party, then ultimately the leadership of the nation. It is very unlikely that Parnell imagined that Gladstone—who had of course denied the 'Hawarden revelations'—would or could give any guarantees under such pressure, and amid inevitable publicity. It is not even likely that Parnell believed that Gladstone's refusal could have much effect on the Irish party, which could appreciate the enormity of the demand. But to the Irish electorate, to which all Parnell's actions were now designed to appeal, Gladstone's refusal to state the terms of his next Home Rule Bill might seem sinister. It would tend to confirm the truth of attacks on liberal sincerity in Parnell's manifesto. At the same time, if the anti-Parnellites refused to seek such guarantees, they would appear less good home rulers than Parnell. This would drive home the other horn of his manifesto: that the party's independence had been weakened by liberal intrigue.

### 4. *Committee Room 15*[2]: *the Opening Days*

*Monday*. When the party met in its room in the House of Commons, on Monday, 1 December, there were 73 members present: the whole party, except for the 6 members in America, 5 members who were reported to be ill and 1 member, Patrick O'Brien, who was in prison for his activities under the Plan of Campaign.[3] One seat, Kilkenny, was vacant.

[1] Letter of 1 Dec. 1890 in Gardiner, *Harcourt*, ii. 88.
[2] The last debates of the whole Irish party under Parnell's chairmanship were universally referred to in the press at the time, and have gone down to history, by the name of the House of Commons committee room in which they took place. Committee Room 15 had been assigned to the Irish party in 1886 and had been used for almost all its meetings since that date.
[3] Sullivan, *Story of Room 15*, p. 17; *F.J.*; *Pall Mall Gazette*, &c., 2 Dec. 1890. *The Times*, same date, gives seventy-four members as present, but this is incorrect. The members reported as ill were Carew, Gilhooly, Lalor, Leahy, and O'Gorman Mahon.

It soon became plain that the anti-Parnellite plan of carrying a resolution terminating Parnell's chairmanship would
not, despite the numerical inferiority of the Parnellites, be
easy to carry out. Parnell was in the chair. The meeting
began with the reading of telegrams: many from National
League branches in support of Parnell, many from more or
less obscure people on both sides, one from Archbishop
Walsh to William Murphy, 'We have been slow to act,
trusting the party will act manfully.'[1] Parnell then ruled that
the resolution before the meeting was still John Barry's
resolution, proposed at the requisitioned meeting of
Wednesday, 26 November: 'That a full meeting of the party
be held on Friday next to give Mr. Parnell an opportunity of
reconsidering his position.' Barry had, of course, intended
'Friday next' to mean 28 November, which was now passed,
but Parnell ruled that it now meant 5 December. This ruling
was the more remarkable in that the meeting, at which
Barry's resolution had been discussed, had ended by carrying a motion to adjourn until 1 December—date of the
adjourned meeting which was now taking place. When
Barry asked leave to withdraw his motion, the chairman
ruled that, in accordance with House of Commons standing
orders—which governed party meetings—the resolution
could not be withdrawn without the unanimous consent of
the meeting. When the point was put to the meeting there
were some 'Noes' and a division was not permitted.[2] The
chairman accepted, however, an amendment by a Parnellite,

[1] *F.J.*, 2 Dec. 1890. The reporters of the *Freeman's Journal* were admitted
to this debate by agreement of both sides and the *Freeman* clippings are preserved in the party's minute books in lieu of a formal minute. The *Freeman's
Journal* had the monopoly of this coverage and sold its report, probably for
a very large sum, to the Press Association. All other newspaper accounts,
including those later issued in pamphlet form (*Pall Mall Gazette*, 'Story of the
Parnell Crisis'; *The Times*, 'The Parnell Split') are therefore based on the
*Freeman* report. D. Sullivan (*The Story of Room 15*) claims that the *Freeman*
report was biased, but does not correct it on any important particular for the
debates of 1–6 Dec. 1890. It may be accepted as substantially accurate, and I
have relied on it for the following account of these debates.

[2] This is one of the matters on which D. Sullivan (*Story of the Parnell
Crisis*, p. 17) claims that the *Freeman* account is 'slanted' in a Parnellite sense.
The dispute is not important, however. The point that Sullivan is trying to
make—that Parnell abused the powers of the chair in defence of his own
position—is amply proved by the allegedly pro-Parnell version of the *Freeman*.

Colonel Nolan, to Barry's resolution. This amendment ran: 'That the question touching the chairmanship of the Irish parliamentary party be postponed until members have had an opportunity of personally ascertaining the views of their constituencies and until the party can meet in Dublin.' The amendment was seconded by Sir Joseph McKenna—a not very happy choice, as that member was a landlord who had had trouble with the Plan of Campaign, and had broken party discipline on that issue.[1]

The hearts of the anti-Parnellites must indeed have sunk as they realized, at the very beginning of the debate, that they would have to fight all the way against partial rulings made by a chairman of whom they all—with the probable exception of John Barry—had long stood in awe. Instead of being engaged in terminating Parnell's chairmanship, they now found themselves discussing an 'amendment' which was in effect a motion for the prolongation of his chairmanship. When they had, no doubt after long debate, got rid of Colonel Nolan's amendment, they would then have to debate a resolution to adjourn—unless in the meantime the chair had accepted further Parnellite amendments. It is true that the anti-Parnellites had, to some extent, brought these troubles on themselves by their actions, first in re-electing Parnell as their chairman, and then in deciding immediately afterwards to remove him from that office.

Colonal Nolan's resolution was, of course, a tactical application of Parnell's strategy: to appeal from the party, which he knew he had lost, to the country, which he thought he might still hold. The proposed move to Dublin was particularly apt, both as an appeal to national sentiment and because Dublin was overwhelmingly pro-Parnell.[2] Colonel Nolan claimed that the adoption of his amendment would avoid a split by means of 'an Irish plebiscite', which might take about three weeks.

It was Sexton who moved the rejection of Colonel Nolan's amendment, thus in effect opening the anti-Parnellite side of

[1] Above, Chap. VIII, p. 263 n. 1.

[2] Of the nine seats which the Parnellites managed to hold in the general elections of 1892—after their leader's death—three were in Dublin city and one in Dublin county. During Parnell's lifetime and before the long clerical denunciations of 1891, Dublin must have been even more strongly Parnellite.

the debate. Having dismissed, as tending to break up the
liberal alliance, Nolan's plan for a plebiscite, he came to
what was, in the anti-Parnellite view, the heart of the matter:
'no service by any leader entitles him to ruin his cause'.
Referring to Parnell's manifesto, he asked for the names of
those whose integrity had been 'sapped' by the liberals. At
this, Parnell rose and replied: 'That section who are intriguing with Mr. Labouchere and Professor Stuart,[1] that
section of the party with whom you and others who ought
to know better have arranged to put me out of my position
in this party.' The reporters record 'cheers and counter-
cheers'.

Sexton rejected this accusation, appealing to his own past
record to show that he had never intrigued with the liberals.
Those who were now opposing Parnell, he said, were those
who had defended the integrity of the party 'under circumstances which would not have made it strange if the independence of any party had been sapped and destroyed'.
He referred to Parnell's long and frequent absences, then
returned to his main theme: 'If the leader is to be retained,
in my judgment the cause is lost.' He ended by saying that,
although he had to urge Parnell's retirement, he had a love
and regard for him such as he could never feel for any other
leader.

John Redmond, in reply, delivered the main statement of
the Parnellite case: a nicely judged blend of principle and
strategy. The principle was that of Irish unity: if Parnell
was deposed, the Irish race would be divided. The strategy
was that of entangling anti-Parnellites with liberals and dis-
crediting both: '. . . if we are asked to sell our leader to
preserve an alliance . . . we are bound to enquire what we
are getting for the price we are paying'. Parnell interjected
a phrase which was to become famous: 'Don't sell me for
nothing. . . . If you get my value, you may change me to-
morrow.' Returning to basic principles, Redmond said that
the deposition of Parnell would finish the Irish party as an
independent party and turn it into a 'discredited and powerless tool' of the liberal party. Finally—ending with some

---

[1] A radical member, active in the Home Rule Union. See above, p. 298.
Both men, Labouchere and Stuart were associates of Healy's.

strategic thrusts—he referred to McCarthy's unsuccessful 'overtures' to Gladstone, and claimed that to yield now to 'English clamour' would cut off American support and ruin the tenants' interests.

Healy, who followed, said that, whatever happened, the party would remain united. Nothing, however, was to be gained by delaying a decision, since Parnell's manifesto presumably contained all he had to say. As regards the content of the manifesto, and notably the Hawarden revelations, he pointed out that the Home Rule Bill of 1886 itself represented an abatement of Irish claims, in order to conciliate English opinion. 'Hear, hear', interjected Parnell. 'And is English opinion now only to be described as clamour?' asked Healy tellingly. He pledged himself to accept no such measure as the bill outlined in Parnell's manifesto, and no measure smaller than the bill of 1886. He reminded the party, however, that the bill of 1886 itself did not give immediate control over constabulary and judiciary, and gave no Irish representation in the imperial parliament. As for the Hawarden conversations, why had Parnell, speaking at Liverpool *after* those conversations, urged his hearers to swell 'the forces of liberalism which will rally at the next general election to the assistance of our grand old leader'. When the laughter which followed this question had died down, Healy followed up his advantage: 'Either Mr. Parnell at Liverpool was false or his manifesto was false.' Parnell interrupted him: 'I will not stand an accusation of falsehood from Timothy Healy and I request him to withdraw his expression.' Healy withdrew out of respect to the chair. This little incident was the first crackle of ill-temper in a debate which, so far, had been dignified, though charged with emotion.

Continuing, Healy asked whether the Irish party itself was so 'bankrupt in the confidence of Mr. Parnell' that he would have told no one of his Hawarden conversations. He scoffed at the charge of intriguing with the liberals; how, for example, could the delegates, across the Atlantic Ocean, fall victims to such intrigues? As for his own Leinster Hall declaration, he was proud of it. 'Aye, we stood up for Mr. Parnell against the bulls of the Pope of Rome (*cheers*). It was not likely we would allow ourselves to be influenced by the declamation of a single Wesleyan pulpit.' But when he saw that the bulk of the liberals were antagonized, he changed.

Why do I defer to English opinion? Why did we defer to it in the settlement of 1886?... We were able to do so because we were led by Charles Stewart Parnell and he was able so to abate the passion and the recollection of wrong and of centuries of suffering on the part of Ireland as to ensure this acceptance, almost without exception, by every body of representatives of the Irish nation. ... There is no hope, there was no hope for Ireland until Mr. Parnell succeeded in obtaining from Mr. Gladstone the promise of a home rule settlement.

But Parnell's name, if he drove out Gladstone, would be of no value.

I say to Mr. Parnell [said Healy in his peroration] that his power is gone. He derived that power from the people. We are the representatives of the people (*loud and prolonged cheers*). Place an iron bar in a coil and electricize that coil and the iron bar becomes magnetized. This party was that electric coil. There (pointing to the chair) stood the iron bar. The electricity is gone and the magnetism with it, when our support has passed away. ... We cannot [he concluded] found our position upon sentiment, upon the claims of friendship, upon anything except the awful necessities that surround us in the presence of a trembling Irish cause.

It is a good gauge of the effectiveness of this remarkable speech—of which only an outline is given above—that Parnell himself immediately rose to reply to it, reminding his audience that it was he who had discovered and trained the orator whom they had just heard. 'Why', he asked the party, in words that must have gone home, 'did you encourage me to come forward and maintain my leadership in the face of the world, if you were not going to stand by me?' He turned on the man who had done most to turn the party from its allegiance, John Barry, 'the leader-killer who sharpens his poniard to stab me as he stabbed the old lion, Isaac Butt, in the days gone by'. He, the leader, was now urged not to resign forever but to retire temporarily; was that proposal as sincere as the election to the leadership? As for the Hawarden conversations, he reminded the party that these conversations were confidential and not definite or final.

He reminded the party again of McCarthy's mission to Gladstone and that Gladstone now knew that 'if these two concessions—control of the constabulary and power to settle the land question—were made, I should retire from public life as a matter of course'.[1] It was important that these concessions should be obtained now, before he, Parnell, was abandoned and while Gladstone was leader of the liberals. Harcourt—then considered likely to be Gladstone's successor—'will give you local government and plenty of coercion'. 'It is not', he ended, 'an unfair thing of me to ask that I should come within sight of the promised land.'

With these four speeches the main lines of the debate were laid down. 'Independence and unity' were the Parnellite watchwords; 'the cause before the leader' was the anti-Parnellite principle. The debating honours had gone to the anti-Parnellites; neither Redmond nor Parnell could match the eloquence of Sexton, and Healy's oratory on this occasion was in a class of its own. But Parnell was not so much concerned with scoring debating points as with his strategy of manœuvring his opponents into the embarrassing position of having to negotiate with Gladstone, necessarily without success, under the eyes of the Irish people. The speeches of Parnell and Redmond were political acts, with a precise strategic end in view; those of Sexton and Healy, by comparison, were declaratory, directed indeed towards ending Parnell's leadership, but not conceived as steps in any plan for so doing. The Parnellites, inferior as they were in numbers and eloquence, still had the advantage of leadership.

Many of the subsequent speakers on each side, in the long debate that followed, merely found different words for the ideas of their leaders; the following account, necessarily abbreviated, takes in only those remarks which opened up new lines of argument or new phases in the tactical struggle.

McCarthy followed Parnell, in order to tell the party about his mission to Gladstone. Gladstone had told him that Parnell was 'absolutely mistaken' on the Hawarden conversations; Parnell and he (said Gladstone) had been in general agreement. As for the present crisis, Gladstone refused to interfere in any way, sign any document, or send

[1] See above, pp. 312–13.

any message. It had been a grave mistake, McCarthy pointed out, not to have told the party earlier about the Hawarden conversations. Parnell, knowing what he knew, after Hawarden, had not been bound to praise Gladstone publicly. If the Hawarden confidence had been so very binding, how could it now be released? Either way, Parnell, said McCarthy, had committed 'a vital error of judgment'; to which Parnell himself interjected 'Hear, hear'. This inconsistency, McCarthy concluded, 'imperilled and must always imperil your leadership and work'.

After this attack—surprisingly damaging, coming from so lethargic a politician—six Parnellite speakers in succession managed to catch the chairman's eye. John O'Connor prophesied that, if Parnell went, Irish public opinion would resolve itself into its conflicting elements; while if he stayed, there was no real danger to the liberal alliance, once the Irish party had shown its independence. O'Hanlon pleaded for a postponement rather than a vote 'to destroy the greatest man Ireland ever saw'. William Redmond—developing Parnell's strategy—claimed that Parnell's position was higher than merely chairman of the party: he was also leader of the Irish people. His deposition—even if it left the party united—would split the Irish people. He asked whether Parnell should be 'cast out' because of facts (the facts of the divorce) which were known before he was re-elected; the people in Ireland who were against Parnell were so because of these facts and not because of the liberal alliance. This last was a telling point, since the anti-Parnellism voiced by the party majority was (of necessity) entirely political, and that of their clerical and other supporters in Ireland was mainly moral and religious.

Mahony undertook to deal with the awkward point of Parnell's 'inconsistency' about Hawarden. It was right to divulge these talks in the present changed circumstances, just as it had been right to keep them secret when Parnell still had a united party in reserve, to keep the liberals up to their home rule pledges. If the party now took its orders from the liberals, it would go on doing so in the future. Dr. Kenny, raising the temperature, said that the liberals were 'hungry for Parnell's blood'. Joseph Nolan said that the question was not one for the English but one entirely for 'the pure Irish race'. After an anti-Parnellite member (Flynn) had intervened to ask for an immediate vote, and another Parnellite (McKenna) had spoken on orthodox Parnellite lines, Edward Harrington rose to make, on the Parnellite side, much the bitterest speech that had yet been made in the debate. Even if the anti-Parnellites had a majority, said the Kerryman, the Irish nation 'would never surrender its chief' to those who would 'decapitate' him and 'lap up his blood'. They would not give in to 'hysterical cries' or to 'the little caucuses in the National Liberal Club, with their dallying hushing, doubting, nodding, prodding, going on for years'. There were men at the present meeting —a shaft aimed at John Barry—whom 'neither 5-line whip nor 40-line whip could get to the house for a critical division', but who emerged now in order to overthrow their leader.

This wild and angry speech was, probably, not part of a preconceived strategy. But it took its cue from the rhetoric of Parnell's manifesto and his speech—'sharpening the poniard'—and, above all, 'English wolves now howling for my destruction'. Rhetoric of this kind, congenial to the readers of *United Ireland*, came rather oddly from Parnell, whose words were usually cool and measured. The new style, which Kenny, Harrington, and others learned so quickly from Parnell, was well suited to the Parnellite strategy, aimed at a final appeal to the country on the cry, 'We are betrayed!' This strategy could not, in fact, be carried out without emotionalism, which is not, of course, to say that the emotions of many speakers were not genuine. We have seen the record, confided to his diary, of Timothy Harrington's feelings as he realized that Parnell's leadership was ending,[1] and we may well suppose that the feelings expressed by Edward—Timothy's brother—were no less sincere. To accept them as such is not incompatible with the belief that it was part of Parnell's strategy to evoke such passions by his own language.

If emotionalism was in the interest of the Parnellites, the interest of the anti-Parnellite members—which many of

---

[1] Above, p. 310.

them forgot—was to keep the debate on the plane of rational argument. Neither the liberal alliance nor the future of the tenants was a good emotional issue, and the party was precluded, by its own previous actions, from drawing on the tremendous emotional reserve behind anti-Parnellism: moral indignation at a detected lapse from an accepted sexual code. The paradox was that, in the party debates, it was the Parnellites who tended to compensate by emotional intensity for inferiority in argument, while in the country— in the campaigns of 1891—the Parnellite arguments, sound as many of them were, were to be lost in a roar of righteous indignation.

The anti-Parnellite speaker, Sheehy, who followed Harrington, brought the debate back to a question of fact: Why were the tenants encouraged to sacrifice so much in the hope of Gladstone's return to office if, all the time, Parnell knew Gladstone would do nothing for them? This pertinent query was followed by some confused exchanges, in which both Parnell and Sexton claimed to have devised the Tenants Defence Association, and a member named Conway produced some purported revelations, denied by Sexton, as to what Sexton had said to him on the boat from Dublin. The debate, mainly as a result of Parnellite provocation, was beginning to show signs of getting out of control.

The next formal speech was by Knox, a young member, belonging to a well-known Protestant landlord family. Knox distinguished himself by being the first to raise the moral issue. Gladstone's letter was *not* the only reason why Parnell should retire; a fundamental reason was that he had wronged 'the purest of existing nations'. The answer to this—that Parnell had been re-elected by the representatives of that nation, in full knowledge of that wrong—was so obvious that the next speaker, a Parnellite, Dr. Fitzgerald, preferred to concentrate, like all previous speakers, on the political question. For the new Parnellite strategy, of 'people versus party', he produced a useful slogan: 'You have no mandate from the Irish people to destroy Mr. Parnell.' The next speaker, Justin Huntly McCarthy, son of the party's vice-chairman, said that this was the darkest day of his life: 'I have great belief in the old-fashioned theory of personal loyalty to a leader.' It was a theory which he did not push too far; he was the only member of the party who, having spoken in support of Parnell's leadership, eventually withdrew with the majority of the party. A more intransigent Parnellite followed: Leamy, who asked, with force, 'What would be our position before the Irish people if, having elected Mr. Parnell unanimously on Tuesday, we on Friday last [*sic*] deposed him at the bidding of an English statesman?'

The debate, on this first day, ended with speeches by two anti-Parnellite members: Webb, a Protestant, and Chance, a member of Healy's 'Bantry band'. Webb made the point that nothing would please Ireland's tory enemies more than the retention of Parnell. Chance said that Parnell's manifesto, with its reference to loss of integrity by a section of the party, implied that, if Parnell stayed, 'many other men would have to go'—including William O'Brien, Dillon, Sexton, McCarthy, and A. O'Connor; he did not mention Healy or Barry. He was interrupted by Campbell, Parnell's secretary, who called him 'a dishonest member', but later withdrew the expression.

The meeting was then adjourned, after a short procedural wrangle, until the following day.

*Tuesday.* When the Irish party met on Tuesday, it knew itself to be the focus of intense interest both in Ireland and in England. The *Freeman's Journal* had devoted twenty-four columns to its report of Monday's proceedings; the English papers—because of the debate's implications for the future of the liberal party—were scarcely less lavish with their space. Committee Room 15 had become the political news-centre of the United Kingdom, and was to remain so until the party had decided Parnell's fate.

Monday's debate had been, on the whole, on a level with the historic importance of the occasion. Tuesday's debate was an anti-climax. Most of the party's ablest and most influential members (along with some others) had already spoken; the main arguments on both sides had been presented. What remained (of this phase of the struggle) was little more than a roll call, a series of personal declarations in justification of a vote to come. The meeting began inauspiciously, with a bicker about the reading of the

American delegates' manifesto (of which the substance had been known since the week-end) and a ruling by the chairman that a remark by Campbell about 'the infamous caucus in the corner' (Healy and his friends) was in order. The first set speeches, by J. J. O'Kelly (Parnellite) and A. O'Connor (anti-Parnellite) added nothing to what had already been said. The next speaker, the blind W. A. Macdonald, although a much less influential member than either O'Kelly or O'Connor, made a more significant contribution. His speech was unique in the debate in that it was a dispassionate and qualified defence of Parnell's leadership. Parnell's manifesto, he said, had been a mistake, but what were the alternatives to him as leader? Sexton was not firm enough, Healy not conciliatory enough to his opponents, Dillon was 'too self-centred', William O'Brien was 'not a great parliamentarian'. Macdonald, after this review, came down not only in favour of Parnell's leadership, but in the direct line of Parnellite strategy: 'Parnell should not relinquish his claim to be leader of the Irish people until the Irish people have dethroned him.'

After Macdonald came orthodox speeches from Corbet and R. Power (Parnellites) and Esmonde and Crilly (anti-Parnellites). The first member to break new ground was M. J. Kenny, an anti-Parnellite. 'You are bound', he pointed out, 'to enter into an alliance with some English party before you can ever obtain home rule for Ireland. . . . Is an alliance with the tories contemplated?' To which Edward Harrington replied: 'If it serves our purpose, yes.' It is interesting that it was the impulsive Harrington who replied so directly, and not Parnell or one of his more seasoned lieutenants. This idea of a 'tory–Parnellite alliance' was, in the circumstances of 1890–91, outside the bounds of possibility. The divorce case, and the use the tory press had made of it, would have made it compromising (as well as unnecessary) for the tories; Balfour coercion made it no less compromising for the Parnellites. In a more remote perspective such an alliance might have become possible, and in the immediate future certain parliamentary combinations on specific subjects were contemplated, as we shall see.

J. F. X. O'Brien, the next speaker, an anti-Parnellite,

started a thoroughly unprofitable wrangle by the claim that Parnell had been re-elected on the understanding that he would resign. The first formal speech, after this dispute had subsided, was made by G. Byrne, a Parnellite, who directed his attack against the agrarian section of the party. The immediate cause of 'the difficulty'—meaning the split—was the problem of financing the Plan of Campaign. Here Byrne certainly touched on a reality, although he probably over-emphasized it. If the Plan members had upheld Parnell's leadership, there might well have been no split, and, if there had been a split, the majority would probably have been for Parnell, thereby greatly changing the whole aspect of the subsequent struggle in the country. And certainly the Plan members—as Sheehy's speech, with abundant other evidence, shows—were powerfully influenced in their decision by their anxiety for the future of the evicted Plan tenants.[1]

Two Parnellite speakers followed: Dalton, with a routine speech, and Harrison, who countered the charge about Parnell's inconsistency as to the Hawarden conversations. Parnell, said Harrison, knew that he, and only he, could 'squeeze' Gladstone when it came to the point. Many an anti-Parnellite, reflecting on 'the alternative leaders', must have felt in his heart the force of Harrison's argument. Two anti-Parnellites spoke next: Tuite, who said nothing new, and Dickson, a Protestant, who referred, like Knox, to 'the moral issue'—on which no Catholic speaker had yet touched. He would be false, he thought, to his religious convictions if he supported Parnell. When Hayden (Parnellite) and P. J. O'Brien (anti-Parnellite) had made typical declarations, Alexander Blane, reputed to be one of the simpler members of the party, achieved the *tour de force* of defending Parnell, on the moral issue, from an extremist Catholic and patriotic point of view. As a Catholic, he said, he was 'ignorant of the existence of the divorce court' and, as a nationalist, he 'refused to believe the evidence of British witnesses'. This defence is exhilarating in its combination of classicism and

---

[1] The unionist press had its own way of expressing this. The Plan of Campaign, in the opinion of the Dublin *Evening Mail* (6 Dec. 1890), was the 'real origin' of the split, for 'if the party broke with Mr. Gladstone the tenants would make peace with their landlords'.

audacity, like certain gambits of Morphy. Not worthy to end on such a note, the debate petered out with more moralizing by yet another Protestant anti-Parnellite, Jordan. When the party divided, there were 44 against Colonel Nolan's amendment and 29 in favour (including the chairman). This was rightly translated: Parnellites 29; anti-Parnellites 44.

### 5. Parnellites and anti-Parnellites

The division in the party remained substantially the same until the end, altering only very slightly in favour of the anti-Parnellites, and this may be a convenient moment to attempt to analyse the make-up of the two sections. The final division was to be 45 : 27 (excluding the chairman), one Parnellite member (J. H. McCarthy) having gone over to the other side. To the anti-Parnellite side may be added five of the American delegates, and to the Parnellite side one of these. The party at this time number 85 in all—there being one vacant seat, in Kilkenny—and that can be broken down as follows :[1]

| | |
|---|---:|
| Chairman . . . . . | 1 |
| Other Parnellites . . . . | 28 |
| Anti-Parnellites . . . . | 50 |
| Absent . . . . . . | 6 |
| | 85 |

[1] *Parnellites*: Blane, Byrne, Campbell, Clancy, Conway, Corbet, Dalton, Fitzgerald, E. Harrington, Harrison, Hayden, Dr. Kenny, Leamy, W. A. Macdonald, Maguire, Mahony, McKenna, Col. Nolan, Joseph Nolan, J. O'Connor, O'Hanlon, J. J. O'Kelly, R. Power, Quinn, J. Redmond, W. Redmond, E. Sheil, and T. Harrington (in America)—28.
*Anti-Parnellites*: Abraham, Barry, Chance, Commins, Condon, Cox, Crilly, Deasy, Dickson, Esmonde, Finucane, Flynn, Foley, Fox, M. Healy, T. M. Healy, Jordan, Kenny, Kilbride, Knox, Lane, McCartan, Justin McCarthy, J. H. McCarthy, P. Macdonald, Swift McNeill, Molloy, Morragh, Murphy, J. F. X. O'Brien, P. J. O'Brien, A. O'Connor, O'Keeffe, Pinkerton, P. J. Power, Reynolds, Roche, Sexton, Sheehan, Sheehy, Stack, Sullivan, Tanner, Tuite, Webb, and Dillon, T. P. Gill, W. O'Brien, T. P. O'Connor, and T. D. Sullivan (in America)—50.
*Absent*: Carew, Lalor, Leahy, Patrick O'Brien, Gilhooly, and O'Gorman Mahon.
Of the absentees all except the last two sided with the Parnellites (after the split was a *fait accompli*) and the Kilkenny seat was won by the anti-Parnellites, giving a final strength of 33 Parnellites (including Parnell) and 53 anti-Parnellites. But for the purpose of the analysis which follows above it seems

What differences can we discern between Parnellites and anti-Parnellites? What truth is there (for example) in the anti-Parnellite claims—made by Davitt and others—that Parnell's followers were 'the men of least prestige and experience in the party'[1] and that most of them 'had financial reasons for upholding him'?[2] And can we measure the force of the Parnellite contention that the anti-Parnellites had been led astray by 'the wire-pullers' of the liberal party?

As regards 'prestige' we can make use of the same methods which we have applied before (Chapter I, &c.), with the difference that the full particulars available for this period on payment of members out of party funds permit us to substitute a precise category ('salaried members') for the 'undefined' group of earlier tables. Table 10 is based on the last division—or 'secession'—of 6 December:

TABLE 10

|  | Anti-Parnellites | Parnellites |
|---|---|---|
| A. 1. Landowners . . . . | 1 | 1 |
| A. 2. Industrialists, merchants, &c. . | 12 | 5 |
| A. 3. Higher professions . . . | 10 | 6 |
| Total upper group . . . | 23 (46%) | 12 (43%) |
| B. 1. Lower employments . . . | 2 | 2 |
| B. 2. Farmers . . . . . | 1 | .. |
| B. 3. Salaried members . . . | 24 | 14 |
| Total lower group. . . . | 27 (54%) | 16 (57%) |

The first, fourth, and fifth categories here (A1, B1, B2) have become insignificant. As regards the second category, the anti-Parnellite preponderance among the 'business' members is more marked than it appears. The Parnellites in this category included only two business men, the others being

preferable to exclude decisions notified after the split had taken place. It seems curious that most of the absentees should have come out on the 'losing side', but it was by no means clear to contemporaries that Parnell was in fact losing. 'William O'Brien and Dillon see quite plainly', noted Harrington in his diary on hearing of Tuesday's division, 'that Parnell with 29 [sic] followers in the house would be much a greater force than any quasi leader that would be set up by the 44 [sic]. . . . Virtually the game is up' (N.L.I., Harrington MSS.: Diary, 6 Dec. 1890).

[1] Davitt, Fall of Feudalism, p. 643. Similar assertions are made by Healy (Letters and Leaders, i. 326, &c.).   [2] Ibid., p. 323.

people of private means. Almost all the business men—and all the substantial ones—were against Parnell. In category A3 most of the lawyers—seven as against three—including all the solicitors, were anti-Parnellites. These proportions may be ascribed either (on the anti-Parnellite view) to the superior acumen of legal and commercial minds, or (on the Parnellite view) to fear of the ill effects, on trade or practice, of taking up an 'anti-clerical' position.

The sixth category (B3) is particularly interesting, in that it disproves an important anti-Parnellite allegation. Healy claimed that Parnell 'had not the support of half a dozen independent M.P.s'.[1] these figures show, not only that he had more than twice that number,[2] but that the 'salaried members' were to be found in about the same proportions on each side. The section with 24 'paid men'—to use Healy's rather lofty expression—out of 50, could hardly afford to sneer at the section which had 14 'paid men' out of 28. But, in fact, with the exception of Healy, they did not sneer. Healy's theory, of course, was that the salaried members on his own side were making a great sacrifice—since Parnell still controlled the 'Paris funds'[3] while the 'paid men' on the other side were hanging on for what they could get. This hardly bears examination and indeed, very shortly after the split, Healy himself was already boasting of the revenue-raising powers of the anti-Parnellites,[4] powers which, given the strenuous episcopal support on which they could count, were quite foreseeable. There is no reason at all to suppose

---

[1] Healy, *Letters and Leaders*, i. 323. The figures in Table 10 for salaried members are based on the salary lists among the J. F. X. O'Brien papers in the National Library of Ireland. Only members who received a regular salary are included in the table. The numbers on each side receiving occasional contributions were also about equal. The Parnellite members classed as salaried include two members—Harrington and Clancy—who were paid officials (of the National League and the Irish Press Agency respectively). Of the party 'salariat' proper (Chap. VIII above, p. 268, n. 1) 24 were anti-Parnellite and 12 Parnellite at the division: 4 were absent, and 4 had resigned, or were dead, by 1890.

[2] Of the 4 members who, though not with him at the time of the secession, later upheld his leadership, 3 were salaried and 1 independent. If these had been included here, Parnell would be credited with 17 salaried and 15 un-salaried supporters—a proportion which would suit Healy's argument better, but still would not justify it.        [3] Chap. VIII above, p. 268, n. 1.

[4] 'There are a number of very grave and honest men on Mr. Parnell's side

that members of the party, in their decision on the leadership, were influenced in any way by their dependence on party funds. Both sides were of course financially injured by the split—which virtually cut off American funds—but that is a different matter.

As far as social standing contributes to prestige, our data give little support to Davitt's opinion about the superiority of the anti-Parnellites.[1] In the less measurable terms of personality, the discrepancy is much more striking. All the most conspicuous members of the party—Dillon, William O'Brien, Healy, Sexton, T. P. O'Connor—were against Parnell. The best known of Parnell's followers was probably John Redmond, and Redmond at this date was a dim light indeed, compared with a Healy or a William O'Brien. The Parnellites included some organizers of great ability— Timothy Harrington, Clancy, Dr. Kenny—but these were what would now be known as 'back-room boys'; they were not among those who were called, in the rather pretentious vocabulary of that time, 'the marshals'. But that very phrase, with its Napoleonic overtones, reminds us of the comparative unimportance of these differences between subordinates, overshadowed as they all were by the towering stature of Parnell.

Davitt speaks not only of prestige, but also of experience, and it is relevant to group the two sections of the party in terms of length of parliamentary service:

### TABLE II

| Period of first election | Anti-Parnellites | Parnellites |
| --- | --- | --- |
| Before 1885 general election   .   . | 16 (32%) | 11 (39%) |
| At 1885 general election   .   .   . | 24 (48%) | 10 (36%) |
| After 1885 general election   .   . | 10 (20%) | 7 (25%) |

Contrary to what one would infer from Davitt's reference to the Parnellites as 'the men of least experience', the 'old

but they cannot raise £30,000 for an election. His opponents in a fortnight raised a far larger sum to found a daily paper' (article 'The Rise and Fall of Mr. Parnell' in *The New Review*, Mar. 1891). On the very day after the split the anti-Parnellites were able to raise 'over £10,000 for current expenses' (*Letters and Leaders*, i. 338).                    [1] Above, p. 327.

members', elected before the general democratization of
1885, had a greater tendency to support Parnell than had
the rest of the party. So, to about the same extent, had the
members returned at by-elections since 1885. These two
groups had one thing in common: they were not products
of the county convention system. The men of 1885, chosen
at county conventions, were 5 to 2 against Parnell, as compared with a proportion of about 4 to 3 in the rest of the
party. In so far as, with such small numbers involved, we
are justified in regarding these proportions as in any way
significant, two interpretations are possible. Since, at the
first general election after the split—and after Parnell's death
—the anti-Parnellites were to sweep the country, leaving
only 9 Parnellites in parliament, it can be argued that, in
1890, the 'convention members', more democratically
chosen, were probably closer to the real mood of the
country than was the rest of the party. This does not
necessarily conflict with what would, I think, be the Parnellite view, that the 'convention members' were closer to
the mood of the clergy, who had played so large a part in
their nomination. One may add that they were almost certainly more influenced by the views of William O'Brien and
John Dillon than were the 'older members'.[1]

The substance of the main Parnellite charge—that the
anti-Parnellites were victims or accomplices of liberal in-
triguers—is hard to measure. This charge, useful though it
was before popular audiences in Ireland, was not simply a
demagogic device. 'The more I reflect upon the present
position', noted Harrington in his diary on 1 December,
'the more am I convinced that even our best men have
suffered in their intense national feeling by too much
association with liberal politicians.'[2] It is hardly possible to
measure something so intangible as the degree of association
with liberal politicians, but the charge did take a more concrete form. Edward Harrington, as we have seen,[3] blamed

---

[1] Of the 4 members who rallied to Parnell after the split, 2—O'Brien and
Carew—were '1885 members'—and 2—Lalor and Leahy—were 'old members', who had belonged since 1880. Of the 2 'post-split' anti-Parnellites one
—Gilhooly—was an 1885 member—and the other a very old member indeed
—the O'Gorman Mahon.
[2] N.L.I., Harrington MSS.                                   [3] Above, p. 321.

the split on 'the little caucuses in the National Liberal Club';
at a meeting of the National League, Parnell's followers had
hissed at the mention of 'that hotbed of whiggery, the
National Liberal Club'.[1] In that club, on the Parnellite
assumption, it was that the liberal 'wire-pullers' had 'sapped
and undermined' a section of the party. It is therefore of
interest to know what members of the party belonged to the
club, and it is fortunate that, through the courtesy of the
club's present librarian, we have that information.

Of the 79 members (including Parnell) whom we are considering here, 36 belonged to the National Liberal Club;
almost all had joined since 1886. Of the anti-Parnellites, 22
—less than half—were members of the club; of the Parnellites, 14, actually a slightly higher proportion.[2] Several
leading anti-Parnellites—notably Dillon, O'Brien, Sexton,
and A. O'Connor—did not belong to the club, while several
of the leading Parnellites—the two Redmonds, Colonel
Nolan, and Dr. Kenny—and Parnell himself, did belong to
this 'hotbed of whiggery'.

While these facts certainly do not tend to confirm the
Parnellite assertions, they cannot be said to disprove them.
Parnell referred, in his manifesto, to 'a section' of the party,
and it was generally understood that he referred to Healy
and his friends. Healy and his brother Maurice, with their
kinsmen Murphy, Chance, and the two Sullivans, all belonged to the club, as did Parnell's most tenacious opponent,
John Barry. Healy's correspondence with Labouchere in
1886[3] might not unfairly be described as intrigue, and in the
congenial atmosphere of 1886–90 he probably remained on

[1] *F.J.*, 3 Dec. 1890. For a nationalist audience, 'whiggery' was virtually
synonymous with treachery.
[2] *Anti-Parnellites*: Barry, Chance, Cox, Dickson, Esmonde, Foley, M.
Healy, T. M. Healy, M. Kenny, Knox, McCartan, Justin McCarthy, J. H.
McCarthy, Swift McNeill, Molloy, Morragh, Murphy, Reynolds, D. Sullivan,
Tanner, T. P. O'Connor, and T. D. Sullivan—22.
*Parnellites*: Campbell, Corbet, Conway, Fitzgerald, Harrison, Dr. Kenny,
Mahony, Col. Nolan, John O'Connor, Parnell, R. Power, John Redmond,
W. Redmond, and Sheil—14.
Only two members—Dickson and Murphy—had belonged before 1886.
These particulars are from a list abstracted from the club's archives and
kindly furnished to the writer, through the good offices of Mr. G. E. Hether-
ington, by the librarian of the National Liberal Club.
[3] Above, Chap. VI, p. 175.

excellent terms with certain liberals. Other members, no doubt, also 'fraternized'. It was, after all, not unnatural that the liberal alliance should bring about greater friendliness between the liberals and members of the Irish party, and that certain Irish members, now more sensitive to English opinion, should consult with liberal friends on matters of common interest—such as the crisis of November–December 1890. From Parnell's point of view, such consultation was 'sapping' and 'wire-pulling'. At most, however, one can attach no more importance to these 'intrigues' (reasonably attributable to only a very few among the anti-Parnellites) than that of accelerating a process which was inherent in the terms of the liberal alliance: a process of becoming more attuned to the large liberal section of English public opinion. The liberal alliance was Parnell's own policy and, when he flouted it, he became its victim.

'Agrarianism' was rightly regarded as an element in anti-Parnellism. Dillon and O'Brien, the most prominent exponents of the Plan of Campaign, and their followers, Condon, Sheehy, Roche, Kilbride, and Lane, were influenced in their opposition to Parnell by concern for the evicted tenants. It is true that certain Parnellites—notably the Harringtons and the Redmonds—had also been active in the Plan, but most of those regarded as 'Plan members'—and particularly those identified with O'Brien's 'New Tipperary'—were anti-Parnellites from the time of Gladstone's letter.

Two other possible dividing elements—the regional and the religious—may be briefly considered. The distribution of constituencies represented (for example) by Parnellites at this time bears no relation to the constituencies which actually returned Parnellites in 1892. Of 4 Dublin city representatives, 3 were against Parnell in 1890, but Dublin returned 3 Parnellites in 1892; similarly the 2 Clare representatives (anti-Parnellites) were dismissed by their constituents in 1892 in favour of Parnellites. The number of Parnellites who were 'out of touch with their constituencies'—as far as can be measured across such a time-gap—was probably greater. No regional basis for the division in the party is discernible.

As far as religion is concerned, it is at first sight paradoxi-

cal—in view of the 'priest-ridden' aspects of the controversy—
that the Protestant members of the party voted against Parnell in a higher proportion—2 to 1—than did the party as a
whole, with its large Catholic majority.[1] It has to be remembered that the outcry against Parnell was originally an expression of Protestant opinion (in England) and that it was
only in its later phases that it became identified with Catholic
'clericalism' in Ireland. The Protestants were, however,
numerically an insignificant section of the party, and did not
include—always excepting Parnell—any of its influential
members. Their actions are worth isolating only as a correc-
tive to the misleading simplification that Parnell was overthrown at the dictation of the Catholic clergy.

In this brief inquiry, we have observed that certain sections seem to have been particularly susceptible to anti-
Parnellism: business men; solicitors; prominent men generally; men who had been selected by conventions; Plan of
Campaign men; Protestants. In itself this aggregation seems
odd rather than illuminating. Reducing it to more general
terms, and ignoring the smaller groups, one can say—with,
again, due reservation in relation to the smallness of the numbers—that the anti-Parnellite grouping consisted in the main
of an alliance between an 'upper' section (including both the
leading politicians and the business men and lawyers) and a
'lower section' made up of the members who had passed
through the convention system. Business men, solicitors,
and 'convention choices' had in common a rather high
degree of sensitivity to the opinions of the Catholic clergy,
so that to this extent the tradition of 'clerical dictation' is
confirmed. 'To this extent', only, for not only the Protestants
but the Plan of Campaign members who had—as Healy said
—'defied the bulls of the Pope of Rome', were against
Parnell. The idea of 'clerical dictation' (at this stage) is an
exaggeration arising from a fact: the fact that, once the
party had begun to split, on a political issue, elements in it
showed a tendency to get on to the side which (for non-

[1] There were, in addition to Parnell, 12 Protestant members. Of these, 8
were anti-Parnellites: Abraham, Dickson, Jordan, Knox, Swift McNeill,
Pinkerton, Tanner, and Webb. Four were Parnellites: Harrison, W. A.
Macdonald, Mahony, and Maguire.

political reasons) was approved by the Catholic clergy. But many, perhaps most, of the anti-Parnellites must have made their decision for reasons which had little to do with either clerical pressure or liberal intrigue. The threatened disruption of the liberal alliance meant, after all, at best, the postponement of victory for the cause in which these men believed: home rule for Ireland.

The composition of the Parnellite grouping is not at all so easy to define by reference to professional or group allegiances—except in so far as, negatively, our analysis of the anti-Parnellite grouping defines it. Healy's attempt at a definition—'the paid men'—is not borne out by the evidence; indeed it is more definitely disproved than the corresponding charge against the anti-Parnellites—of being 'got at' by the liberals—can ever be. The bond that united the Parnellites seems to have been one not of interest or even of policy—although they spoke of policy—but of loyalty to a chief. 'My reason is against Mr. Parnell', Harrington is reported to have said, 'but my heart is with him'.[1] Men who acted on such feelings were not likely to be successful solicitors or business men or to be the 'regular' type of candidate dear to party conventions. They were individualists, whether in the dashing upper-class manner of a Henry Harrison, or with the naïve originality of an Alexander Blane. Men who preferred a leader to the preservation of his policy—for that was in effect the choice before them—were, one fancies, generally more imaginative, less rational, than their opponents, the men of interests and systems. Nor were the Parnellites necessarily mere emotionalists who chose the path of folly. To despise what appeals to the imagination is not, in politics, a rational programme, and the element in the Irish party that could hold the imagination departed with Parnell. 'It appears as if we had the voters and Parnell had their sons', wrote the observant Healy a little later, on being assaulted by some small boys.[2] The sense in which he was right was to be revealed, when the emotional power of Parnellism rose again, without Parnell's policy, in Sinn Féin.

---

[1] F.J., 2 Dec. 1890. He noted, however, policy reasons in his diary.
[2] Letters and Leaders, i. 355 (letter of 23 Feb. 1891).

### 6. *Committee Room 15: the End*

*Wednesday*. When the party met again on Wednesday, 3 December, the day after the defeat of Colonel Nolan's amendment, the business before it was still ostensibly—by the chairman's ruling—John Barry's old resolution for an adjournment 'until Friday'. In reality, as the party and the country knew, the questions were whether Parnell's leadership should be ended, and if so, on what terms.

On this day, however, Committee Room 15 was not the sole centre of political interest. In Dublin the standing committee of the archbishops and bishops of Ireland was meeting to consider Parnell's position. Archbishop Walsh as chairman sent a telegram to McCarthy: 'Important you and members should know bishops issue unqualified pronouncement. Mr. Parnell unfit for leadership, first of all on moral grounds, social and personal discredit as result of divorce court proceedings, also in view of inevitable disruption, with defeat at elections, wreck of home rule hopes and sacrifice of tenants' interests.'[1] In view of earlier episcopal intimations, and of the majority vote against Parnell at the party meeting on the previous day, this message cannot have been altogether unexpected.

The main business at the party meeting on this day was a Parnellite 'compromise' proposal. Clancy, an able and moderate Parnellite, had a new 'amendment' to Barry's resolution. He explained that he had himself been 'staggered' by Gladstone's letter and by the evident drift of English public opinion—with which, as the party's propaganda organizer in England, he was probably more familiar than any other member. None the less, he had voted for Parnell because 'all that we have gained in recent years, including the conversion of Mr. Gladstone himself and the liberal alliance, has been gained by one thing and one thing only— namely the fact and the manifestation of the absolute independence of the Irish party'. To surrender—after the Leinster Hall and other declarations—to Gladstone's letter would mean that 'we would have ceased to be an independent party'. Having been 'squeezed' once, the party would

---

[1] Walsh, *Archbishop Walsh*, p. 418.

be 'squeezed' again; this would be the easier since Parnell's deposition would destroy the party's unity as well as its independence. It was necessary, therefore, to seek a compromise solution. Clancy proposed the 'amendment':

That in view of the difference of opinion that has arisen between Mr. Gladstone and Mr. Parnell as to the accuracy of Mr. Parnell's recollection of the suggestions offered at Hawarden in reference to suggested changes in and departures from the Home Rule Bill of 1886 on the subject of the control of the constabulary and the settlement of the land question, the whips of the party be instructed to obtain from Mr. Gladstone, Mr. John Morley and Sir William Harcourt for the information of the party, before any further consideration of the question, what their views are with reference to these two vital points.

Clancy added that, if assurances were given 'after the manner suggested', Parnell would retire.

This speech (and particularly the last announcement) seems to have had a powerful effect on Parnell's opponents. 'It is the first moment I have had during these terrible days', said Sexton, 'when I seemed to see some hope, however faint.' Warily, however, he asked an important question: Who would be the judge of the satisfactory character of the liberal reply? Would it be the party majority or the chairman?

Healy, in an emotional speech, supported Sexton. 'I wish', he said, 'to make a personal declaration in your regard, Mr. Parnell. I wish to say that, if you feel able to meet the party on these points'—Sexton's questions—'my voice will be the first, at the earliest possible moment, consonant with the liberties of my country, to call you back to your proper place as leader of the Irish race' (*loud and prolonged applause*).

Parnell said nothing.

When Sexton had spoken again, confirming Healy's declaration, Parnell said that he needed time for further consideration before he could answer Sexton's questions. The meeting was adjourned until the following day.

The reception of Clancy's amendment was a small but notable tactical victory for the Parnellites. McCarthy had, after all, gone to Gladstone on this same errand of 'seeking guarantees' only a few days before, and his mission had been fruitless.[1] Now, after the majority of the party had, in effect, voted against Parnell, and while the bishops were hurling thunderbolts from Dublin, this project was successfully revived, and welcomed—although not unconditionally —by the spokesmen of the majority. Parnell's spell was not altogether gone and the description 'anti-Parnellite' was still, in most cases, something of an exaggeration.

*Thursday.* When the party met on the following day, the bishops' address had appeared in the morning papers. It was on the lines of Archbishop Walsh's telegram to Mc-Carthy, but more vehemently expressed. The bishops' decision was not, they explained, based on political grounds but on the facts revealed in the divorce court; Parnell's offence was marked by 'a scandalous pre-eminence in guilt and shame'. Catholic Ireland, so conspicuous for its virtue, would not accept as its leader 'a man thus dishonoured and wholly unworthy of Christian confidence'. The address— which concluded with political reflections, as in Archbishop Walsh's telegram—was signed by the four archbishops and by twenty bishops.

Harrington, on reading the report of the address that evening in America, made a shrewd reflection on its implications: 'Should they [the bishops] succeed in driving Parnell away from the Irish movement they will yet bitterly regret their deed [*and the loss of*] the only conservative force in Irish politics.'[2]

At the party meeting, Parnell showed no obvious signs, as he made his adjourned statement on the Clancy amendment, of being affected by the bishops' pronouncement. He could not, he said—in response to Sexton's questions of the day before—surrender to the party his responsibility of judging the satisfactory character of any liberal assurances. 'My position has been granted to me not because I am the mere leader of a parliamentary party, but because I am the leader of the Irish nation.' In a curious corroboration of Harrington's view of him, he added: '. . . there is no man living if I am gone who could succeed in reconciling the feelings of the Irish people to the Hawarden proposals'. He

[1] Above, p. 312.
[2] N.L.I., Harrington MSS.: *Diary,* 4 Dec. 1890.

had, in addition to Clancy's resolution, a declaratory resolution of his own to propose: 'That in the opinion of the Irish parliamentary party, no home rule bill will be satisfactory and acceptable to the Irish people which will not confer the immediate control of the Irish police on the executive responsible to the Irish parliament and, secondly, which does not confer upon the Irish parliament full power to deal with the land question.' Gladstone, he pointed out, had denied his recollection of the Hawarden conversations, but had not said what the correct version ought to be: 'You are dealing with a man who is an unrivalled sophist.'

'Which?' asked John Barry.

Parnell went on to reiterate his argument about getting 'value for the sacrifice' if he was to be surrendered. The Home Rule Bill of 1886 did not—he admitted—itself give control over the police, but his colleagues had been willing to accept it *pro tanto*. 'It is not fair to throw the whole burden of responsibility on my shoulders in these matters. . . . Mr. Gladstone knows well that, in striking me down, he strikes down the only man who could make that measure acceptable to Ireland.' He would retire if Clancy's resolution and his own were accepted, and if the party after consideration and consultation 'should decide that the liberal leaders' views are in accordance with the views of the party on these points as above expressed'. In addition he proposed that Clancy's amendment should itself be amended to set up a sub-committee, consisting of the whips, plus 5 of Parnell's supporters and 5 of Parnell's opponents, and that the sub-committee should delegate 6 of its members—three from each side—to seek an interview with the three liberal leaders, 'for the purpose of ascertaining whether their views are in accordance with the views of the party as above expressed and whether they will agree to embody those views in the Home Rule Bill and make them vital to the measure'.

This speech was certainly one of the most ill-inspired that Parnell ever delivered. That it was rambling and inconsistent was not necessarily a fatal defect—although it was rather startling that, having begun by refusing to surrender his responsibility to judge whether a measure of home rule was satisfactory, he should in the same speech complain that it was not fair to place the whole burden of such decisions upon him. But that was little more than a debating lapse; it is as a piece of tactics that the speech should be judged. As such, it seems to have been aimed at depriving the 'Clancy compromise' of any chance of success. At least Parnell's opponents can hardly be blamed for seeing it in that light, and for doubting whether Parnell had any sincere intention of retiring on any practicable conditions. Gladstone could hardly have gone any distance to meet the party on the basis of the original Clancy amendment; with these new resolutions, laying down virtual 'surrender terms' for the liberals, agreement became clearly impossible. Such a move could only have the effect of dissipating the atmosphere of the previous day —potentially so favourable for Parnell—and of encouraging those who now needed only a reasonable procedural pretext for obeying the bishops. One may hold that Parnell made a miscalculation here that cost him his last chance of holding the leadership. If he had given a simple affirmative to Sexton's questions, he would have preserved the great goodwill towards him that still existed among the anti-Parnellites, and, at the same time, imposed on his opponents a responsibility that they would have borne uneasily. The liberals were, in the last degree, unlikely to give assurances—in the circumstances—that anyone could find satisfactory. One would think, then, that, without raising procedural difficulties or new conditions, he had a reasonable chance of achieving his tactical purpose: to re-unite his party by 'disillusioning' them with the liberals. In his desire, however, to guard against any possibility of being ousted by a reasonably satisfactory liberal 'assurance', he seems to have played into the hands of those—probably few—among his opponents who utterly distrusted him and were determined that he should be leader no longer.

Healy followed, summarizing Parnell's speech in the words: 'Mr. Parnell has refused to submit this matter to the judgment of the party'. When Parnell denied that, Healy asked whether, then, Parnell would resign if the party got assurances from the liberals and found them satisfactory. 'If the party assume the responsibility', answered Parnell, 'by adopting my resolutions, undoubtedly yes.' Healy asserted that Parnell was now 'shaping his course towards the hillside men'—the fenians—since his earlier policy, the liberal alliance, had 'perished in the stench of the divorce court'. This was the first really offensive personal remark which Healy—or any other member—had addressed to Parnell.

The debate that followed although it covered much of the old ground showed signs on the anti-Parnellite side of a new bitterness. When William Redmond asked rhetorically whether any one would deny that Parnell 'is acting for the love of Ireland alone', John Barry cut in: 'I don't believe he is.' Finally, in response to an appeal from Sexton, Parnell agreed to drop his declaratory resolution, thereby in effect confessing the failure of the curious manœuvre for which he had used his opening speech. Unfortunately, it was easier to drop the declaratory resolution than to restore the relative confidence and friendliness of mood that had existed before that resolution was proposed.

The party now passed Clancy's amendment, altered only to nominate, as well as the whips, six members—Parnell, McCarthy, Sexton, Healy, Redmond, and Leamy—to arrange to obtain the required assurances from Gladstone, Harcourt, and Morley. Only two members—Barry and Chance—voted against this resolution. The meeting then adjourned, and the committee which it had named deputized Sexton, Healy, Redmond, and Leamy to seek an interview with the liberal leaders. They met with an immediate, though partial, rebuff. Gladstone would not permit the Irish party to select the liberal representatives; Harcourt and Morley said it was a matter for Gladstone alone.[1]

*Friday.* On the following day, at 12.30, the party's deputation called on Gladstone. Gladstone explained—rather frigidly, it seems—that there was a 'preliminary bar' in the way of his making any declaration to them. Their terms of reference mentioned a 'difference of recollection' about the Hawarden conversations: 'a difference of recollection', said Gladstone, 'which I do not acknowledge to exist'.[2] He ob-

---

[1] *Pall Mall Gazette*: 'Story of the Parnell Crisis', pp. 82–83.
[2] The account of the negotiations with Gladstone is based on the report which the deputation made to the party on the following day (*F.J.*, 8 Dec. 1890).

jected, also, to linking a discussion of a Home Rule Bill to the question of the leadership. The delegation agreed to report back to the party, in order, if possible, to remove the 'preliminary bar'.

The party met again in the afternoon, rescinded the Clancy resolution, and passed a new resolution, proposed by Redmond and seconded by Sexton, authorizing the same delegates 'to request a conference with Mr. Gladstone for the purpose of representing the views of this party and requesting an intimation of the intentions of himself and his colleagues with respect to certain details connected with the following subjects: First, the settlement of the Irish land question; second, the control of the Irish constabulary force in the event of the establishment of an Irish legislature.' This resolution eliminated, because of Gladstone's objections, the references to Harcourt and Morley and to the 'difference of opinion'.

Armed with these more acceptable terms of reference, the delegates obtained another interview with Gladstone, only to receive what was, in effect, a final negative: 'When the Irish party shall have disposed of this question [of the leadership], which belongs entirely to their own competence, in such a manner as will enable me to renew the former relations, it will be my desire to enter into confidential communication about home rule legislation.' Gladstone added—in words that must have had a ring of irony to some at least of his hearers—that he wished to uphold the independence of the Irish party, without whose approval no home rule scheme could find a chance of acceptance.

If the party had still been in its mood of Wednesday, when the majority had been for a moment swayed by Parnell, it seems likely enough that Gladstone's attitude would have brought about a revulsion in Parnell's favour. Gladstone, after all, had not only refused the required assurances; he had done so with unmistakable contempt, although with elaborate politeness. Before telling the Irish party that he could give them no assurances, he had forced them to change the form of their resolution, and eat their words about the Hawarden talks. It must have been painfully obvious, even to determined anti-Parnellites, that a party no longer led by Parnell, a party which would have overthrown Parnell at Gladstone's bidding, would stand in a new and humbler relation to the liberal party.

It seems, however, that any revulsion in Parnell's favour had been checked by Parnell's own excessive manœuvring on Thursday. The majority was also being braced by episcopal criticism. Hearing of 'the possibility of a compromise' Archbishop Walsh had written to William Martin Murphy: 'Why not think and act boldly? The party, I fear, will otherwise be led into some morass.'[1]

*Saturday.* On the morning of Saturday, 6 December, which was to be the last day of the united party, the archbishop's message was reinforced by strong editorials in the two nationalist weekly papers. 'The clouds have lifted', wrote *United Ireland.* 'The path of duty is clear at last. Ireland or Parnell is now the issue.'[2] *The Nation* carried the same message in more impressive language: 'Never again until new generations are born and grown to manhood will the union that has passed prevail. . . . The leader whom we used to follow is no more.' Tellingly, in relation to Parnell's manifesto, it reminded its readers of the Kilmainham treaty and of Dillon's retirement from politics after it. In point of independence, 'we for our part should prefer the leader [Dillon] who was driven into exile by the disgust which he felt at the ever-memorable proceedings of 1882'.

At the party meeting Sexton announced 'that the majority have made up their minds that these intolerably protracted proceedings must be brought to a close to-day'. After a procedural wrangle and an adjournment, Redmond read the delegates' report on their conversations with Gladstone. At the end of the delegates' report Abraham rose and tried to read a resolution ending Parnell's leadership. J. O'Connor (Parnellite) also rose, and was called by the chairman. Confusion followed. Unable to make himself heard, Abraham handed his resolution to McCarthy, who tried to present it to Parnell. 'Mr. Parnell, who remained standing, tore the

[1] Walsh, *Archbishop Walsh*, p. 420: letter dated 5 Dec. 1890.
[2] *U.I.*, 6 Dec. 1890. This editorial reflected William O'Brien's views. The next issue (13 Dec. 1890) was pro-Parnell, the paper having been 'recaptured' forcibly in the meantime.

resolution from McCarthy's hand saying "I will not receive it".' Amid uproar, Barry called Parnell 'a dirty trickster'. A. O'Connor, an anti-Parnellite but a noted stickler for decorum, appealed for respect for the chair, and asked that J. O'Connor be allowed to speak. Sexton agreed, provided that Abraham should be heard afterwards; Parnell accepted this, on the understanding that O'Connor's amendment would be seconded before Abraham spoke. O'Connor then proposed his 'amendment' to the main resolution, which was still Barry's old proposal to adjourn until Friday. This amendment was in the form of an expression of regret at Gladstone's refusal 'to enter into negotiations . . . except upon the condition that the party shall first remove Mr. Parnell from the chairmanship'. The Irish people, O'Connor claimed, were with Parnell, and would resent this 'attempt at dictation'. As for the anti-Parnellites they were under the leadership of Gladstone. The exchange that followed gave a foretaste of the cruelty which certain anti-Parnellites would use against Parnell in the campaigns in Ireland:

> A. O'Connor: 'He [Gladstone] is not a member of the party.'
> J. Redmond: '. . . The master of the party.'
> T. M. Healy: 'Who is to be the mistress of the party?'

Appalled at this flash from the depths, A. O'Connor appealed to the chair for order. Parnell answered furiously: 'Better appeal to your own friends. Better appeal to that cowardly little scoundrel there that in an assembly of Irishmen dares to insult a woman.' A. O'Connor probably spoke for all but a very small minority of the anti-Parnellites when he rebuked Healy with the words: 'Whatever painful duty we have to discharge, we should discharge it like gentlemen.' J. O'Connor went bravely on with his speech, elaborating a routine Parnellite historical comparison with Grattan's volunteers. J. J. O'Kelly, who seconded, appealed for a friendly spirit of contest, and hoped that a new united party under the same leadership might arise.

It was now, at last, the turn of Abraham to speak and move the resolution which had been entrusted to him at the anti-Parnellite meeting on the previous Sunday (30 November).[1]

---

[1] Above, p. 312.

Abraham stressed—in contrast with a few of the earlier speakers on the same side—that the anti-Parnellites were acting on purely political grounds. Home rule, if Parnell remained leader, 'would be thrust into the dim and distant future'. The general election would be lost. It was for the party to decide what the best course was: 'We, as a party, are the sovereign authority.' He then moved (as an amendment to O'Connor's amendment) the anti-Parnellite resolution: 'That we the members of the Irish parliamentary party declare that Mr. Parnell's tenure of the chairmanship of this party is hereby terminated.' Parnell ruled that this was not an amendment: a ruling which would be hard to reconcile with his acceptance of earlier 'amendments', equally irrelevant to the proposition that the meeting should be adjourned 'until Friday'. 'It is obvious', said A. O'Connor, 'that a determined minority favoured by a chairman who is personally interested (*cheers*) can, if they choose, indefinitely postpone the recording of the decision of the majority. . . . I invite my colleagues to make an end of the business.'

Leamy, for the Parnellites, defended obstruction in principle—with reference to the early history of the party—but denied that it had occurred. The policy of the Parnellites was democratically correct. 'We called on the people to say what they wished and, fortified by their declarations, we voted him into the chair. I was one of those who did it and I will stand by him to the end.'

McCarthy then, in a short speech, put an end to the long debate. After regretting—in an implicit apology for Barry and Healy—the bitter words that had been spoken, he said: 'I see no further use carrying on a discussion which must be barren of all but reproach, ill-temper, controversy and indignity and I will . . . suggest that all who think with me in this grave crisis should withdraw with me from this room.' He then left, with his forty-four followers, leaving Parnell, still in the chair, surrounded by his twenty-seven supporters.[1]

Both sides then formally ratified their own position as the

[1] Newspaper reports differ as to which members were actually in the room at the time—O'Hanlon and Joseph Nolan are omitted from some lists, but as they had earlier spoken and voted for Parnell, and as they remained Parnellites after the split, it may be taken that, whether physically present or not, they were 'with' Parnell in this division.

legitimate continuers of the party. In Committee Room 15 Colonel Nolan declared that the anti-Parnellite majority had exercised 'the right of departing from the party'. Parnell, he said, continued to be chairman. 'Until you are formally deposed from your leadership I will maintain you as leader.' John Redmond in what was—rather remarkably—the first reference to the bishops' address, said that the bishops were not opposing just the Parnellites, but every single member of the Irish party, since the whole party, in full knowledge of the divorce court's verdict, had re-elected Parnell as its chairman. Blane began a disquisition on Judge Keogh and 'Peter the Packer', but was snubbed into silence by Parnell. Parnell then put J. O'Connor's amendment 'regretting' Gladstone's attitude. 'The men who have deserted from our party', he said, 'have deserted on the eve of the day when we were about to return to our country.' They were fleeing from Irish public opinion and false to all their pledges. O'Connor's resolution was then carried and the meeting adjourned.

The anti-Parnellites, meeting simultaneously in Committee Room 14 with McCarthy in the chair, carried two resolutions. The first ran: 'That we, the undersigned, being an absolute majority of the whole number of the Irish parliamentary party declare that Mr. Parnell's chairmanship of this party is hereby terminated.' The second declared 'that the Irish parliamentary party is and always must remain independent of all other parties' and that it would accept no settlement of the home rule question 'except such as satisfies the aspirations of the Irish people'.

The claim to be the only legitimate Irish parliamentary party was important for both sides, since all were pledged 'to sit, act, and vote with the Irish parliamentary party'. Legalistically the Parnellites—who now called their opponents 'seceders'—had the better of the argument since Parnell had not, after all, been deposed from the chairmanship at a meeting of the party. But everyone who had followed the debates—and that meant the whole electorate—could know that the only reason he had not been deposed was that, by an abuse of his powers as chairman, he had refused to allow the motion for his deposition to be put.

Few, probably, outside the ranks of the participants, fully accepted the claims of either section to be regarded as *the* Irish party. Most Irishmen must have recognized the truth of the words in which the Press Association summarized its report of that day's proceedings:

'The old Irish party no longer exists.'

# EPILOGUE

THE story of Parnell's last tragic campaign is well known. With the combined weight of the church, of Gladstone, and of the majority of his own party against him, and with the divorce-court verdict round his neck, he fought and lost three bitter by-elections in Ireland. The struggle in the country, as distinct from that in Committee Room 15, was fought on 'the moral issue', and the influence of the clergy in this phase was, it is generally agreed, decisive. To the Parnellite charge that the priests were under pressure from the hierarchy to work against Parnellite candidates, Archbishop Croke made a quaint retort. 'I hereby positively declare', he wrote, 'that I shall look on all my priests in exactly the same light whether they conscientiously denounce Mr. Parnell or support him—the latter being, I think, impossible.'[1] A few priests did support Parnell, but on the whole 'conscientious denunciation' was the order of the day. Parnell rallied to himself the fenians—John O'Leary and John Devoy spoke out in his support—and the city workers and the young, but electorally he was outmatched. In September 1891 the *Freeman's Journal*, the only remaining powerful champion of Parnell's leadership, was 'captured' for the other side at a meeting of the shareholders. On 6 October Parnell died at Brighton.[2]

Any attempt at a retrospective evaluation of the political actions of Parnell and his party tends to become confused by the entanglement of two sets of issues which are logically separate: the political achievements of the party led by Parnell, and the 1890 crisis about the leadership. That final crisis has hung a curtain of confusion across the memory of Parnell's actions, during his period of power. It may be helpful, therefore, to move backwards in time, and consider first the realities of the split of 1890.

The events of the split have been recorded above in

[1] *F.J.*, 26 Feb. 1891.
[2] For the history of the party after the 'deposition' of Parnell, see F. S. L. Lyons, *The Irish Parliamentary Party, 1890–1910*.

enough detail to enable the reader to form his own judgement upon them. The present writer's opinion—and all that
follows is merely a personal interpretation—is that Parnell's
decision to cling to the leadership, after the verdict of the
divorce court, is indefensible, but that the Parnellite view,
that the party forfeited the substance of its power and independence by abandoning its leader at Gladstone's bidding,
is correct. Once the party, in full knowledge of the divorce
verdict, had reaffirmed its confidence in its leader, it lowered
its status by abandoning that leader for—in effect—the
leader of an English party. If, from that time, the party was
less the ally than the client of the English liberals; if it enjoyed less prestige and confidence among both Englishmen
and Irishmen, these effects flow, in great part, from its own
actions. But to Parnell himself belongs the heavier share of
responsibility. He knew the sacrifices he had asked from his
followers to sustain the 'liberal alliance'; he knew—from the
example of Dilke—the political force, in liberal England, of
moral indignation against an exposed adulterer; he knew
that in Catholic Ireland the same force menaced him,
although there his towering prestige might hold it in check.
It is true that he knew, also, that he was incomparably more
fitted for leadership than any of his possible successors in the
party. But—even setting aside the possibility of his leading
the party from the ranks, under the nominal chairmanship
of some such malleable personality as McCarthy—it is evident, on any rational calculation, that greater dangers,
greater evils waited on retention of the leadership than
would have waited on its abandonment. A united party—
even poorly led—was preferable to a party torn asunder—
and from the time of the 'delegates' manifesto' at least, if
not from that of Gladstone's letter, it was clear that a united
party would not continue to support Parnell's leadership.
Ill-health and feminine influence may have contributed to
Parnell's fatal decision, but on the whole his actions and
language at this time are not those of a weary man, forcing
himself to act at a woman's instigation, but of a man exalted
to combat, delighting in his craft and in a sense—an exaggerated sense—of personal power. There is in him at this
time something of the romantic hero, dazzled by his own

myth, preferring a tragic ending to self-effacement and the continuation of his policy.

For his policy, in the time of his power, had been rational and unromantic. His whole course of action from the time of his election as chairman of the party was—though few contemporaries recognized it as such—a course of reconciliation He assumed the leadership of Davitt's semi-revolutionary 'New Departure' and, with his parliamentary colleagues, turned that movement into a completely constitutional one. He and his party accepted Gladstonian home rule—essentially a compromise between Irish national and English imperial traditions—as a final settlement, and they obtained the approval of the Irish people for this acceptance. Between 1886 and 1890 a united self-governing Ireland, as a willing partner in the British empire, living in harmony with Britain, seemed, to many, well within the bounds of practical politics. There can be no serious doubt that this is what Parnell desired or that—as Cecil Rhodes foresaw when he gave his support to Irish home rule—Parnell's influence would have tended towards 'imperial federation'—the modern concept of the Commonwealth.[1] If, for good reasons, his portrait hangs in the pantheon of Irish patriots along with that of Wolfe Tone, it should not be forgotten—as it sometimes is—that his policy was the antithesis of Tone's. He sought not to break the connexion with England, but to make it more flexible, more efficient, and more acceptable. The achievement of Parnell and his party in converting liberal England to home rule has often been admired, but it is in some ways less notable than their achievement in converting nationalist Ireland to that same policy of compromise. Whether that policy, backed as it was by a great English party and a great Irish party, and by the combined prestige of Gladstone and Parnell, could have succeeded in bringing all Ulster, without serious bloodshed, within the framework of home rule, can obviously never be known. It may be said, however, that no subsequent policy, and no

[1] Cf. R. Barry O'Brien, *Parnell*, pp. 426-30. In an interesting article 'Parnell and his Power' (*Fortnightly Review*, Dec. 1898), J. L. Garvin argued that, if home rule had passed in Parnell's day, 'He would have become at once an imperial force as strong as Mr. Rhodes.'

subsequent combination of leaders, offered such good grounds for hope of a united and self-governing Ireland— or of real and well-founded friendship between England and Ireland.

In spanning the gulf between English and Irish public opinion, Parnell and his party were forced, by sheer historical necessity, to use much duplicity. For English audiences they had to sound more 'loyal' than they really were, while on Irish, and especially Irish American, audiences they had to make a semi-revolutionary or conspiratorial impression. While a William O'Brien wrote seditious articles, or dreamt of kidnapped lord lieutenants and Russian invasions, a J. J. O'Kelly could give a revolutionary some moderate advice in the language of conspiracy, and a Justin McCarthy could assure the lord lieutenant of the essential loyalty of the home rule party.[1] Parnell himself had spoken with several voices, from the 'revolutionary' extreme in the American and Irish speeches, to the extreme of constitutional loyalty in certain English speeches of 1889. While he himself was speaking most constitutionally in the late eighties the English tory press did him the service, in Ireland, of projecting a picture of him as a revolutionary firebrand. Had Parnellism not kept around it—by such means and such accidents—a vague penumbra of revolution, it is doubtful whether sufficient enthusiasm could have been generated in Ireland to make Gladstonian home rule a matter of practical politics. To use again Pareto's useful terms, Parnellism was a system in which the emotional 'residues' of historical tradition and suppressed rebellion could be enlisted in the service of parliamentary 'combinations' of a strictly rational and realistic character. But the driving force of the 'residues' could be successfully directed in the sense of the 'combinations' only under one condition. This was that *the ambiguity of the system must be crystallized in terms of personality*. The leader, in short, had to become a mysterious and awe-inspiring figure. The prestige of achievement, the magnetism of great ability impressively embodied, these drew to the personality of the leader the enthusiasm generated by the revolutionary policies which he was felt to symbolize. Then he was able

[1] Cf. above, pp. 82 and 102.

to carry out, with the aid of his party, and of non-revolutionary elements in the country, his constitutional policy. He remained, in some eyes, a revolutionary, while, to a more discerning few—men like Gray and Harrington—he appeared a far-seeing conservative. Both avatars were necessary to him, and to his movement, and both could find room under a cloak of mystery. It so happened that an air of mystery was not only required by political necessity, but was congenial to Parnell's own reticent character and suited to the enforced secrecy of his domestic life. *Alias* 'Mr. Fox' and 'Mr. Preston', he typified the romantic hero whose *true name* and true intentions are wrapped in obscurity: an obscurity in which he was followed by many who would have abandoned him had they been quite sure of his direction.

It seems that what began as a technique of power, and an adaptation to personal circumstances, grew upon Parnell in such a way that he finished as the servant, instead of the master, of his own legend. Healy, in a cynical but fairly penetrating estimate of his leader's character, saw him as 'a splendid comedian' who, reading in the tory press descriptions of himself as a man of mystery, decided, in Wilde's phrase, 'to live up to the level of his blue china'.[1] This may have been partly true at one stage in the process—and there is something of the 'splendid comedian' about the sombre figure which summoned O'Brien in the fog behind the observatory[2]—but the end was not any kind of comedy. In the end, Parnell acted, not like the cool and rational leader of men that he had been, but like the romantic hero that he had been forced to seem. That was the tragedy.

If this interpretation is valid, the 'Parnell split' was much more than a mechanical division of a party and a people. It represented and it brought about a profound psychological split. The emotional 'residues' and intellectual 'combinations' that Parnellism had equivocally joined now flew apart. The 'residues' first went with Parnell, then left constitutionalism for ever, coming to the surface of politics

---

[1] *Pall Mall Gazette*: 'Story of the Parnell Crisis', p. 90. This was an interview immediately after the split; the assessment is more interesting than anything in *Letters and Leaders of my Day*.
[2] Above, Chap. VIII, p. 246.

again in the rebellion of 1916. The 'combinations' won their empty victory, and dominated a party robbed of its old penumbra and of its power over the young. Split favoured further split; the sight of Parnell 'hounded down by the Catholic priests' confirmed the fears and intensified the revulsions of northern Protestants, and disgusted also those English liberals who had always feared 'a clerical ascendancy'. Englishmen and Protestants easily forgot that the spectacle which repelled them was one which they themselves had been the first—after Parnell himself—to bring about. On the Irish side, in the tradition which formed in the minds of the young, it was Gladstone who suffered injustice, in being remembered, not for devoting his last years to the cause of home rule for Ireland but as the vaguely malevolent 'Grand Old Spider' who figured with the 'English wolves' in the zoology of Parnellite invective. The most tragic spectacle, in 1891, was not that of the doomed hero, but that of a great work laid in ruins: the work of reconciliation which Gladstone and Parnell with their parties seemed, by 1890, to have established on solid foundations.

We have spoken enough of ruins; it remains to speak briefly of the lasting achievements of Parnell and his party. Some of these, though important, were side-effects; it was through no wish of the Irish party, but simply through its actions, that the procedure of the British parliament had to be tightened and its ancient liberties curtailed. Nor did the party intend to serve as a model of disciplined organization to the British parties, although its example probably did have an effect on these.[1] Nor—as we have seen[2]—did the party take any serious interest in the effects of its example, far-reaching though these may have been, among the subject nations of the empire. The direct political results of the party's actions, the results secured within its field of interest, are three.

The first is the revolution in Irish land tenure which began with Gladstone's Land Act of 1881 and was com-

---

[1] 'It was Parnell who first introduced into British politics the notion of a disciplined political party in the modern sense and compelled the British parties in time to imitate him' (Mr. Christopher Hollis, M.P., in *The Tablet*, 19 Jan. 1952). See also Chap. II, pp. 62 sqq.

[2] Above, Chap. I, p. 22.

pleted, in principle, by Wyndham's Act of 1903. The abolition of the old landlordism, the destruction, in Garvin's
words,[1] of 'the bases of the Cromwellian settlement', was a
mighty work, to which the crucial impetus was given by
Michael Davitt's Land League. It could hardly have gained
its victorious momentum, however, without Parnell's
leadership and the prestige of his name—a prestige to which
the elections of 1880, and his own election as chairman of
the Irish party, so largely contributed. More; we can hardly
doubt that the tory 'conversion' to Irish land purchase was
due not only to the success of the agitation of 1880-1, but
also—as the slogan of 'killing home rule by kindness'
implies—to the success of the purely political agitation,
and the danger represented by eighty-six home rulers in
parliament.

The second, and most conspicuous, achievement of the
party was, of course, the effective 'conversion' of Gladstone
and the liberal party to home rule. This achievement was
certainly directly due to the party, and ensured not merely
by its numbers, but by its discipline under strain.[2] By this
great parliamentary triumph, about one-half of the British
electorate found itself—probably rather to its surprise—
committed to the proposition that Ireland should have self-
government. This division in public opinion in Britain was
fateful for the future of the Union settlement.

Harcourt's opinion, that the tory negotiations with Parnell made home rule in the long run inevitable, may be
questioned.[3] It can hardly be questioned, however, that the
'conversion' of the liberals, plus the overthrow of landlordism—the social framework of British rule in Ireland
—did make some degree of self-government inevitable. Parnell and his party, therefore, made a very solid contribution
to the establishment of the modern Irish State, although that
State is not what they, or anyone else on any side, desired.

[1] Above, Introduction, p. 6.
[2] Above, Chap. VI, § 2. It may be that Gladstone's personal 'conversion',
in principle, to home rule was of earlier date, but he could not have attempted
to give practical effect to the principle had it not been for the pivotal position
of the Irish party after the 1885 elections—and also, of course, its moral
authority as representing a great majority of the Irish electors.
[3] Above, Chap. VI, p. 6. See also Chap. III, p. 108, n. 2.

But more than this—and this third achievement of the party has been little noted—their record helped to mould the development of the new State. There had been, after all, little in Irish history, before Parnell, which could endear parliamentary democracy to the people. A people which, with good reason, profoundly distrusted its parliamentary representatives—as the Irish did up to the last quarter of the nineteenth century—could hardly, on winning its freedom by revolution, hope to work a parliamentary democracy; it might not even try to do so. But the concrete achievements of Parnell and his party, and the example of pledged members, not one of whom broke his pledge, seem to have given the people a confidence, and a sense of participation in the democratic process, which they never wholly lost, even when, in 1918, they rejected the party itself. The insurgents of 1918–21 showed, after all, a concern, unexampled in a revolutionary period, for not merely the form but the substance of parliamentary democracy.

There is a certain irony in this heritage of the Parnell movement, for Parnell himself had no particular affection for democracy. 'He was not only not a demagogue', wrote Asquith, 'he was not, and never pretended to be, a democrat.'[1] This was not merely a question of conversation, or of his keeping (as he did) a horse called *Dictator*. The National League, his creation—which might have played a great part in a self-governing Ireland, if home rule had been won in Parnell's day—was a model of authoritarian control under democratic forms.[2] One cannot say what form of government might have developed in a home rule Ireland under Parnell's government, but it would be rash to assume that it would necessarily have been a real—as distinct from a formal—democracy. 'He was dictator'—wrote an admirer, lamenting his fall—'absolute, complete, accepted, acknowledged. Think of his servants voting out the dictator! Why in another age . . . he would have shot them down and he would have been right!'[3] Certainly, no one who reads the Committee Room 15 debates will believe that, if Parnell had then controlled the machinery of a State, he would have

[1] *Fifty Years in Parliament*, i. 185.    [2] Above, Chap. IV, pp. 126 sqq.
[3] O'Hara, *Chief and Tribune*, p. 311.

allowed any majority to remove him, peaceably, from office
in such circumstances. For the adherence of Ireland to parliamentary democracy, we have to thank not the principles
of Parnell, but the example and conduct of the party which
he formed. It may be blamed for grave mistakes and especially for the contribution which, first by indecision and then
by precipitate action, it made to the débâcle of 1890. It may
be blamed also—perhaps not altogether justly—for the inflated oratory which it loved to practise, and which spread
a haze of unreality that still lingers. But exponents of the
whole truth could not survive in politics anywhere; the
members of the Irish party, though not conspicuous for
political candour, were models of what a rank-and-file
democratic politician should be. They were upright and
consistent, faithful to their pledges, disciplined in action,
and courageous in defence of the principles on which they
were elected. They served Ireland well, and might have
served her better if they had not—mainly through his own
fault—lost their leader.

As for the leader, he survives most vividly not by the
memory of his constructive acts, but by the mark which his
romantic image in the last struggle made, and continues to
make, on young imaginations. The young saw him as
Samson pulling down the pillars of the temple—and forgot
that it was a temple he himself had planned and built for his
own people. For the boy James Joyce, Parnell was the
murdered Caesar: *Et tu, Healy!* written when Joyce was
nine, is his first known work, and Parnell is present in all his
major books. In Yeats's old age the image of Parnell, pulled
down by the mob, was an aristocratic symbol:

> But popular rage,
> *Hysterica passio*, dragged this quarry down.
> None shared our guilt; nor did we play a part
> Upon a painted stage when we devoured his heart.[1]

The image of the stage, repelled though it is, is significant,
as is the poem's opening line:

> Under the Great Comedian's tomb, the crowd . . .

[1] 'Parnell's Funeral' in *Collected Poems*, p. 119.

One thinks of Healy's admiring gibe—'a splendid comedian'—and reflects that Parnell had, at least, a great curtain. 'The split' was a natural drama, with a nation participating in it most intensely. It seized certain strong imaginations—I think of Mr. Seán O Faoláin—with a grip that has never loosened, and it is still capable of capturing young minds: 'The class', wrote a Harvard professor who had lectured on Irish patriots, 'were Parnellites to a man.' Did this collective emotional explosion of 1890 help to set free the imaginative forces which, for a time in the early 1900's, made Dublin—the Parnellite city—an important centre of world literature? One cannot prove it to be so, but one does sense in that literature the Parnellite shock. Those who feel—as does the present writer—that the Parnell of the split deviated from politics into literature, may reflect that, in that second field as in the first, he made his power felt:

> And here's a final reason,
> He was of such a kind
> Every man that sings a song
> Keeps Parnell in his mind.

# BIBLIOGRAPHY

## A. PRIMARY SOURCES

### I. *Manuscript Materials*

The most valuable materials in this category are the collections of papers of prominent party members, notably the Harrington and O'Brien Papers in the National Library of Ireland and the Dillon Papers in the Royal Irish Academy (below, 2 and 3).

### 1. *State Paper Office, Dublin Castle*

Irish crimes records, covering the period 1862–72, in four volumes, containing descriptions of fenian suspects, lists of warrants under Habeas Corpus Suspension Act, 1866, &c., Report of the Dublin Metropolitan Police as regards the Irish National Land League (10 Aug. 1880); by Superintendent Mallon ('Mallon's Report'). A six-page report based largely on information given by an anonymous commercial traveller, with an appendix giving brief biographies of prominent leaguers.

Irish National League: Proceedings 1883–91. These are reports furnished by local District Inspectors of the Royal Irish Constabulary on the formation and lapsing of league branches, with general half-yearly summaries by the Crimes Branch, Dublin Castle. The earliest of such summaries are the 'Beckerson Reports' (Jan.–June 1885; Jan.–June 1886).

Particulars and photographs of fenians (undated, pre-1880); includes descriptions of Parnell, Biggar, T. P. O'Connor, and Redmond.

The above papers are of interest for the history of the Land League and National League and for the degree of association of certain members of the party with fenianism. On the latter point they have to be treated with caution because of the police tendency to exaggerate such association.

### 2. *National Library of Ireland*

The collected papers of J. F. X. O'Brien who succeeded Biggar as a treasurer of the parliamentary fund. These include the Parliamentary Cash-book (Nov. 1885–Jan. 1886) and the Account-book of the Irish Parliamentary Fund (1886–90).

These papers are of great importance for the financial history of the party from the end of 1885 on.

The collected papers of Timothy Harrington, secretary of the National League. These include folders of correspondence with Parnell, with Patrick Egan, and with Charles O'Reilly, treasurer of the Irish National League of America; telegrams in connexion with the Galway election of 1886; signed party pledges; documents relating to the foundation of the Irish National League; the 'National League letter-book 1883–8' (as printed for the Special Commission); affidavits in relation to the Paris funds and Harrison's 'American Diary' covering part of the 'split' period.

The Harrington Papers are very useful for the development of the organization of the nationalist movement from the end of 1882 to the end of our period.

The collected papers of William O'Brien and John Redmond.

These contain little of value for our period.

### 3. *Royal Irish Academy*

The papers of John Dillon, which I examined by kind permission of Dr. Myles Dillon, include the party minute-book (Jan. 1886–Dec. 1890); thirty-one miscellaneous notebooks (1880–9), and correspondence with Parnell (1881–2), William O'Brien, and others (1880–5).

Probably the most valuable single collection of papers for this period in the history of the party.

### 4. *British Museum*

Gladstone Papers (Additional MSS. 44086–44835) contain some material of interest in connexion with the Kilmainham treaty (Chapter II, p. 77); Captain O'Shea's parliamentary ambitions (Chapter VI, p. 169); the influence of the Irish party's parliamentary strength (and conjectures about its intentions) on Gladstone's course of action in 1886 (Chapter VI, p. 160), and conversations with Parnell at Hawarden in 1888 and 1889 (Chapter VII, pp. 228 and 235).

This vast collection contains much material relating to Gladstone's Irish policy but relatively little with a direct and significant bearing on the Irish party or its leaders.

Dilke Papers (Additional MSS. 43874–43967).

Some material bearing on the Chamberlain–Dilke overtures to the Irish in 1885 (Chapter III, pp. 90 sqq.).

Campbell Bannerman Papers (Additional MSS. 41206–41252).

Shed some light on the claims of Captain O'Shea (Chapter VI, p. 168).

### 5. *Miscellaneous*

Letters to the writer from the late J. P. Hayden and the late Henry Harrison, formerly members of the party, were helpful on questions of selection and discipline; a letter from Mr. L. J. Kettle, M.I.C.E.I., son of the late Andrew Kettle, a prominent member of the Land League, shed light on an important episode in the 'semi-revolutionary' period (Chapter II, p. 60); information furnished by the librarian of the National Liberal Club, London, was of interest in relation to a controversy of the 'split' period (Chapter IX, p. 79); John Muldoon's account of the Galway election—in the possession of his son, Mr. John Muldoon, and lent to me through the courtesy of Mr. C. S. Andrews— is used in Chapter VI (pp. 179 and 182); from the Davitt Papers in the possession of Dr. T. W. Moody I have been kindly permitted to consult correspondence between Davitt and Richard McGhee (with criticisms of Parnell and his party) and letters from Archbishop Croke to Davitt, including one which is of importance in relation to the hierarchy's attitude on the split (Chapter IX, p. 285).

## ii. *Printed Materials*

### 1. *Parliamentary Papers and other official publications*

Special Commission Act, 1888. Reprint of the shorthand notes on the speeches, proceedings, and evidence taken before the commissioners appointed under the above-named act, London, Stationery Office, 1890. In twelve volumes.

> In investigating the charges of *The Times* against Parnell, the commission attempted to cover the whole field of the 'New Departure' movement. The proceedings, however, are less illuminating than they might be since they were mainly devoted to the tedious demonstration of well-known facts, e.g. that Parnell and his friends encouraged boycotting, and that boycotting was sometimes associated with agrarian crime. I have not thought it wise to rely to any great extent on the evidence given before the commission by Parnell and other prominent members of the party as to their attitudes and activities in the very different political context of six to nine years earlier.

Parliamentary Papers 1880 (382), lvii–1. Return of the election changes, etc. in the general election of 1880.

Parliamentary Papers 1884–5 (259), lxii–271. Return showing the present county and borough constituencies . . . and also the constituencies as constituted by the Redistribution of Seats Act, 1885.

'Queen v. Parnell and others'. Reprints of speeches (at Land League meetings) 1880. In four volumes.

Hansard, 1880–90.

### 2. *Newspapers and periodicals*

The Irish daily newspapers carried regular and voluminous reports throughout the period on the activities of the Irish party both inside and outside parliament. They also carried, as did the Irish weekly newspapers, a great volume of well-informed—and sometimes inspired —commentary on these activities. The Irish provincial press for the period was relatively weak, and even an important local event like the Galway election of 1886 received unilluminating treatment in the local press. The most useful newspapers and periodicals for the purposes of the present study were the following:

Dublin:

Daily
{
*Freeman's Journal* (nationalist).
　I have drawn very heavily on this. Its editor and proprietor,
　E. D. Gray, was a home rule member and its reports on party
　matters are even fuller than those in the other papers.
*Irish Times* (conservative).
*Evening Mail* (conservative).
*National Press* (post-split, anti-Parnellite).
}

Weekly
{
*United Ireland* (left-wing Parnellite).
*The Nation* (right-wing Parnellite).
}

London: *The Times.*
　　　　　*Pall Mall Gazette* (Stead).
　　　　　*Journal of the Home Rule Union* (monthly, 1888–90).

### 3. *Memoirs and other contemporary narratives*

I include here works in treatise form of which the value is mainly of
a memoir character. I omit the voluminous periodical and pamphlet
literature of a purely propagandist character such as the publications of
the 'Irish loyal and patriotic union' (conservative) and the 'Irish press
agency' (nationalist). I also omit the many periodical articles which are
concerned with 'home rule' as a constitutional problem, and not with
the home rule movement as a political fact.

BLUNT, WILFRID S. *The Land War in Ireland, being a Personal Narrative
　of Events.* London, 1912.
　　Contains many valuable extracts from his diary.
CHAMBERLAIN, JOSEPH. *Joseph Chamberlain, a Political Memoir, 1880–92.*
　Edited by C. H. D. Howard, London, 1953.
　　Text from the MS. of the document described by Garvin (below)
　as 'the memorandum of events'. Chapter II deals with the Kilmain-
　ham treaty; Chapter VI with the 'central council' negotiations.
　Captain O'Shea's candidature for Galway is not mentioned.
DAVITT, MICHAEL. *Fall of Feudalism in Ireland.* London and New York,
　1912.
DENVIR, JOHN. *History of the Irish in Great Britain.* London, 1894, 2nd ed.
　　Useful for the history of the Home Rule Confederation of Great
　Britain, of which the author was first general secretary.
DEVOY, JOHN. *Recollections of an Irish Rebel.* London, 1929.
—— *Devoy's Postbag.* Edited by W. O'Brien and D. Ryan. 2 vols.
　Dublin, 1948, 1953.
　　A valuable collection of letters bearing especially on the American
　and 'extreme' connexions of Parnellism.
GARVIN, J. L. Article, 'Parnell and his Power', in *Fortnightly Review*
　(1 Dec. 1888), pp. 625–33.
HAMILTON, LORD GEORGE. *Parliamentary Reminiscences and Reflections,
　1868–1906.* 2 vols. London, 1916 and 1922.
　　Unionist comment.

HEALY, T. M. *Letters and Leaders of My Day*. 2 vols. London, 1928.
   Valuable mainly for day-to-day comments contained in letters to his father, his wife, and his brother Maurice.
—— Articles: 'The Irish Parliamentary Party' in *Fortnightly Review* (1 Nov. 1882); 'The Secret of Parnell's Power', in *Pall Mall Gazette* (23 Dec. 1883); 'The Rise and Fall of Mr. Parnell', in *New Review* (Mar. 1891); interview in *Pall Mall Gazette*, 'Story of the Parnell Crisis' (1891).
HORGAN, JOHN J. *Parnell to Pearse*, Dublin, 1948.
LUCY, SIR HENRY. *A Diary of Two Parliaments*, vol. 2, 1880–5. London, 1886.
—— *A Diary of the Salisbury Parliament, 1885–6*. London, 1886.
   Useful for 'the tone of the House', in relation to the Irish members.
MCCARTHY, JUSTIN. *Reminiscences*. 2 vols. London, 1899.
—— *Story of an Irishman*, London, 1904.
—— *Irish Recollections*, London, 1911.
—— *Our Book of Memories* (with Mrs. Campbell Praed), London, 1912.
   The last of these is useful on the split; the others are verbose and largely uninformative.
MORLEY, JOHN. *Recollections*. 2 vols. London, 1905.
O'BRIEN, LORD. *Reminiscences*. Edited by the Hon. Georgina O'Brien. London, 1916.
O'BRIEN, WILLIAM. *Recollections*. London, 1905.
—— *Evening Memories*. Dublin, 1920.
—— *An Olive Branch in Ireland and its History*. London, 1910.
   The first of these covers the period up to 1883; the second the period 1883–90. Both have to be treated with some reserve especially in relation to Parnell's alleged approval of various revolutionary projects of the author's.
   The third volume deals with the split.
O'CONNOR, T. P. *Memoirs of an Old Parliamentarian*. 2 vols. London, 1929.
—— *The Parnell Movement*. London, 1886.
—— *Gladstone's House of Commons* (1880–5). London, 1885.
O'DONNELL, F. H. *History of the Irish Parliamentary Party*. 2 vols. London, 1910.
   Covers the years 1873–80 in detail with much first-hand information. The years 1880–92 receive about 190 pages and the major events are dealt with from outside and in a rambling and repetitive manner. The book is written from a slightly eccentric, conservative-nationalist point of view and contains some shrewd comments, but is marred by extreme bitterness, personal jealousy of Parnell ('my run-away errand-boy'), and an egoism which leads the writer to magnify the importance of events with which he himself was connected and to distort his own role.
OXFORD AND ASQUITH, EARL OF. *Fifty Years of Parliament*. 2 vols. London, 1926.

PIGOTT, RICHARD. *Recollections of an Irish Journalist.* Dublin, 1882.
> The same Pigott who later became notorious for his forgeries. This work contains attacks on, and inaccurate allegations about, Parnell and the Land League.

ROLLESTON, T. W. Article, 'The Archbishop in Politics', in *Dublin University Review* (Feb. 1886).

STEPHENS, JAMES. Article, 'Ireland and the Franchise Bill', in *Contemporary Review* (May 1884).

SULLIVAN, A. M. *New Ireland.* London, 1884.
> Moderate Parnellite.

SULLIVAN, T. D. *Troubled Times in Irish Politics.* Dublin, 1905.
> Right-wing Parnellite (up to split).

SWIFT MACNEILL, J. G. *What I have seen and heard.* London, 1925.

VICTORIA, QUEEN. *Letters* edited by G. E. Buckle. Second series, vol. iii, 1879–85; third series, vol. i, 1886–9. London, 1930.

4. *Contemporary works of reference*

*Dod's Parliamentary Companion, 1880–9.* Annually.
*Dictionary of National Biography.*
*Annual Register, 1880–91.*
*Thom's Directory, 1880–90.*
*Who's Who, 1879–90.*
*Men of the Time.* 10th ed. 1879. 12th ed. 1887.
*Burke's Landed Gentry of Great Britain and Ireland.* 6th ed. 1879.
*Burke's Peerage and Baronetage.* 42nd ed. 1880.
*A Catalogue of Graduates . . . in the University of Dublin . . . to Dec. 1868 . . .* by James H. Todd, 1869.
*Alumni Dublinenses. A register of the students, graduates etc. . . . in the University of Dublin.* Burtchaell and Sadleir, 1935.
*Alumni Oxonienses, 1715–1886.* Joseph Foster, 1886.
*A Concise Dictionary of Irish National Biography.* John S. Crone, 1928.
*O'Hart's Irish Landed Gentry.* 1887.
*The Industries of Dublin . . . An Account of the Leading Business Men etc.* S. Blackett. Dublin, 1882.

5. *Published collections of documents*

'Documents relating to the Irish Central Board Scheme, 1884–5'. Edited by C. H. D. Howard. *Irish Historical Studies . . .* vol. viii, no. 31 (Mar. 1953).

'Documents relating to the Galway Election of 1886'. Edited by T. W. Moody. *Irish Historical Studies . . .* vol. ix, no. 35 (March 1955).

B. LATER WORKS

1. *General*

ENSOR, R. C. K. *England 1870–1914.* Oxford, 1936.
LOCKER-LAMPSON, GODFREY. *A Consideration of the State of Ireland in the Nineteenth Century.* London, 1907.

MORRIS, W. O'CONNOR. *Ireland, 1798–1898.* London, 1898.
O'CONNOR, SIR JAMES. *History of Ireland, 1798–1924.* 2 vols. London, 1925.
O'HEGARTY, P. S. *A History of Ireland since the Union.* London, 1953.
    The last three works are perceptibly marked by the strong opinions
of their authors on the political issues of their own day.

## 11. *Biographical*[1]

*Balfour, Arthur James.* BLANCHE E. C. DUGDALE. 2 vols. London, 1936.
*Campbell Bannerman, Sir Henry.* J. A. SPENDER. 2 vols. London, 1923.
*Carnarvon, 4th Earl.* SIR ARTHUR HARDINGE. Vol. iii, 1878–89. Oxford, 1925.
    Useful for 'tory alliance' of 1885.
*Carson, Lord.* E. MARJORIBANKS. Vol. i. London, 1932.
*Chamberlain, Joseph.* J. L. GARVIN. 3 vols. London, 1932.
    Criticized cogently by Henry Harrison (below, § III).
*Churchill, Lord Randolph.* W. S. CHURCHILL. 2 vols. London, 1906.
*Davitt, Michael.* D. B. CASHMAN. Glasgow, no date.
—— F. SHEEHY SKEFFINGTON. London, 1908.
    See also *Parnell.*
*Devonshire, 8th Duke (Lord Hartington).* BERNARD HOLLAND. 2 vols. London, 1911.
*Dilke, Sir Charles.* S. GWYNN and G. TUCKWELL. 2 vols. London, 1917.
*Forster, W. E.* T. WEMYSS REID. 2 vols. London, 1888.
*Gladstone, W. E.* JOHN MORLEY. 3 vols. London, 1903.
—— SIR PHILIP MAGNUS. London, 1954.
    See also below, § III.
*Goschen, Lord.* ARTHUR D. ELLIOTT. 2 vols. London, 1911.
*Granville, Lord.* LORD EDWARD FITZMAURICE. 2 vols. London, 1905.
*Harcourt, Sir William.* A. G. GARDINER. 2 vols. London, 1923.
*Healy, Archbishop (of Tuam).* REV. P. J. JOYCE. Dublin, 1931.
*Healy, T. M.* LIAM O'FLAHERTY. London, 1927.
—— MAEV SULLIVAN, Dublin, 1943 (under the title *No Man's Man*).
*Hicks Beach, Sir Michael.* LADY VICTORIA HICKS BEACH. 2 vols. London, 1932.
*Labouchere, Henry.* A. L. THOROLD. London, 1913.
    Very valuable, especially for Healy–Labouchere Correspondence.
*Lansdowne, Lord.* LORD NEWTON. London, 1929.
*Manning, Cardinal.* E. S. PURCELL, 2 vols. London, 1895.
—— SHANE LESLIE. London, 1921 (under the title *Henry Edward Manning, His Life and Labours*).
    For the purpose of the present study the latter biography is by far
the more valuable.

---

[1] Arranged in order of subject, with the biographer's name following. The
titles are in an abridged form.

*O'Brien, William.* MICHAEL MCDONAGH. London, 1928.
*O'Connor, T. P.* HAMILTON FYFE. London, 1934.
*O'Gorman Mahon, The.* DENIS GWYNN. London, 1934.
*Oxford and Asquith, 1st Earl.* J. A. SPENDER and CYRIL ASQUITH. Vol. i. London, 1932.
*Parnell, Charles Stewart.*
—— THOMAS SHERLOCK. Dublin, 1882.
—— R. JOHNSTON. London and Dublin, 1888.
—— T. P. O'CONNOR. London, 1892 (?).
    These early biographies are journalistic in character and contain little of value.
—— R. BARRY O'BRIEN. First edition in 2 vols. London, 1899. One volume edition, London, 1910.
    The references in the text are to the latter edition.
    This is still, despite serious faults, by far the best life of Parnell. The author was an admirer, but not an altogether uncritical one. He relied heavily, however, on undated oral statements made to him by anonymous contemporaries. The biography's usefulness as a source-book is therefore limited, and for the purposes of the present study I have relied on it as little as possible.
—— JOHN HOWARD PARNELL. London, 1916. By his brother. Little information.
—— KATHERINE O'SHEA (Mrs. C. S. Parnell). 2 vols. London, 1914.
    Much valuable political material, especially letters from Kilmainham to the authoress (1881–2).
    The personal information should be considered in the light of the criticisms advanced by Henry Harrison in *Parnell Vindicated* (§ III, below).
—— M. M. O'HARA (*Chief and Tribune; Parnell and Davitt*). Dublin, 1919.
    Some interesting comments on Parnellism.
—— St. JOHN ERVINE. London, 1925.
    Semi-fictional.
—— WILLIAM O'BRIEN (*The Parnell of real life*). London, 1926.
    Refuting Ervine.
—— JOAN HASLIP. London, 1936.
    A readable modern biography, psychological rather than political in its central interest.
—— LEON Ó BROIN (*Parnell: Beathaisnéis*). Ath Cliath, 1937.
    In Irish. Narrative based mainly on R. Barry O'Brien.
*Redmond, John.* DENIS GWYNN. London, 1932.
*Salisbury, Marquis of.* LADY GWENDOLEN CECIL. 4 vols. London, 1921–32.
*Trevelyan, Sir G. O.* G. M. TREVELYAN. London, 1932.
*Walsh, Archbishop.* P. J. WALSH. Dublin, 1928.
    Very valuable for Plan of Campaign and split; also for Chamberlain negotiations of 1885.

III. *Special Studies*

EVERSLEY, LORD. *Gladstone and Ireland.* London, 1912.

HAMMOND, J. L. *Gladstone and the Irish Nation.* London, 1938.

HARRISON, HENRY. *Parnell Vindicated.* London, 1931.

—— *Parnell, Joseph Chamberlain and Mr. Garvin.* London, 1938.

—— *Parnell, Joseph Chamberlain and 'The Times'.* London, 1953.

   Harrison corrected many misinterpretations of Parnell's actions; his work is almost always sound, but on one or two occasions his judgement was clouded by his loyalty to Parnell (see Chapter VI, p. 174, n. 2).

HOWARD, C. H. D. Article, 'The Parnell Manifesto of 21 November, 1885, and the Schools Question', in *English Historical Review* (Jan. 1947). See Chapter III, p. 116, n. 2. Article, 'Parnell, Joseph Chamberlain and the Irish Central Board Scheme', in *Irish Historical Studies*, viii. 32 (Sept. 1953).

LEAMY, MARGARET. *Parnell's Faithful Few.* New York, 1936.

MCCARTHY, M. J. F. *The Irish Revolution.* Vol. i. London, 1912.

   An intelligent but general exposition from a Parnellite point of view.

MANSERGH, NICHOLAS. *Ireland in the Age of Reform and Revolution.* London, 1940.

MOODY, T. W. Article, 'The New Departure in Irish Politics, 1878–9', in *Essays in British and Irish History in Honour of J. E. Todd,* 1949.

—— Article, 'Michael Davitt and the British Labour Movement 1882–1906' in *Transactions of the Royal Historical Society,* series 5, iii. 1953.

O'DONNELL, F. H. *History of the Irish Parliamentary Party.* See above, § 11 (memoirs).

O'NEILL, BRIAN. *War for the Land in Ireland.* London, 1933.

   Marxist. View of the 'Kilmainham treaty' as the bourgeois betrayal of the national-agrarian revolution.

OSTROGORSKI, M. *Democracy and the Organization of Political Parties.* London, 1902.

PALMER, N. D. *Irish Land League Crisis.* Yale, 1940.

   Detailed and well documented.

PELLING, HENRY. *The Origins of the Labour Party.* London, 1954.

POMFRET, J. E. *The Struggle for the Land in Ireland.* Princeton, 1930.

STRAUSS, E. *Irish Nationalism and British Democracy.* London, 1931.

   Marxist. See Chapter III, pp. 109 sqq.

*Bibliographies*

   J. Carty's *Bibliography of Irish History, 1870–1911* (Dublin, National Library of Ireland, 1940) provides an almost complete guide to the relevant literature published before 1940. There are also useful bibliographies in Palmer's *Land Crisis in Ireland* (above, § B. III), Pomfret's *Struggle for Land in Ireland* (above, § B. III), and Joan Haslip's *Life of Parnell* (above, § B. II).

# INDEX

Abraham, W., M.P., 312; moves ending of Parnell's leadership, 342–4.

Anglo-Irish relations, effect on, of divorce crisis, 288.

Anti-Coercion Association, The, 62.

'Anti-Parnellites': in divorce crisis, 285; conference of, 312; composition of, 326 sqq.

Balfour, Arthur: chief secretary, 207; failure to crush Plan of Campaign, 209; and coercion policy, 210; and political prisoners, 211–12; and Catholic education, 236 sqq.; and Purchase Bill, 238.

Ballot Act, 1872, effect in Ireland, 34.

Barry, John, M.P.: and fenian oath, 4; and election of Parnell, 25 n. 4, 29, 62, 124; and divorce crisis, 298, 300 sqq., 314, 318, 321, 331, 340, 342.

Bellingham, A. H., M.P., 151.

Biggar, Joseph, M.P.: and fenian oath, 4; career, 21; and obstruction, 22, 23, 25 n. 4, 29, 31 n. 1, 32, 54; prosecuted and acquitted, 65–66, 74, 83, 128, 135, 140, 146, 154, 157, 168, 173; and Galway crisis, 176 sqq., 249, 254, 268.

Blane, Alexander, M.P., 325, 334, 345.

Blennerhasset, R. P., M.P., 12, 26.

Blunt, W. S.: opinion on Irish members, 158, 226, 242.

Boycott, Captain, harvest of, 55.

Bradlaugh case, and Parnellites, 50, 89.

Burke, T. H., under-secretary, murdered, 82.

Butt, Isaac, M.P., 4; his party, 21; rebukes obstruction, 23, 84, 123, 124–5; and pledging, 140, 318.

Byrne, Garrett, M.P., 25 n. 3, 325.

Callan, Philip, M.P., 23 n. 1.

Campbell, Henry, M.P., 175 181, 323.

Carnarvon, Lord: policy as lord lieutenant, 98 sqq.; discussions with McCarthy and Parnell, 102; question of treaty, 107 n. 1.

Cavendish, Lord Frederick, murdered, 82.

Chamberlain, Joseph, 50, 76, 84, 87; overtures to nationalists, 90 sqq.; proposed visit to Ireland, 99 sqq.; breaks with nationalists, 101, 108; and Protection, 109 sqq.; Irish contempt for, 115, 164, 165, 167, 169; and Galway crisis, 170 sqq., 185, 188, 190, 282.

Chance, P. A., M.P., 257, 305, 323, 331, 340.

Churchill, Lord Randolph: overtures to Irish, 97 sqq.; tactics, 104; popularity, 117; 'Orange card', 189, 192.

Clan-na-Gael (American fenian organization), 3.

Clancy, J., M.P., 285, 289, 301, 329, 335.

Clergy, Irish Catholic: influence in elections, 8; suspect Parnell, 27–28; and electoral organization, 42; and home rule, 43; rally to Parnell's land policy, 54; subscribe to Parnell defence fund, 56; and Land Bill, 68–70; cautioned by Rome, 85; entrust Irish party with defence of Catholic interests, 89–90; and radical overtures, 92 sqq.; and home rule, 96; and Carnarvon, 102, 104 n. 2; and 'vote tory manifesto', 106; in electoral conventions, 129; influence on policy, 157 n. 3; and Galway crisis, 179 sqq.; declare for home rule, 184; call for land reform, 199; and Plan of Campaign, 213 sqq.; and Roman circular, 222–3, 260; and divorce crisis, 281, 283, 297, 304–5, 333; condemn Parnell, 335, 337, 352. *See also* Croke; Healy (Dr.); Manning; McCabe; McHale; Nulty; O'Dwyer; Persico; Walsh.

Commins, Dr. M. P., 25 n. 4.

PRINTED IN
GREAT BRITAIN
AT THE
UNIVERSITY PRESS
OXFORD
BY
CHARLES BATEY
PRINTER
TO THE
UNIVERSITY